THE WEALTH OF A RISING EMPIRE

Yong Liang

THE WEALTH OF A RISING EMPIRE

The Manchu Acquisition of Currencies, People,
Lands and Industries before the Unification of
China (1583-1643)

EBERHARD KARLS
UNIVERSITÄT
TÜBINGEN

TÜBINGEN
LIBRARY PUBLISHING

Bibliografische Information der Deutschen Nationalbibliothek
Die Deutsche Nationalbibliothek verzeichnet diese Publikation in der Deutschen Nationalbibliografie, detaillierte bibliografische Daten sind im Internet über http://dnb.d-nb.de abrufbar.

Die Online-Version dieser Publikation ist auf dem Repositorium der Universität Tübingen frei verfügbar (Open Access).
http://hdl.handle.net/10900/123473
http://nbn-resolving.de/urn:nbn:de:bsz:21-dspace-1234733
http://dx.doi.org/10.15496/publikation-64837

Tübingen Library Publishing 2022
Universitätsbibliothek Tübingen
Wilhelmstraße 32
72074 Tübingen
druckdienste@ub.uni-tuebingen.de
https://tlp.uni-tuebingen.de

ISBN (Hard/Softcover): 978-3-946552-62-8
ISBN (PDF): 978-3-946552-63-5

Umschlaggestaltung: Susanne Schmid, Universitätsbibliothek Tübingen
Coverabbildung: »Tianming Tongbao«, J.H. Stewart Lockhart
Satz: Helena Nebel, Universitätsbibliothek Tübingen
Druck und Bindung: Open Publishing GmbH
Printed in Germany

Table of Contents

Acknowledgements

My gratefulness goes to Professor Hans Ulrich Vogel and Professor Achim Mittag, who supervised this work in the past two years, guiding me to read primary and secondary sources, forming arguments, discerning concepts, improving expression and format. The main structure of the book took its shape during our communication about the Manchu-language sources and was enhanced by Profess Vogel's teaching of research methods and economic history. The chapter of Industries, especially the section of salt, was greatly motivated by his profound research upon China's economy. Professor Mittag's courses of intellectual history and cultural studies also inspired me to write about the ethnic groups during the late Ming time, particularly in the section of Tibetan-Manchu relationship. Their crucial help, care and instructions are engraved in my heart and will not fade away with time.

Professor Lars Peter Laamann, from SOAS University of London, acted as my third supervisor, and directed me to read extensively for enforcing the thesis. One instance is that the section of tobacco was composed during our direct discussion about Manchu economy. Moreover, Professor Laamann's effort of instructing this monograph has started since 2012, when I was fumbling for an academic career in China. I am also thankful that Professor Pamela Kyle Crossley, from Dartmouth College, guided me to read about history, economy and other academic disciplines, in which I have been instructed to better understand the past of East Asia. The section of acquiring the Han Chinese population during Hong Taiji's (man. *hong taiji*; chin. *huangtaiji* 皇太極) reign owes credit to her direction.

Further thanks go to Professor George Bryan Souza for his consistent help and advice upon the idea of Manchu expansion that started in Northeast Asia and finally extended into Central and South Asia. As an insightful mentor, Professor Souza also has been instructing me to manage all sorts of difficulties since my early work on the *Manchus and Their Expansion: Three Eighteenth Century Primers and the Role of Language,* as an attempt of contributing to the academia with Manchu sources for historical studies.

Additional thanks go to Ms Zhang Li 張莉, who has retired from the First Historical Archives of China for teaching me Manchu basic learning, and to Professor Wang Fenglei 王風雷 from Inner Mongolia Normal University and to Professor Baoyindeligen 寶音德力根 from Inner Mongolia University, Professor Heilong 黑龍 from Dalian Minzu University, for teaching me to read Mongol texts. Special thanks go to Professor Zhang Meilan 張美蘭 from Qinghua University for helping me understand the relationship between history, Manchu documents and traditional Han Chinese literature. Their help will not be in vain.

My thankfulness also extends to my colleagues at the Sinology Institute of Tübingen, who exchanged important academic opinions with me in our courses, seminars and colloquiums. Special thanks go to my wife Julia Jie Deng and my son Luke Lujia Liang, for their consistent support along this career track.

23/12/2021, Xi'an International Studies University

Abbreviations

Fe dangse: *Dorgi yamun asaraha manju hergen i fe dangse* a.k.a., *Neige cangben Manwen laodang* 內閣藏本滿文老檔 (Collection of Manchu Old Chronicles Stored in the Grand Secretariat)

Jiudang: *Jiu Manzhou dang* 舊滿洲檔 (The Former Manchurian Chronicles)

Yuandang: *Manwen yuandang* 滿文原檔 (The Original Manchu Chronicles)

man.: Manchu language

chin.: Han Chinese Language

Maps

Illustrations

Tables

1. Introduction

1.1 State of the Field

The Manchus were the ruling elites who dominated China Proper and the vast frontier regions in the Northeast, Central, South and Southeast Asia since 1644. The Qing empire, essentially as a Manchu regime, deserves more attention from the economic perspective. Owen Lattimore spent nine months in the northeast of Asia, conducting a comprehensive research about the economy of Manchuria from 1929-1930. One of his main intentions was to figure out the relationship between economics and transportation, as the Han Chinese, Japanese and Russian rulers were rapidly developing railway, waterway and land forms of transportation. Furthermore, Lattimore also pointed out some modes of economic transformation, such as the Manchus quickly giving up their reindeer economy and adopting the Han Chinese standard of living.[1] Lattimore's research was a swift review of Manchu economy based on fieldwork, but in contrast to this, The Manchu Old Chronicles reveal various models of Manchu economy in history, in a mixture of farming, herding, fishing, hunting, gathering and some sorts of manufacturing industries, which form the main body of my research.

Frederic Wakeman, Jr. reconstructed the decline and fall of the Ming dynasty in comparison with the rise of the Manchu state, in terms of conflicts between the Manchu and Han Chinese frontier people and the integration of Han Chinese into the Manchu institutions. In Wakeman's work, the economic situation of Northeast Asia was briefly analyzed to illustrate the rapid territorial expansion achieved by the Manchus,[2] which inspired scholars to conduct further research for elaborating the state building based on a robust Manchu economy.

In the 1990s, the New Qing History Movement gradually arose in the field dealing with China's late imperial past, stressing the employment of Manchu-language documents into research. As scholars have noted,

---

[1] Owen Lattimore (1932), *Manchuria: Cradle of Conflict,* the Macmillan Company, New York, pp. 13-48.

[2] Frederic Wakeman Jr. (1985), The Great Enterprise: The Manchu Reconstruction of Imperial Order in Seventeenth-Century China, University of California Press, Berkeley, pp. 36-59.

Manchu ethnicity and borderlands are main research themes of this academic school. Evelyn S. Rawski emphasizes that Qing history should be interpreted from a Manchu perspective, rather than from the conventional view of sinicization (*hanhua* 漢化).[3] Mark C. Elliott points out that economics affected the formation of Manchu identity as an ethnic group, especially banner-men who enjoyed certain economic privileges.[4] Manchu ethnic sovereignty was maintained by the Eight Banner system, which sustained the imperial governance throughout the dynasty. Furthermore, scholars who consistently accentuates historical research from a global perspective, such as Pamela Kyle Crossley, highlights that the governance of the Qing empire was built upon the ethnic identity of the Manchu people.[5] William Rowe viewed the "Manchu" identity as historical construct of revisionists, while the Manchu-centered Qing as a different empire than most of the preceding dynasties.[6] Since amounts of people still argue that economy must be subordinate to state, it is quite necessary for scholars to further explore how the Qing dynasty functioned on its economic basis that was closely linked to the ethnicity, banner system and the multinational polity.

In *China Marches West*, Peter C. Perdue addresses the economic history of Later Jin and early Qing during the 1630s, in which the then feeble Manchu army was not yet able to launch a direct unification campaign on the Ming, but mainly resorted to raiding Han Chinese cities and plundering their fields.[7] Perdue points out that the Manchu ambition of state building was constrained in the seventeenth century by their limited logistics and agrarian economies, such as grain harvest failures due to the multiple crises that happened across the globe.[8] The Manchu

---

[3] Evelyn S. Rawski, "Presidential Address: Reenvisioning the Qing: The Significance of the Qing Period in Chinese History", *The Journal of Asian Studies*, 55.4: 829-850.

[4] Mark C. Elliott (2001), *The Manchu Way: The Eight Banners and Ethnic Identity in Late Imperial China*, Stanford University Press, Stanford, California, p. xiv-xvii.

[5] Pamela Kyle Crossley (1999), *A Translucent Mirror: History and Identity in Qing Imperial Ideology*, University of California Press, Berkeley and Los Angeles, California, p. 1.

[6] William Rowe (2009), *China's Last Empire: The Great Qing*, the Belknap Press of Harvard University Press, Massachusetts, p. 6.

[7] Peter C. Perdue (2005), *China Marches West: The Qing unification of Central Eurasia*, The Belknap Press of Harvard University Press, Massachusetts, Cambridge, p. 120.

[8] Perdue, *China Marches West*, p. 120.

expansion is considered by him as a part of the global colonization similar to that carried out by the western powers simultaneously, and thus the study of the Manchu economy provides a critical angle to understand that period of history.

Richard von Glahn declares that in order to boost an economy, three factors are indispensable: an expanding money supply, the regional specialization of production and a sufficient market.[9] In the light of von Glahn's hypothesis, my research will use Manchu-language documents to show that the banner-men, under the leadership of the Manchu elites, acquired large quantities of silver, which formed a sufficient money supply for economic development. Furthermore, the Manchu documents also record the existence of specialized industries, which provided abundant goods for commercial exchange with the Han Chinese and Mongols. Thus, one can see that currencies, industries and markets well underpinned the expansion of Manchu economy.

Based on Han Chinese-language sources, scholars have done remarkable research upon the Ming economy, such as Liang Fangzhong's studies on silver mining, silver circulation, and exclusive taxation in monetary silver as part of the Single Whip Reform (*yitiaobian fa* 一條鞭 法).[10] Yang Liansheng conducted comprehensive research upon the Ming China's import of silver, the relationship between credit, precious metals and paper notes.[11] Ray Huang did comprehensive research on Ming's finance and revenue,[12] with a characteristic of being conservative and rigid since the Hongwu reign (r. 1368-1398).[13] Quan Hansheng studied Ming's international trade and its silver imports in relation to commodity prices in the eighteenth-century China.[14] Zhao Duo's

---

[9] Richard von Glahn (2016), *The Economic History of China: From the Antiquity to the Nineteenth Century*, Cambridge University Press, Cambridge, pp. 295-347.

[10] Liang Fangzhong 梁方仲 (1989), *Liang Fangzhong jingjishi lunwenji* 梁方仲經 濟史論文集 (Collected Papers on Economic History Authored by Liang Fangzhong), Zhonghua shuju, Beijing.

[11] Liu Mengxi 劉夢溪 (1996), ed., *Zhongguo xiandai xueshu jingdian, Hong Ye Yang Liansheng juan* (Academic Classical Works in Modern China, Volumes of Hong Ye and Yang Liansheng), Hebei jiaoyu chubanshe, Shijiazhuang.

[12] Ray Huang (1981), *1587, A Year of No Significance: The Ming Dynasty in Decline*, Yale University Press, Connecticut, New Haven.

[13] Ray Huang (1974), Taxation and Governmental Finance in Sixteenth-Century Ming China, Cambridge University Press, Cambridge.

[14] Quan Hansheng 全漢昇 (2012), *Zhongguo jingjishi luncong* 中國經濟史論叢 (Collection of Essays on China's Economic History), *Zhonghua shuju*, Beijing.

monograph "The Economic History of Qing in the Era of State Founding" (*Qing kaiguo jingji fazhanshi* 清開國經濟發展史) directly addresses the Manchu economy before the unification of China. Guided by Marxist historical views, this book briefly introduces the economic situation of the Jurchen tribes in the northeast regions of the Ming and analyzes the Jurchen, among other topics, the household, slave, and serf economies. The author extensively consulted primary sources, such as local gazetteers, chronicles, veritable records and note-form literature composed by Korean officials of the time.[15]

The above schematic literature review indicates that the economic history of the Ming has been well addressed by scholars, but that there is an urgent need to illuminate the Qing economy from a Manchu perspective. The history of early Manchu economy was often treated solely as a fractional part of Ming history. Scholars in the West have initiated a movement of interpreting Manchu history in Manchu terms, which has inspired me to pursue this project submitted for peer review. Currently some Han Chinese scholars criticize historians of the New Qing History Movement for using insufficient Manchu-language chronicles in their research, and this in spite of these historians' increased use of chronicle documents. This project has consulted and absorbed large quantities of Manchu-language materials to underpin its arguments, and this with the ambition to contribute to the New Qing History Movement with its Manchu-language chronicle orientation.

Additionally, this book attempts to describe the interaction between politics and economics, concerning the dominant roles played by the Manchus in state building during the early seventeenth century. Regarding the theme of Manchu identity, Crossley placed the institutionalization of the Manchu name in the context of empire expansion and decline, which are reflected in *A Translucent Mirror* and *Orphan Warriors*. Elliott illuminated the feature of ethnicity in light of the Eight Banners (man. *jakvn gvsa;* chin. *baqi* 八旗) system, which sustained the Manchu identity throughout the Qing dynasty, according to his *The Manchu Way* and *Ethnicity in the Qing Eight Banners*. Both of

---

[15] Zhao Duo 趙鐸 (1992), *Qing kaiguo jingji fazhan shi* 清開國經濟發展史 (The Economic History of Qing in the Era of State-Founding), Liaoning renmin chubanshe, Shenyang.

the theses stand firmly in perspectives of arguments and present the past on account of extensive literature.

My conviction is that the system of Eight Banners is the body of the state during Nurgaqi's reign, as Meng Sen 孟森 stated (*baqizhe, taizu suoding zhi guoti ye* 八旗者，太祖所定之國體也),[16] and the banners managed the economics on behalf of the khan. In Hong Taiji's time, the structure of state was enlarged by adding the Six Ministries (man. *ninggun jurgan*; chin. *liubu* 六部) and other institutions such as the Three Palace Academies (*neisanyuan* 內三院), and the Ministry of Mongol Affairs (man. *monggo jugan*; chin. *menggu yamen* 蒙古衙門) that was renamed as Court of Colonial Affairs (man. *tulergi golo be dasara jurgan*; chin. *lifanyuan* 理藩院). The administration of economics was mainly carried out by the Six Ministries, which represented the state and the khan. The function of the Eight Banners was gradually confined to military affairs, in which its power was balanced by the khan and the Ministry of War (*bingbu* 兵部). The Manchus may have developed this political structure from the previous Jin dynasty (1115-1234), which created a dual system to organize the Jurchens by units of Battalion-Company (*meng'an mouke* 猛安謀克), and administrating China Proper by Mobile Presidential Council (*xingtai shangshusheng* 行台尚書省).[17] Nevertheless, the Eight Banners remained distinct Manchu characteristics and enjoyed certain level of autonomy, which was regarded as a state within a state.[18] Thus, I believe that the Manchu identity closely linked to the banner system and state building, with economics included. In this regard, the chapter Acquisition of Industries will give some further accounts.

Other relevant definitions of China, Jurchen, Jin, Manchu and Great Qing should also be briefly spelled out for facilitating the comprehension of this book. In the late Ming period, the Jurchens, as the predecessor of Manchus, were excluded from the constituents of people in China. The

---

[16] Meng Sen 孟森 (1959), *Baiqi zhidu kaoshi* 八旗制度考實 (Evidential Research on the Eight Banners System), collected in *Ming Qing shi lunzhu jikan* 明清史論著集刊 (Collected Papers on the Treatise of Ming-Qing History), Zhonghua shuju, Beijing, p. 218.

[17] Herbert Franke and Denis Twitchett, (eds.) (1994), *The Cambridge History of China: Alien Regimes and Border States, 907-1368*, vol. 6, the Press Syndicate of the University of Cambridge, Cambridge.

[18] Meng Sen, *Baqi zhidu kaoshi*, p. 218.

"Records of Military Accomplishments of Wanli" says that sable furs came from Kaiyuan and its northeast, between which the distance is thousands of *li*.[19] According to the Ming rule, markets of Kaiyuan were open from the first to the fifth day of each month. Barbarians on the river transported them for sale in the Tianshan region of the northeast, and annually they entered China on the first days of the seventh, eighth and ninth months (*diaopi zi kaiyuan dongbei shuqianli er yuan jiang shang zhi yi, fanzhi dongbei tianshan jian, sui yi qiu qi ba jiu yue yi ru zhongguo* 貂皮自開原東北數千里而遠江上之夷，販之東北天山間，歲以秋七八九月一入中國).[20] This document was composed in 1612, revealing the geographical difference between the northeast frontier inhabited by the barbarians (*yi* 夷) and China in context of business transactions. Zhang Nai 張鼐, who was a Metropolitan Graduate (*jinshi* 進士) in 1604, was sent on a diplomatic mission to Liaodong in 1620. Later he commented that the Ming court had lost the influence of China in the first place and accordingly looked at the Jurchens as a state beyond control. Hardly people realized that, as Zhang described, among all barbarians, the Jurchens were only one kind, which is in size of a pellet ball, and the string of manipulation or overthrow was in our China's hand in the first place (*wo xian shi zhongguo zhi shi, er sui shi nu wei bukezhi zhi guo. Buzhi nu yu zhongyi zhong buguo danwan zhi yizhong er, caozong er diandao zhi xiansuo, yuanzai wo zhongguo zhi shou* 我先失中國之勢，而遂視奴為不可制之國。不知奴於眾夷中不過彈丸之一種耳，操縱而顛倒之線索，原在我中國之手).[21] Such comments tell that the Han Chinese intellectuals considered Jurchens as a type of tribal people or foreigners, who were subordinate to China's central governance. Nonetheless, Zhang Nai admitted that the Jurchens had gained power that is independent of the Ming regime.

When Matteo Ricci (b. 1552-1610) was in the Ming empire, he found out that China was Cin (*Qin* 秦), referred by people in ancient Vietnam

---

[19] The Chinese measurement unit *li* is about five hundred meters.

[20] *Wanli wugonglu* 萬曆武功錄 (Records of Military Accomplishments of Wanli), composed by Qu Jiusi 瞿九思(circa 1580), collected in *Qing ruguanqian shiliao xuanji yi* 清入關前史料選輯 1 (Compilation of Selected Historical Materials before the Qing Entered through Shanhai Pass), vol. 1, compiled by Pan Zhe 潘喆 et al., edition Beijing: Zhongguo renmin daxue chubanshe, 1984, pp. 27-28.

[21] *Liao yi lüe* 遼夷略 (Strategies for Pacifying the Liao Barbarians), composed by Zhang Nai 張鼐(1572-1630), *Qing ruguanqian shiliao xuanji yi*, p. 90.

and Thailand, from whom the Portuguese settlers learned this name and called it China; meanwhile the Japanese called it Tang 唐, Tartars called it Han 漢 and Muslims called it Cathay (*Qidan* 契丹).[22] Beside the Muslims in Central Asia, this Cathay notion of China has been well accepted in the Mongol and Russian languages up to today. The concept of *Zhongguo* 中國 in modern history has been explained by Chen Bo, in comparison to the European notion of China.[23] Zhao Gang argued that the earliest Manchu references adopted the Ming view and treated the Ming empire and the Han group as equivalent.[24] Here we may find that the early Manchu view equates the Ming empire (man. *daiming gurun;* chin. *damingguo* 大明國) with the Han Chinese state or people (man. *nikan gurun;* chin. *hanren* 漢人 or *hanrenguo* 漢人國), which highlights the ethnic identity of Han Chinese state and people in the late Ming period.

As for the Jin state-building, the Ming intellectual Mao Ruizheng 茅瑞徵 deemed that the Jurchens built their own state, named as Jin (1115-1234), for the conviction that gold is solid and sustainable with a white color. The Wanyan 完顏 tribe, as the ruling tribe that unified the Jurchens, highly regarded the color of white and therefore named the state as Great Jin (*yi jin jian buhuai, sebai, er wanyanbu se shang bai, sui hao dajin yan* 以金堅不壞，色白，而完顏部色尚白，遂號大金焉).[25] In the early seventeenth century when the Jurchens rose again as a formidable power, Mao judged that Nurgaqi usurped the khan-ship and the state title of Later Jin, wearing a yellow robe and becoming the emperor (*nu'erhachi ... jian hao houjinguo han, huangyi chengzhen* 奴兒哈赤…僭號後金國汗，黃衣稱朕…).[26] In the eyes of the Ming Han

---

[22] *China in the Sixteenth Century: The Journals of Mathew Ricci (1583-1610)*, written by Matteo Ricci and Nicolas Trigault, translated from the Latin by Louis J. Gallagher, S. J. Random House, New York, 1953, p. 5.
[23] Chen Bo (2016), "The Making of 'China' out of 'Zhongguo' ", *Journal of Asian History*, 50.1:73-116.
[24] Zhao Gang (2006), "Reinventing China: Imperial Qing Ideology and the Rise of Modern Chinese National Identity in the Early Twentieth Century", *Modern China*, 32. 1: 3-30.
[25] *Dongyi kaolüe* 東夷考略 (Evidential Research upon the Eastern Barbarians) composed by Mao Ruizheng 茅瑞徵 (circa 1601), *Qing ruguanqian shiliao xuanji yi*, p. 47.
[26] Dongyi kaolüe, Qing ruguanqian shiliao xuanji yi, p. 47.

Chinese scholars, the legitimacy of the new Jurchen regime remained controversial, being different from the antecedent Jin dynasty.

Nonetheless, the Manchu-language sources depicted a different scenario. In 1616 when Nurgaqi was fifty-eight years old, surrounded by the Jurchen chieftains (man. *beile* or *beise* as a plural form; chin. *beile* 貝勒) and leaders of the Eight Banners, he ascended the throne and was honored as the Great Bright Khan Appointed to Nourish All Lands (*fulgiyan muduri aniya, sure kundulen han i susai jakvn se de, ... jakvn gvsai beise ambasa, geren be gaifi duin dere duin hoxo arame jakvn bade ilifi, ... amban geren gurun be ujikini seme sindaha genggiyen han*).[27] In the "Manchu Veritable Records" which were written in Hong Taiji's reign, Nurgaqi's honorary title was modified as the Bright Khan to Nourish All Lands, with a reign title as Mandate of Heaven (*...geren gurun be ujire genggiyen han...aniyai gebu be abkai fulingga sehe*).[28] The Manchu expression of *aniyai gebu* corresponds with the Han Chinese term *nianhao* 年號, which must a strategy adopted by the Jurchens to befriend their Han Chinese partners and to confront the Ming rival.

The title of the regime was consistently used as the Gold State (man. *aisin gurun;* chin. *jinguo* 金國) during Nurgaqi's reign and the first half of Hong Taiji's reign. For example, in 1613, three years before Nurgaqi openly announced his khan-ship, the scribe recorded that because of the heavenly grace, the Wise Respectable Khan gathered great amounts of people and held the authority of Gold state for administration (*abkai kesi de sure kundulen han amba gurun be isabufi, aisin doro be jafafi banjire de, ...*).[29] This passage indicates that Nurgaqi declared to inherit the legacy of the previous Jin dynasty. In the second year of Hong Taiji's reign (1628), a diplomatic letter sent by the Korean government shows that the state title of the Jurchens was Gold, just like Joseon for the Joseon people (*wesihun gurun i qolo aisin serengge, meni gurun i qoohiyan sere adali*).[30] This Korean document translated in Manchu

---

[27] *Neige cangben manwen laodang* 內閣藏本滿文老檔 (Collection of Manchu Old Chronicles Stored in the Grand Secretariat), compiled by Wu Yuanfeng 吳元豐 (b. 1956) et al., edition Shenyang, Liaoning minzu chubanshe, 2009, pp. 195-198.

[28] *Manzhou shilu* 滿洲實錄 (The Manchu Veritable Records), collected in Qing shilu 清實錄 (The Qing Veritable Records), edition Beijing: Zhonghua shuju, p. 187.

[29] *Jiu Manzhou dang* 旧滿洲档 (The Former Manchurian Chronicles), edition Taipei: Taibei gugong bowuyuan chuban, 1969, p. 58.

[30] *Fe dangse*, p. 4317.

language is solid proof that Gold, as the state title, was firmly recognized by its neighboring country Korea.

Nonetheless, it was difficult for the Jurchens to maintain their inheritance. According to Hong Taiji's decree announced in the regions of Hebei province, the Ming emperors Tianqi and Chongzhen once repeatedly humiliated Hong Taiji, by ordering him to stop using the emperor title of the Gold State and the jade seal made by himself. Surprisingly, Hong Taiji tried to reconcile, claiming himself not an emperor but a khan, and asked the Ming to make a seal for him. However, the Ming authority did not permit his request (*tian ki han, qung jeng han, geli gidaxame aisin gurun i hvwangdi sere be naka, enquleme araha doron be naka sehe manggi, bi inu aqara be buyeme hvwangdi sere be nakafi han seki, suwe doron arafi bu, buhe doron takvraki seqi, geli ojorakv ofi, ...*).[31] Thus we can see the title, as a political legitimacy, was highly valued in the pre-industrial society.

The Ming emperors and officials always kept in mind that the previous Jin (1115-1234) had terminated the Northern Song dynasty (960-1127) by force. When attacking the Dalinghe fortification in 1631, the Ming army resisted fiercely. In order to moderate the tension, Hong Taiji wrote to Zu Dashou 祖大壽, the general in charge of defence, declaring that the Ming emperors are not the descendants of Song emperors and we, Hong Taiji himself and his late father Nurgaqi, are not descendants of the previous Jin emperors (*daiming han, sung han i hvnqihin waka, be geli nendehe aisin han i hvnqihin waka*).[32] During the war, such a statement made by Hong Taiji is more like a military strategy to win the battle, rather than an official decree for fundamental change. As Crossley contended, the royal clan of the previous Jin was Wanggiya (Wanyan 完顏), which was a tribe (man. *gurun*; chin. *bu* 部) in the twelfth century, before and during the wars of unifying the Jurchens. But the royal clan descended into a tribe again after the fall of Jin dynasty.[33] As for the Aisin Gioro clan (man. *hala*; chin. *xingshi* 姓氏 or *zongzu* 宗族) that dominated the Later Jin, according to Nurgaqi's own statement, is the people of the Gold Clan that descended from heaven (*abkaqi*

---

[31] *Fe dangse*, p. 4590.

[32] *Fe dangse*, p. 5513.

[33] Pamela Kyle Crossley (1987), Manzhou Yuanliu Kao and the Formalization of the Manchu Heritage, *The Journal of Asian Studies*, 46.4: 767.

wasika aisin gioro halangga niyalma).[34] Here, the original expression *halangga* means people who bear the same surname, or, as Elliott pointed out, the notion of *hala* consists of families that belong to the same surname or clan.[35] Furthermore, *halangga* also refers to a large group of people in the same ethnic identity, such as the Manchu language is the root of people who have Manchu surnames (*manju gisun serengge, manju halangga niyalmai fulehe da*).[36] The parallel Han Chinese translation of *manju halangga niyalmai* in the original document is *manzhouren* 滿洲人, representing the ruling community that grew exponentially after the Manchu unification of China.

In the seventeenth century, there was a pronounced need of a new identity for the Jurchens to expand their enterprise of unification. In the early reign of Nurgaqi, the term of Manchu (man. *manju*; chin. *manzhou* 滿洲) appeared in the annals dated in 1613. The scribe wrote that the Wanli emperor of the Ming dreamed three times in a row over one night, and in his dreams a person, who looks like a girl of a different surname, sat on him and poked him with a spear. The next day Wanli consulted with knowledgeable men, who said that "the girl-looked person is the wise khan of the Jurchen Manchu state, who will take over the throne of your majesty" (*terei onggolo nikan i wan li han, emu dobori ilanggeri ini beye de emu enqu halai sargan jui adali banjiha niyalma aktalame yalubi, gida jafafi ini beyebe gidalame tolgika bihe sere, jai qimari sara sara xu niyalma de fonjire jakade, sargan jui adali nioji manju gurun i sure han, han sini soorin be durimbi seme henduhe biheni*).[37] Here one can see that the word Jurchen (man. *nioji*; chin. *nüzhi* 女直) is on a par with Manchu, as identities for one state. Therefore, in this book, I use Jurchen-Manchu as the original term to describe historical events.

It is worth noting that the name of *nioji* corresponds with *nüzhi* 女直, not *nüzhen* 女真. According to the Ming scholar Mao Ruizheng, the Jurchens of the Black Water tribe (*heishui buluo* 黑水部落) were categorized into the Civilized Jurchen (*shu nüzhen* 熟女真) who lived in

---

[34] *Manwen yuandang* 滿文原檔 (The Original Manchu Chronicles), vol. 10, edition Taipei: Taibei gugong bowuyuan chuban, 2005, vol. 1, p. 22.

[35] Elliott, *The Manchu Way*, p. 50.

[36] *Qingwen zhiyao jiedu* 清文指要解讀 (Guidance of Essential Elements of Manchu Language), edited by Zhang Huake 張華克, edition Taipei: Wenshizhe chubanshe, 2005, p. 1.

[37] Jiu Manzhou dang, pp. 81-82.

the southern regions and the Uncivilized Jurchen (*sheng nüzhen* 生女真) who lived in the north. The Civilized Jurchens registered their households in the Liao regime and the uncivilized did not. Due to an evasion of mentioning the word *zhen* 真, which is also in the name of the seventh emperor Yelü Zongzhen 耶律宗真, *nüzhen* 女真 was changed to *nüzhi* 女直 (*youshi heishui buluo zainanzhe ji qidan, hao shu nüzhen. zaibeizhe buruji, hao sheng nüzhen. hou bi xingzong hui, gai nüzhi* 由是黑水部落在南者籍契丹，號熟女真。在北者不入籍，號生女真。後避興宗諱，改女直).[38] The Manchu-language chronicles written before 1644 adopted both *nioji* and *juxen* to address the Jurchen (man. *juxen*; chin. *zhushen* 諸申) identity.

The identity of Manchu appeared frequently after Hong Taiji ascended the throne. Besides Gold, Manchu was also used for referring to the state's name. On the eighth day of the first month in 1627, which is the first year of Hong Taiji's reign, in the name of the Khan of the Manchu state, an imperial decree was sent to Yuan Chonghuan 袁崇煥, the Grand Coordinator of Ningyuan (*ningyuan dutang* 寧遠都堂). However, the original expression was "Gold State's Khan's letter" (*aisin gurun i han i bithe*),[39] and the script was written without diacritical marks. The word *aisin* was blackened and replaced with *manju*, which has a diacritical mark on the vowel *u*. Therefore, this modification must be conducted after the spring of 1632, when Scholar (man. *baksi;* chin. *bakeshi* 巴克什) Dahai took an order to improve the scripts with diacritical marks. Nonetheless, not all names of *aisin* were changed into *manju*. Both of them were consistently adopted to make reference to the state and its people.

The Manchu word *gurun* has multiple meanings, covering tribe, confederation, state, country, people, land, dynasty, regime, nation and empire, etc. The definition of *gurun* expands in the course of history. In the early stage of state building, *manju gurun* usually meant tribe, state and people. Critical evidence is a story dated on the sixth day of the fifth month in the ninth year of Hong Taiji's reign (1635), which is considered as the earliest record about the origin of Manchu. The chronicle says that,

iqe ninggvn de, sahaliyan ula ergi hvrha gurun de qooha genehe ambasa qeni dahabufi gajiha ambasa sain niyalma be han de aqabura

---

[38] Dongyi kaolüe, Qing ruguanqian shiliao xuanji yi, p. 45.
[39] *Manwen yuandang*, vol. 6, p. 4.

doro, ... qooha de dahabufi gajiha mukesike gebungge niyalma alame, mini mafa ama jalan halame bokori alin i dade bolkori omode banjiha. mini bade bithe dangse akv. julge banjiha be ulan ulan i gisureme jihengge. tere bolkori omode abkai ilan sargan jui engvlen, jenggvlen, fegvlen ebixeme jifi enduri saksaha benjihe fulgiyan tubihe be fiyanggv sargan jui fegvlen bahafi anggade axufi bilgade dosifi beye de ofi bokori yongxon be banjiha. terei hvnqihin manju gurun inu.[40]

On the sixth day, the officials who led the army to unify the Hvrha tribe in the direction of Black River [man. *sahaliyan ula*; chin. *heilongjiang* 黑龍江] returned. The officials and the good people [who surrendered] saluted to the Khan, ... Among the captives brought back by the army, there was a person whose name is Mukesike, and he said that "for generations my ancestors originally lived around the Bolkori lake [*tianchi* 天池] under the Bokori mountain [*changbaishan* 長白山]. There were no written documents in my place. According to tradition by words. Three Celestial Daughters, Engvlen, Jenggvlen and Fegvlen, came down to the Bolkori lake for bathing. The supernatural magpie delivered a red fruit, and the youngest daughter Fegvlen got it, put it in mouth and swallowed it. She got pregnant and gave birth to Bokori Yongxon, whose descendants are Manchu.

From the passage, the tribe *hvrha gurun* is a federation of Jurchen people who spoke Jurchen language, or a similar dialect, with regional coherence and self-governance, as Crossley stated in her analysis of formalization of the Manchu heritage.[41] An interesting phenomenon is that, based on the text, the Manchu forefather got his surname from the mountain where he lived. A reasonable doubt is that the story could be made up by the war prisoner to please the khan Hong Taiji. Lin Shixuan 林士鉉 assumed that if the word Manchu was not modified by the chronicle clerk, then the concept of Manchu had already been known in the region of Black River.[42] Regarding the three Celestial Daughters, Lin argued that the story was related to Shamanism and the legend of Mongol ancestors, whose stories share many similarities, such as mountain, lake,

---

[40] *Manwen yuandang*, vol. 9, pp. 160-162.

[41] Crossley, Manzhou Yuanliu Kao and the Formalization of the Manchu Heritage, p. 767.

[42] Lin Shixuan 林士鉉 (2009), *Qingdai Menggu yu Manzhou zhengzhi wenhua* 清代蒙古與滿洲政治文化 (Political Culture of Mongol and Manchu in Qing Dynasty), Guoli zhengzhi daxue lishixuexi, Taipei, p. 37.

a celestial lady bringing forth a boy, bird, etc.[43] Thus, the name of Manchu may signify greater political intentions, especially with a phonetic link to the Manjusri Buddha in both Chan and Tibetan Buddhism.

A few months later, on the thirteenth day of the tenth month in 1635, the khan Hong Taiji finally declared that "the tribes of our state were originally Manchu, Hada, Ula, Yehe and Hoifa, which were mistakenly called as Jurchen by the ignorant people. The Jurchens are descendants of Sibe's Qoo Mergen, which has nothing to do with us. From now on all people must address us with the original name Manchu. Those who call us Jurchens will be punished" (*tere inenggi, han hendume musei gurun i gebu daqi manju, hada, ula, yehe, hoifa kai. tere be ulhirakv niyalma juxen sembi. juxen serengge, sibei qoo mergen i hvnqihin kai. tere muse de ai dalji. ereqi julesi yaya niyalma musei gurun i da manju sere gebu be hvla. Juxen seme hvlaha de weile*).[44] Shortly after, on the twenty-fourth day in his palace, Hong Taiji officially announced that the name of the people (state) is Manchu (*orin duin de amba yamun gisun. gurun i gebu be manju sembi*).[45] Meng Sen argued that since Nurgaqi's reign, those unified tribes, such as Hada, Ula and Hoifa still used their own tribal names for identification, and therefore, Hong Taiji adopted Manchu as a new identity to unify all the previous tribes.[46] What interesting is that in the same announcement, Hong Taiji still used the word Jurchen to address his own people, stipulating that those Jurchens who are exclusively controlled by banner chieftains must be called Jurchens of a certain banner chieftain (*gvsai beise de salibuha gisun. tere gvsai beilei juxen sembi seme geren de ejebume hvlaha*).[47] This official document legalized the ownership of chieftains upon their subordinate Jurchens, which can confirm Elliott's thesis of the Jurchen's social status as semi-free or dependent.[48] Meng Sen pointed out that this edict was Hong Taiji's strategy to elevate the Manchu identity while confine the

---

[43] Lin Shixuan, Qingdai Menggu yu Manzhou zhengzhi wenhua, pp. 37-39.
[44] *Manwen yuandang*, vol. 9, p. 408.
[45] *Manwen yuandang*, vol. 9, p. 416.
[46] Meng Sen 孟森 (1992), *Manzhou kaiguo shi* 滿洲開國史 (History of the Manchu State-Founding), Shanghai guji chubanshe, Shanghai, p. 10.
[47] *Manwen yuandang*, vol. 9, p. 416.
[48] Elliott, The Manchu Way, p. 51.

Jurchen status to the lowly people.[49] In short, with a consistent emphasis of Manchu identity, Jurchen was used less and less in the remaining Hong Taiji's reign and after the unification of China, the Qing ruling elites prohibited people from mentioning the name of Jurchen and only accepted the identity of Manchu.

The state's name experienced further changes. "The Draft of Veritable Records of Qing Taizong" says that on the eleventh day of the fourth month in 1636, Hong Taiji offered sacrifices and reported to the Heaven and Earth. Then he accepted the honorific title, which is the Generous, Gentle, Benevolent, and Sacred Emperor. The name of the state was established as Great Qing and the reign title is changed to Chongde as in the first year (*yiyou, shang yi shou zunhao, jigao tiandi. Shou kuanwenrensheng huangdi zunhao, jian guohao yue daqing, gaiyuan wei chongde yuannian* 乙酉，上以受尊號，祭告天地。受寬溫仁聖皇帝尊號，建國號曰大清，改元為崇德元年).[50] The same text is repeated in "The Veritable Record of Taizong Wen Emperor" without modification.[51] The "Draft of Qing History" paraphrased the expression without changing the core message, which says that in the first year of Chongde, on the eleventh day of the fourth month in summer, the emperor offered sacrifices to the Heaven and Earth, and then performed a ceremony to accept the honorific title. Next the emperor established the name of Great Qing for unifying the lands under heaven and changed the reign title to Chongde (*chongde yuannian, xia siyue yiyou, jigao tiandi, xing shou zunhao li, ding you tianxia zhihao yue daqing, gaiyuan chongde* 崇德元年，夏四月乙酉，祭告天地，行受尊號禮，定有天下之號曰大清，改元崇德).[52]

Nonetheless, the "Original Manchu Chronicles" on the same date did not mention the changes of state's name and reign title. The Manchu text says on the eleventh day, the khan led the chieftains and officials to offer

---

[49] Meng Sen, Manzhou kaiguo shi, p. 10.

[50] *Qingtaizong shilu gaoben* 清太宗實錄稿本 (The Draft of Veritable Records of Qingtaizong), collected in *Qingchu shiliao congkan* 清初史料叢刊 (Historical Materials for the Early Qing), vol.3, liaoning daxue lishixi, edition Shenyang: Liaoning daxue chubanshe, 1980, p. 83.

[51] *Taizong wen huangdi shilu* 太宗文皇帝實錄 (The Veritable Records of Taizong Wen Emperor), excerpted from *Qingshilu* 清實錄 (The Qing Veritable Records), vol. 2, edition Beijing: Zhonghua shuju, 1986, pp. 360-361.

[52] *Qingshigao* 清史稿 (The Draft of Qing History), vol. 2, composed by Zhao Erxun 趙爾巽 et al., Zhonghua shuju, 1977, p. 55.

sacrifices to the throne of the Heaven's Khan. After finishing the sacrifice, the khan sat on his big throne (*juwan emu de han geren beise ambasa be gaifi abka i han i soorin de weqehe. weqeme wajiha manggi. han amba soorin de tehe*).[53] On the thirteenth day, because of the grand political event, the sacred khan sat on his big throne in the palace, where a banquet was held for the chieftains and officials from palace and provinces (*juwan ilan de enduringge han amba soorin de tehe urgun i doroi amba dasan i yamun de dorgi tulergi geren beise ambasa be amba sarin sarilaha*).[54] On the fifteenth day, according to their ranks, the khan rewarded the Manchu, Mongol and Han Chinese officials with the depository silver because of the ceremony of accepting the grand name (*ineku tofohon de han amba gebu be alime gaiha doroi manju, monggo, nikan geren hafasa de ku menggun tuqibufi jergi bodome xangnaha*).[55] None of these three messages mentioned the state's name of Great Qing and the change of reign title. The Manchu expressions, such as "the grand political event" and "the grand name", are rather vague, even within the context. However, in the diplomatic document written to the Joseon king, on the same day, the scribes adopted the Great Qing (man. *daiqing*; chin. *daqing* 大清) as the official name of the state (*daiqing gurun i han i bithe qoohiyan gurun i wang de unggihe*),[56] but still referred to Hong Taiji as the khan in the following months. The title of emperor (man. *hvwangdi*; chin. *huangdi* 皇帝) was used to address Nurgaqi, the deceased father of Hong Taiji, in an elegy written on the third day of the eleventh month in 1636, for thanking Nurgaqi's bless upon the wars of defeating the Ming army (*iqe ilan de enduringge han doroi baturu jiyvn wang, daiming gurun de qooha genefi heqen hoton gaiha, qooha gidaha urgun be ama dergi taizu de alame tai miyoo de weqehe tere bithei gisun ... ama dergi taizu ... enduringge hvwangdi*).[57] The reason that Hong Taiji kept the title of khan but addressed his departed father as emperor could be out of respect. Nevertheless, the title of emperor was used consistently throughout the Qing dynasty after 1644.

---

[53] Manwen yuandang, p. 118.
[54] *Manwen yuandang*, vol. 10, p. 119.
[55] *Manwen yuandang*, vol. 10, p. 121.
[56] *Manwen yuandang*, vol. 10, p. 122.
[57] *Manwen yuandang*, vol. 10, pp. 557-558.

Thus we can see that the Manchu-language chronicles reveal an intention to maintain an accordant and coherent Manchu identity, with minor modifications but without abrupt diversions. The complicated identities of the Jurchen-Manchu state, supreme leaders, and people coexisted in the fast process of imperial expansion in relation to other cultures. The Koreans called the Jurchens under Nurgaqi's leadership as Jianzhou Tatars (*Jianzhou dazi* 建州猹子),[58] in which the made-up word 猹, instead of the original 韃, has a radial of dog to show contempt upon the barbarians. The term Jianzhou was a Han Chinese garrison that was subordinate to the Ming central government and therefore, the Manchus seldom used this term in their official documents. "The Manchu Veritable Records" even made a clear affirmation that "Manchu" is the right name for the state and the Ming mistook it as Jianzhou (*qiguo dinghao manzhou... nanchao wuming jianzhou* 其国定號滿洲…南朝误名建州).[59] Such a statement manifests distinction between the Manchu and Han Chinese discourses in politics, history and academics.

1.2 Research Questions, Methods and Aims

What is economy in a Manchu perspective? The Manchu-language chronicles show that the Jurchen-Manchu regimes focused on the acquisition of currencies, people, lands and industries before the unification of China. My hypothesis is that, being similar to the other global powers like the British, French and Russians, the Manchus launched military campaigns to expand their territories, defeating the Koreans, Mongols and Han Chinese for tributary and taxation purposes. Chronicle documents do support the hypothesis that the Manchu expansion, though it clearly lacked a maritime dimension, generally falls into the category of continental expansion.

Besides the acquisition of wealth achieved by military expansion, how did the Manchus develop their economy? Manchu, Han Chinese and Korean documents also demonstrate that multiple modes of economic

---

[58] *Mingdai Man Meng shiliao* 明代滿蒙史料 (Manchu-Mongol Historical Materials of the Ming Dynasty), *Lichao shilu chao* 李朝實錄抄 (Selected Compilation from the Veritable Records of the Li Court), vol. 23, edition Tokyo: 文海出版社有限公司印行 (Wenhai Publishing Co., Ltd.), 1953, p. 32.

[59] *Manzhou shilu* 滿洲實錄 (The Manchu Veritable Records), excerpted from *Qing shilu* 清實錄 (The Qing Veritable Records), vol. 1, edition Beijing: Zhonghua shuju, 1986, p. 8.

sectors, such as hunting, gathering, fishing, husbandry, farming and many other kinds of manufacturing industries in forms of mining, smelting, salt production and textile industry, etc. Such chronicle evidence confirms the mixed pattern of the Manchu economy, which was robust and resilient to survive all kinds of natural calamities and military defeats.

Research methods consists of analysis, interpretation and critical appraisal of Manchu chronicles. The analysis of Manchu texts involves identifying and categorizing the patterns of economic activities, such as acquiring and distributing currencies, lands, human population and various industries. Interpretation is to highlight hypotheses based on analysis, which appear as the arguments being addressed in various places of this book. Sources written in other languages, especially Han Chinese and Korean will naturally be taken into consideration for criticism and evidence confirmation. Thus, one can conclude that historical research is a process characterized by an attempt for knowing the past and identifying historical events, that is, to critically evaluate from multiple perspectives how past events and decision-makings may have taken place.

As Jörn Rüsen pointed out that scholars could question the principle of historical thinking and then investigate the determinant factor of the scientific nature of the science of history. In this regard, method is the criterion of scientificity, which is addressed as a comprehensive and fundamental principle of historical knowledge (*Man kann auch der historischen Methode als Prinzip des historischen Denkens fragen und untersucht dann den bestimmenden Faktor der Wissenschaftlichkeit der Geschichtswissenschaft; Methode ist dann das Kriterium der Wissenschaftlichkeit, sie wird im Sinne von Descartes als umfassendes und fundamentales Prinzip der historischen Erkenntnis angesprochen*).[60] Specifically speaking, terminological study is employed to determine some crucial terms in economic activities. For example, the meaning of a Manchu word *jiha* varies in different context. Whether it means copper coin or a unit of measurement for silver is being analyzed in the following chapter. Grammatical analysis is extensively used for translating the Manchu texts into English. As a Tungusic language, it does not require a verb to form the predicate of a sentence. For a simple

---

[60] Jörn Rüsen (1988), *Historische Methode,* Herausgegeben von Christian Meier und Jörn Rüsen, Deutscher Taschenbuch Verlag, München, p. 67.

instance, the statement of *lama, tanggvt i niyalma* can directly goes as "the lamas are Tibetan people", by inserting a linking verb for translation. Grammar rules change along the historical course. Before 1644, the scribes used *bi* as a suffix to a verb stem, for indicating certain actions that will happen in a successive order, but the Qianlong scholars in the process of re-transcribing changed some of them into *fi*, which has been used as a standardized grammar rule up to now. Obviously, these grammatical modifications can help researchers better understand the time sequence of historical events with a clearer focus on the core message.

Most of the economic activities were recorded as written texts, along with oral communications of the people during the time. The language used by the scribes for note taking is vernacular, which was based on the Jurchen dialect being spoken in Nurgaqi's homeland that was addressed as *Jianzhou* 建州 in the Han Chinese historical and academic discourse. After taking over the Ming's Liaodong region, the local Han Chinese merchants suffered from looters, who could be some Jurchen soldiers or Han Chinese bandits. Nurgaqi issued decrees to encourage both the Jurchen and Han Chinese people to arrest the robbers: *durime niyalma be juxen saqi, juxen jafa, nikan saqi, nikan jafa* (if Jurchens saw the robbers, Jurchens catch them; if Han Chinese saw the robbers, Han Chinese catch them). In textual analysis, these colloquial words reflect a quick response of the Later Jin state to protect the market.

Content analysis surveys the whole collection of Manchu annals written before 1644 for identifying patterns that could help illuminate the economy of a rising empire. The acquisition of currencies, people, lands and industries from the Later Jin's neighbors frequently appears in the Manchu texts, which draws my attention to from the structure of this book. Combining with the relevant events kept by the contemporary Han Chinese and Korean literati, comparative analysis is applied to interpret the significance of economic growth championed by the Later Jin state. In consideration of secondary sources, theories of economics are being explored in a historical context, which may result in a further investigation upon the relationship between state and economy.

Statistical analysis, especially in form of table chart, is intensively employed for analyzing the Manchu acquisition of people from their neighboring regions. Though circa ten years of Manchu-language chronicles were missing, the existing documents are sufficient for me to make a survey of the population growth under the Jurchen-Manchu regime within certain time periods. Economy, essentially, is human activities of producing, exchanging, distributing and consuming goods, upon which other factors are involved for various purposes. However, without human beings, economy cannot take place. Thus, it is reasonable to understand that the early Jin-Qing scribes kept detailed records of their acquisition of human beings, and the number ranged from one person to hundreds of thousands.

One of the main aims of this research, as a case study, is to adopt a specific Manchu perspective in looking at the past of Northeast Asia's development and to reinterpret the history of Manchu economy mainly based on Manchu chronicles and historiographical documents. Another aim is to enhance the critical use of Manchu documents and integrate it into research, thus opening new horizons for promoting a better understanding of Manchu history. Translating the Manchu-language chronicles into English will also be one of the further goals of this project and thus will make Manchu sources accessible for a wider academic public.

1.3 Source Criticism

Manchu economy in the pre-unification era remains mysterious in research due to the insufficient use of Manchu-language chronicles. Scholars mainly studied the economy of Ming China based on Han Chinese-language documents, with little reference to the Manchu economy before 1644, particularly from a Manchu-centered perspective. Extraordinary work has been conducted about Ming China's economic activities, for instance, the circulation of paper notes and silver currency, monetary and fiscal policies, commercial exchange in relation to metals, salt, grains, silk, porcelain and other products. The prosperity of the Ming economy, partially as a result of the global trading system, has been well recognized in academia. Nonetheless, the Manchu state, as Ming China's rival in Northeast Asia, deserves more attention with regard to its economic dimensions.

Generally, people believe that the rise of the Manchus was unstoppable because of their military advantages. Recently, however, scholars have also started to analyze the Manchu expansionism more from aspects of political institutions and economic achievements. Moreover, the publication of Manchu-language chronicles has promoted the research of Manchu history and provides ample support in elucidating its dimension of political economy. An early publication is *Manwen laodang* (1607-1637) published by Tōyō Bunko in Tokyo from 1955 to 1963, with seven volumes translated by Kanda Nobuo et al.. In 1969, the National Palace Museum in Taipei fortification of Taiwan published the ten volumes of the "Former Manchurian Chronicles" (*Jiu Manzhou dang* 舊滿洲檔, abbreviated as *jiudang* in this monograph). This was followed in 2005 by the ten volumes of the "Original Manchu Chronicles" (*Manwen yuandang* 滿文原檔, abbreviated as *yuandang*), which are photocopies of the original chronicles composed by Jurchen-Manchu writers. *Jiudang* and *Yuandang* are nearly identical documents, chronicled from 1607 to 1636, with minor differences such as printing technique. In 2009, Liaoning Minzu Press published the twenty volumes of "Collection of Manchu Old Chronicles Stored in the Grand Secretariat" (*Neige cangben Manwen laodang* 內閣藏本滿文老檔, abbreviated as *fe dangse*), with annotations, romanization and Han Chinese translation of the Manchu texts. Compared with *Jiudang* and *Yuandang*, *fe dangse* also started with 1707 and ended in 1636, but lacked the chronicle of 1635. These publications fueled research of Qing history with broader vision and evidence, with excellent prospects, especially for exploring the Manchu economy before 1644. Personally, I have read all these primary Manchu sources repeatedly for identifying their discrepancies, and I translated numerous passages into English for strengthening my arguments about ethnicity and economic history. Additionally, these Manchu-language chronicles contain information about specific interactions between Manchus and Mongols, which reveal that the Manchu leaders took serious the lessons taught by the decline and fall of the Mongol empire, especially concerning monetary and fiscal policies.

Moreover, Korean sources provide a unique angle for evaluating the Manchu economy from a third-party perspective. Official documents, such as "The Veritable Records of the Chosŏn Court" (*Lichao shilu* 李朝 實錄) informs us not only about diplomatic communications, but also on commercial transactions between Korea and the Later Jin. Private documents, taking Li Minwan's "Records of Hearings and Seeings in Jianzhou" (*Jianzhou wenjian lu* 建州聞見錄) for example, along with his "Daily Records in Prison" (*Zhazhong rilu* 柵中日錄) telling his experiences as a war prisoner after the battle of Sarhv, offers the author's personal insights, thus being helpful for reconstructing the economic history of the early Manchu state. Another private source is Zhao Qingnan's "Miscellaneous Records during the Turmoil" (*Luanzhong zalu* 亂中雜錄), which provides valuable economic information about the Manchu state circa 1637, i.e., the period when Hong Taiji ordered to invade Korea again.

Korean sources are indispensable for the academia to develop a holistic view when interpreting the late Ming and early Qing history. As Meng Sen ascertained, the Qing state avoided the claim that once it was the enemy of the Ming, and accordingly, some historical events, or facts in Meng's term, were completely eradicated from the Ming's Veritable Records (*shilu* 實錄). Consequently, "History of Ming" (*Mingshi* 明史) lacks consulting a large number of scripts that were recorded in the Veritable Records, which awaits today's scholars to supplement and emend (*qingdai huicheng yu ming wei diguo, yijiang shilu suozai shishi jinshan, mingshi sui wei quelou yida bufen zhishu, er youdai jinzhi zhi buding yi* 清代諱稱與明爲敵國，宜將實錄所載事實盡刪，明史遂爲闕漏一大部分之書，而有待今日之補訂矣).[61] Though Korea was unified by the Manchus and became a dependent state of the Qing empire for most of the time, large amounts of historical writings survived the Qing's censorship. The rise of the Jurchen-Manchu state was well documented in the Korean source, which provides valuable evidence for scholars to reconstruct the economic activities of the time.

Han Chinese sources consist of official chronicles, local gazetteers, veritable records, and literary collections. Guan Xiaolian's "Compiled Translation of Manchu Chronicles Kept by the Early Qing Palace Historiographic Academy" (*Qingchu neiguoshiyuan manwen dang'an yibian* 清初內國史院滿文檔案譯編) presents comprehensive details about the Manchu economy during Hong Taiji's reign. Shen Guoyuan's "Narration and Records of the Two Reigns" (*Liangchao congxin lu* 兩朝從信錄) gives Han Chinese opinions of how to deal with the rise of the

---

[61] Meng Sen 孟森 (1934), *Mingyuan Qingxi tongji* 明元清系通紀 (Comprehensive Chronicles of Narrating the Qing's Genealogy according to the Ming's Notation System) zhengbian juan 6, the Jingtai reign, edition Beijing: Guoli beijing daxue chubanshe, p. 3.

Manchu state, especially in the aspect of fiscal matters. Local gazetteers such as the "Complete Records of Liao" (*Quan Liao zhi* 全遼志) and "Records of unification by the Great Ming" (*Daming yitong zhi* 大明一統志) are rich sources for obtaining economic data regarding the Late Ming Liaodong province, which eventually was unified by Nurgaqi. Official historiography and veritable records, e.g., the "History of Ming" (*Mingshi* 明史) and the "Ming Veritable Records" (*Ming shilu* 明實錄) respectively, likewise offer Han Chinese perspectives for an appraisal of the Manchu economy. Finally yet importantly, literary collections such as the "Compilations of Statecraft in the Ming Dynasty" (*Ming jingshi wenbian* 明經世文編) that contain articles compiled by Chen Zilong, depict a strong Manchu economy that posed formidable threats upon the Ming China.

In light of the above primary sources, this project is going to explore the dimension of Manchu political economy in its relationship to currencies, land, people and industries. Indeed, although the Manchu economy grew exponentially in terms of procurements achieved by military success, it nonetheless also flourished because of an expanding money supply, robust industries and flourishing markets. The Manchu economy developed rapidly along with the expansion of the Manchu state, starting first with tribal strife, but quickly growing into an entity that transcended ethnic identities. The significance of political transformation was closely tied to the Manchus' economic acquisitions, while at the same being underpinned by the growth of its military industries.

As for the definition of chronicle in this monograph, conventionally I followed the name of the documents that were re-transcribed in the Qianlong reign (r. 1736-1796), which reads as *dorgi yamun asaraha manju hergen i fe dangse*. The literal meaning is "inner-cabinet collected Manchu word's old chronicles". The word of *dangse* takes its origin in the Mongolian word *dangsa*, whose script looks slightly different but conveys the same meaning.[62] Correspondingly it goes with the Han Chinese expression *dangzi* 檔子. In the Manchu-language annals that were written before the unification of China, the concept is "the regular documents". The first scribe of these scripts, Erdeni, who kept these official records and wrote that "all this good governance established by

---

[62] Shan Shikui 單士魁 (1978), *Qingdai dang'an congtan* 清代檔案叢談 (Collected Talks about the Archives of the Qing Dynasty), Zijincheng chubanshe, Beijing, p. 7.

the wise great and bright Khan were remembered, written and collected as the regular documents" (*sure amba genggiyen han i ilibuha eiten haqin i sain doro be, erdeni baksi ejeme bitheleme gaiha, an i bithe ere inu*).[63] Another original concept consists of laws and documents, which were also written by Erdeni, stating that "Erdeni, the scholar who recorded laws and wrote documents, said that the Han people's emperor Wanli ..." (*kooli be ejeme bithe araha erdeni baksi hendume, nikan gurun i wan li han, ...*).[64]

According to Shi Shouqian 石守謙, *Jiudang* is a photocopy of the original scripts, but the actual appearance is not sufficiently presented and therefore, *Yuandang* is reproduced in a way of microfilming.[65] Personally I compared these two publications and found out that their contents are identical and the latter is in a better shape for reading. In comparison with these two Taipei versions, *Fe dangse* lacks the documents that were composed in the ninth year of Tiancong (1635). But this loss can be compensated by the Han Chinese translation of "Compiled Translation of Manchu Chronicles Kept by the Early Qing Palace Historiographic Academy" (*Qingchu neiguoshiyuan manwen dang'an yibian* 清初內國史院滿文檔案譯編), which contains the missing annals of *Yuandang, Jiudang* and *Fe dangse*.

Regarding the disparities, the scribes of *Fe dangse* corrected the spelling errors during the process of transcribing and did evidential research about the names of people and places.[66] Furthermore, achievements made by the original annals writers, such as Erdeni's effort of composing the scripts and Dahai' improvement upon the writing system, were added in the Qianlong transcript of *Fe dangse*. Therefore, researchers can benefit from these supplemental materials. By and large, these three sources are identical in almost every case of describing historical events, starting from 1607 and ending in 1636. Thus, one can believe that *Fe dangse* was a copy on the basis of *Yuandang*, with corrections and supplements.

In aspect of script, the early texts of *Yuandang* (a.k.a., *Jiudang*) was written in the Old Manchu Script (man. *tongki fuka akv hergen*; chin. *lao*

---

[63] Jiu Manzhou dang, p. 129.
[64] *Fe dangse*, p. 392.
[65] *Manwen yuandang*, vol. 1, p. i.
[66] *Fe dangse*, pp. 3-4.

manwen 老滿文), whose alphabet was designed by Gagai and Erdeni on the command and inspiration of Nurgaqi in 1599.[67] The old script was based on Mongol alphabet that has no diacritical marks to distinguish certain pronunciations in writings. In the first month of 1632, Hong Taiji's commanded Daihai to add circles and dots upon the Twelve Heads (man. *juwan juwe uju*; chin. *shi'er zitou* 十二字頭), which is the Manchu alphabet chart, to clarify the confusion in reading (*juwan juwe uju... aisin gurun i sure han i ningguqi aniya niyengniyeri ujui biyade, han i hesei dahai baksi tongki fuka sindame temgetulehe, ...*).[68] Consequently, part of the *Yuandang* was written in an interchanging state, struggling with the proper use of diacritical marks. In late Hong Taiji's reign, the scribes handled the improved writing system more skillfully, which is now recognized as the New Manchu Script (man. *tongki fuka sindaha hergen*; chin. *xin manwen* 新滿文). *Fe dangse* was transcribed entirely with the new script by the Qianlong scholars.

The texts of *Fe dangse* are relatively authoritative. For instance, Nurgaqi's first born, Argatu Tumen, had conflicts with his four brothers and five ministers, who later brought these disputes to Nurgaqi. The Khan's response to these nine people is that "your words are orally reported and how could I remember? Write a script and bring it to me." Each of the four brothers and five ministers wrote a document about their sufferings and reported to the Khan (*han hendume, suweni ere gisun be anggai alaqi, bi ya be ejere, bithe arafi gaji seme henduhe manggi, duin deo sunja amban qani joboho be emte bithe arafi han de alibuha*).[69] Documents were composed as evidence to verify accusations among the leaders of state. Nevertheless, this research adopts chronicle, instead of archive, for translating the word *dangse,* due to the chronicled records of the annalists.

The following text directly mentioned the name of Manggvltai, who was the fifth son of Nurgaqi, but when referring to Hong Taiji, the writer used *duinqi beile* (the Fourth Chieftain) for respecting his higher status.[70] In the *Original Manchu Chronicles*, the names of these two brothers were

---

[67] *Manzhou shilu*, pp. 110-112.
[68] *Fe dangse*, pp. 5790-5792.
[69] *Fe dangse*, pp. 83-84.
[70] Fe dangse, p. 90.

paralleled as *manggvltai taiji hong taiji*,[71] from which we know that Hong Taiji's name could be only one word *hong*, since *taiji* is a title for honoring the leaders of Mongol or Jurchen groups.[72] Thus, the credibility of the documents were dubious because certain narrative was evidently modified after Hong Taiji took over the khan-ship. I looked into the *Jiudang* (a.k.a. *Yuandang*) and found that the original expression was *hong taiji*,[73] which was the authentic name of Nurgaqi's eighth son, who was crowned as the Fourth Chieftain and gained the throne after Nurgaqi's death. When the Qinglong literati re-transcribed the original documents, they correspondingly changed Hong Taiji's name into the Fourth Chieftain to honor his khan-ship. Even though the original message in the context was not compromised, the modification of expression still confirms the purpose of manipulating the readers for believing something else, as Lars Peter Laamann and Hans Ulrich Vogel communicated to me in private communications. Nonetheless, large amounts of economic activities were still reliable as historical events, which can be verified by comparison to the Ming and Korean sources.

Another interesting phenomenon is that Nurgaqi's name never appeared in these Manchu-language chronicles. The chronicle writers referred to Nurgaqi as khan. Nurgaqi's younger brother was written as Xurgaqi in *Fe dangse* in the New Manchu Script, with a dot as diacritical mark to pronounce the *g* sound, so that we have reason to believe that his older brother's name must pronounce in a similar or same way. The corresponding reference of Xurgaqi in *Yuandang* and *Jiudang* was written in the original Old Manchu Script and therefore, one cannot determine whether the name should pronounce as Xurgaqi, Xurhaqi or Xurkaqi without diacritical marks.

Nonetheless, according to the "Manchu-language Biography of the Founding-father Lofty Emperor" (*manwen taizu gao huangdi benji shu* 滿文太祖高皇帝本紀書), the name of the founder of Later Jin is spelled as Nurhaqi,[74] with a circle as diacritical mark, without considering the

---

[71] *Manwen yuandang*, vol. 1, p. 34.

[72] Further evidence is the name *Hong Baturu*, in which *baturu* means a brave man or warrior. *Baturu* was often bestowed to the people who fought courageously in wars and is still widely used for naming the males in Mongolian regions.

[73] Jiu Manzhou dang, p. 68.

[74] *Manwen taizu gao huangdi benji shu* 滿 文 太 祖 高 皇 帝 本 紀 書 (The Manchu-language Biography of the Founding-father Lofty Emperor), author unknown,

Han Chinese tradition of avoiding the mention of superior's name. This Manchu-language biography was a copy produced in 1819, in which the syllables of Nurhaqi is close to the modern Han Chinese pronunciation of Nu'erhachi 努爾哈赤. Yet, Nurgaqi is adopted in this book in consideration of the official spelling of his younger brother Xurgaqi's name, which was also confirmed by the Qianlong scholars.

The "Manchu Veritable Records" (*Manzhou shilu* 滿洲實錄) is another major source to underpin my research. As the first volume of the "Qing Veritable Records" (*Qing shilu* 清實錄), these annals were composed in Manchu, Han Chinese and Mongol languages simultaneously. According to the preface in the photocopy of Zhonghua Book Company 中華書局, the first edition of the Manchu Veritable Records was finished in 1635,[75] which deserves more discussion. The name of the Khan, Hong Taiji, was erased or evaded in texts of all three languages, which means that the authors had a clear sense of tabooing the supreme leader's name. However, passages of *Jiu Manzhou dang* written in 1636 still directly referred to the Khan as Hong Taiji, which says that "Hong Taiji, your subordinate of the Great Qing, submitted a report to the Heaven and Earth" (*daiqing gurun i amban hong taiji abka na de wesimbure gisun ...*).[76] As Giovanni Stary stated, the first reign title of Hong Taoji (man. abkai sure; chin. tiancong 天聰) must have been mistaken as "Abahai" as Hong Taiji's name.[77] This narrative proves that the "*Manchu Veritable Records*" must be finalized after 1636. Furthermore, one can see that languages reflect different ideologies when reading these three languages. When narrating the mother of the Manchu forefather, the Manchu text said "heaven's daughter" (*abkai sargan jui*), which is the same as the Mongol expression (*tegeri-in ükid*), but the Han Chinese text used the word "fairy" (*xiannü* 仙女),[78] which leads to the concept of superstition rejected by Confucianism. Another example is that when locating the birthplace of the Manchu people, the Manchu text said "the sun-rising side" (*xun dekdere ergi*), which is the same as the

---

collected by The Kyoto University Research Centre for the Cultural Sciences, a copy in 1819, pp. 6-8.

[75] Manzhou shilu, pp. 1-2.

[76] Jiu Manzhou dang, p. 5329.

[77] Giovanni Stary (1984), The Manchu Emperor "Abahai": Analysis of an Historiographic Mistake, *Central Asiatic Journal*, 28. 3: 296-299.

[78] Manzhou shilu, p. 4.

Mongol (*naran urguku jug*). But the Han Chinese expression is "northeast" (*dongbei* 東北),[79] which reflects that the Han Chinese author may have brought the Han Chinese sense of location into the text. Beides, the Mongol text has a different narrative than the Manchu and Han Chinese. One example is that, in the Manchu and Han Chinese texts, the mother told the son to settle the chaotic state (man. *faquhvn gurun*; chin. *luanguo* 亂國), while the corresponding Mongol text only refers to the Manchu people (*manju olon*).[80] The chapter of the Acquisition of Lands heavily depends on this source because of its systematic records of territorial expansion.

Besides the Manchu-language documents, Manchu sources that were translated into Han Chinese were also adopted in large quantities. The "Compiled Translation of Manchu Chronicles Kept by the Early Qing Palace Historiographic Academy" (*Qingchu neiguoshiyuan manwen dang'an yibian* 清初內國史院滿文檔案譯編) can sufficiently complement the records that were missing in the original Manchu-language chronicles, ranging from 1633 to 1643. In my book, this source particularly helps with the statistics of population that was acquired in Hong Taiji's reign. One of my future projects is to access the original documents for verifying the relevant numbers in quotation, and also for translating a holistic English version of Manchu-language annals that were produced before 1644, so that a better study on the early Qing history can be expected.

The evidence for writing this book is mainly extracted from my own translation of the Manchu-language annals. A large number of passages in the Manchu-language chronicles were translated from Manchu into English for reinforcing the thesis of what Manchu economy is. Nonetheless, this monograph is not a comprehensive reconstruction of the early Qing economics, nor a general history of the Manchu regime in the pre-unification era. Materials were selected in view of economic activities for state-building in the Manchu way, and more Manchu-language texts will be translated and added into this book with following improvements.

---

[79] Manzhou shilu, p. 4.
[80] Manzhou shilu, p. 5.

1.4 Plans for Further Studies and Publication

This book formally started in 2017 under the guidance of Professor Hans Ulrich Vogel and Professor Achim Mittag, who have encouraged me to read primary Manchu-language documents and other sources as well as secondary literature for developing hypotheses, forming arguments, and dealing with theories in historiography and political economy. I am very grateful that my supervisors have given me all the necessary support for advancing the research project in sustainable ways.

Besides this introduction, the book divides into four main chapters: "Acquisition of Currencies", "Acquisition of People", "Acquisition of Lands", and "Acquisition of Industries". The chapter of currencies covers analysis of copper coins minted by the Later Jin state and its acquisition of silver in the Ming's Liaodong region. The chapter of people reconstructs the process that Nurgaqi and Hong Taiji subjugated the Jurchen tribes, the Ming's Liaodong people, Mongol nomads and some Koreans. The chapter of lands reviews Nurgaqi's endeavor of unifying the Jurchen realm and the unification of the Ming's Liaodong region. Hong Taiji carried out the subjugation of Korea and the Mongol Chakhar confederation (Inner Mongolia) and then upgraded himself as the Qing Emperor for owning these wide territories. The chapter of industries covers various traditional economies engaged by human hands, which also fits into the Latin definition of industry. The rise of the Manchu state started upon the Jurchen conventional economy, which consists of herding, farming, fishing, hunting and gathering. Some Jurchen people maintained animal husbandry after the demise of the Mongol rule, some sustained agriculture as sedentary communities, and some, including Nurgaqi himself, kept hunting, gathering, fishing and conducting commercial transactions from time to time. Accompanying the military expansion, this comprehensive structure of industries transformed the Jurchen-Manchu society into a resilient organization, which allows the regime and people to survive natural calamities and to overcome all sorts of challenges. The acquisition of Han Chinese industries in the Liaodong region, such as military works, greatly strengthened the Later Jin's military capacity for further encroaching the Ming's remaining areas beyond the pass.

More secondary literature, in the fields of historiography, linguistics, politics, economics, military history and religious studies, should be integrated into the arguments of this book. The function of currencies can be further elucidated in the traditional context of political economy, in which the state competed against the merchants for the control of copper and silver in regards of mining, refining, minting, circulating and reclaiming. After the unification of the Ming, paper notes were issued in the Shunzhi reign (r. 1644-1661) for a short while, but paper currency did not appear in the Later Jin and early Qing regime before 1644. Did the Jurchen-Manchu state learn the lessons from the Mongol Yuan, or the Han Chinese Ming? Alternatively, was there a need of printing paper notes because the state had already acquired sufficient silver? Reasons could be far more complicated and it is worth further exploration based on sources written in multiple languages.

Military industries will expand in light of great masses of primary and secondary literature. The available Manchu annals provide little information of recruiting the Han Chinese crafts men for casting cannons, but the concurrent Manchu documents kept by some other Manchu administration, with their corresponding Han Chinese chronicles, may reveal much evidence for studying the firearm manufacture. Secondary literature written in Han Chinese and western languages supply insightful knowledge of technology, scientific theories and the spread of firearms from Europe to Asia, which can help this monograph gain a wider view of history as a reflection of the past. In the age of the Internet, I have great opportunities of accessing different primary sources and secondary literature that present a global perspective of studying the past and pursuing a holistic interpretation.

Considerable amounts of passages in the early Manchu annals written before 1644 have already been translated, quoted and paraphrased into this book. A promising project is to translate the whole collections of these Manchu-language documents into English, which will provide the academia with more comprehensible materials as primary source after coming off the press. I am thankful to the efforts of Tübingen Library Publishing (TLP) for promulgating this book and long for more collaborations with TLP to publish more works in Asian Studies. Professor Wang Qilong, an insightful scholar from Shaanxi Normal University and Xi'an International Studies University, and many colleagues across the globe are inspiring me to integrate different academic disciplines into International and Regional Studies, which is an interdisciplinary work concerning fundamental and practical research. I hope our joint effort will be published by TLP for promoting humanities as science.

There are different academic landscapes in regards of studying the past of East Asia, such as Chinese Studies, which involves Manchu, Mongol, Tibetan and Turkic Studies, Oriental Studies and Global History. This book, in a personal expectation, will serve as a catalyst to encourage myself for greater pursuit of historical science in all of these disciplines. It is never too late to start learning about the past and the past always reflects directions for human beings to make a better future.

2. Acquisition of Currencies

2.1 Introduction

This chapter tries to present a Manchu view of what happened in the early seventeenth century when the Jurchen-Manchu state rose up to acquire precious metals from the Ming's Liaodong region. Evidence is mainly extracted and quoted from the Manchu-language annals, which convey very different messages from the Han Chinese-language documents of the time. For example, activities of Li Chengliang 李成梁 and Li's family did not appear in the annals written solely in Manchu language, but in the *Manchu Veritable Records* that was composed in Manchu, Han Chinese and Mongol languages. Neither did the Manchu-language documents explain why silver flooded into the Liaodong region during the Ming period. Based on the sources written in western and Han Chinese languages, scholars such as Kenneth Swope, postulated the ascent of Li Chengliang's family in connection with Americas' silver flowing into Ming's coffers,[81] which reinforced the Han Chinese military defence in northeast frontiers. Nonetheless, Lin Man-houng argued that Asian silver also flowed into China in the sixteenth century,[82] which boosted the Ming's economy, with the Liaodong region included. Frontier security remained severe through out the Ming dynasty. The government had to dispatch large numbers of army in the northern frontiers for the defence against the Mongols and Jurchens. Since the second half of the sixteenth century, the annual military expenditure increased from two million *liang* silver to four million and therefore, silver imported from the southeast coast of China flooded into the northern borderlands, as Mio Kishimoto declared.[83] Accordingly, this book attempted to present how silver in the Ming Liaodong regions ended up in the Jurchen-Manchus' treasury.

---

[81] Kenneth Swope (ed.) (2005), *Warfare in China since 1600*, The Cromwell Press, Trowbridge, Wiltshire, 2005, p. 11.

[82] Lin Man-houng (2006), *China Upside Down: Currency, Society and Ideologies, 1808-1856*, Harvard University Asia Center, Cambridge Massachusetts, p. 30.

[83] Mio Kishimoto 岸本美緒 (2010), *Hou shiliushiji wenti yu Qingchao* "後十六世紀問題" 與清朝 (The Problems of the Post-sixteenth Century and the Qing Dynasty), collected in *Qingchao de guojia rentong* 清朝的國家認同 (State's Identity of the Qing Dynasty), edited by Liu Fengyun 劉鳳雲 and Liu Wenpeng 劉文鵬, Zhongguo renmin daxue chubanshe, Beijing, p. 307.

Recent scholarship has pointed out that silver surged into China during the last century of the Ming, which prompted rapid commercial expansion because of the increasing demand of China's porcelain and silk in Europe and Americas.[84] Nonetheless, few traces of international trade with Japan and European countries can be detected in the Manchu-language documents. From a Jurchen-Manchu stance, commercial transactions mainly took place with the Ming China, Korea and the neighboring Mongol tribes. Barter trade still remained as a popular way of business exchange in the first half of the seventeenth century, besides minor commodities being conducted in various amounts of silver. The Manchu documents show that silver functioned as the main medium of revenue and commerce in the northeast Asia during Nurgaqi (r. 1616-1626) and Hong Taiji's reign (r. 1626-1643). Being similar to the Ming state, silver acquired by the Jurchen-Manchus also circulated in an uncoined form before 1644 and down to the end of imperial era,[85] largely as ingots. A small quantity of brass coins were also issued by the regime, presumably for the significance of declaring sovereignty against the Ming and over the other ethnic groups in the region. Furthermore, quantities of copper was demanded for military industry, especially in Hong Taiji's time.

Little evidence, from either Korean or Han Chinese source, points out that the Later Jin and early Qing state before 1644 ever issued paper currency. According to the Manchu annals, currencies that circulated in the Jin-Qing empire appeared in three forms: coin (man. *jiha*; chin. *qian* 錢), silver (man. *menggun*; chin. *yin* 銀) and gold (man. *aisin*; chin. *jin* 金). The following chapters aim to analyze the acquisition, distribution and functions of gold and silver, and to introduce a concise imperial opinion regarding the true wealth of an empire, which is people, rather than the precious metals.

2.2 Coin as a Fractional Currency

The usage of coin is recorded little in the official documents of the Later Jin state and only a few passages mention the existence of coin. The

---

[84] Richard von Glahn (2013), Cycles of Silver in Chinese Monetary History, collected in Billy K. L. So (ed.), The Economy of Lower Yangzi Delta in late Imperial China: Connecting Money, Markets, and Institutions, Routledge, London, p. 31.

[85] Richard von Glahn, Cycles of Silver in Chinese Monetary History, p. 45.

state's mintage appears in the northeast Asia according to these early Manchu annals, unlike the pervasive private mintage of copper coins in southwest China during the late Qianlong period.[86] One piece of positive evidence is:

iqe juwe de, menggun elgiyen ofi, jiha be takvrarakv seme alara jakade, jiha hungkerere be nakabuha.[87]

On the second day [of the fifth month in the tenth year of the Genggiyen Han, 1625], because [people] reported that silver was abundant, [and thus people] would not use coins, [therefore, the state] stopped casting coins.

This text indirectly confirms silver as the main medium for commercial exchange and state's payment in the Later Jin. The context of the early Manchu annals shows little evidence about the relationship between currencies and production of industries. It would be too early to argue that a primitive form of managed monetary system was established in Nurgaqi's regime, since the idea of a managed system is mainly utilized by modern societies, in which the circulation of goods and services were facilitated by issuing an amount of money.[88] Nonetheless, an affirmative message is that the state circulated both silver and coins as currencies for the imperial operation, and the amount of coins were minted to supplement the circulating silver.

It is unlikely that the state stopped casting coins due to the shortage of copper caused by a high demand in military industry. Both Manchu and Han Chinese documents written before 1644 confirm that cannon manufacture did not start until the fifth year of Sure Han (1631), which is in Hong Taiji's reign. Neither do the documents support that the Jurchen-Manchus experienced scarcity of copper in Nurgaqi's reign. The reason of stopping the cast of coin simply could be the sufficient quantity of silver in circulation, as the Manchu text indicates.

---

[86] Lin Man-houng, *China Upside Down*, p. 35.
[87] *Fe dangse*, pp. 2978-2979.
[88] Lin Man-houng, *China Upside Down*, p. 7.

Wang Zhonghan 王鍾翰 considered Heaven's-Mandate-Khan-Cash (*tianming hanqian* 天命汗錢) as physical evidence of copper coin cast in Nurgaqi's reign.[89] As for the material components of the coins, Dai Jianbing 戴建兵 claimed that there were multiple formats, exquisitely minted of bronze (*qingtong* 青銅), copper (*hongtong* 紅銅) and brass (*huangtong* 黃銅).[90] The design of Jurchen coin falls into the category of oriental system, being inscribed with written characters, plus a square hole in the center, rather than being decorated with images of animals and plants as on the occidental coins.[91]

Illustration 1: A copper coin minted in Nurgaqi's reign with Manchu inscriptions that read abkai fulingga han jiha, meaning Heavenly-Mandate-Khan money

[89] Wang Zhonghan 王鍾翰 (1957), *Qingshi zakao* 清史雜考 (Miscellaneous Research on Qing History), Renmin chubanshe, Beijing, p. 13.

[90] Dai Jianbing 戴建兵 (2011), *Zhongguo huobi wenhuashi* 中國貨幣文化史 (History of China's Currency Culture), Shandong huabao chubanshe, Ji'nan, pp. 158-159.

[91] Lin Man-houng, *China Upside Down*, p. 31.

Illustration 2: A copper coin minted in Nurgaqi's reign with Han Chinese inscriptions that read tian ming tong bao, meaning Heavenly-Mandate-universal treasure.

Peng Xinwei 彭信威 specified that when Nurgaqi established his own state in 1616, he ordered to cast two kinds of coins, with both Manchu and Han Chinese inscriptions.[92] The Manchu-inscription coin weights more than six grams, and its diameter ranges from 28 to 29 millimeters, being slightly bigger than the Han Chinese-inscription coin.[93] This description can be confirmed by the official records, which says that in the beginning of the first founder Nurgaqi's reign, the state minted coins named as *tianming tongbao,* which were classified into two types: Manchu and Han Chinese. The Manchu type is bigger than the Han Chinese. Hong Taiji, whose Han Chinese reign title is Tiancong, followed this institution (*taizu chu, zhu tianmingtongbao, bieyi manhanwen wei erpin. manwen yipin zhi jiao hanwen yipin wei da. tiancong yin zhi* 太祖初，鑄天命通寶，別以滿漢文爲二品。滿文一品質較漢文一品爲大。天聰因之).[94] However, the exchange rate between copper coins and silver ingots of the time remained unclear in these official documents.

Specifically speaking, the Manchu inscription *abkai fulingga han jiha* means heaven's-mandate-khan-cash, and the Han Chinese *tianming tongbao* 天命通寶 means heaven's-mandate-universal-treasure. The

[92] Peng Xinwei 彭信威 (1958), *Zhongguo huobishi* 中國貨幣史 (History of Currencies in China), Shanghai renmin chubanshe, Shanghai, p. 521.

[93] Dai Jianbing, Zhongguo huobi wenhuashi, p. 158.

[94] *Qingshigao* 清史稿 (The Draft of Qing History), complied by Zhao Erxun 趙爾巽 (1844-1927), et al., 1928, juan 120, edition Beijing: Zhonghua shuju, 1976, p. 3641.

Manchu passage quoted above juxtaposes "*menggun*" and "*jiha*" as parallel currencies, confirming the existence of coin. Another proof is the phrase of "*jiha hungkerere*", which is a typical expression of "minting coins". Therefore, this passage does justify coin as a currency circulating in the Jin-Qing empire. Nonetheless, only a few passages indicate coin as a medium of exchange. The word "*jiha*" appeared in one passage which was documented in the sixth month of the seventh year of Abkai Fulingga (1622) :

iqe nadan de, lio fujiyang bithe wesimbume... aqafi tehe nikan, gai jeo de lio fujiyang de habxanafi... mini ujihe ulgiyan be, amba ulgiyan de emu juwe jiha maktame bufi, gidame jafafi wambi seme uttu habxara jakade.[95]

On the seventh day, Regional Vice Commander [man. *fujiyang*; chin. *fujiang* 副將] Liu reported to the throne... the Han Chinese who lived together [with the Jurchens] came to Gai Zhou and brought a lawsuit to the Regional Vice Commander Liu... "The pigs I raised were taken away and killed [by the Jurchens], who threw one or two coins as payment for the big pigs. For this reason [I] sue [them]."

The phrase *emu juwe jiha* were one or two coins as a negligible compensation for the grown pigs, which also imply that coin stores very little value in circulation. In the third month of the the next year, Xajin, who was an Assistant Regional Commander (man. *canjiyang*; chin. *canjiang* 參將), robbed forty pigs from some Han Chinese people. Later, he got accused and was sentenced to pay forty *liang* silver to the owners (*xajin canjiyang be ini booi hehe gerqilame, nikan de dehi ulgiyan... dehi ulgiyan de dehi yan...*).[96] From this passage, we can know that one grown pig was worth as least one *liang* silver as a reasonable price and thus the indemnity of one or two coins was far blow people's expectation.

However, according to a private communication with Hans Ulrich Vogel, the expression of *emu juwe jiha* can be translated to "one or two *qian* of silver", which regards *jiha* as a measure of weight. This is a sound argument and my defence is that in the Manchu language, when *jiha* is used alone, it means brass coin, as the previous passages indicate. In other passages, *jiha* also refers to a small amount of silver when it is

---

[95] *Fe dangse*, pp. 1868-1869.
[96] *Fe dangse*, p. 2080.

accompanied by another word *menggun* as a combination of *jiha menggun*. Such as:

... nirui ejen beiguwan i uksin hadaha de, juwe jiha menggun bu...[97]

To make an armor for the Battalion Commander [man. *nirui ejen*; chin. *niulu ezhen* 牛錄額真] and the Defense Officer [man. *beiguwan*; chin. *beiyu* 備御], [it costs] two *qian* silver.

This passage affirms that "*jiha*" is used as a unit of measuring silver, rather than a medium of exchange. Other than this, little evidence has been found to confirm further usage of "*jiha*" in the Manchu chronicles dated before 1636. Though the Manchus seldom used cash coins, when Hong Taiji took over the khan-ship, he still mint coins out of political purpose, with Manchu inscriptions *sure han ni jiha* on the front, which means the wise khan's money; with *juwan* and *emu yan* on the back, which means equivalence with ten cash coins and one *liang* in correspondence as nominal value of weight. Peng xinwei 彭信威 argued that Hong Taiji's coins completely simulated the manufacturing style of the Ming's Tianqi coin, and the Manchu inscription was written in the new script too, with diacritical marks, while Nurgaqi's coins were inscribed in the old script without diacritical marks.[98] However, according to the coins collected in China Numismatic Museum (*Zhongguo qianbi bowuguan* 中國錢幣博物館), it is positive that Hong Taiji's coins were still inscribed in the old script, without any diacritical marks on the spellings of *sure, han, jiha* and *juwan*.[99] The Manchu word *juwan* is interpreted as ten cash (*dangshi* 當十),[100] which could reflect the state's shortage of copper reserve in the Hong Taiji's reign. My personal understanding is that *juwan* could be converted to ten cash coins (*zheshi* 折十), simulating the Ming's official coin. If so, the reason for copper scarcity could be out of the ongoing wars with the Ming that resulted in embargo, or, the Later Jin state had realized the importance of firearms and then started to hoard copper for weapon manufacture.

---

[97] *Fe dangse*, p. 1184.

[98] Peng Xinwei, *Zhongguo huobi shi*, pp. 521-522.

[99] According to the diacritical marks designed by the Jurchen scholar Dahai in 1632, there should be a dot on the vowel "u", "e" and a circle on the combination of "ha" if these words were inscribed in the new Manchu script.

[100] Dai Jianbing, Zhongguo huobi wenhuashi, p. 159.

Illustration 3: A coin minted in Hong Taiji's reign

The left image is the front side of a copper coin minted in Hong Taiji's reign with Manchu inscriptions that read *sure han ni jiha,* meaning the Bright-Khan's money; the middle image is the back side of a copper coin with Manchu inscriptions that read *juwan emu yan,* meaning the nominal value of ten-cash and the nominal weight of one *liang* copper. The *emu yan* or one ounce (*yiliang* 一兩) should not be the actual weight but a regulation of government. The frequent wars between the Later Jin and Ming must have severely affected the supply and consumption of copper and therefore, the regime of the Later Jin minted the ten-cash coins in a simulation of the Ming's fiscal policy, such as the Tianqi reign. The Jurchen ten-cash coins could imply that the copper coins actually circulated in the market as a medium to facilitate commercial transaction and its worth of one *liang* copper could prove that the Jurchen-Manchu state tried to intervene the market by stipulating the actual value of copper coin with its nominal.

Coins convey messages, as Barakatullo Ashurov's research upon the Sogdian coins that bear Christian motifs,[101] and the coins minted in Nurgaqi and Hong Taiji's reign also represent the sovereignty of a new rising regime that acted independently and defiantly against the Ming empire. Politics and economics are the two sides of one coin, and politics exerted great impacts upon economics in our case. The collapse of the Ming's economy, due to the failures of fiscal policies and natural

---

[101] Barakatullo Ashurov (2018), "Coins Convey a Message: Numismatic Evidence for Sogdian Christianity", *Central Asiatic Journal*, 61.2: 257-295.

calamities, directly led to the fall of the central government when facing the challenge of farmer's insurrection. Nonetheless, the Later Jin survived all sorts of crises and its monetary policy deserves greater attention.

Neither did Nurgaqi nor Hong Taiji issue paper notes. The early Manchu documents did not specify the reasons why the state and people exclusively relied on the precious metals as currencies within the Later Jin empire. One reason could be that the previous Jin dynasty (1115-1234), which was founded by the forefathers of the same Jurchen race, over-issued paper currency and caused its value to plummet dramatically. The "History of Jin" (*jinshi* 金史) says:

……鈔法屢變，隨出而隨壞……天興二年十月印天興寶會於蔡州，自一錢至四錢四等，同見銀流轉，不數月國亡。[102]

... the decree of paper notes frequently changed, and when a new one was issued, it immediately became corrupted... In the tenth month of the second year of Tianxing [1233], paper currency, named as Tian Xing Bao Hui, was issued in Caizhou, and it was classified into four degrees from one to four *qian* [of silver]. It circulated along the ongoing silver, but the state perished in a few months.

Since both Nurgaqi and Hong Taiji often looked into the previous Jin dynasty in search of examples for improving governance, they should have heard of such failures of over-issuing paper currency. Another passage from "History of Jin" tells that silver was a more reliable current than coin:

向以物重錢輕，犯賊者計錢論罪則太重，於是以銀爲則。[103]

Since long ago, goods have been valued heavily and coins lightly. For criminals, if their crimes were punished by paying coins, [the coins] would be too heavy [in weight]. Therefore, [the state] should take silver as the standard.

These passages may help to explain why neither paper note nor coin adopted as the main currency in the Later Jin due to the consequence of inflation and its insufficiency of measuring values. Furthermore, both the Yuan and Ming are the recent examples of undermining their authority by over-issuing paper notes. Besides the inflated economy, the Ming also

---

[102] Tuotuo 脫脫 et al., Jin Shi 金史 (The History of Jin Dynasty), edition Beijing: Zhonghua shuju, 1975, pp. 1087-1090.

[103] *Jinshi*, p. 1088.

suffered from casting coins in poor quality. In Feng Menglong's time (b. 1574-1646), coins were mint in such a small size that even one hundred items cannot make a handful (*bai bu ying wo* 百不盈握) and they broke into pieces once being dropped on the ground (*zhi di ji sui* 擲地即碎).[104] The small-sized coins and the inferior hardness imply a severe shortage of copper supply during the late Ming period. The reason of copper scarcity could be the depletion of mines and high demand in firearm producing for wars against the Jurchen-Manchu invasion. Consequently, coins in such low quality would impose negative impacts on commercial transactions. In the Ming dynasty, as Richard von Glahn analyzed, brass coin was a fractional currency that supplemented silver for daily transactions,[105] and the Later Jin was in the same situation, due to massive quantities of silver circulating in regions of the northeast Asia. Dai Jianbing declared that few coins minted in Hong Taiji's reign have been handed down to today,[106] and the reason could be that very few coins were minted by the state, or copper was used mainly for military purpose, as the following passages will argue.

Moreover, the Later Jin was constantly at war with all its neighboring lands and thus all sorts of metals, such as copper, were in urgent need of making weaponry. Zhao Duo 趙鐸 speculated that most of the copper was preferred to make cannonballs during the Later Jin period and thus very little was used for minting coins as subsidiary money.[107] Nonetheless, according to a private communication with Hans Ulrich Vogel, most of the cannonballs in the preindustrial society could be made of rocks or mint out of the metal lead, which also corresponds well with the records of *qianzi* 鉛子 in the concurrent Han Chinese documents. In the following chapter of traditional economies, we can also find that cannon making became a predominate industry in Hong Taiji's reign, which consumed large quantities of copper. Therefore, it was more

---

[104] Feng Menglong 馮夢龍, *Feng menglong quanji* 馮夢龍全集 (The Complete Works of Feng Menglong), Book 15, edition Nanjing: Fenghuang chubanshe, 2007, p. 243.

[105] Richard von Glahn, *An economic history of China: from antiquity to the nineteenth century*, Cambridge University Press, Cambridge, 2016, p. 307.

[106] Dai Jianbing, Zhongguo huobi wenhuashi, p. 159.

[107] Zhao Duo 趙鐸, *Qing kaiguo jingji fazhanshi* 清開國經濟發展史 (The Economic History of Qing's Empire-Building), Liaoning renmin chubanshe, Shenyang, 1992, p. 341.

practical for the state to prioritize silver and gold as the main currencies over copper cash and paper notes.

2.3 Acquisition of Gold and Silver

2.3.1 Acquisition through Wars

Both Nurgaqi and Hong Taiji demanded large quantities of gold and silver from the Ming as a condition of truce. No solid evidence confirms that the Ming ever sufficiently met their requests. Consequently, the Jurchen Manchus launched long-lasting wars to attack the Ming's Liaodong region, and acquired numerous gold and silver to fuel further military operations.

In the first month of the fourth year of the Gengiyen Han (1619), Nurgaqi attacked the Yehe tribe and looted large amounts of people and animals (*sohon honin aniya aniya biyai iqe juwe de, genggiyen han i qooha, yehe de geneme jurgan ... hoton de dosime genere niyalma morin ihan be gaifi gajiha*).[108] As Yehe's ally, the Ming sent an army for rescue but it was not successful (*... nikan qooha, yehe i gaxan de isinjifi, nikan qooha, yehe i juwe hoton i qooha aqafi afaki seme gvnifi, ohakv ...*).[109] After the victory, Nurgaqi sent a message to the Ming's officials, demanding three thousand *liang* silver and three hundred *liang* gold as a condition to stop the war (*... dain nakarakv ainaha... ilan minggan yan menggun, ilan tanggv yan aisin gaji seme bithe arafi unggihe*).[110]

Nurgaqi's request was responded with fierce military retaliation from the Ming and its dependency Korea, which was known as the Battle of Sarhv (*Sa'er'hu zhi zhan* 薩爾滸之戰). Within two months, the Ming sent two hundred and seventy thousand soldiers to attack Sarhv via four routes, but the war turned in the Jurchen-Manchus' favor: five thousand Korean soldiers surrendered (*sunja minggan solho dahame*)[111] and three routes of the Ming army were annihilated (*ilan jugvn i qooha be gemu waha*).[112] Following the victory of Sarhv, Nurgaqi ordered his troops to bring down the Ming's Kaiyuan fortification (*Kaiyuan shi* 開原市) and the result was significant:

---

[108] *Fe dangse*, p. 333.
[109] *Fe dangse*, p. 335.
[110] *Fe dangse*, pp. 335-336.
[111] *Fe dangse*, p. 284.
[112] *Fe dangse*, p. 387.

... keyen i heqen i ninggureme qoohai ying hadafi iliha, olji ulin aisin menggun, ihan morin eihen losa be, heqen i dolo meni meni tatan i teisu isibuha... ilan dedume olji ulin isibuqi wajihakv, qoohai morin de gemu aqiqi wajihakv ofi, tere heqen de baha morin eihen losa de gemu aqifi, ihan sejen de tebuqi wajihakv geli funqehe ...[113]

The army camped on the town walls, and all the captured treasure, such as gold, silver, cattle, horses, donkeys, and mules, were gathered inside the fortification where the troops stationed... after three nights, the obtained treasure was still not distributed over. All military horses were employed to ship the booties back but still could not finish the work. Thus, all the horses, donkeys and mules in the fortification were drafted, and even oxcarts were used to transport. However, there was still leftover...

Kaiyuan was a significant commercial fortification in the Ming' northern territory. Since Yongle (r. 1403-1424), the early Ming time, there were three horse markets set up in the Liaodong region, and two horse markets were established in Kaiyuan's region, being located forty *li*, twenty kilometers, away from the fortification (*mashizhe, shi yongle jian. liaodong she shi san, er zai kaiyuan, yi zai guangning, ge qu cheng sishili* 馬市者，始永樂間。遼東設市三，二在開原，一在廣寧，各去城四十里).[114] Remarkable wealth had accumulated in the fortification along the two hundred years of historical course. The Jurchens' harvest was abundant. Gold and silver were considered more importantly than the other spoils, so the precious metals were confiscated to the Eight Chieftains. The rest, such as silk and satin embroidery, were divided by the soldiers (... *tere dain de aisin menggun suje gequheri be, jaka ambula baha, gvwa jaka be gemu geren qooha neigen baha, aisin menggun be tulergi niyalma bahakv, gemu jakvn booi beise baha...).*[115]

Two years later, on the thirteenth of the eleventh month of the sixth year of the Genggiyen Han (1621), Daixan, the First Chieftain (man. *amba beile*; chin. *dabeile* 大貝勒), visited the magistrate of silver treasury (man. *menggun ku i da*; chin. *yinku zhang* 銀庫長), took sixty-six thousand *liang* silver away, rewarded the officials who had

[113] *Fe dangse*, pp. 441-442.
[114] *Mingshi* 明史 (History of Ming), vol. 92, Beijing edition: Zhonghua shuju, 1980, p. 2277.
[115] *Fe dangse*, pp. 456-457.

actual positions, and distributed the rest to the military men *(ineku tere inenggi, amba beile, menggun ku i da de genefi, ninggun tumen ninggun minggan yan menggun gajifi, juxen i hergen baha hafasa de bumbi, qoohai niyalma de salambi seme gajiha).*[116] Sixty-six thousand *liang* silver is a large number. The form of silver is not specified in the text, and a sensible speculation is ingots in this time period.[117] This passage implies that the Jurchens acquired large quantities of silver after taking over the Ming's Liaodong region and furthermore, the Later Jin had established their own treasury to store currencies.

The Ming government transported large quantities of silver into the Liaodong region for defending against the Jurchens. After taking over the Guangning fortification (Guangning cheng 廣寧城) in the third month of the eighth year of the Genggiyen Han (1623), Nurqaqi commanded all his men that had stopped building town walls in order to search silver that was buried by the Han Chinese. A small amount, such as two or three hundred *liang*, could be kept by the finders. As for a large amount of one thousand or ten thousand, finders could keep half of it *(ilan biyai iqe inenggi, guwangning de unggihe bithe, heqen sahara be nakaha, qoohai niyalma gemu guwangning ni heqen i dorgi tulergide aika umbuha eye baime fete, juwe ilan tanggv yan bahaqi, baha niyalma gemu gaikini, minggan yan tumen yan bahaqi, baha niyalma de emu hontoho bumbi...).*[118]

One month later, the officials delivered sums of discovered precious metals, which are nine hundred and thirty *liang* silver, and six *liang* seven *qian* gold *(alban i fetehe menggun uyun tanggv gvsin yan, aisin ninggun yan nadan jiha benjire jakade...)* .[119] The expression of *fetehe* means the action of digging in a past tense, and thus confirms some results of searching activity.

Silver was also obtained from Korea after some military conflicts, but the amount was negligible. On the sixth day of the fourth month in the eighth year of the Genggiyen Han (1623), a Regional Vice Commander Lenggeri led four hundred guards, captured one hundred and thirteen men, and brought back two hundred and fifty *liang* silver that was distributed

---

[116] *Fe dangse*, pp. 1241-1242.
[117] Lin Man-houng, *China Upside Down*, p. xxiii.
[118] *Fe dangse*, pp. 2084-2085.
[119] *Fe dangse*, p. 2183.

to the troops (*solho i ergi de lenggeri fujiyang, duin tanggv xanggiyan bayarai niyalma be gaifi anafu tenefi gajihangge, emu tanggv juwan ilan niyalma ... gajiha bihe ... juwe tanggv susai yan menggun be, gehehe bayarai niyalma de buhe*).[120]

After Nurgaqi's death, Hong Taiji carried on the same policy to blackmail the Ming for precious metals. In the first month of the first year of the Sure Han (1627), Hong Taiji wrote to Yuan Chonghuan (袁崇煥), who was the Grand Coordinator of Ningyuan (*ningyuan dutang* 寧遠都堂), and asked for one hundred thousand *liang* gold and one million *liang* silver as the gift for reconciliation (*manju gurun*[121] *i han i bithe, yuwan amba niyalma de unggihe... te suwe meni uru be safi, juwe gurun i doro aqaki seqi, aqara doroi aisin juwan tumen yan, menggun tanggv tumen yan...*).[122] If reconciliation was realized, Hong Taiji would offer ten Eastern Pearls (man. *tana*; chin. *dongzhu* 東珠), one thousand pieces of mink fur and one thousand *jin* ginseng roots each year as presents. As an exchange, the Ming should annually deliver ten thousand *liang* gold and one hundred thousand *liang* silver to the Later Jin (*doro aqame wajiha manggi, juwe gurun ishunde benere doroi aniyadari be tana juwan, seke emu minggan, orhode emu minggan gin benere, suwe, aisin emu tumen yan, menggun juwan tumen yan...*).[123]

Two months later, Yuan Chonghuan politely replied that the Middle Country was vast and the Ming Emperor owned everything to nurture the Jurchens in four directions; but the previous letter demanded too much and therefore it was against the Heaven (*dulimba i amba, han i duin juxen be gosime ujire de, tere jaka akvn, tere be hairambio, duleke bithe de akv, ambula gaiqi, abka be jurqembi...*).[124] Thus, Yuan declined indirectly, and correspondingly, Hong Taiji agreed to reduce half of the amount, but the annual tribute would remain the same.[125]

Before Yuan made any further response, Hong Taiji had launched a punitive expedition upon Korea (*fulahvn gvlmahvn sure han i suqungga*

---

[120] *Fe dangse*, pp. 2192-2193.

[121] In the *Jiu Manzhou dang*, it was written as the "Gold State" (man. *aisin gurun*; chin. *jinguo* 金國) in the first place. Later the word "*aisin*" (gold) was erased and changed to "*manju*" (Manchu). *Jiu Manzhou dang*, p. 2563.

[122] *Fe dangse*, pp. 3786-3794.

[123] *Fe dangse*, p. 3795.

[124] *Fe dangse*, p. 3833.

[125] *Fe dangse*, p. 3861.

aniya, solho gurun be dailaha ...).[126] After defeating Korea, an agreement between the two countries was reached in Pyongyang and the Manchu army pulled back (... *ping r'ang de gashvha qi amasi, manju i qooha bederere de...).*[127] Soon the Manchu State suffered from a severe hunger and even cannibalism happened among its people (*gurun yuyume ofi ... irgen niyalmai yali be inu jeke ...).*[128] Consequently, the Manchus did not launch intense military activities against the Ming for a short while.

Two years later, in the twelfth month of the third year of the Sure Han (1629), Hong Taiji raided the surroundings of Beijing and sent officials to the Gu'an District (Gu'an xian 固安縣) for collecting gold, silver and other treasure (*tere inenggi gu an hiyan hoton i aisin menggun sain ulin be bargiya seme, emu gvsai emte ulin i niyalma be unggihe).*[129] One month later, the officials reported that there were twenty thousand *liang* silver at the Prefecture treasury and five thousand *liang* at the District treasury (*tofohon de, jifu i ku be neime ... menggun i ton juwe tumen yan seme alaha ... jihiyan i ku de sunja minggan yan bi seme alaha ...).*[130] These spoils were insignificant compared with Nurgaqi's time.

In the following years, Hong Taiji shifted his focus on unifying the Mongol tribes who had not surrendered yet. On the first day of the sixth month in the sixth year of the Sure Han (1632), Hong Taiji ordered his military force to raid the Mongols who lived near the Ming's Shahukou frontier (man. *xurgei duka*; chin. *shahukou* 殺虎口), which is the modern Youyu county of Shuozhou fortification in Shanxi province (Shanxisheng Shuozhoushi Youyuxian 山西省朔州市右玉縣). According to the report, the Mongols fled into the Ming's Shahukou fortification (*dayaqi tabunang, korqin i ukxan, manjuxiri be gamame nikan jasei xurgei dukai teisu i baising de tabqin genefi, tere ba i monggo burulafi nikan i jasei xurgei hoton de dosikabi seme alanjiha manggi, iqe inenggi...).*[131] The Manchu army managed to retrieve the booties from the Ming officers (*nikan i fujiyang jasei ninggude tefi musei ambasai baru hendume, ulin*

---

[126] *Fe dangse*, p. 3884.
[127] *Fe dangse*, p. 3953.
[128] *Fe dangse*, p. 4045.
[129] *Fe dangse*, p. 4618.
[130] *Fe dangse*, pp. 4691-4692.
[131] *Fe dangse*, p. 6221.

ulha ai jaka be gemu bure...),[132] but there were only one thousand six hundred *liang* silver acquired through this military act (... *menggun emu minggan ninggun tanggv yan...*).[133]

Within the same month in 1632, the Manchu State reached a truce agreement with the Ming. On the twenty-eighth of the sixth month, a Grand Coordinator Chen and a Regional Commander Dong attended the ceremony, negotiated peaceful terms and offered small amounts of gold and silver as presents *(orin jakvn de, siowan fu i xen du tang, dung zung bing guwan, doro aqara jalin de beyede alifi manju i emgi doro aqame toktofi... doro aqaha doroi aisin susai yan, menggun sunja tanggv yan...).*[134]

To sum up, we can resort to a memorial written by Hu Gongming 胡貢明, who was a Han Chinese Cultivated Talent from the Bordered Red Banner of the time. Hu reported to Hong Taiji on the twenty-ninth of the first month of the sixth year of the Sure Han (1632), and said that the Later Jin could collect very few tribute and taxes due to its narrow territory with a sparse population, and therefore, the state had to rely on soldiers and cavalries to loot treasury (廂紅旗相公胡貢明奏……我國地窄人稀，貢賦極少，全賴兵馬出去搶些財物).[135] This is a direct evaluation between an official and his supreme leader about the imperial economic growth, admitting that the Later Jin developed its economy on the looted wealth from the neighboring lands. Lin Man-houng proclaimed that Spain firmly took over the Philippines as its colony in 1571, and after that silver circulated from the Spanish America to the Philippines, from which it flowed into the Ming China.[136] Lin also pointed out that Japan was another major supplier of silver to the Ming China due to its considerable consumption of Chinese silk in the sixteenth century, and the Portuguese merchants exported both Spanish and Japanese silver into

---

[132] Fe dangse, p. 6229.

[133] *Fe dangse*, pp. 6221-6244.

[134] *Fe dangse*, pp. 6313-6315.

[135] Hu Gongming 胡貢明, *Hu Gongming chenyan tubaozou* 胡貢明陳言圖報奏 (Hu Gongming's Memorial of Reporting and Returning the Imperial Kindness), excerpted from *Qingchu shiliao congkan disizhong* 清初史料叢刊第四種 (The Fourth Collection of Historical Materials for the Early Qing), *tiancongchao chengong zouyi* 天聰朝臣工奏議 (Official Memorials of the Tiancong's Reign), liaoning daxue lishixi, edition Shenyang: Liaoning daxue chubanshe, 1980, pp. 9-10.

[136] Lin Man-houng, *China Upside Down*, p. 63.

China.[137] Now it is becoming clear that this foreign currency finally reached its destination, which is in the Manchu coffer.

2.3.2 Acquisition through Mining

Besides wars, mining is another major source of obtaining gold and silver. The "*Manchu Veritable Records*" tell that:

sohon ulgiyan aniya... ilan biya de aisin menggun feteme urebume sele wereme urebume deribuhe.[138]

In the year of the light yellow pig (1599)... in the third month, [the Jurchen authority] started to exploit, smelt gold and silver, panning-wash [man. *werembi*; chin. *taoxi* 淘洗] and smelt iron.

This is the earliest record, which proves that Nurgaqi started to build his own financial power by extracting gold and silver. The mining technology could be ashing-blowing method, which was popularly adopted by the miners in the late Ming, Korea and Japan during the time.[139] In the following decades, this mining industry grew stronger and brought remarkable revenue to his state.

juwan de, du tang ni bodofi wesimbuhe bithe, emu aniya, emu hahai alban i tuqirengge, alban i jeku, alban i menggun, qoohai morin de ulebure liyoo, uhereme ilan yan, ilan yan menggun be bodofi, aisin werere ninggun tanggv haha de, emu aniya ilan tanggv yan aisin gaimbi, menggun urebure emu tumen haha de, ilan tumen yan menggun gaimbi.[140]

On the tenth [of the second month in the eight year of the Genggiyen Han, 1623], the Grand Coordinator calculated and reported that annually each man's taxes, with official grains, official silver and fodder for military horses included, [can be converted to] three *liang* silver in total. Calculating by three *liang* silver, annually [the government] should take three hundred *liang* gold from the six hundred gold-panning men, and take thirty thousand *liang* silver from the ten thousand silver-smelting men.

This passage implies that the yield of gold and silver from the mining industry could be considerable because the manpower of panning gold

---

[137] Lin Man-houng, *China Upside Down*, p. 62.

[138] Manzhou shilu, p. 112.

[139] Lin Man-houng, *China Upside Down*, p. 59.

[140] *Fe dangse*, pp. 2010-2011.

and smelting silver is over ten thousand combined. Besides, the tax charged by the government is also measured in gold and silver, which indicates an abundant circulation of precious metals. The scribes did not record the actual quantity collected from mining in the following years, but the figure should not be disappointing.

2.3.3   Contribution from Military Leaders

The third source of obtaining gold and silver is the contribution made by some military officers and commoners. On the twelfth day of the fourth month of the Genggiyen Han (1621), the Grand Commandant (man. *xeobei*; chin. *shoubei* 守備) of Aihe (man. *aiha*; chin. *aihe* 靉河) visited Nurgaqi with his three guards. They brought ten *liang* gold, ten rolls of silk, thirty clothes and two horses *(han de, aiha i xeobei, ilan xeo pu be gajime, juwe yan aisin, juwan suje, gvsin etuku, juwe morin benjime juwan juwe de isinjifi)* .[141] One month later, Wang Fengqing, a commoner from Qianshan (man. *qiyan xan*; chin. *qianshan* 千山), contributed ten *liang* gold to the treasury *(qiyan xan i wang fung qing sei, han de beye dahabumbi seme, juwan yan aisin gajime aqanjiha)*.[142] In the following month, Zhang Yuwei, the Mobile Corps Commander of Gaizhou *(gaizhou youji* 蓋州遊擊*)*, contributed one thousand three hundred sixty-eight *liang* and five *qian* silver *(juwan ninggun de, gai jeo i iogi jang ioi wei benjihengge, menggun emu minggan ilan tanggv ninju jakvn yan sunja jiha...)*.[143]

Generally, the amount of such contributions is small in comparison with the booties collected from the wars. It is reasonable to assume these officers obtained their silver from military operations, too.

2.3.4   Tribute from Korea

The fourth source of acquiring precious metals would be the gifts from Korea. In the later period of Nurgaqi's reign, the Later Jin constantly pressed the Korean government to surrender a Ming general Mao Wenlong 毛文龍, who often took refuge in Korea and attacked the Jurchens' home front from time to time. To ease the tension, on the sixth day of the second month in the eighth year of the Ginggiyen Han (1621),

---

[141] *Fe dangse*, p. 941.
[142] *Fe dangse*, p. 981.
[143] *Fe dangse*, p. 980.

the Korean King sent envoys three times and brought silver, silk, noil cloth (man. *miyanqeo*; chin. *mianchou* 綿綢), and paper, etc., as gifts (*solho i ilan jergi elqin jihe hafan i han de gajiha menggun, qeqeri, miyanqeo, hooxan... menggun emu tanggv yan...*),[144] but the amount of one hundred *liang* silver was relatively small (*menggun emu tanggv yan*).[145] A Korean official Wu Shisan also delivered two hundred *liang* silver as gift, but its silver content was low, so the Jurchens ordered him to take back (*uxisan i gajiha juwe tanggv yan menggun be ehe, hvlaxambi seme i amasi gamahabi*).[146]

Soon after Hong Taiji ascended the throne, he defeated Korea by military force. On the eighteenth day of the eleventh month in the sixth year of the Sure Han (1632), he sent envoys to Joseon and commanded one hundred *liang* gold, one thousand *liang* silver, all sorts of silk and one hundred pairs of water buffalo horns as an annual tribute (*juwan jakvn de, manju gurun i sure han, baduri, qahara, dungnami be qoohiyan gurun de takvrafi, aniyadari emu aniya emu jergi aisin tanggv yan, menggun minggan yan, haqin haqin i miyanqeo minggan, ... mukei ihan i weihe emu tanggv juru...*).[147]

One month later, the Jurchen envoys reported that the Korean king would only submit one tenth of the required tribute, except for the gold, silver and water buffalo horns which were not native products of Korea. As a response, Hong Taiji ordered to expel the Korean emissary (*juwan nadan de, solho de genehe baturi iogi, qahara, dungnami isinjifi gisun wesimbume, solho gurun i wang gaji sehe ton i jaka be juwan ubu de emu ubu benjire, aisin menggun weihe ere ilan haqin i jaka, meni gurun qi tuqire jaka waka seme ojorakv seme wesimbuhe manggi. sure han, jurgan de hese wasimbufi... solho be halbuhakv boxofi unggihe*).[148]

However, in the coming years Hong Taiji seemed to accept Koreans' offer. In the fourth month of the first year of Wesihun Erdemungge (1636), the Koreans delivered large amounts of tribute, and there was no gold, silver and water buffalo horns on the list.[149]

---

[144] *Fe dangse*, pp. 1985-1986.
[145] *Fe dangse*, p. 1987.
[146] *Fe dangse*, p. 1988.
[147] *Fe dangse*, p.6519.
[148] *Fe dangse*, pp. 6554-6556.
[149] *Fe dangse*, pp. 6872-6875.

2.3.5 Acquiring Gold through Trade

Gold was relatively plenty but in a big demand, therefore, the Later Jin state had to exchange silver for gold. On the nineteenth day of the ninth month in the sixth year of the Genggiyen Han (1621), Nurgaqi ordered his sons-in-law to take five hundred *liang* silver for trading gold. An acceptable price is five or four *liang* silver for one *liang* gold and the price should not be higher or lower than this *(juwan uyun de, fusi efu, si uli efu de wasimbuha gisun, fusi efu, sunja tanggv yan menggun, si uli efu, sunja tanggv yan menggun jafafi aisin uda, sunja yan, duin yan menggun de, emu yan aisin bahaqi, gaisu,tereqi fulu ekiyehun ume bure...).*[150] Thus, we can see that a reasonable ratio between gold and silver, in Nurgaqi's opinion, is one to four or five. Two years later, an official statement of the Later Jin government set the ratio at one to six *(... ilan yan menggun be bodofi, aisin werere ninggun tanggv haha de, emu aniya ilan tanggv yan aisin gaimbi...).*[151] This passage indicates that for paying the same amount of annual tax, the gold miner paid 0.5 ounce gold and the silver miner paid 3 ounces silver. The rate is one to six.[152] In the beginning Nurgaqi paid less silver for gold but later the price rose to six, which tells that the demand of gold was still there. As Hans Ulrich Vogel suggested in a private communication, Nurgaqi ordered his son-in-law to conduct this gold-silver exchange business, which may not be a general trade but a state exchange or a fair trade. Nevertheless, the rise of gold price is still obvious.

Compared with the other parts of the world, gold was relatively cheap and silver was expensive in the Ming China. According to Richard von Glahn's research, "... China's gold/silver ratio remained well below the international rate until the 1640s ..."[153] Peng Xinwei 彭信威 studied Gu Yanwu's "Daily Accumulation of Knowledge" (*ri zhi lu* 日知錄), along with the records kept by the East Indian Company, and pointed out that the gold/silver ratio in the late Ming period is ranging from one to eight

---

[150] *Fe dangse*, pp. 1192-1193.

[151] *Fe dangse*, pp. 2010-2011.

[152] The Manchu text says "for paying three ounces silver as tax to the government, the six hundred gold miners pay six hundred ounces gold and ten thousand silver miners pay thirty thousand ounces silver." Thus the rate between gold and silver, according to the official tax regulation, is one to six.

[153] Richard von Glahn (1996), *Fountain of Fortune, Money and Monetary Policy in China, 1000-1700*. University of California Press, Berkeley, p. 128.

or ten.[154] Thus, one can assume that the ratio offered by Nurgaqi, one to four or five might lead to failure.

Nonetheless, as a commercial exchange, Nurgaqi's decree emphasized that the trade must be conducted on the principle of free will: buy gold from those who are willing to sell and do not force people to sell if they are not willing to. Bring silver back if trade is not successful. If some people give gold free, do not accept *(tere qihangga niyalma, gaikini, qihakv niyalma be, ume ergeleme udara, menggun amasi benju, menggun gaijurakv aisin bure niyalmai aisin be ume gaijara)*.[155] The reason why Nurgaqi refused the free gold is not specified in the chronicles, but clearly he wanted to conduct business by rules.

As a summary, one can see that the Later Jin state accumulated substantial precious metals through military acts. Unlike the Ming government, the Jurchen-Manchus did not issue any paper notes or bonds to borrow resources for funding the wars. Peer Veries compared the high Qing's economy with Europe's fiscal military states from 1680s to 1850s, and considered military Keynesianism as a mode of "deficit spending" to categorize some European countries' economy.[156] Taking it from here, one can also infer that the early Qing's economy before 1644 was similar to the high Qing period, which was still based on accumulation and unification, rather than issuing credits to fund wars for territory expansion.

Besides mining, most of the precious metals came from the acquisition of the Ming's Liaodong region. China never was a country known for producing abundant silver. According to Quan Hansheng 全漢昇, the Ming China annually obtained substantial quantities of silver, which is approximately 1.3 million pesos, through trading with the New World via the Philippines in the early seventeenth century.[157] Peter C. Perdue's estimation is that, through European and Japanese traders, at least 7,300 metric tons of silver flooded into the Ming dynasty during its

---

[154] Peng Xinwei 彭信威 (1958), *Zhongguo huobi shi* 中國貨幣史 (The History of China's Money), Shanghai renmin chubanshe, p. 503.

[155] *Fe dangse*, pp. 1193.

[156] Peer Vries (2015), State, Economy and the Great Divergence, Great Britain and China, 1680s-1850s, Bloomsbury, London, p. 213.

[157] Quan Hansheng 全漢昇 (2012), *Zhongguo jingjishi luncong* 中國經濟史論叢 (Collection of Essays on China' Economic History), vol. 1, Zhonghua shuju, Beijing, p. 495.

last century.[158] Furthermore, as von Glahn said, by the early seventeenth century, silver had become a major commodity in global trade and the Ming China had a great appetite for it; the price of silver was relatively higher in China and foreign traders exported a mass of silver into China's market, with an estimation of 115 tons per year of the time, or much higher figures according to other scholars.[159] All these academic analysis has confirmed that the Ming China had become a treasury for silver before the Manchus rose up. Due to the monstrous quantities of silver available per capita circulating in the territory, the Ming's Premier Zhang Juzheng 張居正 (b. 1525-1582), finally recognized silver as the official means of collecting tax.[160] Since the forty-six year of the Wanli emperor (1618), the Ming government started to raise taxes under the name of Liao Rations (*liaoxiang* 遼餉) in order to cope with warfare against the Jurchen-Manchus.[161] In the tenth month of the Taichang reign (泰昌,1620), an official from the Ministry of Justice, Wei Yingjia 魏應嘉, reported that over one year, eight million *liang* silver had been used as military expenditure in the Liaodong region, besides the two million granted by the late emperor Wanli (*chu xiandi suo fa er bai wan wai, yi nian zhi wai yi yong guo xiang yin ba bai yu wan liang yi* 除先帝所發二百萬外，一年之外已用過餉銀八百餘萬兩矣).[162] Thus, besides purchasing war supplies within the China proper, considerable amount of silver circulated into the Liaodong region to finance the wars, and some of them eventually ended up in Nurgaqi's treasury.

---

[158] Perter C. Perdue (2005), *China Marches West, The Qing unification of Central Eurasia,* the Belknap Press of Harvard University Press, Canada, p. 380.

[159] Richard von Glahn (2016), *An economic history of China: from antiquity to the nineteenth century,* Cambridge University Press, Cambridge, p. 308.

[160] *Ming Shi* 明史 (History of Ming), vol. 7, compiled by Zhang Tingyu 張廷玉 et al., Zhonghua shuju, 1974, p. 1902.

[161] *Ming Shi,* p. 1903.

[162] Shen Guoyuan 沈國元, *Liangchao congxin lu* 兩朝從信錄(The Narration and Records of the Two Reigns), excerpted from *Qing ruguanqian shiliao xuanji* 清入關前史料選輯 (The Selected Historical Materials before the Qing Entered through Shanhai Pass), vol. 2, compiled by Pan Zhe (潘喆), et al., edition Beijing: Zhongguo renmin daxue chubanshe, 1989, p. 127.

2.4 Distribution of Gold and Silver

2.4.1 Rewarding Military Forces

As spoils, gold and silver were often rewarded to the officials and officers who had significant achievements in battlefields.

tere dain de aisin menggun suje gequheri be, jaka ambula baha... uju jergi geren i ejen ambasa de, juwete tanggv yan menggun, sunjata yan aisin, jai jergi gvsai ejen ambasa de, emte tanggv yan menggun, juwete yan aisin, ilaqi jergi ambasa de, gvsita yan menggun, duiqi jergi ambasa de, tofohoto yan menggun, sunjaqi jergi ambasa de, juwanta yan menggun, ningguqi jergi ambasa de, sunjata yan menggun, nadaqi jergi nirui ejete de, ilata yan menggun, jakvqi jergi sonjoho bayarai qoohai kirui ejete de, nirui jangisa de, juwete yan menggun xangnaha.[163]

In this battle [of Kai Yuan 開原 in the fourth year of Genggiyen Han, 1619], gold, silver, satin embroidery and such things were abundantly acquired. Each of the first-rank-lord officials [man. *geren i ejen ambasa*; chin. *zong ezhen dachen* 總額真大臣] received two hundred *liang* silver and five *liang* gold. For the second-rank banner-lord officials, each of them received one hundred *liang* silver and two *liang* gold. Each of the third-rank officials received thirty *liang* silver. Each of the fourth-rank officials received fifteen *liang* silver...

The battle of Kaiyuan was one of the major victories achieved by the Later Jin state over the Ming. The passage reveals that the officials of the first and second ranks were bestowed with a small amount of gold and from the third rank downward, only silver was given.

Bestowing silver to the officers, officials and soldiers frequently appeared in the chronicles. After unifying the Ming's Hedong region (man. *birai dergi*; chin. *hedong* 河東) in spring of the sixth year of the Genggiyen Han (1621), large quantities of silver were given to the military officers and soldiers:

zung bing guwan de juwete tanggv yan menggun... fujiyang de emte tanggv susaita yan menggun... canjiyang de jakvnjuta yan menggun... iogi de susaita yan menggun... nirui ejen, beiguan, xanggiyan bayarai kirui ejen, beiguwan i jergi baksi, emu jergi, orita yan menggun... xanggiyan hiya, bayara, daise beiguwan, olbo i niyalma, emu jergi, tofohoto yan

---

[163] *Fe dangse*, pp. 456-457.

71

menggun... xanggiyan giyajan bayara, fulgiyan bayarai uju, niru boxoro qiyanzung, qiyanzung ni jergi baksi, emu jergi, juwanta yan menggun...[164]

Each Regional Commander received two hundred *liang* silver... each Regional Vice Commander received one hundred and fifty *liang* silver... each Assistant Regional Commander received eighty *liang* silver... each Mobile Corps Commander received fifty *liang* silver... twenty *liang* silver for each of the Battalion Commanders, Defense Officers, Flag-Commanders of the White Defensive Army [man. *bayara*; chin. *hujun* 護軍], and the clerks [man. *baksi*; chin. *bakeshi* 巴克什] in the rank of Defense Officer... fifteen *liang* silver for each of the White Guards, Defensive Army, Acting Defensive Officer and Cotton-armor soldiers who are in the same rank...

It is outspoken that the obtained silver, as the universal medium, was fairly divided according to military ranks that relate to the battle achievements. Furthermore, a Han Chinese source reveals that Nurgaqi advocated sharing of booty, which may not be the real case but an ideal statement that promotes a good relationship among the community members. On the eleventh day of the second intercalary month of 1621, after building up the Sarhv fortification, Nurgaqi addressed his subordinates, mentioning that the servants worked on agriculture and shared their harvested food with their masters, and accordingly the masters should share the acquired wealth, including silver, and hunted prey with their servants (*pu suoshi zhi nongye, yu zhu gongshi, er zhu suohuo zhicai ji suotian zhi wu, yi dang yu pu gongzhi* 僕所事之農業，與主共食，而主所獲之財及所畋之物，亦當與僕共之).[165] Combined with the previous passages, this passage tells a booty sharing between the rulers and their subordinates during the time.

Besides bestowing silver after the major achievements, individual rewards were also given to the officers for specific performances. In the sixth month of the sixth year of the Genggiyen Han (1621), the Mobile Corps Commander Aita captured some Korean and Han Chinese people.

---

[164] *Fe dangse*, pp. 887-889.

[165] *Qingtaizu wu huangdi shilu* 清太祖武皇帝實錄 (The Veritable Records of the Forefather Martial Emperor), collected in *Qing ruguanqian shiliao xuanji yi* 清入關前史料選輯 1 (Compilation of Selected Historical Materials before the Qing Entered through Shanhai Pass), vol. 1, compiled by Pan Zhe 潘喆 et al., edition Beijing: Zhongguo renmin daxue chubanshe, 1984, p. 364.

Accordingly, he was promoted to an Assistant Regional Commander, being rewarded with five hundred *liang* silver *(tere gung de, aita be wesibufi canjiyang obuha, sunja tanggv yan menggun ...)*.[166]

Besides military officials, soldiers were rewarded with small amounts of silver for their military performance, too. Three months after Aita's reward, two hundred enemy soldiers arrived at the landing place of Niang Niang Gong 娘娘宮 by five boats. One Battalion Commander of Dongjing (man. *dung ging ni emu bezung*; chin. *dongjing bazong* 東京 把總) led eighty people and defeated the enemy. Therefore, the commander was rewarded with five *liang* silver, so was Hoto, a Jurchen person. Twenty *liang* silver was rewarded to a man who died of injuries. Twenty *liang* silver was rewarded to each person who captured the enemies alive. Moreover, each military man was rewarded with five *qian* silver *(niyang niyang gung ni ba i dogon de, sunja jaha i juwe tanggv qooha jifi, dung ging ni emu bezung, jakvnju niyalma be gaifi, afafi gidaha seme, bezung de sunja yan, hoto de sunja yan, feye de buqehe emu niyalma de orin yan, dain i niyalma be weihun jafaha niyalma de orin yan, jai geren qoohai niyalma de sunjata jiha menggun xangnaha)*.[167]

2.4.2 Rewarding Mongol Allies

During Nurgaqi's time, substantial gold and silver were bestowed to the Mongols for maintaining the alliance relationship. On the second day of the fourth month in the seventh year of the Genggiyen Han (1622), Nurgaqi received the Mongol chieftains as guests from the Chakhar tribe and rewarded five *liang* gold and two hundred *liang* silver to each prince; three *liang* gold and one hundred *liang* silver for each of the second-rank chieftains. In total, the Mongol leaders received 87 *liang* gold and 3,400 *liang* silver *(iqe juwe de, qahar qi jihe beise de buhengge, beise de sunjata yan aisin, juwete tanggv yan menggun... jai jergi de ilan yan aisin, tanggv yan menggun... ilaqi jergi de juwete yan aisin, susaita yan menggun... uhereme ton, aisin jakvnju nadan yan, menggun ilan minggan duin tanggv yan...)*.[168] Again, gold's quantity was much less than silver comparatively.

---

[166] *Fe dangse*, p. 1045.
[167] *Fe dangse*, pp. 1152-1154.
[168] *Fe dangse*, pp. 1815-1817.

Sometimes, small amounts of silver were also bestowed to the Mongol envoys and their refugees. Just two months later, regarding the emissaries of Aohan tribe, eight *liang* silver was given to the leader and three *liang* to each of the followers *(orin ninggun de, aohan i elqin de, ujulaha niyalma de jakvn yan, kutule de ilata yan menggun xangname buhe...)*.[169]

The chronicles also indicate that Nurgaqi was very generous to the Mongols who married into his family. His son-in-law Enggeder was a typical example. When Enggeder's emissary Babai was departing on the fourteenth of the second month in the eighth year of the Genggiyen Han (1623), Nurgaqi sent a letter and declared that besides the previously bestowed bond-servants of eight thousand men, annually five hundred and twenty *liang* silver will be given to the imperial son-in-law, his brother, the princess, and their three sons *(enggeder efu i babai bithe benjime jifi, juwan duin de amasi genehe, unggihe bithe gisun... efu, gege, sini emu deo, ilan jui de, uhereme jakvn minggan haha de, emu aniya sunja tanggv orin yan menggun...)*.[170]

Nurgaqi highly valued his relationship with Enggeder. Soon this Mongol son-in-law was rewarded again. In the ninth year of the Genggiyen Han (1624), the Khan held a great banquet in the Eight-Angled Palace and gave ten *liang* gold to Enggeder and Manggvltai respectively *(han jakvn hoxonggo ordo de tuqifi amba sarin sarlame, enggeder efu, manggvltai de buhengge, juwanta yan aisin...)*.[171]

Besides, gold was also given to some important female figures who married into Mongols to form the alliance relationship. On the twenty-fourth day, a prince Udahai's sister married into Dalai, the brother of Gurbusi. Four cattle and five goats were killed to celebrate the event. Nurgaqi went out of the gate of his palace and ordered to perform all sorts of plays. Nurgaqi bestowed two hundred *liang* silver and five *liang* gold to the princess who was getting married *(orin duin de, udahai age i non be gurbusi efu i deo dalai de bume, duin ihan sunja honin wafi, han, duka de tuqifi, haqin haqin i efin efibume sarilaha, gege de juwe tanggv yan menggun, sunja yan aisin...)*.[172]

---

[169] *Fe dangse*, p. 1900.
[170] *Fe dangse*, pp. 2014-2021.
[171] *Fe dangse*, p. 2790.
[172] *Fe dangse*, pp. 2800-2801.

Like his father, Hong Taiji also used precious metals as a tie to maintain relationships with the Mongol leaders. On the first day of the twelfth month in the second year of the Sure Han (1638), officials Sonin and Ajuhv were assigned to the Mongol Tusiyetu Khan with a letter, which indicates that the Tusiyetu Khan made peace with the Later Jin state after the Chakhar Mongol tribe's incursion. As rewards, a daughter from the imperial family married into the Tusiyetu Khan with gifts of abundant Eastern Pearls, gold, five thousand *liang* silver and all sorts of items for daily usage (*jorgon biyai iqe de, sonin, ajuhv be tusiyetu han de takvraha bithei gisun, sure han i bithe, tusiyetu han de unggihe... qahar bedarehe manggi, aqaki seme jihe de, simbe gosime jui be bume mujakv kuntuleme, tana, aisin... sunja minggan yan menggun, niyalmai baitalara eiten haqin i jaka be gemu bufi unggihe....).*[173]

The above passage tells that through intermarriage, the Tusiyetu Khan became a son-in-law of the Jurchen imperial family. Two years later, this Mongol Tusiyetu Khan was rewarded again for maintaining alliance with the Later Jin. On the twenty-fifth day of the fifth month in the fifth year of the Sure Han (1631), Tusiyetu and his wife, a Jurchen princess, came back to pay respect. Hong Taji gathered his brothers and officials at the study of the emperor, giving a pair of gold cups and ten *liang* gold as gifts (*orin sunja de, tusiyetu efu, gege de jihe doroi aika bume, han, manggvltai beile, taijisa, ambasa, bithei boode isafi tuwame buhe... aisin i hvntahan emu juru... aisin juwan yan...).*[174]

Forming the alliance with the Mongols allowed the Jurchens to secure their home front when they attacked Joseon. On the nineteenth of the eleventh month in the first year of Wesihun Erdemungge (1636), Hong Taiji decided to launch another round of military expedition upon Joseon (*juwan uyun de, qoohiyan be dailambi...).*[175] To consolidate the alliance, Hong Taiji bestowed silver to a number of Mongol leaders while he decided to attack the Koreans. On the twenty-sixth day, he rewarded the Mongol tribe of Aru Khalkha with one hundred *liang* silver for Sunggai... sixty *liang* silver for the Chief Lama Xoloi Bandi... sixty *liang* silver for Lama Darhan from Ujumuqin, and forty *liang* silver for Lama Eljitu Gabqu (*orin ninggun de, aru i kalka i gurun de xangname buhengge...*

---

[173] *Fe dangse,* pp. 4347-4351.
[174] *Fe dangse,* pp. 5275-5276.
[175] *Fe dangse,* p. 8312.

sunggai de menggun emu tanggv yan... xoloi bandi da lama de menggun ninju yan... ujumuqin i darhan lama de menggun ninju yan... eljitu gabqu lama de menggun dehi yan...).[176]

2.4.3 Rewarding Individual Han Chinese and Korean People

Most Han Chinese military officers and soldiers were already rewarded along with the Jurchens after military acts. Nonetheless, some special examples were made by the scribes to distinguish their special contributions in the historical course.

In the sixth month of the sixth year of the Genggiyen Han (1622), Li Qingcai was rewarded with five hundred *liang* silver for finishing his commission diligently and well (*li qing sai be, afabuha weile de kiqebe sain seme, sunja tanggv yan menggun xangnaha*).[177] One month later, Nurgaqi bestowed one hundred *liang* silver to the Mobile Corps Commander Zhao, and twenty *liang* for his assistant (*han, jeo iogi be saixafi, tanggv yan menggun xangnaha, takvrafi jihe jung giyvn de, orin yan menggun xangnaha*).[178] At the end of the year, three *liang* silver was rewarded to each of the Han Chinese Outer Gentlemen (man. *wailan*; chin. *wailang* 外郎) who were teaching at the Eight Banners (*gvsin de, jakvn gvsai bithe taqibure nikan wailan de, emu wailan de ilata yan menggun buhe*).[179]

From the first to the fourth month of the Sure Han (1627), the Later Jin defeated Korea. The Korean king's brother was also brought to the Later Jin as the hostage (*... solho gurun be dahabufi, solho han i deo be gajiha...*).[180] On the sixteenth day of the seventh month, the Korean envoys returned to Korea. Hong Taiji bestowed sixty *liang* silver to the Korean King's brother and ninety *liang* to the released Korean official Jiang Honglie (*juwan ninggun de, solho i elqin xen jeng hv, piyoo lan ying se genere de... deo de ... ninju yan menggun... sindafi unggihe hafan giyang hung liyei de uyunju yan menggun unggihe*).[181]

---

[176] *Fe dangse*, pp. 8314-8318.
[177] *Fe dangse*, p. 1048.
[178] *Fe dangse*, p. 1097.
[179] *Fe dangse*, p. 1405.
[180] *Fe dangse*, p. 3965.
[181] *Fe dangse*, pp. 4069-4071.

2.4.4 Special Rewards, Compensations, and State Payment

After taking over the Liaodong region, Nurgaqi decided to move the Jurchen households from Sarhu to Liaodong. When the work was successfully conducted, each of the Grand Coordinators and Regional Commanders was bestowed with fifty *liang* silver and three *liang* gold; each of the Regional Vice Commanders with forty *liang* silver and two *liang* gold; each of the Assistant Regional Commanders and Mobile Corps Commanders thirty *liang* silver and one *liang* gold; each of the Defense Officers with twenty *liang* silver *(sarhv qi liyoodung de boigon gurime jime... du tang, zung bing guwan de susaita yan menggun, ilata yan aisin xangnabuhe, fujiyang de dehite yan menggun, juwete yan aisin buhe, canjiyang, iogi de gvsita yan menggun, emte yan aisin buhe, beiguwan de orita yan menggun...).* [182]

This record was documented in the eleventh month of the sixth year of the Genggiyen Han (1621), confirming that the bestowed gold was much less than silver in quantity. Compared with the Kaiyuan battle, officials were rewarded with less precious metals. Still, both of these events prove that gold was only rewarded for the notable achievements.

Before the sixth year of the Sure Han (1632), when the three degrees of the Regional Vice Commanders died in battlefield, their families received the same amount of silver as compensation. The same principle was also applied to the Assistant Regional Commanders and Mobile Corps Commanders. From the first month of the sixth year, a first-rank Regional Vice Commander will be compensated with eight hundred and twenty *liang* silver; ten *liang* silver decreased for the next degree. A first-rank Assistant Regional Commander will be compensated with six hundred and twenty *liang* silver; and ten *liang* silver decreased sequentially for the other two degrees *(neneme dain de akv oho hafasa de burengge, fujiyang ilaqi jergi bime emu adali, canjiyang iogi de emu adali bihe, te ereqi amasi, uju jergi fujiyang de jakvn tanggv orin yan, jai jergi de juwanta yan ekiyeniye, uju jergi canjiayang de ninggun tanggv orin yan, jai juwe jergi de juwanta yan ekiyeniye).* [183]

During Hong Taiji's reign, a system has been formed to pay the officials salary according to their ranks. On the seventh day of the twelfth

---

[182] *Fe dangse*, pp. 1273-1274.
[183] *Fe dangse*, pp. 5881-5882.

month in the sixth year of Sure Han (1632), Ran Sehui, a Plain-yellow Bannerman, did not receive grains and silver in accordance with his rank. According to the regulation, his yard was supposed to have a gate. Therefore, he brought this situation as a lawsuit to the Khan. Afterwards, Behei, Kamtu, Dondohoi and Loxo reported to the Khan that silver and grains had been given to Ran as a young man of a good family (man. *siyang gung*; chin. *xianggong* 相公), and a gate had been built for his yard *(iqe nadan de, gulu suwayan i ran se hvi, jeku akv, hafasai jergi de menggun buhekv, booi hvwa de duka akv seme han de habxaha manggi, behei, kamtu, dondohoi, loxo, han de alafi siyang gung sei jergi de menggun buhe, jeku buhe, hvwa de duka arabuha)*.[184]

Through the distribution of silver, one can see that silver served as the major agent of measuring people's contribution. Political systems were established to include Jurchens, Mongols and Han Chinese people as beneficiaries. It is obvious that the empire-building of the Later Jin gradually took place on the foundation of precious metals, which marked a difference than the early Ming regime that issued paper notes.

2.5 Usages of Gold and Silver

Throughout the whole chronicles, silver functioned as the major means for the rulers to manage the empire: acquiring booties from battles, rewarding and punishing the officials, officers, soldiers and commoners, collecting taxation, conducting commerce, demanding tribute from other countries, and so on. Most of these political and economic activities were conducted with the incentives of silver.

2.5.1 Punishments Compensated in Silver

In the beginning of the "Original Manchu Chronicles", a war between the Ula tribe and Nurgaqi's broke out. This event was also re-transcribed in the *fe dangse*, which recorded that Nurgaqi had asked an official, whose name is Qangxu, to protect his son in the battlefield, but Qangxu failed to carry out the order. Initially Qangxu was sentenced to death, but Nurgaqi's younger brother interceded and thus, Qangxu's death penalty was exempted, but one hundred *liang* silver was forfeited as punishment

---

[184] *Fe dangse*, pp. 6543-6544.

(... *beyebe wara be nakafi, qangxu gebungge amban de, tanggv yan i weile araha...*).[185]

Forfeiting silver was also a means of law enforcement. In the sixth year of the Genggiyen Han (1621), Artai was accused for hunting improperly and was fined nine *liang* silver accordingly (*artai be abalaha seme nirui niyalma gerqilefi, geqilehe juxen hokoho, uyun yan i weile araha*).[186] Another case is that Xumuru was fined twenty *liang* silver because he had not prosecuted his battalion men after they broke law (*xumuru be, nirui niyalmai weile be xajin de gajifi alabuhakv seme, orin yan i weile araha*).[187]

On the fourth day of the eleventh month in the sixth year of the Genggiyen Han (1621), Neodei was fined twenty-five *liang* silver for beating people and then commanded his foot soldiers to beat people (*iqe duin de, neodei be niyalma tantaha, yafahan niyalma be tvbuhe seme*).[188] The imperial son-in-law Darhan was fined thirty *liang* silver for dividing fruit trees without a group discussion and then taking in the Han Chinese people who were not permitted to settle down by government. Another case is that Unege was fined thirty *liang* silver for interrogating without permission (*orin sunja yan menggun gaiha. darhan efu be geren i hebe akv tubihe moo be dendere, iqihiyara unde siden i nikan be ujibuhe seme, gvsin yan i weile gaiha, unege be enquleme weile beidehe seme, gvsin yan i weile gaiha*).[189]

On the thirtieth day of the fourth month in the fourth year of the Sure Han (1630), a letter was sent to the Qian'an District (Qian'an 遷安縣), regulating that according to the prince who is in charge, the crime of concealing people is considered as stealing. Therefore, he who breaks the law will be flogged with his ears pierced. The escapee's original owner should not demand silver for the case. The wealthy people are allowed pay silver to atone the crime and the silver goes to the government. For those who are less wealthy, they can choose to pay silver or accept punishment of flogging (*gvsin de, qiyan an de unggihe bithe gisun, beile hendume, niyalma gidaha weile de hvlhai weile, tantafi juwe xan toko,*

---

[185] *Fe dangse*, p. 14.
[186] *Fe dangse*, p. 834.
[187] *Fe dangse*, p. 835.
[188] *Fe dangse*, p. 1223.
[189] *Fe dangse*, pp. 1223-1224.

niyalmai ejen menggun gaijara be naka, sain niyalma tantara mooi jalin joolime menggun buqi, siden de gaisu, yebken niyalma weile bahaqi, menggun bure moo alire be imbe sonjobu ...).[190]

2.5.2   Silver as a Means of Commercial Transactions

In the ninth month of the sixth year of the Genggiyen Han (1621), an official Yegude took an order to oversee the bow makers. The chronicles record that to process an armor for a Battalion Commander or a Defense Officer, it costs two *qian* silver; to process an armor for an acting Defense Officer or a Regimental Commander (man. *qiyanzung*; chin. *qianzong* 千總), it costs one *qian* silver for each; to process ten official armors, a prince should pay one *liang* silver; it costs one *qian* silver for making a bow and five *fen* for repairing a damaged one (*yegude de beri faksi be iqihiya seme afabuha, nirui ejen beiguwan i uksin hadaha de, juwe jiha menggun bu, daise beiguwan, qiyanzung ni uksin hadaqi, emte jiha menggun be aqan bu, alban i juwan uksin hadaha de, beise emu yan menggun bumbi, emu beri arabuqi, emu jiha bu, bijaha beri be dasabure de, sunja fun bu*).[191] This passage tells that transactions of government procurement was conducted in silver, which better facilitate transactions in large amounts.

Another passage tells that the non-governmental commercial transactions with the Han Chinese were also proceeded in silver. On the first day of the second month in the fifth year of the Sure Han (1631), Liu Wuge (man. *lio wuge*; chin. *Liu Wuge* 劉五哥)'s five men arrived on foot from the South. The number of goods they brought are: one hundred and eighteen rolls of Maoqin blue cloth (man. *moqin*; chin. *maoqinbu* 毛青布), which are worth seventy-one *liang* silver; fourteen and a half *jin* mercury which is worth forty-three *liang* and five *qian* silver; two and a half *jin* welding agent, which is worth seven *liang* and five *qian* silver; rouge powder, combs, and fine-toothed combs, which are worth three *liang* silver; forty-eight thousand needles which are worth ten *liang* silver; one roll of Peng Silk (man. *pengduwan*; chin. *pengduan* 彭緞) and one roll of voile (man. *xa*; chin. *sha* 紗), which are worth five *liang* silver; one *jin* Cinnabar, which is worth two *liang* silver; one hundred and eighty bundles of tobacco, which are worth four *liang* silver. In total, one

---

[190] *Fe dangse*, pp. 4970-4971.
[191] *Fe dangse*, pp. 1184-1185.

80

hundred and forty-six *liang* silver was paid (*juwe biyai iqe de, julergi lio wuge i sunja niyalma yafahan hvda gajime jihe, gajiha hvdai ton, moqin lamun emu tanggv juwan jakvn de menggun nadanju emu yan, toholon muke juwan duin gin emu hontoho de dehi ilan yan sunja jiha, hangnara okto juwe gin emu hontoho de nadan yan sunja jiha, fiyan, ijifun, merhe de ilan yan, ulme duin tumen jakvn minggan de juwan yan, pengduwan emke, xa emke de sunja yan, qinuhvn emu gin de juwe yan, dambagu emu tanggv jakvnju sefere de duin yan, ede uheri emu tanggv dehi ninggun yan buhe*).[192]

Further chronicle records prove that certain amounts of silver were spent on trade in the bordering regions. In the tenth of the fifth month in the first year of Wesihun Erdemungge (1636), eight people of Eleken and Loojin with the other eight followers were allocated with one thousand *liang* silver and went to the frontier gate for trade (*ineku dere inenggi, eleken, loojin be dabume jakvn niyalma, jakvn kutule de siden i ku i emu minggan yan menggun bufi duka de hvda unggihe*).[193] The transaction site is called "*duka*" in the Manchu language, which means "gate" in the frontier region. Since many of the Mongol tribes were considered as alliance, one can reasonably assume this *duka* site as a border with the Ming. Due to the ongoing wars between the Ming and the Later Jin, such commercial records were very rare in the Manchu chronicles. Nonetheless, silver invested in business with the Mongols was substantial.

On the seventeenth of the fifth month in the first year of Wesihun Erdemungge (1636), an official named Gulugudei and a leading official from Tumet tribe, along with servants and silver owners, were sent to Hohhot (man. *huhu hoton*; chin. *huhehaote* 呼和浩特) for trade. Every banner had at least ten thousand *liang* silver with them (... *tesei yaya emu gvsai hvdai menggun tumen yan qi wesihun funqehe de, gulugudei si tumet i ujui amban i fejergi niyalma be ini menggun i ejen be gamame, huhu hoton de genefi sain i hvdaxaqi...*).[194]

Peter C. Purdue pointed out that scholars' recent analysis had recognized the Ming China's role as the world silver sink.[195] The above

---

[192] *Fe dangse*, pp. 5291-5293.
[193] Fe dangse, pp. 7085.
[194] *Fe dangse*, pp. 7122-7124.
[195] Perdue (2005), p. 380.

passages at least confirm that the Later Jin also functioned as a "silver sink", in which large amounts of the Ming's silver settled down and was redistributed to the Jurchens and Mongols, with very little flowing back to the Ming. Here one needs to notice that in the sixteenth century, the merchants of the Ming controlled the supply of silver,[196] but in the Later Jin, the state exercised a strong hand upon the circulation of currencies.

2.5.3 Means of Gifts, Bribery, Entertainment, Money-lending, Government Relief and Mortuary Objects

In the sixth month of the eighth year of the Genggiyen Han (1623), a lawsuit was brought to Nurgaqi's firstborn prince, disclosing the bribery activities among the military officers, high-rank officials and the imperial son-in-law. Even the fourth prince Hong Taiji was involved:

amba beile de, fu jeo i beiguwan wang bin i alaha gisun, ha sing wang de, emu jerde morin, menggun susai yan bufi, wang du tang de benehe... lo san sa jorgon biyai orin emu de, sain aisin juwan yan... li dai qeng de juwe yan aisin... bi ji sai de aisin juwan yan... jai yung ning giyan i beiguan li diyan kui geli alame, sahaliyan indahvn aniyai jakvn biyai juwan uyun de, li diyan kui mini aisin orin yan du tang gaiha, wang iogi sambi... tere gisun be geren beidesi beise de duile seme afabufi duileqi, urgvdai efu jabume, aisin serengge, neneme juwan yan aisin be li diyan kui, aita bene sehe seme benjihe manggi, bi gvnime, aita minde kimun bihe, ere aisin be gerqileki seme geodebume benjihebi dere seme duiqi beile de tuwabuha, duiqi beile hendume, unenggi aita benjiqi ai sain, ere aisin be taka asara, weile tuqire be tuwaki seme henduhe ...[197]

To the Big Prince, the Defense Officer of Fuzhou [man. *fu jeo*; chin. *Fuzhou* 復州] Wang Bin reported, "Once [I] gave a red horse and fifty *liang* silver to the Grand Coordinator Wang through a person Hasingwang... On the twenty-first of the twelfth month, ten *liang* good gold [was given] to Lo Sansa... two *liang* gold to Li Dacheng... ten *liang* gold for Bi Zhisai..." Moreover, the Defense Officer of Yongningjian [man. *yung ning giyan*; chin. *Yongningjian* 永寧監] Li Diankui reported that, on the nineteenth day of the eighth month in the Black-dog year, the Grand Coordinator took twenty *liang* gold from me, Li Diankui. The Mobile Corps Commander Wang knows [this matter] ... This case was

---

[196] Lin Man-houng, *China Upside Down*, p. 40.
[197] *Fe dangse*, pp. 2428-2434.

submitted to all the judges and chieftains for inspection, and the Imperial Son-in-law Urgvdai answered, "The gold was delivered first by Li Diankui, who said it was sent by Aita. After delivering, I thought that Aita and I had some grudges and this gold could be a trap set [by him to] accuse me. Therefore, [I] took [this gold] to the fourth prince [Hong Taiji]. The fourth prince said, 'Indeed [if it were] sent by Aita, what benefit [it would be]. This gold should be put away for the moment, and [we] see what crimes would happen' ..."

This law case turned very complicated, implicating many chieftains and certainly, it reached Nurgaqi. As punishment, Nurgaqi discharged Urgvdai from the position of Grand Coordinator. Nurgaqi was also saddened for Hong Taiji's involvement, criticized him of being unwise and advised him to behave moderately with justice. Finally, Nurgaqi ordered Hong Taiji to compensate all the loss caused by Urgvdai, with ten *liang* gold and three hundred *liang* silver deposited to the treasury (*duiqi beile de juwan yan aisin, ilan tanggv yan menggun gaifi ku de sindaha*).[198]

One passage tells that silver also functioned in the business of pawnshop and money lending. On the third day of the first month in the ninth year of the Genggiyen Han (1624), Nurgaqi declared that the government intervened and all the Jurchen and Han Chinese pawnshops must be closed (*iqe ilan de wesimbuha bithei gisun, han hendume, juxen nikan damtun i puseli be gemu naka*).[199] One of the reasons is that pawn is pledged for silver, which causes thieves and bad people to steal clothes in order to exchange for silver (*damtun jafafi menggun buqi, hvlha ehe niyalma weri etuku be hvlhafi, damtun jafabufi menggun gaifi ukambi*).[200] Furthermore, Nurgaqi ordered money lending of silver must be stopped, too. Moneylenders must collect their debts before the tenth day of the first lunar month and they can accuse the debtors if they cannot return. After the tenth day, the debts will be collected by those who know the internal situation (*jai menggun juwen sindara be inu gemu naka, juwen sindaha niyalma, aniya biyai juwan qi ebsi gaime waqihiya, burakvqi jafafi habxa, juwan be tulike de, hetu saha niyalma gaisu*).[201] The decree

---

[198] *Fe dangse*, p. 2444.
[199] *Fe dangse*, p. 2719.
[200] *Fe dangse*, pp. 2719-2720.
[201] *Fe dangse*, p. 2720.

did not justify the reason of stopping money lending in silver, but the following passages dealt with the problems that occurred in tax collection.[202] Thus, one can assume that the government tried to regulate the financial market to protect the revenue, though hardly effective means is observed. Besides bestowing gold to the Jurchen and Mongol leaders, silver and gold were also used a reward for entertainment purpose. On the second day of the first month in the eight year of the Genggiyen Han (1623), Khalkha Mongol Chiefs, Sengge Tabunang and his brother Monggo Tabunang, led forty households, escaped and surrendered to Nurgaqi. On the third day, Nurgaqi ascended the Big Yamun, put on all sorts of plays and held a huge feast for the new comers. Fifty *liang* silver was granted to the Han Chinese who performed the plays (*iqe juwe de, kalka i monggo sengge tabunang, deo monggo tabunang, dehi boigon gajime ukame jihe. iqe ilan de, han, amba yamun de tuqifi, haqin haqin i efin efibume amba sarin sarilaha, tere efin efihe nikasa de susai yan menggun xangname buhe*).[203]

On the second day of the first month in the Green-Cattle Year (1625), Nurgaqi gathered his wives, all the chieftains of the Eight Banners and their wives, the Mongol chieftains and their wives, the Han Chinese officials and their wives, to the Taizihe River (man. *tai zi ho*; chin. *taizihe* 太子河) to play football on ice. The Khan and his wives sat in the middle place and stipulated the others to run from the two sides. The people who arrived first would win the game and received gold and silver. Later, every portion of twenty *liang* silver and one *liang* gold was deposited in twelve places, and the Khan ordered all the daughters, the wives of the small Taiji officials and the Mongol wives to run. Finally, one *liang* gold and five *liang* silver were rewarded to each of the twelve women (*... juwan juwe hehe de emte yan aisin, sunjata yan menggun buhe ...*).[204]

For a long time a Ming general, Mao Wenlong 毛文龍, posed a severe threat on the home front of the Later Jin. In the ninth month of the first year of the Sure Han (1627), Wang Zideng 王子登, an Regional Vice Commander of the Bordered Yellow Banner was sent to Mao for peace talks. Wang told Mao that the Khan (Hong Taiji) had distributed one hundred thousand *liang* silver to the flood victims. For every six *mu*

---

[202] *Fe dangse*, pp. 2720-2723.
[203] *Fe dangse*, pp. 1913-1914.
[204] *Fe dangse*, pp. 2921-2924.

flood-damaged land, one *dan* (man. *hule*; chin. *dan* 石) grains would be given (... *wang zi deng bi alame, han i juwan tumen be tuqibufi irgen de salaha, yaya muke de eyehe usin i jalin emu qimari de emu hule buhe ...*).[205]

The following passage tells that the Jurchen-Manchus had a custom of burying gold and silver with the dead:

juwan duin de, han de weilere jurgan i aliha amban munggetu gisun wesimbume hendume, weilengge manggvltai, degelei juwe beile i giran sindaha aisin menggun i tetun be gaifi, be asarahabi, tere be ainambi seme gisun wesimbure jakade...

On the fourteenth [of the first month of Wesihun Erdemungge, 1636], the minister [man. *aliha amban*; chin. *chengzheng* 承政] Munggetu of the Ministry of Works reported to the Khan and said, "The gold and silver vessels, which were buried with the corpses of the two sinful chieftains Manggvltai and Degelei, were taken out. We have put them away. Thus [we] reported to the throne, asking how to dispose ..."

The accurate amount of gold and silver vessels is unknown, however, given the high social status of the deceased, one can speculate that plentiful precious metals were buried. Otherwise, Hong Taiji would not be bothered to retrieve them.

2.6 Conclusion

The above analysis shows that the Later Jin state mainly acquired currencies through wars, in large quantities of silver and gold. Some currencies were obtained from mining, tribute and trade, but the quantity was dwarfed in comparison with the income generated by military operations. While currencies were being accumulated, military men were rewarded to launch new rounds of military expeditions for acquiring more wealth. Briefly, the official Manchu documents stipulate that the Later Jin state exerted a high-level control of silver ingots, by owning and distributing them. Private supply and ownership of silver stay were recorded little in the government chronicles. Based on the official documents, one can see that the rise of the Jurchen-Manchu state was partially due to the state's steady dominance over its silver reserve and distribution.

---

[205] *Fe dangse*, pp. 4228-4230.

On the thirtieth day of the fourth month in the fourth year of the Sure Han (1630), Hong Taiji asked three military leaders about their captives during the war. The three leaders answered that they had captured more than the previous two wars. Hong Taiji said that he would not take pleasure in obtaining much gold, silver, silk and other treasure, but in obtaining many people. The reason is that gold, silver, silk and other treasure finally will be consumed, but people will not. Even just one or two persons were captured, they would become people of the Jin state, and the children born by them will also become Jurchens (... *ilan taiji, qeni yabuha feliyehe babe alafi unggihe gisun be han de alaha manggi, han fonjime, nenehe juwe jergi jihe olji qi ere fonji ambula dere, tede nenehe mudan qi ere fonji nikan labdu gajihabi sehe manggi, han hendume, bi aisin menggun suje ulin labdu baha seme urgunjerakv, niyalma labdu baha serede urgunjembi, aisin menggun suje ulin serengge, manara wajire jaka, niyalma wajimbio, emke juwe bahaqi, gemu gurun i tuwali, tede banjiha juse, gemu musei juxen ombi kai seme henduhe).*[206]

This passage indicates that Hong Taiji believed that manpower functioned more important than the precious metals or varieties of treasure in the process of state building. The above analysis also implies that the strategies of acquiring the Ming's land and wealth were essentially carried out by the military leaders and soldiers, which are the "people" in Hong Taiji's opinion. Thus, Hong Taiji was convinced that the endless wealth of an empire is the ever-growing population that brings worthy pleasure to him.

The above chapters also suggest that the administration of the Later Jin state was operated based on precious metals, which are silver and gold, rather than brass coins and paper notes. Compared with the precedent Jin, Yuan dynasties and its rival Ming, this new uprising empire functioned on the accumulated physical wealth, not credit. In the early stage of empire building, this strategy sufficiently underpinned the Jurchen-Manchu military expansion over the other land powers.

Throughout the Manchu annals, one can see that these unifying elites were strengthening the state by accumulating three major components: precious metals as currencies, human population and lands, which are the foundation of economic development in an ancient society. Acquiring

---

[206] *Fe dangse*, pp. 4973-4974.

silver and gold is just the beginning to initiate a great enterprise. The Manchu-language chronicles were composed on governmental statistics, which tell little about civilian or market economy. This political economy is limited within a Manchu perspective, on which one cannot assume its rivalry, the Ming, was weaker fiscally or economically.

3. Acquisition of People

3.1 Introduction

Imperial population grew exponentially through wars. Nurgaqi integrated other Jurchen tribes, Mongols and Han Chinese into his reign mostly through wars and superior living conditions. Hong Taiji unified Korea, secured his home front and then bypassed the Great Wall to acquire more people in the northern part of Ming's territory, such as the surrounding regions of Beijing. Based on chronicle records and relevant secondary sources, this section aims to present the state building effort of the Jurchen-Manchus through assimilating different peoples into one regime and transforming them to provide the power base for a greater enterprise.

Before taking over the Ming territories, the Jurchen-Manchu economy was a mixture of hunting, gathering, farming and herding. Investment of more human labor can help increase productivity dramatically. The ruling elite heavily valued human population, as the foundation to develop economy and expand territories. Thus, this treatise includes the integration of human populations as an economic factor.

This chapter divides into three major sections, all dealing with integration: Integrating the Jurchens, Integrating the Mongols, and Integrating the Han Chinese. Each section is divided into two parts: one is about Nurgaqi's achievement and the other Hong Taiji's. Since there are only a few chronicle passages of subjugating the Korean people, they are analyzed towards the end as a shorter section.

3.2 The Foundation of a Rising Enterprise

Fe dangse begins with a military expedition for acquiring more people:

qooha be waki seme tumen qooha be unggifi tosoho, tere tosoho qooha be aqaha manggi, hvrhan hiya ini gajire sunja tanggv boigon be, alin i ninggude jase jafafi, emu tanggv qooha be tuqibufi boigon tuwakiyabuha ... emu ama de banjiha juwe fujin sargan buhe bujantai gvwaliyafi, qooha heturefi, boigon ganaha emu amhan juwe efu be waki seme tosoho, bujantai tumen qooha be abka wakalaha ... sure kundulen han i dehi uyun se de. hvnin aniya ilan biyai orin de ...[207]

---

[207] *Fe dangse*, pp. 5-9.

This passage says "in order to kill (our) army, (the Ula tribe, our enemy) sent ten thousand soldiers for an ambush. After encountering the enemy troops in an ambush, the Royal Guard, Hvrhan, located (the captured) five hundred households at the mountain top, built barricades, and dispatched one hundred soldiers for protection." Based on the same description in the *"Qing Veritable Records"*, these five hundred households were subjugated from Fio fortification of the Warka tribe in the Eastern Sea (... *dergi mederi warkai aiman i fio gebungge hoton* ...).[208] On the way back, they were intercepted by Bujantai, who was a leader of the Ula tribe, a tribe that spoke the same language as Nurgaqi's. Bujantai was Nurgaqi's son-in-law, being married with Nurgaqi's two daughters. Later Bujantai betrayed Nurgaqi repeatedly and now ambushed his army, trying to kill Nurgaqi and his two sons-in-law. According to the above passage, Heaven condemned Bujantai's army and therefore he lost this battle. The event happened in the Year of the Lamb (1607), when Nurgaqi was forty-nine.

After defeating Bujantai, Nurgaqi diverted his attention to the tribes, which belonged to his son-in-law:

tere ula i qooha be gidaha manggi, warka i hesihe, fenehe goloi niyalma kemuni ula i bujantai be dahafi bihe, sure kundulen han hendume, muse emu gurun kai, ba i goro de, ula gurun de dalibufi, suwe ula de dahafi banjiha dere, musei emu gurun i han, tuqifi ula i qooha be gidaha kai, te musei emu gurun i han de daha seqi, daharakv ofi, ineku tere aniya sunja biyade, ini fiyanggv deo joriktu beile, eidu baturu, fiongdon jargvqi, hvrhan hiya de, minggan qooha be afabufi unggifi, hesihe, omoho, suru, fenehe tokso, tere golo be suqufi waqihiyame gaifi, juwe minggan olji gajiha.[209]

After the Ula army had been defeated, the Warka people's Hesihe and Fenehe regional circuits still depended on the Ula's leader Bujantai. The Wise and Bright Khan said, "We are one country, but your place is remote, and is separated by the Ula tribe. Therefore, you have to depend on Ula for a living. The Khan of our country has defeated the Ula's army, now you should surrender to our country's Khan." They did not surrender, [the Khan sent] his younger brother Prince Joriktu, Warrior Eidu, Adviser Fiongdon, and Guard Hvrhan, leading one thousand soldiers to subdue

---

[208] *Qing shilu,* vol. 1, Zhonghua shuju, 1986, p. 127.
[209] *Fe dangse,* pp. 14-15.

the regional circuits of Hesihe, Omoho, Suru and Fenehe village. Those regional circuits were all taken and two thousand captives were brought back.

This passage tells that Nurgaqi tried to convince the tribes of *hesihe and fenehe* who affiliated to *ula*, saying that they belonged to one unified country in the first place. However, this strategy did not work, so Nurgaqi had to deploy military force to integrate those tribes into his realm. All these events were kept as the earliest chronicle records, exemplifying the value of human populations and their rights in the political thinking of the the Jurchen-Manchu political convictions. Nevertheless, why were populations so important for them just then?

After unifying the Kaiyuan fortification, on the way home, Nurgaqi and his army arrived in a place named Niowanggiyan Dabagan (*Qingheling* 清河嶺). He ordered a person, named as Menggetu, to deliver a letter to the princes of the five Khalkha Mongol tribes. The letter read,

... bithe i gisun, julgei niyalma jakvnju tumen nikan, dehi tumen monggo, mukei ilan tumen juxen seme mafari gisurere be donjiha bihe, jakvnju tumen nikan, ini gurun be elerakv komso seme, mini gurun be ajigen seme gidaxame, wara be wara, gaijara be gaijara bifi...).[210]

I heard the ancestors said that there were eight hundred thousand Han Chinese, four hundred thousand Mongols and thirty thousand Jurchens who live by the riverside. Eight hundred thousand Han Chinese still consider their country not big enough, and attack our small country, by slaughtering and plundering anyone at will.

Certainly, the figure of eight or four hundred thousand is not accurate, but a means of comparing states in different sizes. The passage suggests that a large population is an advantage that can help to gain superior over the weaker ones. Similar records appeared frequently in the early Manchu chronicles, such as:

(tere gisun i karu uyun biyai iqe sunja de, Kalka i sunja tatan i geren beise i elqin de unggihe, bithei gisun, be alin i golo hada i dalda de tefi banjime, jakvnju tumen nikan, dehi tumen monggo amba gurun de, bi emu ajige hitahvn i gese weile be arahakv bihe...).[211]

---

[210] *Fe dangse*, pp. 458-459.
[211] *Fe dangse*, pp. 651-562.

On the fifth of the ninth month, envoys sent a letter to Mongol princes of Kalka's five tribes and the letter says, we [the Jurchens] live in mountain valleys and shades, and I (Nurgaqi) has never done anything wrong to offend eight hundred thousand Han Chinese and four hundred thousand Mongols...

Such an expression is humble, since Nugaqi just started his enterprise. Clearly, he understood his disadvantage, which is a small population in comparison with the Han Chinese and Mongols. Though he communicated in a modest way, the Mongols mocked him back. On the twenty-second day of the tenth month in the fourth year of Nurgaqi's reign (1619), a large Mongol tribe, the Chakhar, sent their envoys with a *hese*, an imperial decree, to tease Nurgaqi who was the Lord Revered Bright Khan of the thirty thousand Jurchens living by rivers (*... qahar i elqin i gajiha bithei gisun, dehi tumen monggo gurun i ejen baturu qinggiz han i hese, mukei ilan tumen juxen i ejen kundulen genggiyen han, jilgan akv sain i tehebio seme fonjime unggihe...*).[212]

As a retaliation, on the seventeenth day of the first month in the next year (1620), Nurgaqi replied to the Chakhar Khan with a specific analysis of the Mongol populations under Chakhar's control:

aniya biyai juwan nadan de, qahar i han i unggihe bithei karu unggihe bithei gisun, qahar i han sini unggihe bithe de, dehi tumen monggo i ejen baturu qinggiz han, mukei ilan tumen juxen i ejen kundulen genggiyen han de bithe unggihe seme arahabi, sini dehi tumen monggo i geren be minde ainu qoktolombi, bi donjiqi, daidu heqen be gaibure de, dehi tumen monggo be gemu nikan de gaibufi, damu ninggun tumen burulame tuqike seme donjiha, tere ninggun tumen monggo gemu sinde akv kai, ordoz emu tumen, juwan juwe tumet emu tumen, asot yungsiyebu emu tumen, tere iqi ergi ilan tumen gurun sinde dalji akv, ini qisui enquleme yabure gurun kai, hashv ergi ilan tumen gurun gemu sinde bio, ilan tumen gurun akv bime, dehi tumen seme julgei fe gisun i qoktolome, mini gurun be komso, damu ilan tumen seme fusihvlara be, abka na sarkv bio, sini gurun i gese dehi tumen geren akv, sini beye gese baturu akv, mini gurun be komso seme, mini beye be oliha seme, abka na gosifi, hoifa i gurun, ula i gurun, yehe i gurun, fusi, niowanggiyaha, keyen, qilin, jakvn amba ba be abka na minde buhe kai ...[213]

---

[212] *Fe dangse*, p. 572.
[213] *Fe dangse*, pp. 615-69.

On the seventeenth day of the first month, [Nurgaqi] sent a letter to Chakhar's Khan and the letter says, "Chakhar's Khan, in the letter you sent, [you said that] the Lord Brave Qinggiz Khan of four hundred thousand Mongols wrote to the Lord Revered Bright Khan of thirty thousand Jurchens in riverside. How could you be so arrogant to me? Because of your four hundred thousand Mongols? I hear that when Daidu [man. *daidu*; chin. *dadu* 大都] was taken over, four hundred thousand Mongols were all captured by the Han Chinese, and only sixty thousand escaped. Those sixty thousand Mongols are not all yours: Ordoz tribe has ten thousand, the Twelve Tumet tribe has ten thousand, Asot Yungsiyebu tribe has ten thousand. These thirty thousand Right-wing people have nothing to do with you, but are tribes who decide to move by free will. Are the Left-wing's thirty thousand people all yours? [You] do not even have thirty thousand people, but just boast by some ancient and old words of having four hundred thousand, [in order to] despise my thirty thousand people. Don't Heaven and Earth know that? I do not have four hundred thousand people like yours, neither are we strong as you; my people are despised, and my body is weak. However, Heaven and Earth bless me. Big eight places, such as Hoifa tribe, Ula tribe, Yehe tribe, and places like Fusi [man. *fusi*; chin. *fushun* 撫順], Niowanggiyaha [man. *niowanggiyaha*; chin. *qinghe* 清河], Keyen [man. *keyen*; chin. *kaiyuan* 開原] and Qilin [man. *qilin*; chin. *tieling* 鐵嶺], have been bestowed to me by Heaven and Earth ..."

The message is clear: The Chakhar Khan is exaggerating his population and Nurgaqi has achieved great success by bring some Jurchen tribes and Han Chinese regions under his control. This Jurchen leader also admitted that his great enterprise had started with subjugating some Jurchen and Han Chinese people in the first place and gradually extended his power into the Mongol regions. Franz Michael argued that before 1644 the Manchus were not barbarians as certain sources and scholars claimed, but an ethnic group that successfully built a frontier civilization, which absorbed Han Chinese and Mongol cultural elements.[214] The following passages will present the process of merging

---

[214] Franz Michael (1942), The Origin of Manchu Rule in China: Frontier and Bureaucracy as Interacting Forces in the Chinese Empire, John Hopkins Press, Baltimore, pp. 86-110.

different frontier peoples under one governance, focusing more on a perspective of military unification.

3.3 Integrating Jurchen Tribes

3.3.1 Integrating Jurchens into Nurgaqi's Regime

When the Ming dynasty (1368-1644) was founded, the Jurchens established political ties with the Han Chinese regime in Nanjing. The *"Ming Veritable Records"* says that in the fifteenth year of Hongwu (洪武, i.e. 1382), several Commanders of a thousand (*qianhu* 千戶) who served the previous Yuan came from Jurchen regions to surrender. These leaders reported that from Liaoyang 遼陽 to Fochuhun 佛出渾, the land stretches over three thousand and four hundred *li*. Their former subordinates all lived between Fochuhun and Qilielian 乞列憐, and they would deliver the imperial decrees, and make them submit to the Ming rule. The Ming emperor granted their petition, and bestowed silk fabrics woven with gold thread to them (*gu yuan jinghai qianhu ... zi nüzhen lai gui. yan liaoyang zhi fochuhun zhidi, sanqian sibai li ... zi fochuhun zhi qilielian, jie jiu suo bu zhi di, yuan wang yu qi min, shizhi lai gui. zhao xu zhi, ci yi zhijin wenqi* 故元鯨海千戶...自女真來歸。言遼陽至佛出渾之地，三千四百里，... 自佛出渾至乞列憐，皆舊所部之地，願往諭其民，使之來歸。詔許之，賜以織金文綺).[215]

According to Guanjie and Li Yanguang's research, the Ming government established firm control over the northeastern territories, reaching into the modern Heilongjiang Province (黑龍江省) and Sakhalin (庫頁島).[216] However, the Ming empire's governance over the mid and downstream of Heilongjiang and Songhuajiang 松花江 became increasingly weaker and weaker since the mid fifteenth century, and the Han Chinese addressed these local dwellers as "seven-surname savages" (*qixing yeren* 七姓野人).[217] "The Common Genealogy of Eight Banner Manchu Clans" (*baqi manzhou shizu tongpu* 八旗滿洲氏族通譜) was compiled in the ninth Qianlong year (1744), collecting 1,114 Manchu

---

[215] *Ming taizu shilu*, zhongyang yanjiuyuan lishi yanjiusuo jiaoyin, Juan yi si er, Taibei, 1962, pp. 2235-2236.

[216] Guanjie, Li Yanguang (eds.) (1991), *Manzu tongshi*, Liaoning minzu chubanshe, Shenyang, pp. 23-25.

[217] Manzu tongshi, p. 26.

surnames,[218] in which most families were the aboriginal inhabitants who lived among the vast plains, forests, rivers and mountains in northeastern China. In the words of Peter C. Perdue said, "... a tribal people dispersed through the forests and fields of China's northeast frontier".[219]

The *"Manchu Veritable Records"* depicted Nurgaqi's humble beginning of state building. To avenge the death of his grandfather and father, Nurgaqi started to attack Nikan Wailan (man. *nikan wailan*; chin. *nikan wailang* 尼堪外郎), who was a local power broker and a vital link between the Ming and the Jurchens. All he had to start with were the thirteen armors left behind by his father *(taizu sure beile mafa ama i karu be gaime, ini amai werihe juwan ilan uksin i nikan wailan be dailame deribuhe)*.[220] Later, Jurgaqi's soldiers recruited some one hundred soldiers with thirty armors *(tere fonde taizu sure beile i qooha emu tanggv, uksin gvsin bihe)*,[221] and slowly built up his influence.

Among the Jurchen tribes, Nurgaqi's power grew steadily, gradually unifying his neighbors. In the Year of the Lamb (1607), Nurgaqi launched a war against the tribe of Hoifa, took over its fortification, captured and killed the overlord Baindari and his son. At this moment, the Hoifa who had lived in the Hvrki mountains for generations, perished, and its people were taken away (... *tere honin aniya uyun biyai juwan duin de, hoifa i hoton be kafi afame gaiha, hoton i ejen baindari beile i ama jui be bahafi waha, tere hvrki hada de, hoifa i niyalma ududu jalan halame banjiha gurun be efulefi gajiha)*.[222]

Soon afterwards Nurgaqi reported to the Wanli Emperor of the Great Ming, arguing that in the previous Jin dynasty a Warka tribe had dispersed, entered the border zone with Korea and lived there ever since *(julge aisin han i fonde samsiha warka gurun, solho de dosifi, solho i jase i jakarame tehe warka be...)*.[223] According to a Korean source, indeed there were indeed certain Jurchen tribes that had been assimilated into the Korean realm, namely in the first year of Yongle (1403):

---

[218] *Baqi manzhou shizu tongpu* 八旗滿洲氏族通譜 (The Common Genealogy of Eight Banner Manchu Clans), edition Shenyang: Liaoshen shushe, 1989, p. 874.

[219] Peter C. Perdue, *China Marches West, The Qing unification of Central Eurasia,* the Belknap Press of Harvard University Press, Canada, 2005, p. 109.

[220] Manzhou shilu, p. 32.

[221] Manzhou shilu, p. 33.

[222] *Fe dangse*, p. 22.

[223] Fe dangse, p. 28.

辛未三府會議女真事。皇帝敕諭女真吾都里、兀良哈、兀狄哈等、招撫之、使獻貢。女真等本屬于我，故三府會議。[224]

In the sixth month of the third year of Taizong [太宗],[225] the Three Highest Administrative Institutions (*Sanfu* 三府) met to discuss the Jurchen matter. The emperor notified the Jurchen tribes of Wuduli, Wuliangha and Wudiha, etc., pacified them and commanded them to pay tribute. The Jurchens and their peers belonged to us in the first place, so therefore, the three highest institutions held a conference to discuss.

Now Nurgaqi wanted to claim these people back. The Wanli emperor ordered the Korean king for an investigation and found one thousand Warka households (*sure kundulun han baiqame gemu gaji seme, amba nikan gurun i wan li han de bithe wesimbume habxaha manggi, wan li han, solho i han de hendume baiqabufi, julgei jalan de samsiha ududu jalan i waliyabuha warka gurun be, solho han baiqafi ...*).[226] The Korean source also confirmed this event, which says,

老（乙）可赤有名於建州韃子之中，浸浸有強大之勢，今已十餘年矣。今者作為文書，辭說張皇。先為刷還我國之民，曲示禮意，...[227]

Nurgaqi enjoys fame among the Jianzhou Tartars. Gradually [he] has gained strong power, which has sustained for over ten years now. Nowadays in the diplomatic documents composed [by his subordinates], his expression is very aggressive. Previously for retrieving people from our nation, [he] indirectly expressed his etiquette and kindness.

The Manchu source stated that those Jurchens were sent back to Nurgaqi in the second month of the Light-yellow Chicken year (1609), when Nurgaqi was fifty-one years old (*sure kundulen han i susai emu se de, sohon qoko aniya juwe biyade, warka gurun i minggan boigon be tuqibufi elgeme unggihe*).[228]

"*The Manchu Veritable Records*" also reconfirmed this historical matter by saying that in the second month (of 1609), the Manchu state's Taizu Bright Khan sent a letter to the Great Ming state's Wanli Khan, and claimed that people of the Warka tribe, who live along the border with

---

[224] Mingdai Man Meng shiliao, vol. 14, p. 139.

[225] The original document indicates the year is the third year of Taizong (李朝太宗實錄三年), which accordingly is the first year of Ming's Yongle reign (1403). 辛未 is the sixth month according to the lunar calendar in this context.

[226] *Fe dangse*, pp. 28-29.

[227] Mingdai Man Meng shiliao, p. 23.

[228] *Fe dangse*, p. 29.

Korea, all belonged to him and he thus wanted them back. The Wanli Emperor ordered the Korean King to investigate, and later, the Korean King sent one thousand households back (*juwe biya de, manju gurun i taizu kundulen han daiming gurun i wan li han de bithe unggime, solho i jasei jakarame tehe warka aiman i niyalma, gemu miningge kai tere be baiqafi minde bu seqina seme habxaha manggi, wan li han solhoi wang de elqin takvrafi gemu baiqabufi minggan boigon tuqibufi unggihe*).[229]

At the end of the year 1609, Nurgaqi attacked the Huye tribe, defeated it and took two thousand captives back (*huye i golo be suqufi, tere golo be gemu gaiha, juwe minggan olji baha*).[230] In the eleventh month of the next year (1610), Nurgaqi sent his army to four regional circuits of Namdulu, Suifun, Ningguta and Nimaga, registered their people, and took them back. The captives were ordered to leave first, while the army was dispatched to the Yalan regional circuit, took it over and brought ten thousand people back (... *namdulu golo, suifun golo, ningguta golo, nimaqa golo, ere duin golo niyalma be gemu boigon arafi gajime jurafi, boigon be juleri unggihe, qoohai niyalma amasi genefi, yaran golo be jorgon biyade suqufi gemu gaiha, tumen olji bahafi gajiha*).[231]

In the next year, Nurgaqi sent troops to regional circuits of Urguqen and Muren, defeated them and brought one thousand captives back (... *urguqen muren golo be suqufi gemu gaiha, minggan olji baha*).[232] The tribe of Hvrha had been desired for a long time. In the twelfth month of the year 1611, Nurgaqi's soldiers subdued the regional circuit of Hvrha, bringing back two thousand captives and five hundred households. The "*Manchu Veritable Records*" can verify the same event, which says

jorgon biya de, han i hojihon hohori efu, eidu baturu, darhan hiya ere ilan amban de juwe minggan qooha afabufi, weji i aiman i hvrhai golo be dailame genefi jagvtai hoton be ilan inenggi kafi, daha seqi daharakv ofi afame hoton de dosifi emu minggan niyalma be waha, juwe minggan olji baha, terei xurdeme golo be dahabufi tulexen erexen gebungge juwe amban, sunja tanggv boigon be dalime gajiha.[233]

---

[229] Manzhou shilu, pp. 140-141.
[230] *Fe dangse*, pp. 36-37.
[231] *Fe dangse*, p. 38.
[232] *Fe dangse*, p. 44.
[233] *Manzhou shilu*, pp. 145-146.

In the twelfth month, three officials, the Khan's son-in-law Hohori Efu, Eidu the Brave, Darhan Guard, along with two thousand soldiers, had a military expedition against the Hvrha regional circuit. [Hvrha]'s Jagvta fortification was besieged for three days. [The Jurchens] asked [the Hvrha] to surrender but they refused. Therefore, [the Jurchens] took over the fortification, killed one thousand men and obtained two thousand captives. The surrounding areas all surrendered. Two officials, Tulexen and Erexen, brought five hundred households back.

The text in the "*Manchu Veritable Records*" is almost identical with its corresponding part in *Fe dangse*, which demonstrates that different editors had confirmed the same event.

The tribe of Ula was a strong adversary of Nurgaqi. The leader is Bujantai, who was captured by Nurgaqi in a war, but was pardoned and married into Nurgaqi's three daughters. Bujantai's Ula tribe grew rapidly and posed a severe threat to Nurgaqi's enterprise. Nurgaqi resented that, and finally in the twenty-second day of the ninth month in the Year of the Rat (1612), he sent an army from the Khan's fortification to attack the Ula tribe (*tede korsofi ineku tere singgeri aniya uyun biyai orin juwe de, han i heqen qi qooha jurgan*).[234] Four months later, the army demolished Ula's enterprise, which had been accumulated for generations. Its capital was occupied and the whole tribe was obtained. The army camped in the capital for ten days, divided the captives, registered ten thousand households and took them back (*ula gurun de ududu jalan halame han seme banjiha doro be efulefi, amba heqen be baha, gubqi gurun be gemu bahafi, juwan dedume amba heqen de ing hadafi olji dendehe, tumen boigon arafi gajiha...*).[235]

When the Ula tribe was defeated, Bujantai's army was annihilated, and he escaped alone to the Yehe tribe (*bujantai emhun beye burulame tuqifi ini geren qooha be wabufi ... yehe de genehe manggi*).[236] Hence, Nurgaqi launched another military operation, took over nineteenth villages and brought three hundred households back (*uhereme amba anjigen juwan uyun gaxan be gaifi... ilan tanggv boigon arafi gajiha*).[237] In the eleventh month, five hundred soldiers were sent for an expedition.

---

[234] *Fe dangse*, pp. 48-49.
[235] *Fe dangse*, p. 72.
[236] *Fe dangse*, pp. 96-97.
[237] *Fe dangse*, p. 102.

In the twelfth month, Sirin was subjugated, and later the Yaran tribe. One thousand people were captured, registered into two hundred households and were brought back (*omxon biyade, sunja tanggv qooha be unggifi, jorgon biyade sirin be suquha, tereqi genefi yaran gurun be suqufi minggan olji baha, juwe tanggv boigon arafi gajiha*).[238]

In the eleventh month of the Green-Rabbit year (1615), when Nurgaqi was fifty-seven years old (*niohon gvlmahvn aniya, sure kundulen han i susai nadan se de ...*),[239] he summoned two thousand men. On the twentieth day of the twelfth month, they started to attack the Ehe Guren (*omxon biyade, juwe minggan qooha unggifi, jorgon biyai orin de, ehe guren be suqufi*).[240] In the end, ten thousand Ehe people were captured and registered into five hundred households (*tumen olji baha, sunja tanggv boigon araha*).[241]

Due to his significant achievements of subjugating the neighboring tribes, in the Red-Dragon year (1616), when Nurgaqi was fifty-eight years old, he crowned himself as the Khan of *abka geren gurun be ujikini seme sindaha genggiyen han,*[242] which means "the bright Khan appointed by the Heaven to nourish all people". Peter C. Purdue also depicted this glorious moment in his *China Marches West*, pointing out that Nurgaqi was "consolidating his claim to the Mongolian traditions of leadership".[243] Indeed, the coronation of Khan had its origins in the steppe culture. According to the *Fe dangse*, up to the moment of his coronation, Nurgaqi's accomplishment was mainly based on integrating the Jurchen and Han Chinese people. Subduing the Mongols would happen in a few years. Now, by the mandate of Heaven, Nurgaqi was legitimized to subjugate more people into his regime.

Seven months later, he ordered to attack the Sahaliyan tribe that lived along Sahaliyan River (*nadan biyai juwan uyun de qooha jurafi*).[244] Sahaliyan River literally means Black River, which is today's Heilongjiang (黑龍江). The war stretched into the tenth month, when the

---

[238] *Fe dangse*, p. 115.
[239] Fe danbgse, p. 119.
[240] *Fe dangse*, p. 142.
[241] *Fe dangse*, p. 144.
[242] Fe dangse, p. 197.
[243] Perdue, China Marches West, p. 122.
[244] *Fe dangse*, p. 211.

Black River froze fifteen or twenty days earlier than usual. The scribe wrote,

julge sahaliyan ula, omxon biyai tofohon de orin de amala juhe jafambihe, sunggari ula, omxon biyai juwan de tofohon de sunja inenggi amala juhe jafambihe, amba genggiyen han i qooha genehe aniya, juwan biyai iqereme juhe jafara jakade...

In the past, the Black River usually froze from the fifteenth day to the twentieth day in the eleventh month; the Heavenly River [man. *sunggari ula*; chin. *Songhua jiang* 松花江] would freeze from the tenth to the fifteenth day in the eleventh month. In the year when the Great Bright Khan's army arrived, [the river] froze in the beginning of the tenth month.

This may reveal important information as the Little Ice Age, which corresponds with Bret Hinsch's research on the climate change during the late Ming, when temperature became comparatively colder from 1608 to 1617, according to Yuan Xiaoxiu's diary. [245] The later chronicles reconfirmed that Black River froze earlier by fifteen to twenty days compared to the past (*sahaliyan ula an i juhe jafara tofohon orin i inenggi onggolo juhe jafahangge*).[246] Nurgaqi's troops crossed the frozen river easily and soon subdued the Sahaliyan tribe. Thirty-six villages were abolished along with the Bojiri fortress (*bojiri xurdeme gvsin ninggun gaxan be gemu gaifi*),[247] but the number of captives was not mentioned.

In the Light-Red Snake year (1617), when Nurgaqi was fifty-nine years old (*fulahvn meihe aniya, genggiyen han i susai uyun se de*),[248] he decided to subjugate the people who scattered along the Eastern Sea. On the eighteenth day of the first month, four hundred military men were dispatched for the mission (*juwan jakvn de, duin tanggv qooha be, dergi mederei jakarame tefi daharakv samsifi bisire gurun be gaisu seme unggihe*).[249] In the sixth month, all the escaping fugitives were gathered and in total, there were three thousand captives, who were registered into

---

[245] Lan Yong 藍勇 et al. (2003), "Qihoubianqian he zhongguo lishi" 氣候變遷和中國歷史 (Climate Change and History of China), *Zhongguo lishi dili luncong* 中國歷史地理論叢 (Collections of Essays on Chinese Historical Geography), 18.1: 63.

[246] *Fe dangse*, pp. 218-219.

[247] *Fe dangse*, p. 218.

[248] *Fe dangse*, p. 221.

[249] *Fe dangse*, p. 225.

one hundred households. Afterwards the army returned (*ninggun biyade, burulame tuqifi guwehengge be waqihiyame gaiha, uhereme ilan minggan olji baha, tanggv boigon araha, tereqi qooha bedereme jihe*).[250]

Non-military ways were also adopted to increase population by attracting people with generous treatment. On the tenth day of the tenth month, Nurgaqi heard that Nakada, an official from the Hvrha tribe in the east, was leading one hundred households to come and surrender. He sent two hundred men to receive them (*juwan biyai de, dergi hvrha gurun i nakada gebungge amban, ujulafi tanggv boigon dahame jimbi seme, juwe tanggv niyalma be okdome unggihe*).[251] The one hundred households arrived on the twentieth. After the Bright Khan went to his yamun, the Hvrha people kowtowed and met the Khan; the Khan received them with a ceremony and a magnificent banquet (*tere tanggv boigon hvrha orin de isinjiha, genggiyen han yamun de tuqifi, hvrha gurun hengkileme aqaha manggi, aqaha doroi amba sarin sarilaha...*).[252] After the banquet, the Hvrha people were ordered to split into two groups: those who wanted to go home stood on one side and those who would stay permanently on the other (*tereqi amasi ini boode genere niyalma be emu ergide ilibuha, enteheme jihe niyalma be emu ergide ilibufi*).[253] Those who stayed were abundantly rewarded with bondservants, horses, cattle, clothes, houses, and other daily necessities, according to their ranks. For example, each of the eight leading officials was bestowed with ten couples of bond-servants, ten horses for riding, ten oxen for cultivating lands and fur coats sewed with satin embroidery and leopard skin as rims (*ujulame jihe jakvn amban de, takvra seme juwanta juru aha, yalu seme juwanta morin, tari seme juwanta ihan, yarga hayame gequheri burime jibqa dahv, sekei mahala...*).[254] Many of those who were leaving witnessed the abundant rewards and decided to stay (*tuttu buhe be safi, boode amasi genembi sehe niyalma ambula genehekv tehe*).[255]

However, those who returned did not escape from the fate of being subdued. On the twenty-sixth day of the first month in the fourth year of the Genggiyen Han (1619), Nurgaqi sent one thousand soldiers, led by

---

[250] *Fe dangse*, p. 227.
[251] *Fe dangse*, p. 322.
[252] *Fe dangse*, p. 322.
[253] *Fe dangse*, p. 323.
[254] *Fe dangse*, p. 323.
[255] *Fe dangse*, pp. 325-326.

the official Muhaliyan, went to the Hvrha tribe in the east, and collected the rest of people who still remained there (*orin ninggun de, muhaliyan gebungge amban de emu minggan qooha be adabufi, xun dekdere ergi hvrha gurun i funqehe tutahangge be waqihiyame gaisu seme unggihe*).[256] On the eighth day of the sixth month, Muhaliyan and the soldiers returned, bringing back one thousand households, two thousand men and six thousand family members (*xun dekdere ergi hvrha gurun i funqehe tutaha be waqihiyame gaisu seme unggihe muhaliyan i emu minggan qooha, ninggun biyai iqe jakvn de amasi isinjiha, emu minggan boigon, juwe minggan haha, ninggun minggan anggala gajime jidere de...*).[257]

The above passages are significant records that depict the integration of the Jurchen tribes who spoke the same language, except for Yehe, which was regarded by Nurgaqi as a Jurchen tribe speaking a different language (*yehe, muse oqi, enqu gisun i juxen gurun kai*).[258] From this point onward, Nurgaqi shifted his focus on assimilating the Mongol and Han Chinese people, to lay a greater foundation for his enterprise. Nonetheless, occasionally some tribal people from Hvrha and Warka came to surrender. On the fifth day of the second month in the tenth year of the Genggiyen Han (1625), three leaders named Tayu, Garda, and Fukana, leading 112 men from Huvha tribe and 222 men from Warka tribe, surrendered to Nurgaqi (*iqe sunja de, tayu, garda, fukana i gajiha hvrha i emu tanggv juwan juwe haha, warka i juwe tanggv orin juwe haha, han de hengkileme aqaha*).[259]

Months later, two leaders named as Yahv and Kamdani brought households from the Gvwalqa tribe. Nurgaqi travelled ten *li* to welcome them. The number of people they brought back is 1,900, with 540 men included (*iqe uyun de, han, gvwalqa i boigon be, yahv, kamdani gajime jidere de, han tuqifi juwan ba i dubede okdofi... gajiha anggalai ton, emu minggan uyun tanggv, haha sunja tanggv dehi*).[260]

---

[256] *Fe dangse*, p. 337.
[257] *Fe dangse*, p. 422.
[258] Fe dangse, p. 137.
[259] *Fe dangse*, p. 2960.
[260] *Fe dangse*, pp. 3008-3009.

The following chart displays Nurgaqi's major achievements:

Dates in Lunar Calendar	Original Residence	Number of Migrants or captives	Number of Households	Remarks	Page numbers in *Fe dangse*
20/03/1607	Warka		500		p. 1.
05/1607	Warka	2,000			p. 15.
02/1609	Korea		1000		p. 29.
12/1609	Yaran	10,000			p. 38.
02/1611	Urguqen and Muren	1,000			p. 44.
12/1611	Hvrha	2,000	500		p. 46.
22/09/1612	Ula		10,000		p. 72.
10/09/1613	Yehe		300		p. 102.
12/1614	Sirin	1,000	200		p. 115.
20/12/1615	Ehe Guren	10,000	500		p. 143.
06/1617	the Eastern Sea	3,000	100		p. 227.
10/10/1618	Hvrha		100		p. 322.
08/06/1619	Hvrha	8,000	1,000		p. 422.
17/02/1621	Warkaxi	114			p. 807.
21/01/1625	Warka	370			p. 2946.
05/03/1625	Hvrha and Warka	334			p. 2960.
09/08/1625	Gvwalqa	1900		With 540 men included	p. 3009.
04/10/1625	the Eastern Sea	600	1500		pp. 3031-3032.
Total		40,318	15,700		

Table 1: Jurchen migrants and captives in Nurgaqi's reign

Sometimes the calculated households and people are overlapped, so our analysis mainly depends on the number of migrants and captives in the following chapters. The chart shows that Nurgaqi acquired 40,318 people and 15,700 households as captives from the wars. Three tribes, Yaran, Ehe Guren and Hvrha, contributed nearly three-fourths population as war prisoners, and the rest was mainly from the Eastern Sea. Regarding the households, more than two thirds of the total amount consisted of the Ula tribe, followed by one thousand Warka households handed over by Korea. If each household consists of roughly five people, then Ula could be the biggest population contributor with 50,000 people.

In 1613, When trying to settling down the seizure of the khanship among his sons, Nurgaqi mentioned that five thousand households were granted to his two eldest sons who were born by the same mother (*sini neneme mutuha emu eme de banjiha ahvn deo juwe jui de, sunjata minggan boo gurun...*).[261] As for the children who were born by the other wives, the number of granted bondservants and imperial decrees for trade decreased successively (*mini hanji sargan de banjiha geren juse de, gurun ejehe ai jaka be gemu komso buhe kai*).[262] In 1615, after subjugating many rival tribes, such as Yaran, Hvrha, Ula and Yehe, Nurgaqi gathered his people and counted their number. Three hundred men are assigned into one battalion, and each battalion has one leader (*sure kundulen han i isabuha amba gurun be, gemu neigen teksileme dolofi, ilan tanggv haha be emu niru arafi, niru de emu ejen sindafi...*).[263] One can see that most of the acquired Jurchen populations were assimilated into the banner system and became part of the military force. According to Wang Zhonghan 王鍾翰, the Jurchens being assimilated into the Eight Banners during Nurgaqi's reign were named as Old Manchus (man. *fe manju*; chin. *fo manzhou* 佛滿洲), which is distinguished from the New Manchus (man. *iqe manju*; chin. *yiche manzhou* 伊徹滿洲) integrated into banners during Hong Taiji's reign.[264] This also leads to our next chapter.

---

[261] Fe dangse, p. 87.
[262] Fe dangse, p. 88.
[263] *Fe dangse,* p. 156.
[264] Wang Zhonghan 王鍾翰 (1997), *Qingshi xinkao* 清史新考 (New Evidential Research on Qing History), Liaoning daxue chubanshe, Shenyang, pp. 50-51.

3.3.2   Integrating Jurchens into Hong Taiji's Regime

In Hong Taiji's reign, Usita was commanded to subdue the regional circuits of Nooro and Aran, which originally belonged to the Warka tribe. On the fourth day of the third month in the first year of Wesihun Erdemungge (1636), messengers of Usita delivered a letter, saying that one hundred and twenty Warka men were captured, along with two hundred and ten women, and seventy superior-class women. The total number of captives was four hundred and twenty (*iqe duin de, warka i nooro, aran golo de qooha genehe usita i takvraha elqin i gajiha bithe, haha emu tanggv orin, erei hehe juwe tanggv juwan, deji hehe nadanju, erei anggala ton duin tanggv orin...*).[265]

One month later, on the tenth day of the fourth month in 1636, two military leaders under two White Banners, named Hvsintai and Holdon, returned from the expedition of Warka. As for the captives, they brought back one hundred fifteen men, one hundred forty women, and fifty-seven children. In total, the number reached three hundred and twelve (*juwan de, warka de qooha genehe juwe xanggiyan i Hvsintai, Holdon isinjiha, esei bahafi gajiha hahai ton emu tanggv tofohon, hehe emu tanggv dehe, ajige juse susai nadan, uheri anggalai ton, ilan tanggv juwan juwe...*).[266]

Five days later, Usita and the other leaders who also went to subdue Warka tribe sent back a report, which says the eight banners captured 1,860 men, and one hundred forty five women. The total number is 2,800 (*warka de qooha genehe usita sei unggihe bithe, jakvn gvsai baha hahai ton, emu minggan emu tanggv ninju, deji hehe emu tanggv dehe, uheri anggalai ton, juwe minggan jakvn tanggv...*).[267] On the same day, two leaders under the two Red Banners, Dojiri and Hvsi, returned. They captured three hundred seventy-five men, two hundred sixty-two women, and one hundred eighty-five children. The total number is seven hundred ninety-five (*tofohon de, warka de qooha genehe juwe fulgiyan i dojiri, hvsi qooha isinjiha, esei bahafi gajiha hahai ton, ilan tanggv nadanju sunja haha, hehe juwe tanggv ninju juwe, ajige juse emu tanggv susai jakvn, uheri anggala ton, nadan tanggv uyunju sunja...*).[268]

---

[265] *Fe dangse*, pp. 7678-7679.
[266] *Fe dangse*, pp. 6889-6890.
[267] *Fe dangse*, p. 6904.
[268] *Fe dangse*, p. 6906.

Dates in Lunar Calender	Original Residence	Number of Migrants or captives	Number of Households	Page numbers in *Fe dangse*
12/12/1632	Ujala	700		p. 6552.
04/03/1636	Warka	420		p. 6779.
10/04/1636	Warka	312		p. 6890.
15/04/1636	Warka	3,595		p. 6904.
27/04/1636	Warka	601		p. 6988.
02/05/1636	Kamnigan	29		p. 7013.
05/05/1636	Warka	982		pp. 7028-7029.
Total		6,639		

Table 2: Jurchen migrants and captives in Hong Taiji's early reign

The chart shows that nearly ninety percent of the migrants was from the Warka tribe. Ujala consisted of one tenth, with an insignificant percentage from Kamnigan. Notably, the number of households was not recorded in this period.

The previous charts are derived from the chronicle passages from the "Manchu Old Chronicles" (man. *fe dangse*; chin. *manwen laodang* 滿文老檔). The following analysis was conducted according to the "Compiled Translation of Manchu Chronicles Kept by the Early Qing Palace Historiographic Academy" (*qingchu neiguoshiyuan manwen dang'an bianyi* 清初內國史院滿文檔案編譯). These translated chronicles are incomplete due to some missing years, which will be better explained at the end of this article.

Dates in Lunar Calendar	Original Residence	Number of migrants or captives	Number of Households	Page numbers in Qingchu neiguoshiyuan manwen dang'an yibian
23/01/1633	Ujala	565		p. 4.
15/09/1634	Hvrha	1,490		pp. 109-110.
14/04/1635	Warka	9,785		p. 159.
25/04/1635	Ninggvta	1,216		p. 160.
06/05/1635	Sahaliyan bira	2,000		p. 160.
07/05/1635	Warka	116		p. 164.
18/05/1635	Warka	1,216		p. 166.
25/04/1638	Warka	315		p. 304.
06/12/1638	Hvrha		90	p. 398.
15/03/1640	Warka	303		p. 453.
21/06/1640	Sahaliyan bira	4,819		p. 454.
13/11/1642	Sunggari	1,458		p. 496.
16/01/1643	Sunggari	1,565		p. 507.
Total		14,967	90	

Table 3 Jurchen migrants and captives in Hong Taiji's later reign

This chart shows that nearly eighty percent of migrants were obtained from the Warka tribe, with one quarter of the captives from the regional circuit of Sahaliyan bira, which is today's Heilongjiang Province. Nearly twenty percent were acquired from the Sunggari area. The scribes recorded only ninety households in this time.

Peter C. Perdue describe this integrating process as "The predominant theme in most studies of the rise of the Manchus has been the transformation of the clan society of the Manchu tribes into a centralized bureaucratic state."[269] Comparatively, the integration of the Jurchen tribes was almost completed by Nurgaqi, leaving a few tribes, such as Warka, for Hong Taiji to unify. However, Wang Zhonghan pointed out that, even after 1644, some tribal peoples, such as Solon (man. *solon*;

---

[269] Perdue, *China Marches West*, p. 109.

chin. *suolun* 索倫)[270], Sibe (man. *sibe*; chin. *xibo* 錫伯), Dahvr (man. *dahvr*; chin. *dahu'er* 達瑚爾)[271] and Heje (man. *heje*; chin. *hezhe* 赫哲)[272] were incorporated into the banner system, but they were not assimilated into the Manchu family.[273] Most of the subdued tribes spoke the same language as Nurgaqi, with the Yehe tribe as an exception. These Jurchen tribes formed the main body of the Eight-Banner system, which was the foundation for Nurgaqi and Hong Taiji to subjugate the Mongols and Han Chinese as a higher purpose. In total, the number of Jurchens being integrated into the Later Jin state reached 63,958.

3.4 Integrating Mongol Tribes

3.4.1 Integrating Mongols into Nurgaqi's Regime

Nurgaqi started his enterprise with a strenuous beginning. Only a few Mongols came to join his vision. Therefore, almost every Mongol defection was detailed in the Manchu chronicles. On the thirtieth day of the second month in the fifth year of the Genggiyen Han (1620), twenty-six households of eighty Mongol refugees came to surrender, along with their children, wives, and animals. Originally they belonged to Jongnon, who was a tribal leader of the Jarut Mongols (*monggo i jarut gurun i jongnon beile i monggo, orin ninggun boigon, jakvnju anggala niyalma, juse sargan ulha gajime ukame, gvsin de isinjiha*).[274] On the eighth day of the eighth month, twenty-seven households of the Neiqi Khan from the Jarut Mongol place came to yield (*monggol i jarut ba i neiqi han qi orin nadan boigon, iqe uyun de ukame jihe*).[275] Ten days later, eight households escaped from Neiqi Beile of the Jarut Mongol tribe, came and surrendered to Nurgaqi (*monggo i jarut ba i neiqi beile qi, jakvn boigon ukame jihe*).[276]

One after the other, Mongols left their original tribes and surrendered to Nurgaqi. On the seventh day of the third month, seven households escaped from the Mongol Bagadarhan's tribe, came and surrendered to

---

[270] A modern name is Evenks (*Ewenkezu* 鄂溫克族).
[271] A modern name is Daur People (*dawo'erzu* 達斡爾族).
[272] The Russian name is Nanai people.
[273] Wang Zhonghan, *Qingshi xinkao*, p. 52.
[274] *Fe dangse*, pp. 775-776.
[275] *Fe dangse*, p. 788.
[276] *Fe dangse*, p. 798.

Nurgaqi (*ilan biyai iqe nadan de, monggo i bagadarhan i nadan boigon ukame jihe*).[277] On the eleventh, three men and two women, escaped from the tribe of Babai taiji, who was Mongol Beile Joriktu's son: all migrated to Nurgaqi's state (*juwan emu de, monggo i joriktu beile i jui babai taiji qi, ilan haha juwe hehe, ninggun morin gajime jihe*).[278]

On the seventh day of the fourth month, one hundred twenty men with ninety-eight households came and surrendered. Originally, they belonged to the Mongol Barin tribe that was under Dureng beile's reign. (*iqe nadan de, monggo i barin dureng beile i uyunju jakvn boo, emu tanggv orin haha...*).[279] On the sixteenth day of the eleventh month, four Mongols and five Han Chinese escaped by horses to surrender; on the same day, another four Mongols came from Guangning to surrender (*juwan ninggun de, guwangning qi duin monggo, sunja nikan, uheri uyun niyalma morin yalufi ukama jihe, tere inenggi, jai geli duin monggo guwangning qi ukame jihe*).[280] Five days later, forty-seven men and women from the Bayot Mongol tribe came to yield. They brought forty-seven sheep, thirty-six oxen, twenty-six carts and one horse (*orin emu de bayot gurun i monggo haha hehe dehi nadan, honin dehi nadan, ihan gvsin ninggun, sejen orin ninggun, morin emken gajime ukame jihe*).[281] On the same day, forty-nine Mongols in two groups escaped from the Guangning fortification, came and surrendered. Nugaqi went to his yamun and held a banquet to receive them all (*guwangning qi emu inenggi juwe jergi dehi uyun han i beye yamun de tuqifi, jihe ukanju de sarin sarilaha*).[282]

In the following years, small groups of Mongols successively joined Nurgaqi's regime. The Manchu chronicles detailed all of them. The beneath grid chart calculates the Mongols being integrated in Nurgaqi's time.

---

[277] *Fe dangse*, p. 839.
[278] *Fe dangse*, pp. 840-841.
[279] *Fe dangse*, p. 934.
[280] *Fe dangse*, p. 1252.
[281] *Fe dangse*, pp. 1271-1272.
[282] *Fe dangse*, p. 1272.

Dates in Lunar Calendar	Original Residence	Number of migrants or captives	Number of House-holds	Page numbers in *Fe dangse*
09/08/1620	Jarut		27	p. 788.
19/08/1620	Jarut		8	p. 798.
30/09/1620	Jarut	80	26	pp. 775-776.
07/03/1621	Bagadarhan		7	p. 839.
11/03/1621	Babai taiji	5		p. 841.
07/04/1621	Barin	120	98	p. 934.
16/11/1621	Guwangning	8		pp. 1251-1252.
21/11/1621	Bayot	47		p. 1271.
21/11/1621	Guwangning	49		p. 1272.
24/11/1621	Guwangning	5		p. 1287.
27/11/1621	Bayot	6		p. 1300.
29/11/1621	Kalka i Nangsuk	2		p. 1314.
06/12/1621	Kalka	1		p. 1331.
12/12/1621	Kalka	2		p. 1346.
14/12/1621	Kalka	4		p. 1351.
17/12/1621	Joriktu	8		p. 1355.
17/12/1621	Nangsuk	8		p. 1355.
18/12/1621	Bagadarhan	2		p. 1355.
20/12/1621	Bagadarhan	10		p. 1377.
21/12/1621	Hvng Baturu, et al.		35	p. 1381.
24/12/1621	Bayot	115	80	p. 1392.
04/01/1622	Urut	460		p. 1429.
06/01/1622	Kalka i Nangsuk	16		p. 1435.
07/01/1622	Anggai taiji, et al.	100		p. 1445.
09/01/1622	Kalka i Nangsuk	17	3	p. 1452.
11/01/1622	Kalka i Bagadarhan	21		p. 1456.
16/01/1622	Bayot	35		p. 1492.
27/01/1622	Kalka i Dureng, et al.	649		pp. 1527-1528.

Table 4: Mongol migrants and captives in Nurgaqi's reign

Dates in Lunar Calendar	Original Residence	Number of migrants or captives	Number of House-holds	Page numbers in *Fe dangse*
03/02/1622	Qahar	63		pp. 1543-1546.
04/02/1622	Qahar	6		p. 1560.
07/02/1622	Mongol tribes		10-20 on a daily basis	p. 1583.
17/02/1622	Sereng beile	95		p. 1633.
14/03/1622	Kalka i Joriktu and Sereng	22		pp. 1753-1754.
14/03/1622	Bagadarhan		10	pp. 1754.
27/03/1622	Kalka i Joriktu	11		p. 1803.
04/04/1622	Kalka i Joriktu	44		p. 1821.
11/04/1622	Kalka i Joriktu	6		p. 1837.
18/04/1622	Barin	22		pp. 1854-1855.
10/06/1622	Neiqi	7		p. 1875.
02/01/1623	Kalka i Monggo Sengge Tabunang		40	p. 1913.
08/01/1623	Monggo gurun i Kalka i labasihio taiji		40	p. 1931.
12/02/1623	Monggo i bahvn beile and Baigal beile		48	p. 2013-2014.
19/02/1623	Monggo i Barin	20	20	p. 2032.
24/02/1623	Barin i Nangnuk	24		p. 2060.
29/02/1623	Kalka	4		p. 2077.
30/02/1623	Aohan	4		p. 2079.
06/03/1623	Kalka	40		p. 2106.
13/03/1623	Korqin	58		p. 2114.

Table 4: Mongol migrants and captives in Nurgaqi's reign

Dates in Lunar Calendar	Original Residence	Number of migrants or captives	Number of House-holds	Page numbers in *Fe dangse*
14/03/1623	Kalka	3		p. 2122.
14/04/1623	Barin	10		p. 2122.
19/04/1623	Jaisai	3		p. 2227.
30/04/1623	Jaisai	50		p. 2276.
01/05/1623	Neiqi	2		p. 2277.
03/05/1623	Joriktu	21		p. 2314.
03/05/1623	Monggo	1,280		p. 2315.
04/06/1623	Bagadarhan	40		p. 2403.
08/01/1624	Jaisai	28		p. 2750.
07/05/1625	Barin		10	p. 2984.
Total		5,321	462	

Table 4: Mongol migrants and captives in Nurgaqi's reign

The chart shows that in the successive six years, from 1620 to 1625, there were 5,321 people and 462 households who were assimilated into Nurgaqi's realm. Nearly one fourth of the migrants were registered under the name of Monggo, with twelve percent being obtained from the Khalkha tribe. The rest evenly came from other small tribes. Sometimes the scribes only recorded the registered households, without calculating the exact number of people. Therefore, the actual figure of refugees and captives should be higher than the above finding.

3.4.2 Integrating Mongols in Hong Taiji's Regime

When Hong Taiji took over the throne, he immediately launched military expeditions against Korea. Meanwhile, he frequently negotiated with the Ming's general Yuan Chonghuan 袁崇煥 for peaceful terms integration. Under such political circumstances, although many Mongols came to surrender, the actual figures were not well kept. The available numbers are displayed as following:

Dates in Lunar Calendar	Original Residence	Number of migrants or captives	Number of House-holds	Remarks	Page numbers in *Fe dangse*
18/08/1627	Qahar	39			p. 4084.
15/02/1628	Qahar i Dolot	11,200			p. 4163.
24/02/1628	Qahar		200		p. 4165.
23/05/1628	Guteita-bunang	10,000		With humans, camels, horses, oxen and sheep included.	p. 4195.
07/08/1628	Qahar i Alakqot	700			p. 4314.
15/09/1628	Qahar	30			p. 4332.
11/10/1628	Qahar	100			p. 4501.
06/06/1632	Qahar	18,915			p. 6245.
07/06/1632	Qahar	8,250			pp. 6254-6257.
10/06/1632	The Ming	318		Mongols who escaped to the Ming	p. 6260.
18/06/1632	Qahar	1			p. 6292.
29/08/1632	Qahar	18			p. 6448.
05/10/1632	Qahar	9			p. 6470.
19/11/1632	Qahar	84			p. 6521.
25/02/1636	Mooming-gan	547	270		pp. 6758-6759.
20/03/1636	Mooming-gan		99	With 37 women	pp. 6839-6840.
Total		50,240	569		

Table 5: Mongol migrants and captives in Hong Taiji's early reign

The above chart shows that nearly eighty percent of the Mongol migrants and more than one third of households were from the Chakhar tribe. Another significant contributor were the Guteitabunang, making up nearly one fifth of the percentage.

From the third to the fourth year of Sure Han (1629-1630), Hong Taiji shifted his focus to the Han Chinese and personally led the army to attack Beijing and its surrounding areas. Up to the fifth year of Sure Han (1631), the scribes kept very few records of Mongol defections. In the seventh month of the fifth year (1631), Hong Taiji concentrated on battling the Ming's Dalinghe 大凌河 region.

After the Dalinghe Battle, more and more Mongols came to surrender. Years later, on the sixteenth day of the tenth month in the first year of Wesihun Erdemungge (1636), Hong Taiji sent officials to form an alliance with the Khorchin Mongols (... *juwan biyai juwan ninggun de korqin de qulgame genefi*).[283] The officials reported that there were 6,539 armored soldiers, 22,308 households, and 448 companies (*uheri uksin i ton ninggun minggan sunja tanggv gvsin uyun booi ton juwe tumen juwe minggan ilan tanggv jakvn boo, duin tanggv dehi jakvn niru*).[284]

On the sixth day of the eleventh month, Hong Taiji sent his uncle Asidarhan and Dayaqi tabunang to register the companies of Outer-Vassal Mongols (man. *tulergi goloi monggo*; chin. *waifan menggu* 外藩蒙古) as his allies (*iqe ninggun de, tulergi goloi monggo i niru banjibume genehe asidarhan nakqu, dayaqi tabunang isinjiha*).[285] The result was 19,580 households and 384 companies (*ere uheri booi ton, emu tumen uyun minggan sunja tanggv jakvnju boo, irui ton ilan tanggv jakvnju duin inu*),[286] plus 5,456 armored soldiers (*uhereme uksin i ton, sunja minggan duin tanggv susai ninggun uksin*).[287]

In total, up to the year 1636, there were 832 Mongol companies, 41,888 Mongol households and 11,995 armored soldiers under Hong Taiji's leadership, as an minimal estimation.

In Hong Taiji's later reign, there were still large amounts of Mongols coming to join his state. The following chart has been developed from the

---

[283] *Fe dangse*, p. 8167.
[284] *Fe dangse*, pp. 8193-8194.
[285] *Fe dangse*, p. 8125.
[286] Fe dangse, p. 8168.
[287] *Fe dangse*, p. 8171.

"Compiled Translation of Manchu Chronicles Kept by the Early Qing Palace Historiographic Academy" (*Qingchu neiguoshiyuan manwen dang'an bianyi* 清初內國史院滿文檔案編譯). Again, the record is not complete because some chronicles were damaged during certain historical periods.

Dates in Lunar Calender	Original Residence	Number of migrants or captives	Number of House-holds	Remarks	Page numbers in Qingchu neiguo-shiyuan manwen dang'an bianyi
22/01/1634	Kalka	936			p. 58.
19/02/1634	Sirhaxibtu	217			p. 67.
21/04/1634	Sonomu	115			p. 77.
09/06/1634	Qahar	153			p. 87.
09/06/1634	Qahar		1,000		p. 87.
21/06/1634	Qahar	2,700			p. 90.
23/06/1634	Qahar		63		p. 90.
14/08/1634	Asut	15		This month is an intercalary month.	p. 104.
20/03/1635	Qahar	1400		With their wives, children and animals.	p. 156.
27/05/1635	Qahar		1,500		p. 167.
04/06/1635	Monggo	600	1,380		p. 170.
24/06/1635	Qahar	6,833			p. 176.
03/07/1641	Monggo	35			p. 458.
12/04/1642	Taxan	186			p. 467.
Total		13,190	3,943		

Table 6: Mongol migrants and captives in Hong Taiji's later reign

115

Compared with Chart Five, one can find that the same pattern repeated. Nearly eighty percent of migrants came from the Chakhar tribe. In the ninth year of Sure Han (1635), a Han Chinese official Chen Jin 陳錦 wrote a memorial to Hong Taiji, confirming that "Chakhar Mongols came successively from afar and the military force increased daily, so our country grew significantly stronger" (*chaha'er menggu yuanlaizhe luoyi, bingli rizeng, woguo da qiang* 察哈爾蒙古遠來者絡繹，兵力日增，我國大強).[288] Another two significant contributors were the Khalkha and Sanggar, but the ratio is lower than one percentage. As for households, Chakhar tribe contributed over sixty-five percent, with the rest being registered under the name of "Monggo". To sum up, combining the two above charts above, one can see that Chakhar alone contributed nearly eighty percent of the Mongol migrants to the Later Jin.

Up to this moment, the number of Mongol migrants and captives is therefore 68,751, without counting the households. As Rawski said, the power of Chinggis derived from a loosely incorporated tribal confederation in the steppe,[289] and now this authority was shifting to the supreme Manchu leader.

3.5 Integrating Han Chinese

3.5.1 Integrating Han Chinese into Nurgaqi's Regime

In the Yellow-Horse Year (1618), when Nurgaqi was sixty years old (*suwayan morin aniya, amba genggiyen han i ninju se de ...*),[290] he gathered one hundred thousand men from the Eight Banners to attack the Ming. The time was scheduled on the Snake Hour of the Tiger's Day, which is the thirteenth day of the fourth month (*duin biyai juwan ilan i tasha inenggi meihe erinde, jakvn gvsai juwan tumen qooha, nikan be dailame genere de*).[291] Two days later, Nurgaqi led the army and besieged the Fusi fortification (man. *fusi*; chin. *fushun* 撫順), where the

---

[288] *Qingchu neiguoshiyuan manwen dang'an yibian* 清初內國史院滿文檔案譯編 (Compiled Translation of Manchu Chronicles Kept by the Early Qing Palace Historiographic Academy), translated and compiled by Guan Xiaolian et al., edition Beijing: Guangming ribao chubanshe, 1986 p. 143.

[289] Evelyn S. Rawski, "Presidential Address: Reenvisioning the Qing: The Significance of the Qing Period in Chinese History", *The Journal of Asian Studies*, 55. 4: 835.

[290] Fe dangse, p. 233.

[291] *Fe dangse*, p. 249.

Mobile Corps Commander (man. *iogi hergen i hafan*; chin. *youji* 遊擊)
Li Yongfang 李永芳 was stationed (*tofohon i qimari han i beye, iogi hergen i hafan i tehe fusi heqen be kame de*).[292] After a short battle, Commander Li dressed himself in official robes, rode a horse, got out of the fortification and surrendered to Nurgaqi (... *iogi li yung fang teni dahame, amba etuku etuhei morin yalufi heqen tuqike manggi...*).[293] The next day, the Eight Banner troops gathered at the west side of the Fusi fortification, divided three hundred thousand people and animals as their booties, and registered people into one thousand households (*juwan ninggu de, fusi heqen i xun tuhere ergi bigan de, jakvn gvsai qooha aqafi amasi bederefi... gvsin tumen olgi be dendeme minggan boigon araha*).[294] At this point, the Eight-Banner Han Chinese Artillery Troops (man. *ujen qooha*; chin. *baqi hanjun* 八旗漢軍) had not yet been established, as the captives were assigned to the various (high-low) officials of different ranks, led by Commander Li according to the Ming institution (*kemuni ini nikan gurun i kooli amba ajige hafan ilibufi, ini da ejen iogi lii yung fang de bufi kadalabuha*).[295]

In the unification of Fusi, a Han Chinese captive made significant compact in historical court. His name is Fan Wencheng (范文程), who voluntarily surrendered to Nurgaqi with his brother Fan Wencai (范文寀). In the coming decades, one can see that both Nurgaqi and Hung Taiji regarded highly of Fan Wencheng and consulted him in the unification of Lüshun, Pingdao, Korea, Mongol tribes and the Ming China (*tianming sannian, taizu ji xia fushun, wencai, wencheng gong ye taizu ... shang fa ming, qu liaoyang ... wencheng jie zai xingjian ... zishi po lüshun, shou pingdao, tao chaoxian, fuding menggu, wencheng jie yumou* 天命三年，太祖既下撫順，文寀、文程共謁太祖...上伐明，取遼陽...文程皆在行間...自是破旅順，收平島，討朝鮮，撫定蒙古，文程皆與謀).[296]

Crossely believed that Fan Wencheng and other Liaodong Nikans were crucial to help the Manchu rulers earn loyalty from the Han Chinese

---

[292] *Fe dangse*, p. 260.

[293] *Fe dangse*, p. 265.

[294] *Fe dangse*, pp. 266-267.

[295] *Fe dangse*, p. 289.

[296] *Qingshigao*, compiled by Zhao Erxun et al., vol. 232, Zhonghuashuju, Beijing, 1977, pp. 9350-9351.

throughout the whole Qing dynasty.[297] Moreover, these Han Chinese farmers provide am economic foundation for the regime to establish all sorts of institutions and expand its territories.

On the twentieth of the seventh month in the third year of the Genggiyen Han (1618), the Later Jin's army attacked Niowanggiyaha (man. *niowanggiyaha*; chin. *qinghe* 清河). On the twenty-second day, the army took over Niowanggiyaha and captured three thousand people (*nadan biyai orin de, niowanggiyaha de qooha genere de... orin juwe de, niowanggiyaha i heqen be afame gaiha... ilan minggan olji baha...*).[298] On the twenty-fifth day of the ninth month, the army looted a place named Hui An Pu (man. *hvi an pu*; chin. *hui an pu* 會安堡), located in the north of Fusi fortification, and captured one thousand people (*uyun biyai orin sunja de, fusi amargi hvi an pu golo be dabqilame dosifi, minggan olji baha...*).[299]

Besides providing human resource, these Han Chinese dwelling districts constituted ideal places for Jurchens to secure food supplies. On the twelfth day of the sixth month in the fifth year of the Genggiyen Han (1620), Nurgaqi led the troops to plunder grain silos. They entered the Fushun regional circuit and reached a suburb place which was ten *li* away from the Shenyang fortification (man. *simiyan*; chin. *shenyang* 瀋陽). One hundred Ming soldiers were killed and four thousand were captured (*juwan juwe de, jeku gaime yafaha qooha be gamame, fusi golo be qooha dosifi, simiyan i heqen de juwan ba i dubede isitala fekesifi, nikan qooha be tanggv isime waha, duin minggan olji baha ...*).[300]

The human population acquired from the Han Chinese regions is substantive. On the twenty-first day of the eighth month in the fifth year of the Genggiyen Han (1620), Nurgaqi launched an attack upon the Ming, and besieged the two cities of Yilu (man. *ilu;* chin. *yilu* 懿路) and Puhe (man. *puho;* Chin. *puhe* 蒲河). Soon the Eight Banners moved onto Shenyang fortification and captured eight thousand people (*orin emu de, nikan de qooha dosifi, ilu, puho gebungge juwe hoton be kaqi ... simiyan*

---

[297] Pamela Kyle Crossley (1999), *A translucent mirror: history and identity in Qing imperial ideology*, University of California Press, Berkeley and Los Angeles, California, p. 126.

[298] *Fe dangse*, pp. 301-304.

[299] Fe dangse, p. 318.

[300] *Fe dangse*, p. 702.

heqen i baru baime geneqi... tere qooha de baha jakvn minggan olji be...).[301]

At the time, possessing human beings was considered as great asset. A Han Chinese Defense Officer Ying Tinglu delivered four villains to the regime as a contribution, which was reported to the Khan by three Jurchen leaders. Nurgaqi replied that if the Defense Officer committed some crime in the future, this achievement could be regarded as his atonement (*kubuhe lamun gvsai nikan beiguwan ing ting lu, duin guwanggun be benjihe seme turgei, torai, bakiran, han de alafi, amala weile tuqiqi gung okini, ejeme gaisu seme gaiha*).[302]

To increase population, in the second month of the seventh year of the Genggiyen Han (1622), Nurgaqi made announcements to the Han Chinese who lived beyond the Shanhai Pass by declaring that the Ming emperor was fatuous and therefore was condemned by the Heaven. If those moved back into the Shanhai Pass, there would be no provision of food, clothes, houses and lands for cultivating. If they stayed between the Shanhai Pass and Guangning fortification, it would impossible to make a living because the Mongols would rob them. Nurgaqi pointed out that the Mongols themselves had no food to eat and no clothes to wear, and all people would die of being bitten by lice. If they moved into the east of Liaodong River, the Bright Khan would provide them with houses to live, food to eat and lands for work. "The Khan is fair to take care of all people and the Heaven favors him. Don't you know that? The remaining people should all cross the river and submit to the Bright Khan..." (*xanaha i tulergi niyalma, suwe xanaha dosime geheqi, suweni han be abka wakalafi farhvn ofi, suwende jetere jeku, dere boo, tarire usin iqihiyame barakv kai, xanaha i tule guwangning de isitala, suwe bihe seme bibumbio, monggo gamambi kai, monggo de jetere jeku, eture etuku bio, qige de buqembi kai, birai dergi liyoodung ni bade geneqi, genggiyen han, tere boo, jetere jeku, tarire usin iqihiyame bumbi kai, gurun ujire genggiyen ofi, abkai gosire be suwe ainu sarkv, funqehe tutaha niyalma biqi, gemu bira doome liyoodung ni bade genggiyen han be baime jio...*)[303]

---

[301] *Fe dangse*, pp. 730-740.
[302] *Fe dangse*, p. 2770.
[303] *Fe dangse.* pp. 1546-1548.

The following chronicle records show that large amounts of Han Chinese submitted to Nurgaqi and were bestowed with lands for cultivation. A grid chart may help us with an overview of Nurgaqi's achievements.

Dates in Lunar Calendar	Original Residence	Number of migrants or captives	Number of House-holds	Remarks	Page numbers in *Fe dangse*
13/04/1618	Fusi 撫順		1,000	With 300,000 humans and domestic animals	p. 267.
12/06/1620	Fusi 撫順	4,000			p. 702.
21/08/1620	Simiyan 沈陽	8,000			p. 740.
04/03/1621	Simiyan 沈陽	1			p. 835.
06/03/1621	Simiyan 沈陽	1			p. 838.
10/03/1621	Fung ji pu 奉集堡	2			p. 840.
26/03/1621	Haijeo 海州	15			p. 878.
25/05/1621	Jengjiyang 鎮江	1,000			p. 999.
17/11/1621	Guwangning 廣寧	7			p. 1252.
23/12/1621	Simiyan and Liyoodung 沈陽、遼東	1,665			p. 1391.
04/01/1622		8			p. 1428.

Table 7: Han Chinese migrants and captives in Nurgaqi's reign

Dates in Lunar Calendar	Original Residence	Number of migrants or captives	Number of House-holds	Remarks	Page numbers in *Fe dangse*
04/01/1622		8			p. 1428.
08/01/1622	Guwangning 廣寧	2			p. 1451.
16/01/1622	Guwangning 廣寧	1			p. 1491.
07/02/1622	Ginjeo 錦州	149			p. 1581.
09/02/1622	Io tun Wei heqen	13,401			p. 1586.
14/02/1622	Guwangning 廣寧	600			p. 1616.
17/02/1622	Ginjeo 錦州	20,550			p. 1635.
18/02/1622	Iqe heqen 新城	280			p. 1641.
18/02/1622	Be tu qang and Jeng an pu 白土場、鎮安堡	21,150		9,238 men	p. 1642.
15/03/1622	Guwangning 廣寧	2,900			p. 1756.
15/03/1622	Guwangning 廣寧	210			p. 1757.
15/03/1622	Iqe heqen 新城	49		With four soldiers in armor	p. 1758.
05/04/1623	Mio ma wai and Qing tai ioi	140			pp. 2184-2185.

Table 7: Han Chinese migrants and captives in Nurgaqi's reign

Dates in Lunar Calendar	Original Residence	Number of migrants or captives	Number of House-holds	Remarks	Page numbers in *Fe dangse*
08/04/1623	Julergi 南方	1,000			p. 2199.
07/07/1623	Sio yan 岫岩	6,700			p. 2592.
13/01/1624	Kubuhe lamun gvsai nikan beiguwan Ing ting lu 鑲藍旗漢備御 贏廷祿	4			p. 2770.
Total		81,835	1,000		

Table 7: Han Chinese migrants and captives in Nurgaqi's reign

The chart shows that Ginjeo, Be tu qang and Jeng an pu constitute fifty percent of the Han Chinese migrants and captives. Another significant contributor was Lo tun Wei, which makes up sixteen percent. Large cities, such as Fusi, Guwangning and Sioyan, were also noticeable contributors. A remarkable fact is that the number of households was not kept, and the population of Han Chinese captives is far greater than the Mongols. Regarding the thousands of households who were captured at Fushun, they were assigned to Li Yongfang, the former Mobile Corps Commander of the Ming, to govern according to the previous Ming institution (*fusi heqen qi dahame jihe minggan boigon ... kemuni ini nikan gurun i kooli amba ajige hafan ilibufi, ini da ejen iogi li yongfang de bufi kadalabuha*).[304]

Mark C. Elliott contended that many of these early Han Chinese subjects were totally transformed by the Jurchen culture and the acculturation was so successful that the only remnant trace is in

---

[304] *Fe dangse*, pp. 288-289.

genealogical terms,[305] which are their Han Chinese names and family trees. Li Yongfang married into Nurgaqi's family, by receiving the oldest daughter of Abatai, who was Nurgaqi's son (*han i jui abatai de banjiha amba sargan jui be ... fusi iogi de bume ...*).[306] Thus, in the later Manchu annals, Li Yongfang often appeared as the Fusi Efu, the Imperial Son-in-law of Fushun, in the generation of Nurgaqi's grandchildren.

After taking over the Liaodong region, part of the Han Chinese captives were assigned to the Jurchen officials and officers. For example, each of the Jurchen Grand Coordinators and Regional Commanders was allocated with three thousand, each of the Jurchen Regional Vice Commanders with 1,700, each of the Jurchen Assistant Regional Commanders and Mobile Corps Commanders with one thousand, and each of the Jurchen Defense Officers with five hundred Han Chinese men (*birai dergi nikan gurun be dendefi, juxen i dutang, zung bing guwan de ilan minggan haha buhe, fujiyang de emte minggan nadan tanggv haha buhe, canjiyang iogi de emte minggan haha buhe, beiguwan de sunjata tanggv haha buhe*).[307] These Han Chinese people, very likely as Elliott suggested, were completely assimilated into the Jurchen population. For those who were granted to the Han Chinese officers in the Later Jin regime, their population is slightly larger, with four thousand for each of the Regional Commanders, three thousand for each of the Regional Vice Commanders, and two thousand for each of the Assistant Regional Commanders and Mobile Corps Commanders (*nikan i zung bing guwan de duin minggan haha buhe, fujiyang de ilata minggan haha buhe, canjiyang, iogi de juwete minggan haha buhe*).[308] It is possible that these Han Chinese subjects still remained their original cultural identity, but historians may hold different opinions since many Han Chinese soldiers were commanded by Jurchen-Manchu officers in the later historical course.

---

[305] Mark C. Elliott (2005), *Ethnicity in the Qing Eight Banners*, collected in *Empire at the Margins: Culture, Ethnicity, and Frontier in Early Modern China*, edited by Pamela Kyle Crossley, Helen F. Siu, and Donald S. Sutton, University of California Press, California, p. 43.
[306] Fe dangse, p. 290.
[307] *Fe dangse*, pp. 1429-1430.
[308] *Fe dangse*, pp. 1430-1431.

3.5.2 Integrating Han Chinese in Hong Taiji's Regime

On the thirteenth day of the eleventh month in the third year of Sure Han (1629), the Jurchen army arrived in Ji Zhou 薊州, which is part of modern Tianjin. Some soldiers captured a Cultivated Talent (man. *xusai*; chin. *xiucai* 秀才) and let him deliver a message for summoning the Han Chinese military officers and all the commoners to surrender (*juwan ilan de, gi jeo de isinjiha, emu xusai be bahafi, hoton i ejen dooli, qoohai hafasa geren irgen be daha sere bithe jafabufi unggihe ...*).[309] Four days later, the army reached the Ming Emperor's horse-ranch institution, which is twenty *li* away from Beijing. The horse ranch is five *li* away in the south, which is quite a large area surrounded by walls. The horses had been taken away before the Jurchens arrived. But the leader of the ranch, along with two eunuchs and some three hundred people, were besieged and finally surrendered (*juwan nadan de, qooha jurafi beging heqen de orin ba isinahakv, han i adun ulebure pu de isinafi ing iliha, tere pu i julergi sunja ba i dubede, han i geren adun ulebure heqen amba, emu dere juwe ba funqembi, tere bihe minggan funqeme morin be juwan nadan i qimari gamahabi, adun i ejen, juwe taigiyan, niyalma ilan tanggv funqeme horibufi dahaha ...*).[310]

After looting Beijing's surrounding, on the ninth day of the second month in the next year (1630), officials Asan, Yangxan and Lungsi, et al., were sent to Pan giya keo (Panjiakou 潘家口) for registering two hundred forty households, including six hundred men (*pan giya keo be iqihiyame genehe asan, yangxan, lungsi sei iqihiyaha boo juwe tanggv dehi jakvn, haha ninggun tanggv*).[311]

One year later, another large-scale campaign was initiated. On the twenty-seventh day of the seventh month in the fifth year of Sure Han (1631), Hong Taiji started to attack Dalinghe fortification 大凌河城. Frederic Wakeman reconstructed the whole process of besieging Dalinghe, which was one of the largest battles in the Later Jin period.[312] Besides the Jurchen and Han Chinese troops, Hong Taiji summoned his Mongol allies to help. However, faced with these cavalries, Dalinghe

---

[309] *Fe dangse*, pp. 4583-4584.
[310] *Fe dangse*, pp. 4595-4596.
[311] *Fe dangse*, pp. 4792-4793.
[312] Frederic Wakeman, Jr. (1985), *The Great Enterprise*, University of California Press, London, pp. 170-194.

turned to be a hard bone to chew. Finally, according to Wakeman's research, Hong Taiji relied heavily on his Han Chinese collaborators and won the war.[313] The scribes did not record the exact number of Han Chinese captives, but only large numbers of death.

After the decisive battle of Dalinghe, Hong Taiji frequently ordered his generals to plunder the Ming cities, such as Jin Zhou and Song Shan in Liaodong province, in order to obtain more people. The achievements varied. On the tenth day of the tenth month in the fifth year of Sure Han (1631), they only brought one Defense Officer and sixteen people back (*juwan de, turgei, namtai de minggan qooha adabufi, ginjeo, sung xan i ergi de tabqin unggifi ... emu xeobei, juwan ninggun niyalma bahafi gajiha*).[314] Sometimes the Han Chinese would surrendered on their own initiative. Just two days later, an Assistant Regional Commander (man. *canjiang*; chin. *canjiang* 參將) surrendered himself with two hundred thirty-nine men and three hundred thirty nine women (*juwan juwe de, ioi zi jang tai i ejen canjiyang wang ging dahaha. haha juwe tanggv gvsin uyun, hehe juse ilan tanggv gvsin uyun ...*).[315]

Finally, Hong Taiji fixed his eyes on a big fortification--Jang giya keo (Zhangjiakou 張家口), which is a vital communication and commercial center between the Ming and Mongols territories. After successive wars, on the twenty-ninth of the sixth month in the sixth year of Sure Han (1632), the Jurchen and Mongol winners divided the spoils into five shares (*tere inenggi, jang giya keo i duka de gaiha ulin be sunja ubu sindafi...*).[316] Ten banners seized 20,158 people, and the Outer Mongolian princes obtained 6,435 (*juwan gvsai baha olji niyalma juwe tumen emu tanggv susai jakvn ... dulergi monggo beise i baha olji ton, niyalma ninggun minggan duin tanggv gvsin sunja ...*).[317] In total, the number is 26,593.

In the seventh month of the first year Wesihun Erdemungge (1636), the Jurchens crossed the Ming's border for the sake of plundering. Eight days later, the troops met in Yan king jeo (Yanqing Zhou 延慶州 *dosika jakvnqi inenggi, yan king jeo de aqaha ...*).[318] Seventeen banners

---

[313] Wakeman, *The Great Enterprise*, pp. 168-170.
[314] *Fe dangse*, pp. 5607-5608.
[315] *Fe dangse*, pp. 5608-5609.
[316] *Fe dangse*, p. 6316.
[317] *Fe dangse*, pp. 6341-6342.
[318] *Fe dangse*, p. 7502.

125

obtained 3,418 people (*juwan nadan gvsai baha olji, niyalma ilan minggan duin tanggv juwan jakvn* ...).[319] Combined with people acquired by the Banner Mongols, the total number is 4,112.

The campaign continued. Three months later, the Jurchen army attained 73,290 people from Beijing's surrounding regions (*niyalma nadan tumen ilan minggan juwe tanggv uyunju* ...).[320] A comprehensive view displays beneath:

Dates in Lunar Calender	Original Residence	Number of migrants or captives	Number of House-holds	Remarks	Page numbers in *Fe dangse*
13/11/1629	Gi jeo 薊州	2			p. 4583.
14/11/1629	San ho hiyan 三河縣	1			p. 4584.
15/11/1629	Tung jeo 通州	9			p. 4587.
17/11/1629	Han i geren adun ulebure heqen 明帝牧馬堡	300			p. 4596.
09/02/1630	Pan giya keo 潘家口	600	248		pp. 4792-4793.
17/04/1630	Dalingho 大凌河	23			p.4926.
07/05/1630	The Ming 明	50			p.4997.
08/08/1631	Dalingho 大凌河	11			p.5470.
10/08/1631	Dalingho 大凌河	144			pp.5472-5473.

Table 8: Han Chinese migrants and captives in Hong Taiji's early reign

---

[319] *Fe dangse*, p. 7517.
[320] *Fe dangse*, p. 7766.

Dates in Lunar Calender	Original Residence	Number of migrants or captives	Number of House-holds	Remarks	Page numbers in *Fe dangse*
12/08/1631	Dalingho 大凌河	32			p.5488.
13/08/1631	Dalingho 大凌河	69			p.5495.
10/10/1631	Ginjeo and Sung xan 錦州、松山	17			p.5608.
12/10/1631	Ioi zi jang tai 于子章台	578			pp.5608-5609.
13/10/1631	Je giya pu 翟家堡	100			p.5611.
14/10/1631	Qen hing pu 陳興鋪	45			p.5613.
25/10/1631	Ginjeo and Sung xan 錦州、松山	8			p.5624.
04/01/1632	Tang ho pu 湯河堡	29			p.5762.
29/01/1632	The Ming 明	30			p.5948.
30/06/1632	Jang giya keo 張家口	35,390			pp. 6351-6359.
07/12/1632	Ginjeo 錦州	2			p.6545.
24/04/1636	Haijeo 海州	107			pp. 6985-6986.
23/05/1636	Sio yan 岫岩	3			p.7139.

Table 8: *Han Chinese migrants and captives in Hong Taiji's early reign*

Dates in Lunar Calender	Original Residence	Number of migrants or captives	Number of House-holds	Remarks	Page numbers in *Fe dangse*
19/07/1636	Yan king and Yvn jeo 延慶、雲州	4,112			pp. 7501-7523.
04/08/1636	Haijeo 海州	54			pp. 7599-7600.
08/09/1636	Beging's surrounding areas 北京周邊	73,290		Combined with domestic animals, the final figure is 181,256	pp. 7733-7766.
14/09/1636	Beging's surrounding areas 北京周邊	(179,820) It must be a repetitive record, and therefore it is excluded from counting		With domestic animals included	p. 7783.

Table 8: Han Chinese migrants and captives in Hong Taiji's early reign

Dates in Lunar Calender	Original Residence	Number of migrants or captives	Number of House-holds	Remarks	Page numbers in *Fe dangse*
28/09/1636	Beging's surrounding areas 北京周邊	(180,000) It must be a repetitive record and therefore it is excluded from counting		With domestic animals included	p. 7826.
				The last three figures are repetitive and only 73,290 is counted as human population, while the remaining number as animals	
Total		115,016	248		

Table 8: Han Chinese migrants and captives in Hong Taiji's early reign

129

This chart demonstrates that nearly sixty-four percent of the Han Chinese population was acquired from Beijing and its surroundings. Nearly thirty-one percent was from Jang giya keo (Zhangjiakou 張家口). The Last two figures were overlapped with the last but third, manifesting the great military achievements by the Jurchens in the northern territory of the Ming. Comparatively, the number of household is insignificant.

The available Manchu chronicles, *Dorgi yamun asaraha manju hergen i fe dangse* 內閣藏本滿文老檔 (The Version of Manchu Old Chronicles Stored by the Grand Secretariat), ended in the first year of Wesihun Erdemungge (1636). Large quantities of Manchu files are missing, ranging from the seventh year of Sure Han to the eighth of Wesihun Erdemungge (1633-1643), except for the first year of Wesihun Erdemungge (1636). The First Historical Archives of China published "Compiled Translation of Manchu Chronicles Kept by the Early Qing's Palace Historiographic Academy" (*Qingchu neiguoshiyuan manwen dang'an yibian* 清初內國史院滿文檔案譯編), which covers most of years mentioned above. However, the sixth year of Sure Han (1632) and the sixth year of Wesihun Erdemungge (1641) are still absent. Moreover, chronicles of each year were all damaged to different degrees.[321]

The following chart was developed from the chronicles kept by the Early Qing's Palace Historiographic Academy, from which a complete calculation is not feasible.

---

[321] Qingchu neiguoshiyuan manwen dang'an yibian, p. 1.

Dates in Lunar Calendar	Original Residence	Number of migrants or captives	Number of Households	Page numbers in Qingchu neiguoshiyuan manwen dang'an yibian
28/01/1633	Mingludao 明鹿島	173		p. 5.
23/03/1633	Ningyuang 寧遠	1		p. 9.
23/05/1633	Liaodong 遼東	3,000		p. 16.
14/07/1633	Lüshunkou 旅順口	5,302		p. 26.
18/08/1633	Shichengpu 石城堡	20		p. 32.
01/09/1633	Shanhaiguang 山海關	4,213		p. 34.
12/09/1633	Chaoxian 朝鮮	29		p. 37.
27/01/1634	Changshandao 長山島	1,100		p. 59.
27/01/1634	Guangludao 廣鹿島	3,500		p. 59.
05/02/1634	Mingguo 明國	3871		p. 61.
19/06/1635	Huangchengdao 黃城島	68		p. 174.
26/08/1635	Mingbian 明邊	76,200		p. 187.
27/02/1638	Shichengdao 石城島	2,454		p. 284.

Table 9: Han Chinese migrants and captives in Hong Taiji's later reign

131

Dates in Lunar Calendar	Original Residence	Number of migrants or captives	Number of Households	Page numbers in Qingchu neiguoshiyuan manwen dang'an yibian
01/11/1638	Kaizhou 開州	703		p. 384.
01/11/1638	Dafupu 大福堡	337		p. 384.
02/11/1638	Jinzhou 錦州 Ningyuan 寧遠	1,090		p. 385.
05/11/1638	Wulihe 五里河	200		p. 386.
11/11/1638	Molongguan 模龍關	272		p. 387.
01/04/1639	Lianshan 連山		People, horses, oxen, donkeys, mules and sheep make up the number of 1,000.	p. 412.
11/04/1642	Tashancheng 塔山城	1,414		p. 467.
11/04/1642	Xingshan 杏山	6,838		pp. 467-468.
05/11/1642	Ningyuan 寧遠	102		p. 492.
09/11/1642	Qiantunwei 前屯衛	289		p. 492.
Total		111,074		

Table 9: Han Chinese migrants and captives in Hong Taiji's later reign

From the above one can see that Xingshan 杏山 is the greatest contributor, making up nearly twenty percent of the migrants. Circa fifteen percent of the migrants were from Lüshunkou 旅順口, which makes the second largest contributor. The third would be Shanhaiguan 山海關, which makes up almost twelve percent of the Han Chinese migrants. Other significant contributors were Liaodong 遼東 and Guangludao 廣鹿島. The rest were relatively inconsiderable. Plus the 115,016 migrants in Hong Taiji's early reign, we reach a total figure of 229,090 that was acquired in Hong Taiji's reign. Crossley quoted a figure from Zhu Chengru, who estimated that Hong Taiji collected over a million Han Chinese people through five campaigns in ten years' time.[322] The large amounts of Han Chinese population provided sufficient labor for general material production, allocation and transportation in wartime.

Even so, An Shuangcheng's research indicates that when Nurgaqi established the Eight Banners, there were 308 Manchu companies, 76 Mongol companies and 16 Han Chinese companies,[323] from which we know that the Han Chinese soldiers counted as four percent of the banner population. Later, large amounts of Mongol and Han Chinese were assimilated into the banner system. During the Manchu unification of China, as Richard J. Smith found out, the Manchu soldiers constituted half of the military force,[324] which implies a significant increasing population of the Han Chinese soldier. To the fifth year of Shunzhi (1648), the Han Chinese military men accounted for more than seventy-five percent of the banner men.[325] Thus, we can assume a vigorous growth of Han Chinese population during Hong Taiji's time, which can confirm Crossley's research. Nonetheless, An Shuangcheng pointed out that the number of Han Chinese soldiers decreased gradually after the unification.[326] For most of the Qing time, as Richard J. Smith claimed, the Manchu banner-men outnumbered their Mongol and Han

---

[322] Crossley, *A translucent mirror*, p. 184.

[323] An Shuangcheng 安雙成 (1983), "Shun Kang Yong sanchao baqi ding'e qianxi" 順康雍三朝八旗丁額淺析 (A Preliminary Analysis of the Eight Banners Active Registration in the Shunzhi, Kangxi and Yongzheng Periods), *Lishi Dang'an* 歷史檔案 (Historical Archives), 1. 2:101.

[324] Richard J. Smith (1974), Chinese Military Institutions in the Mid-Nineteenth Century, 1850-1860, *Journal of Asian History*, 8. 2: 122-161.

[325] An Shuangcheng, Shun Kang Yong sanchao baqi ding'e qianxi, p. 101.

[326] An Shuangcheng, Shun Kang Yong sanchao baqi ding'e qianxi, p. 102.

Chinese peers.[327] This phenomenon demonstrates that the banner system remained as a Manchu-established, Manchu-led, and Manchu-hosted regime that underpinned the Qing empire.

3.6 Integrating Korean People

Though large numbers of Koreans had settled in northeast China, only a few Manchu chronicle passages have mentioned the subjugation of Korean people. One early record is from the fourth year of Genggiyen Han (1619), when the Korean king sent twenty thousand soldiers to help the Ming for the battle in Sarhv (Sa'erhu 薩爾滸). The war turned in Manchu favor. On the fifth day of the third month, the Korean marshal Giyang Gong Liyei (Jiang Hongli 姜弘立) and his five thousand soldiers came down a hill and surrendered to Nurgaqi (*jai qimari iqe sunja i inenggi, solho i du yuwanxuwai hergen i amba hafan giyang gong liyei, sunja minggan qooha be gaifi dahame alin qi wasifi ...*).[328]

A Korean source also confirmed this military failure. In the meantime, the fifteenth ruler of Korea, Li Hui 李琿, wrote that Jiang Hongli reconciled with the Jurchens after being defeated; he wished he could be released when peaceful terms were quickly reached (*gu zhanbai zhi hou, deyi kuan hao, ruo sucheng heyi, ze chendeng keyi chugui* 故戰敗之後，得以款好，若速成和議，則臣等可以出歸).[329] However, among five thousand military men who came to help the Ming, only four officers and an interpreter were sent back to Korea. The rest remained in the Later Jin (*tere nikan qooha de dafi jihe solho i sunja minggan qooha be dahabufi, gajiha duin hafan, emu tongse, uhereme sunja niyalma be sindafi unggime ...*).[330]

The other particular record is that in the fourth month of the eighth year of Genggiyen Han (1623), a Regional Vice Commander Lenggeri, with four hundred White Armored Soldiers under his leadership, who

---

[327] Richard J. Smith (1974), Chinese Military Institutions in the Mid-Nineteenth Century, 1850-1860, *Journal of Asian History*, 8. 2: 136.

[328] Fe dangse, p. 383.

[329] *Qingchu shiliao congkan diqi zhong* 清初史料叢刊第七種 (The Seventh Compilation of Early Qing Historical Materials), *Chaoxian Lichao shilu zhong de nüzhen shiliao xuanbian* 朝鮮李朝實錄中的女真史料選編 (Selected Compilation of Jurchen Historical Materials in Veritable Records of Korea's Chosŏn Court), Wang Zhonghan jilu, edition Shenyang: Liaoing daxue chubanshe, 1978, p. 280.

[330] *Fe dangse*, p. 406.

captured one hundred and thirteen Koreans in the bordering region (*solho i ergi de lenggeri fujiyang, duin tanggv xanggiyan bayarai niyalma be gaifi anafu tenefi gajihangge, emu tanggv juwe ilan niyalma...*).[331]

Another record cites a military expedition upon Korea in the first year of Sure Han (1627 *fulahvn gvlmahvn sure han i suqungga aniya, solho gurun be dailaha*).[332] After unifying Yi Zhou 義州, the Manchu army took over An Jeo Heqen (Anzhou Cheng 安州城), killed the defenders when attacking the fortification, but afterwards released the captives to join their families (*... heqen be afara de wabuhai dabala, baha manggi, qoohai niyalma be emkeqi wahakv, gemu meni meni boode hehe juse de aqana seme sindafi unggihe ...*).[333] Furthermore, the Manchu source claims that after the Covenant of Pyongyang, the Manchu army returned along the main road without plundering anything (*ping rang de gashvha qi amasi, manju i qooha bederere de, solho i umai jaka be neqihekv, amba jugvn be jafafi qooha bederehe*).[334] This large-scale military incursion is also verified by a Korean source, the "Veritable Records of King Renzu of the Chosŏn Court" (*Lichao renzu shilu* 李朝仁祖實錄), which says, "The Jurchen army seized Yi Zhou last night" (*nubing zuoye gongxian yizhou* 奴兵昨夜攻陷義州), but again, the source did not point out that Korean people were taken away.

Ten years later, Hong Taiji launched another expedition against Korea. The Manchu scribes kept every detail of the achievement, including the annual tribute offered by the Korean king after the war.[335] Once more, there were no records of bringing Korean captives back to the Later Jin. This largest invasion of Korea happened in 1636. On the eleventh day of the fourth month, Hong Taiji held a ceremony to officially change the state's name to DaQing and the reign title to Chongde, but the Korean emissaries refused to salute. For this reason, Hong Taiji plotted a war for punishing Korea.[336] Six months later Hong Taiji personally led the army and besieged the Korean king in South Seoul (Nan hancheng 南漢城) on the twenty-ninth of the twelfth

---

[331] *Fe dangse*, p. 2192.
[332] Fe dangse, p. 3884.
[333] *Fe dangse*, p. 3892.
[334] *Fe dangse*, pp. 3953-3954.
[335] Qingchu neiguoshiyuan manwen dang'an yibian, pp. 226-255.
[336] *Qingshigao*, vol. 2, pp. 55-58.

month.[337] On the first day of the second month in the next year, Hong Taiji rewarded his officials with people, animals, money and all sorts of wealth they looted from Ganghwa Island (Jianghuadao 江華島).[338] In the "Draft of Qing History" (*Qingshigao* 清史稿), Hong Taiji specifically informed Dorgon (duo'ergun 多爾袞) not to raid populations who had already surrendered (*yu duo'ergun deng jin lüe xiang min* 諭多爾袞等禁掠降民).[339]

Strategically, Korea had to be secured before the Manchus could move southward to attack the Ming. Repeatedly, the Jurchen-Manchus intruded Korea and finally Korea completely submitted to the Qing authority. Nonetheless, the available Manchu sources provide little information about bringing large amounts of Korean people back to the Qing state.

As Crossley pointed out that, the early Qing ruler-ship derived from peoples of the northeast regions who submitted to Nurgaqi and Hong Taiji's governance, including the Han Chinese, Mongols and the hunting peoples of upper Jilin and Heilongjiang. This integration can be considered as an ordering process that culminated in the first Qing emperor-ship in 1636 and finally resulted in the unification of China.[340] this monograph confirms that the unification of Korea was also included into the empire building initiated by the Manchus.

Finally, yet importantly, quite a few Tibetan lamas also joined the Jurchen-Manchu regime, mostly on their own initiative. Tibet was mentioned as *tanggvt* in the early Manchu annals. Tibetan lamas were significant religious and political figures due to their grand impact upon the Mongol nomads through preaching Tibetan Buddhism. On the first day of the first month in 1622, the Khan Nurgaqi, leading the Eight-banner chieftains and officials, went out the fortification to worship in Shamanistic sites (man. *tangse*; chin. *tangzi* 堂子) and temples. Afterwards, the Khan returned to his administrative office and sat on his throne. The Eight-banner chieftains led the banner officials to kneel in front of the Khan and wished him for a long life. Subsequently, the Mongol son-in-law Enggeder, son-in-law Manggol and secondary

---

[337] Qingchu neiguoshiyuan manwen dang'an yibian, p. 231.
[338] Qingchu neiguoshiyuan manwen dang'an yibian, p. 244.
[339] *Qingshigao*, vol. 2, p. 60.
[340] Crossley, *A translucent mirror*, p. 47.

Mongol chieftain (man. *taiji*; chin. *taiji* 臺吉) Gurbusi led the Mongol people to kneel; Next, Fuxi son-in-law Li Yongfang and Si Uli son-in-law Tong Yangxing led the Han Chinese officials to kneel; Last, two lamas from the country of Tibet and four Korean officials knelt; In a proper sequence they all knelt in front of the Khan *(sahaliyan indahvn aniya biyai iqe inenggi, han, jakvn gvsai beise ambasa be gaifi, heqen tuqifi tangse de miyoo de hengkilehe, tereqi amasi bederefi yamun de tehe manggi, jakvn gvsai beise, geren ambasa be gaifi, han be se baha seme hengkilehe, beise i sirame monggo i enggeder efu, manggol efu, gurbusi taiji, geren monggo be gaifi hengkilehe, terei sirame fusi efu, si uli efu, nikan i geren hafasa be gaifi hengkilehe, terei sirame tanggvt gurun i juwe lama, solho i duin hafan hengkilehe, tuttu jergi jergi han de hengkileme wajiha manggi ...).*[341] The passage tells the position of Tibet in the political order set up by the Jurchens: banner-men come first, Mongol allies second, Han Chinese subjects third, Tibetan lamas fourth and Korean envoys fifth. This is one of the earliest official contact between Tibet and the Later Jin. Tibetan lamas could have realized the rise of the Jurchen power and hence came to seek protection.

On the sixth day of the eleventh month in 1625, some lamas came to Nurgaqi for a living because they had heard of Nurgaqi's generosity and meanwhile the Mongol chieftains mistreated them. Sahalqa, a Mongol tribe that was subordinate to the lamas, also left their home place and followed their spiritual leaders to submit to the Khan. As a reward to the Sahalqa people who came along with the lamas, their descendants will be exempted from corvee for all generations; they will only be imprisoned for capital crime; they will be pardoned for robbery and endless favor will come. Such benevolence was written on the imperial edicts, which were bestowed to one hundred thirty-two people. On the early Manchu annals, there were original commentary, which says that the lamas were people from the country of Tanggvt, who came to the place of the Mongol Khorchin chieftains for a living. Later they heard that the Bright Khan respected lamas, and therefore they came to Liaodong *(iqe ninggunde, lama, monggo i beise be ujire ehe, han be ujire sain seme, han be baime jidere de, lama i sahalqa sa banjiha ba, jeke muke be waliyafi lama be dahame jihengge, tereqi jilakan ai bi, ere jihe gung de*

---

[341] *Fe dangse*, pp. 1411-1412.

137

lama be dahame jihe sahalqa sabe, gemu juse omosi jalan halame alban de ume dabure, buqere weile bahaqi giyala, ulin gaijara weile bahaqi waliya, gosire doro be ume lashalara seme bithe arafi, emu tanggv gvsin juwe niyalma de ejehe buhe. lama, tanggvt i niyalma, monggo gurun i korqin i ba i beise be baime jifi bihe, genggiyen han i kundulere be safi, liyoodung de baime jihe).[342] Mark C. Elliott pointed out that Nurgaqi competed against the Lingdan Khan of the Chakhar Mongol confederation over the patronage of Tibetan Buddhism.[343] These two passages could serve as historic evidence that marked the significant beginning of the Later Jin regime to sponsor the propagation of Tibetan Buddhism, which was carried on by the successive Manchu rulers.

Nurgaqi's successor, Hong Taiji, remained a cautious attitude upon the negative influence of lamas, which represented the Gelug school of Tibetan Buddhism that was widely believed by the Khalkha and Chakhar Mongols. In 1632, Hong Taiji personally commanded the army to attack the Chakhar confederation, but the Khan Lingdan fled away without resistance. On the ninth day of the fourth month in 1634, he promulgated a decree that warns the Jurchens not to give up their native language. In Hong Taiji's opinion, it is impossible to undertake a great enterprise by employing languages of other countries. The Mongols abandoned their Mongol language and adopted the Lama Language for names and titles, which caused their state to decline.[344] However, just one month later, when Lama Manjushri Hotogtu came to visit, Hong Taiji travelled to the suburb for reception and shook the Lama's hands.[345] The impact of Tibetan Buddhism was substantial. On the twenty-seventh day of the tenth month in 1634, when Hong Taiji offered a sacrifice to his late father, Nurgaqi, he claimed that after being defeated by the Jurchen army, the khan of Chakhar led his people to escape towards Tanggvt.[346] When some of the remaining Chakhar tribes came to surrender, Hong Taiji sent two lamas to receive them.[347] So far, it is outspoken that these lamas of Tibetan Buddhism functioned as religious and political figures, which

---

[342] *Fe dangse*, pp. 3052-3054.
[343] Elliott, Ethnicity in the Qing Eight Banners, p. 40.
[344] Qingchu neiguoshiyuan manwen dang'an yibian, p. 74.
[345] Qingchu neiguoshiyuan manwen dang'an yibian, p. 80.
[346] Qingchu neiguoshiyuan manwen dang'an yibian, p. 118.
[347] Qingchu neiguoshiyuan manwen dang'an yibian, p. 121.

played critical roles in the construction of empire led by the Jurchen-Manchus.

On the twenty-fourth day of the twelfth month in 1634, the Jurchen scribes wrote that during the time of Kublai Khan in the Mongol Yuan dynasty, Lama Phagspa molded a gold statue of Mahakala, who was viewed as the destroyer of the world in Buddhist belief. Later this statue was moved to the Chakhar tribe for worship. When the Khan of Chakhar escaped and his people surrendered, Lama Mergen, who is a Tibetan from Kyigudho in Kham,[348] took the statue to the Later Jin. Hong Taiji sent another lama to bring Mergen back to the capital Mukden, Shenyang.[349] This event marked as a milestone that the Later Jin successfully replaced the Mongols, as the new guardian of Tibetan Buddhism.

On the twelfth day of the eighth month in 1638, the gold statue brought by Mergen was placed at True Victory Temple (*shisheng si* 實勝寺) in the west of Mukden, which took three years of construction. This grandeur episode was also mentioned by Elliott in his *The Manchu Way*.[350] At the east and west sides of the temple, two stone tablets were erected. The text of the tablet on the east side was inscribed with Manchu language in the front and Han Chinese in the back. The text of the tablet on the west side was inscribed with Mongol language in the front and Tibetan in the back. The text briefly reviewed the propagation of Buddhism in East Asia and now the Khan of the Great Qing empire has become its protagonist. Hong Taiji also led the princes, chieftains, Mongol and Han Chinese officials to worship the statue.[351] In modern scholarship, this event was considered as the start of relationship between Tibet and the Later Jin.[352] Nonetheless, to the Jurchen-Manchu leaders, the political significance overrides the religious rituals and soon, the Khan ordered his subordinate princes and officials to enhance the practice of Shamanism and Manchu language.[353] The Manchus must remain their unique identity in the process of expanding their ideology of integrating different peoples into their regime.

---

[348] Tibet and Manchu, p. 1.
[349] Qingchu neiguoshiyuan manwen dang'an yibian, p. 126-127.
[350] Elliott, *The Manchu Way*, p. 480.
[351] Qingchu neiguoshiyuan manwen dang'an yibian, p. 354-357.
[352] Tibet and Manchu: An Assessment of Tibet-Manchu Relations in Five Phases of Historical Development, DIIR publications, Dharamsala, 2008, p. 1.
[353] Qingchu neiguoshiyuan manwen dang'an yibian, p. 397.

Four months after worshiping in the temple, on the twenty-ninth day of the twelfth month in 1638, Hong Taiji exercised strict discipline to control the lamas. Those who did not obey the rules were punished. One lama, who committed adultery but refused to get married, was castrated.[354] On the seventh day of the tenth month in 1639, Hong Taiji sent a document to the Khan of Tibet, inviting some Buddhist sages to propagate the Buddhist doctrines among the people under the heaven, of course, in Hong Taiji's favor.[355] Up to this moment, the Khan of the Great Qing empire openly declared to act as the patron of Buddhism, which would bring greater impact upon the people who encounter Buddhist teachings. Numerous Mongols, Han Chinese, and Tibetans would gradually realize that the power of the Manchu Khan is emerging through the chanting of sutra. The successive Tibetan Buddhist leaders and Manchu rulers consolidated this unique relationship for the purpose of placating the Mongol tribes, which described as "teacher-patron" or "priest-patron" relationship in modern scholarship.[356] Zhuang Jifa 莊吉發 described this political collaboration as the a relationship between the Qing central government and Gelug School of Tibetan Buddhism (*huangjiao* 黃教).[357] Along with many works conducted in modern academia, this research also confirms that the Manchu empire is different from the previous dynasties built by the Han Chinese rulers. As Yu Yingshi argues, the dominant philosophy in late imperial China is the New Chan Buddhism, New Taoism, and Neo-Confucianism, which all took its origin in Baizhang huaihai 百丈懷海's new religious theories and practice.[358] In comparison, the Manchu philosophy in aspect of state building consists of Shamanism to strengthen the Manchu identity, Confucianism to rule the Han Chinese, and Tibetan Buddhism to govern the Mongols and Tibetans. The philosophical divergence between the Han Chinese dynasty and the Manchu state is quite outspoken up to this point.

---

[354] Qingchu neiguoshiyuan manwen dang'an yibian, p. 405.

[355] Qingchu neiguoshiyuan manwen dang'an yibian, p. 431.

[356] *Tibet and Manchu*, preface, pp. i-ii.

[357] Zhuang Jifa 莊吉發 (1997), *Qingshi lunji (er)* 清史論集 （二） (Collection of Treatise on the Qing History, 2), Wenshizhe chubanshen, p. 303.

[358] Yu Yingshi 余英時 (2010), *Zhongguo jinshi zongjiao lunli yu shangren* 中國近世宗教倫理與商人 (China's Early Modern Religious Ethic and Merchants), Lianjing chuban shiye gufen youxian gongsi 聯經出版事業股份有限公司 (Linking Publishing Company), Taipei, pp. 41-85.

3.7 Distributing Captives

When the Ming government was busy fighting the Japanese for their invasion of Korea, Nurgaqi took the moment and started his own enterprise, by subjugating the Jurchen-speaking tribes first. Those acquired Jurchens were the foundation of the banner system, upon which the Later Jin state was built. In the early unification of some cities at the Ming's border, the Han Chinese captives are in a small number, and quickly they were assimilated into the Jurchen societies. Typical examples are Cao Yin's forefathers as Spence stated,[359] and the Fan Wencheng brothers as Crossley researched.[360] Generally, the acquired population, especially after the unification of the Ming's Liaodong region, was distributed to the banners or stayed in their homelands for farming. On the second day of the first month in 1622, Nurgaqi went out of his office and proclaimed that once he ordered the Han Chinese officials to sent the captives back to where their parents were, but the Han Chinese officials did not agree (*han, yamen de tuqifi nikan i geren hafasai baru hendume, suwembe dahaha qooha be, gemu meni meni ama emete bade sindafi seqi ojorakv*).[361] However, the Han Chinese officials took tens of thousands people to the places of Xincheng and Aihe on the grounds that they might not be captured again after being released (*tere be sindafi unggifi, jai be qooha be adarame bahambi seme unggirakvqi, iqe hecen, aiha i baru genere de, suwe udu tumen gamaha bihe*).[362] Nurgaqi did not thoroughly investigated this issue, but he pronounced that the Han Chinese officials were corrupt, wrong and could no longer be trusted (*ulin gaifi tuttu wakaqi ai, nikan suwende, be te akdarakv*).[363] Obviously the Han Chinese officials secretly hid a large number of war prisoners for personal gain and Nurgaqi had to tolerate them.

On the fourteenth day of the first month in 1622, some ten thousand Han Chinese captives were captured from the Ming general Mao Wenlong and half of them were rewarded to the Jurchen soldiers who went to wars, with the other half for the officers ranging from the Grand

---

[359] Jonathan D. Spence (1966), *Ts'ao Yin and the K'ang-hsi Emperor: Bondservant and Master,* Yale University Press, New Haven.

[360] Crossley, A Translucent Mirror.

[361] *Fe dangse*, p. 1414.

[362] Fe dangse, pp. 1414-1415.

[363] *Fe dangse*, p. 1417.

Coordinator to the Grand Commandant (*mao wen long be dabqilafi gajiha tumen olji isinjiha, tere tumen be, dulin be genehe qoohai niyalma de buhe, dulin be du tang, zung bing guwan qi fusihvn, xeobei qi wesihun xangname buhe*).[364] After the unification of the Liaodong region, the Later Jin regime must deal with the large population of the dwellers. On the twenty-seventh of the first month in 1622, the government sent a decree, ordering the Han Chinese civilians who came from the east of the Liao River to return to their original places, and people who came from Guangning, which is at the west of the Liao River, could seek refuge with their existing relatives if they wanted (*orin nadan de, nikasa de wasimbuha gisun, birai dergi liyoodung ni ba i niyalma bira doome jihengge, suwe meni meni bade bedereme gene, jai birai wargi guwangning ni ba i niyalma, niyaman hvnqihin bisire niyalma, qihangga oqi, niyaman hvnqihin be baime gene*).[365] The government cannot sponsor such a great number of people to make a living.

War was cruel. On the fourth day of the second month in 1622, Nurgaqi sent a document to the Grand Coordinators, said that he marched the army towards Shanhai Pass and burned all cities along the way (*han i bithe, du tang de juwe biyai iqe duin de wasimbuha, han, xanaha i baru geneme, xi san xan qi dalingho, xolingho, sung xan, hing xan, ta xan de isitala tuwaqi, gemu tuwa sindafi gamahabi*).[366] Consequently, all people of the nine garrisons had to cross the Liao River and move to the Liaodong region under command, so did the people of the two garrisons in Jinzhou (*bisire uyun wei niyalma be bira doome liyoodung ni bade unggi, ginjeo i juwe wei be liyoodung de unggi ...*).[367] The administration of people was carried out by the Banner Companies, through which all men of Liaodong were counted and divided into three parts, with one for garrison, two for farming in Liaodong (*emu nirui liyoodung de tehe haha be dabume, ilan ubu arafi emu ubu tekini, juwe ubu haha liyoodung de usin weilekini*).[368] According to a letter sent by Nurgaqi to his Vice Regional Commander Munggatu on the eighteenth day of the second month in 1622, some households were allocated to places where they can

---

[364] *Fe dangse*, p. 1473.
[365] *Fe dangse*, pp. 1523-1524.
[366] *Fe dangse*, p. 1555.
[367] *Fe dangse*, p. 1556.
[368] *Fe dangse*, p. 1569.

be accommodated, otherwise, they must be sent to live beyond the border (*han i bithe, juwe biyai juwan jakvn de wasimbuha, munggetu fujiyang, si unggihe boigon i joriha bade baktara be tuwame tebu, baktandarakvqi, ... jase tuqitele beneme tuwame tebume*).[369] As for the men who came from Guangning, after counting, they were bestowed to the officers of Guangning according to ranks and the rest were given to the Mongol chieftains who came to surrender (*guwangning qi jihe haha tolome wajiha manggi, guwangning ni hafasa de hergen bodome haha bufi, fucehe haha be monggo i jihe beise de bu*).[370] One can see that distributing the captives is a way to cultivate the khan's popularity among the leaders of the state.

Large amounts of the Han Chinese were also massacred when the hidden refugees were discovered by the authority. On the twenty-sixth day of the sixth month in 1623, the Grand Coordinators sent a document to the Company Commanders, stating that in the past there were seven thousand men in Fuzhou 復州 (*du tang ni bithe, orin ninggun de geren qiyanyung de wasimbuha, ...fu jeo i teile da toloro de, nadan minggan haha bihe*).[371] But some people of Fuzhou came to indict that there were eleven thousand more than the original counting (*fu jeo i niyalma ubade gerqileme, fu jeo heqen de da toloho nadan minggan haha qi, fulu emu tumen emu minggan haha ohobi*).[372] The First Chieftain was sent to check, verifying that indeed there were eleven thousand more men comparing with the original account, so the Fuzhou people were killed (*amba beile be tuwana seme unggifi tuwaqi, hahai ton, da toloho qi emu tumen emu minggan fulu, ... fu jeo i niyalma be wahangge tere inu*).[373] Furthermore, people of any other places would be dealt in the same way if they sheltered the refugees (*yaya ba i niyalma, fu jeo i adali fulu niyalma be gidafi, inu tere kooli ombikai*).[374] It is reasonable to assume that quite a number of people were slaughtered in unrest times without being allocated for new settlement.

In Hong Taiji's time, massacre was prohibited for the purpose of better managing the newly acquired regions. After taking a new place,

---

[369] *Fe dangse*, p. 1639.
[370] *Fe dangse*, p. 1685.
[371] *Fe dangse*, pp. 2523-2524.
[372] *Fe dangse*, pp. 2524-2525.
[373] *Fe dangse*, pp. 2525-2526.
[374] *Fe dangse*, p. 2526.

soldiers were not allowed to disturb the Ming residents. But the Second Chieftain Amin violated Hong Taiji's order. When unifying the Zhenzi town, Amin drove the Han Chinese captives to the fortification Yongping, where they were divided by the Eight Chieftains and became bond-servants (*jeng zi zheng sere hoton ... nikan be yongping de gajifi, jakvn boo dendeme gaifi aha arahabi*). [375] But soon Hong Taiji considered Amin's act as one of his major crimes, which challenged his authority and imprisoned Amin with provision of clothes and food (*etungge jengge bufi, loo de horifi ujimbi*).[376] Though this event was part of the power struggle between Hong Taiji and Amin, one can still see that the Later Jin regime faced a situation of upgrading its administration by easing the conflict with the Han Chinese subjects.

When the relationship with the Ming was on a relatively peaceful term, Hong Taiji moved his sight on the Chakhar Mongols, which is roughly today's Inner Mongolia. After successive wars, a large number of Mongol population were integrated into the Later Jin regime, and the captives were divided by the armored soldiers of each Banner (*olji niyalma be meni meni gvsai uksin bodome dende*).[377] Hong Taiji also reinforced his command of distributing the captives by banners (*han hendume, niyalma be meni meni gvsai dende*).[378] Subsequently, these Mongol nomads greatly strengthened the Later Jin's cavalry, by providing large sums of soldiers and horses.

In Nurgaqi's time, the Jurchen population that was incorporated into the banners were called Old Manchus (man. *fe manju*; chin. *jiumanzhou* 舊滿洲) and in Hong Taiji's time, New Manchus (man. *iqe manju*; chin. *xinmanzhou* 新滿洲). These Jurchen people constituted the body of Eight-Banner Manchus (man. *gvsai manju*; chin. *baqi manzhou* 八旗滿洲). Comparatively, only a small part of the Han Chinese population were assimilated into the banner system, which were under the name of Eight-Banner Han Chinese Artillery Troops (man. *ujen qooha*; chin. *baqi hanjun* 八旗漢軍), while the majority remained as civilians (man. *irgen*; chin. *minren* 民人). A great number of Chakhar Mongols, along with the Horqin Mongols who had already formed alliance with the Later Jin,

---

[375] *Fe dangse*, p. 5095.
[376] *Fe dangse*, p. 5107.
[377] Fe dangse, p. 6225.
[378] *Fe dangse*, p. 6226.

made up of the Eight-Banner Mongols (man. *gvsai mongol*; chin. *baqi menggu* 八旗蒙古). The ownership of banner (*gvsai*) overrides the ethnic identity as a fixed rule throughout the Qing dynasty. It was not until the Qianlong reign, Manchu Banners (*manzhou baqi* 滿洲八旗), Mongol Banners (*menggu baqi* 蒙古八旗) and Han Chinese Banners (*hanjun baqi* 漢軍八旗) started to appear in some Han Chinese-language documents as inappropriate terms. Still, the official Manchu-language documents always stayed with the fixed rule of highlighting the character of banner.

3.8 Conclusion

In Nurgaqi's reign, the Later Jin gradually subdued different Jurchen tribes under its ruling, while unifying the neighboring Han Chinese regions. Thus, a solid foundation was laid for overwhelming the Mongol tribes. Meanwhile, both Nurgaqi and Hong Taiji attracted great numbers of Mongol people into their regime, and most of them were from the Chakhar tribe, as we have analyzed.

Because his father had already subjugated most Jurchen tribes, Hong Taiji was able to concentrate his military campaign against the Han Chinese and Mongols. Combining both the Han and Mongol forces, the Jurchen-Manchus marched south to besiege Beijing and plundered its surrounding regions.

The above nine grid charts can roughly represent the acquired populations, though chronicle records for two years are missing. Overall, the subdued Jurchens counted 61,924 people, Mongols 68,751 and the Han Chinese 307,925. An approximate ratio of these three peoples would be 1:1:5.

In other words, both Nurgaqi and Hong Taiji integrated 61,924 Jurchens from other tribes into his realm, 68,751 Mongols and 310,925 Ming people. Sometimes the scribes only recorded people by counting the households. In addition to the figures from the missing two years, the actual figures of acquired population could be much higher. The number of the Han Chinese people is immense. Many cities in Liaodong entirely surrendered to Nurgaqi, but the numbers of population were not recorded. As Albert Feuerwerker said, research on any premodern society lacks of reliable and systematic statistical data for measurements. [379] In our Manchu case, this is very true since the Manchu scribes only recorded things that they heard or understood. One must admit that there is large quantities of historical data awaiting for scholars to discover.

Though calculations are incomplete, these numbers are still helpful. Within certain times, these numbers can approximately reflect the percentages of population growth and constitution under the direct control of the Later Jin-Qing state.

---

[379] Albert Feuerwerker (1984), The State and the Economy in Late Imperial China, *Theory and Society*, Elsevier Science Publishers, Amsterdam, 13.3: 297-326.

4. Acquisition of Lands

4.1 Introduction

The definition of economy varies in history. The Han Chinese expression of Jingji (經濟) stands for Jing shi ji min (經世濟民), which better corresponds with "statecraft". Ancient China's history of economy was well kept as "food and products" (*shi huo* 食貨) in the official history books, including institutions of lands, human population, tax, corvee, transportation, money, market and state's budget, etc.. This concept of governance, in aspects of political economy and fiscal administration, highlights the rulers' responsibility for providing economic welfare to their people, as Richard Von Glahn stated.[380] Salt and iron (*yan tie* 鹽鐵) were the fundamental components in Han Chinese dynasties such as Han and Song. By manipulating the provision of salt and iron, the state manages its control over vast lands, especially people who live in the remote regions. The Han Chinese language documents, both official and private, also show that salt and iron were important goods that the Jurchens still needed to purchase from the Ming and Korea. What is economy on a Manchu term? Through reading the Manchu-language chronicles, one can see that the ruling elite pursued three elements: currency, population and lands, which were acquired by the Manchus through wars for the purpose of territorial expansion, without highlighting the Confucian idealism in the first place. Silver and gold were used to fuel greater battles, so were people and lands, except for the tax intention shared by the Ming. The rest economic elements, such as manufacturing industries, mining, farming and animal husbandry, were subject to these three basic factors.

This section aims to examine the chronicle records, which help us reconstruct the process of acquiring lands for the great Qing enterprise. Most of the sources come out of the *Manchu Veritable Records*, which was compiled after the year 1635, when the identity of the state and people officially changed into Manchu. For this reason, the Jurchen identity was modified as Manchu by the compilers. In most cases, this

---

[380] Richard von Glahn (2019), Modalities of the Fiscal State in Imperial China, *Journal of Chinese History*, 29.4: 1.

book still uses the identity of Jurchen for describing historical events that happened before 1635, but some cases still adopt Manchu for corresponding with the expression of sources.

Nurgaqi started his enterprise by building up a small community, which was organized as banners of military units, by integrating Jurchen tribes that lived beyond the borders of Ming's Liaodong province. This community expanded into a multi-ethnic state when more and more Mongols and Han Chinese elite came on board. Reinforced by different ethnic powers, this new regime expanded its territory exponentially. With more lands under control, resources were better coordinated for greater expansion. From an economic perspective, lands and cities are the locations where resources accumulate. War is an effective means to boost economic growth for state building. Nurgaqi unified the Jurchen-speaking lands and then unified the Ming's Liaodong province. His successor Hong Taiji subjugated Korea twice and integrated Chakhar, which is also called Inner Mongolia, into the governance. These territorial expansions greatly assembled resources to equip the Manchus for the unification of the Ming.

4.2 Unifying Jurchen Lands

In the Han Chinese historical view, Nurgaqi's tribe is called Jianzhou nüzhen (建州女真) and Nurgaqi was entitled as Dragon-Tiger General (*Longhu jiangjun* 龍虎將軍). For example, in a letter to his friend, Xiong tingbi (熊廷弼), the Ming's Grand Minister Commander in Liaodong (*liaodongjinglüe* 遼東經略), said,

寧遠顧思各家，敕書無所屬，悉以與奴酋，且請爲龍虎將軍以寵之。於是奴酋得以號召東方，收名家故地遺民歸於一統，而建州之勢合矣。[381]

Li Chengliang [Ningyuan Earl, 寧遠伯] considered the situation of each clan and found no means to dispatch the Imperial Decrees. Therefore, he gave all of them to the Chief Nu [nu qiu 奴酋, Nurgaqi]. Furthermore, Li asked [the central government] to entitle Nurgaqi with Dragon-Tiger General as an imperial honor. Thus, the Chief Nu was able

---

[381] *Mingjingshiwenbian* 明经世文编 (Compilations for Ordering the World in the Ming Dynasty), compiled by Chen Zilong 陈子龙, vol. 408, *Xiongjinglüeji*, edition Beijing: Zhonghua shuju, 1962, p. 5287.

to summon people in the East, unifying the outstanding clans, former regions and remnant inhabitants, so that the power of Jianzhou formed.

Besides, in the Han Chinese historical discourse, the Jurchens were divided into three regions according to where they lived: Jianzhou nüzhen 建州女真 who lived around the Ming's Jianzhou garrison, Haixi nüzhen 海西女真 who lived in the valley of Songhua River, and Yeren nüzhen 野人女真 that literally means the wild Jurchens who lived beyond regions of Jianzhou and Songhua River. These three terms indicate a relationship that the Jurchens were subordinate to the Han Chinese authority and therefore, these terms were not adopted in the Manchu documents. In the official Manchu perspective, there were all sorts of small tribes, which were independent from Nurgaqi's Manchu regime. They were tribes in Suksuhu River (Sukesuhuhebu 蘇克素護河部), Hunehe River (Hunhebu 渾河部), Wanggiya (Wanyanbu 完顏部), Donggo (Dong'ebu 董鄂部), and Jeqen's place (Zhechenbu 哲陳部); the Neyen (Nayin 訥殷) and Yalu River (Yalujiang 鴨綠江) tribes in Changbaishan 長白山; Weji (Woji 窩集), Warka (Wa'erka 瓦爾喀), and Kvrka (Ku'erka 庫爾喀) in the Eastern Sea, and the Ula (Wula 烏拉), Hada (Hada 哈達), Yehe (Yehe 葉赫), and hoifa (Huifa 輝發) tribes in the Hvlun Land (*hulunguo* 呼倫國 or *hulunbu* 扈倫部) (*tere fonde babai gurun faquhvn ofi, manju gurun i suksuhu birai goloi aiman, hunehe birai goloi aiman, wanggiyai goloi aiman, donggoi goloi aiman, jeqen i bai aiman, xanggiyan alin i goloi neyen, yalu giyang ni aiman, dergi mederi goloi weji warka kvrkai aiman, hvlun gurun i ulai goloi aiman, hadai goloi aiman, yehei goloi aiman, hoifai goloi aiman babade ...*).[382]

---

[382] *Manzhou shilu* 滿洲實錄 (The Manchu Veritable Records), excerpted from *Qingshilu* 清實錄 (The Qing Veritable Records), vol. 1, edition Beijing: Zhonghua shuju, 1986, p. 19.

Map 1: Jurchen tribes in the early sixteenth century

As Gertraude Roth Li argued that, most of these Jurchen tribes were pacified by the Ming government for the purpose of dominating the Mongols as a traditional policy of playing off one barbarian group to control another (*yi yi zhi yi* 以夷制夷).[383] When Nurgaqi started to unify these tribes, he was twenty-five years old, with a few soldiers and amours at his side to fight against the conflicting neighbors. The first one was Ehe kuren (*sure kundulen han sunja se qi, ehe kuren de eljeme dain dailara de qooha uksin komso bihe*).[384] In the Manchu-language chronicles, the earliest event was dated on the twentieth day of the third month in the year of the Lamb (1607), when Nurgaqi was forty-nine years old (*sure kundulen han i dehi uyun se de, honin aniya ilan biyai orin de*).[385] Twenty-four years of records were missing, but they can be found in *The Manchu Veritable Records* (man. *yargiyan kooli*; chin. *manzhoushilu* 滿洲實錄), which was first composed in Hong Taiji's reign (1626-1643) as the official but unoriginal chronicle.

The Manchu Veritable Records says that Nurgaqi wanted to revenge against Nikan Wailan for the death of his grandfather and father, with only thirteen armors inherited from his father (*taizu sure beile mafa ama i*

---

[383] Gertraude Roth Li (2002), State Building before 1644, in *The Cambridge history of China: vol. 9 Part I: The Ch'ing Empire to 1800*, ed. Willard Peterson, Cambridge University Press, Cambridge, pp. 11-12.

[384] *Fe dangse*, pp. 176-177.

[385] *Fe dangse*, p. 9.

karu be gaime, ini amai werihe juwan ilan uksin i nikan wailan be dailame deribuhe, taizu sure beilei orin sunja se de sahahvn honin aniya juwari dulimbai biya de, nikan wailan be dailame qooha jurafi geneqi ...).[386] Later he recruited some one hundred men with thirty sets of armors, and took over Nikan Wailan's fortification, Turun (*taizu sure beile nikan wailan i turun i hoton be gaime genere de... taizu sure beile tere turun i hoton be afame gaifi bederehe, tere fonde, taizu sure beile i qooha emu tanggv, uksin gvsin bihe*).[387] Nurgaqi's enterprise started with victories and soon he defeated another enemy Nomina and Naikada brothers, and gained their fortification Sarhv. However, this fortification betrayed Nurgaqi immediately (*taizu sure beile qooha niyalma tere gida jangkv be bahafi uthai nomina naikada ahvn deo qoohai niyalma be gemu wafi sarhvi hoton be gaifi... sarhvi hoton be dasafi taizu sure beile qi geli ubaxaha*).[388] Even so, this is the very first large fortification Nurgaqi ever acquired according to the official Manchu documents. From this moment on, Nurgaqi started his arduous journey of unifying people and land and finally took over the Ming's territory in the next few decades.

The Donggo Tribe was a tough one to unify. Nurgaqi was shot in the neck by an arrow and he nearly died in the war of acquiring the fortification Onggolo (*taizu sure beile ini meifen de hadaha... senggi ilirakv...*).[389] After the wound healed, Nurgaqi launched another attack and took over the fortification (*taizu sure beile feye johiha manggi, qooha genefi onggolo i hoton be afame gaiha*).[390]

In the ninth month of the Green Chicken year (1585), Nurgaqi vanquished Antu Gvwalgiya (Antugua'erjia 安圖瓜爾佳), a fortification of Suksuhu Tribe, and killed its leader Nomhon; the army returned afterwards (*taizu sure beile qooha genefi suksuhu aiman i antu gvwalgiya be afame gaifi, hoton i ejen nomhon be wafi qooha bederehe*).[391]

In the middle summer month of the Red-Dog year (1586), Nurgaqi sent his army and subjugated Hunehe Tribe's lands and castles (*fulgiyan

---

[386] Manzhou shilu, p. 32.
[387] Manzhou shilu, p. 32-33.
[388] Manzhou shilu, p. 35.
[389] Manzhou shilu, p. 51-52.
[390] Manzhou shilu, p. 54.
[391] Manzhou shilu, p. 61.

indahvn aniya, juwari dulimbai biya de, taizu sure beile qooha genefi, hunehe aiman i boihon xanqin be afame gaiha).[392]

In the Fire-Red Pig year (1587), based on the previous success, Nurgaqi constructed a three-layer fortification with government offices, buildings and watchtowers, which located on a hill in the southeast between two rivers named as Xoli and Hvlan Hada; on the twenty-fourth day in the sixth month, he set up administration to stop bad, disturbing, theft and other unlawful things; thus law and order were established (*fulahvn ulgiyan aniya taizu sure beile xoli anggaqi hvlan hadai xun dekdere julergi giyaha birai juwe siden i ala de ilarsu hoton sahafi, yamun leose tai araha, ninggun biyai i doro be toktobume ehe faquhvn, hvlha holo be nakabume xajin kooli be ilibuha).*[393]

Soon Nurgaqi launched a punitive war upon the leader Artai of Jeqen tribe, and took over Artai's castle and killed the fortification's leader Artai (*taizu sure beile, qooha gaifi jeqen i aiman i artai be dailame genefi, artai xanqin be afame gaifi, hoton i ejen artai be waha).*[394] Next Nurgaqi led the army to attack the Dung fortification, and forced its leader Jahai to surrender (*taizu sure beile qooha gaifi, jahai gebuengge amban be dailame genefi, dung ni hoton be afame gaifi, hoton i ejen jahai be dahabufi gajiha).*[395] This marked the end of the Jeqen tribe.

Besides military campaigns, marriage is another way to bond the tribes together. In the fourth month of the Yellow-Mouse year (1588), Hvrgan Beile, the son of Khan Wan of Hada's tribe, married his daughter to Nurgaqi; The bride was escorted by her brother Daixan (*hadai gurun i wan han i jui hvrgan beilei amin jeje gebungge sargan jui be ini ahvn daisan beile, taizu sure beile de sargan benjire de).*[396] The tension with the Hada tribe was temporarily eased.

During the time, the leader of Suwan place, Solgo, surrendered to Nurgaqi, along with his subordinate Jurchen people (*tere fonde suwan i bai ejen solgo gebungge amban ini harangga juxen irgen be gaifi dahame jihe manggi).*[397]

---

[392] Manzhou shilu, p. 62.
[393] Manzhou shilu, p. 66.
[394] Manzhou shilu, pp. 66-67.
[395] Manzhou shilu, p. 68.
[396] Manzhou shilu, p. 69.
[397] Manzhou shilu, p. 71.

Up to this year (1588), the scribes concluded that Juerchen leaders were pacified one by one and the surrounding lands were completely subjugated. From now on, the Manchu state became strong and powerful. During the time, Nurgaqi sent emissaries to the Ming's Wanli emperor every year. On peaceful terms, Nurgaqi received five hundred imperial permits for conducting trade and paying tribute. The scribe said the land produced bright pearls, ginseng, three kinds of fox fur, such as black and red; and furs of mink, lynx, leopard, tiger, sea-beaver, otter, snow weasel, and Siberian weasel. There were all sorts of pelts for people to wear. At four entrances of Fushun 撫順, Qinghe 清河, Kuandian 寬甸 and Aiyang (靉陽) people were trading and acquiring treasure. The Manchu state became wealthy and honorable (*tuttu golo goloi ambasa be elbime dahabure, xurdeme gurun be dailame waqihiyara, tereqi manju gurun ulhiyen i etuhun hvsungge oho tere fonde daiming gurun i wan li han de aniya dari elqin takvrame hvwaliyasun doroi sunja tanggv ejehei ulin be gaime gurun qi tuqire genggiyen tana, orhoda sahaliyan boro, fulgiyan ilan haqin i dobihi seke, silun, yarha, tasha, lekergi, hailun, ulhu, solohi, haqin haqin i furdehe be beye de etume, fuxun xo, qing ho, kuwan diyan, ai yang duin duka de hvda hvdaxame ulin nadan gaime, manju gurun bayan wesihun oho*).[398]

This passage can be confirmed with Xiong Tingbi's letter to his friend, which says

...自建州之勢合而奴酋始疆。自五百道之貢賞入，而奴酋始富。[399]

Since the Jianzhou power came into being, the Chief Nu [Nurgaqi] emerged as a strong power. Since [he received] the five hundred [imperial decrees] to pay tribute and received rewards, the Chief Nu became wealthy.

Xiong pointed out that when the surrounding tribes were unified by Nurgaqi, resources were integrated, and the Jurchens appeared as a formidable force. When Nurgaqi's grandfather and father were killed by a mistake in 1583, the Ming authority gave him thirty imperial decrees as compensation, along with their dead corpses, thirty horses and an appointment letter of governor (*nikan i daiming gurun i wan li han i*

---

[398] Manzhou shilu, pp. 71-73.

[399] *Ming jingshi wenbian* 明經世文編 (Compilations of Statecraft in the Ming Dynasty), vol. 408, compiled by Chen Zilong 陳子龍 (1608-1647), edition Beijing: Zhonghua shuju, 1962, p. 5287.

juwan emuqi sahahvn honin aniya... taizu sure beile de sini mafa ama be qoohame waha weile waka endebuhe seme, ama mafai giran, gvsin ejehe, gvsin morin benjihe, jai geli nememe dudu ejehe benjihe manggi).[400] These imperial decrees were passports and licence for the Jurchens to conduct business with the Han Chinese people in large cities. Nurgaqi had thirty imperial decrees in 1583 and five years later, he unified the tribes in Jianzhou region and owned five hundred of them (*wu bai dao* 五百道) as verified in both the Manchu and Han Chinese sources.

In the same year (1588), Nurgaqi led the army and attacked the Wanggiyai tribe, whose fortification was easily unified and its leader Daidu Mergen was killed (*tere aniya taizu sure beile qooha gaifi wanggiyai hoton be dailame... tereqi qooha julesi dosime genefi, wanggiyai hoton be afame gaifi, hoton i ejen daidu mergen be waha*)[401]

To sum up, these first five tribes, Suksuhu River, Hunehe River, Wanggiya, Donggo and Jeqen, were conventionally named by the Han Chinese as Jianzhou Jurchen (*jianzhou nüzhen* 建州女真),[402] which were unified by Nurgaqi as his top priorities. Next, the three tribes in Changbaishan 長白山, which are Neyen, Yalu River, and Juxeri (*tere fonde xanggiyan alin i aiman i juxeri...*),[403] were also subdued into the Manchu reign afterwards.

While maintaining a peaceful relationship with the Ming, Nurgaqi took every opportunity to integrate the other Manchu tribes into his reign. In the Light-Yellow Ox year (1589), Nurgaqi launched a punitive attack on Ningguqin, who was the leader of Joogiya fortification. After the war, the fortification was taken, Ningguqin was killed and the Jurchen army returned (*sohon ihan aniya, taizu sure beile joogiyai hoton i ejen ningguqin janggin be dailame ... tereqi hoton be afame gaifi hoton i ejen ningguqin janggin be wafi, qooha bederehe).*[404]

In the year of the light-white rabbit (1591), Nurgaqi sent some military force to attack the Yalu River circuit, which belonged to the White Mountain (Changbaishan 長白山) tribe. The circuit was completely unified (*xahvn gvlmahvn aniya, taizu sure beile, xanggiyan*

---

[400] *Manzhou shilu*, pp. 26-29.

[401] Manzhou shilu, p. 74.

[402] Yan Chongnian 閻崇年 (1983), *Nu'erhachi zhuan* 努爾哈赤傳 (Biography of Nurgaqi), Beijing chubanshe, Beijing, pp. 36-37.

[403] Manzhou shilu, p. 82.

[404] Manzhou shilu, pp. 75-77.

alin i aiman i yalu giyang ni golo de qooha unggifi tere golo be
waqihiyame gaifi gaijiha).[405]

In the ninth month of the year of the light-black snake (1593), nine
surrounding tribes formed an alliance to attack Nurgaqi. The leaders were
Bujai and Narimbulu from Yehe, Menggebulu from Hada, Mantai and his
brother Bujantai from Ula, Baindali from hoifa, Unggadai, Manggvz and
Minggan from Mongol Khorchin, Sibe tribe, Gvwalqa, Yulengge from
Juxeri in White Mountain, Seowen and Sekesi from Neyen (*sahahvn
meihe aniya ... tere aniya uyun biya de, yehei gurun i bujai beile,
narimbulu beile hadai gurun i menggebulu beile ulai gurun i mantai beile
deo bujantai beile, hoifa gurun i baindari beile amargi nvn i korqin i
monggoi gurun i unggadai beile, manggvz beile, minggan beile, sibei
aiman, gvwalqa i aiman, manju gurun i xanggiyan alian i juxeri goloi
ejen yulengge, neyen i goloi ejen seowen, sekesi uheri uyun halai gurun
aqafi ilan jugvn i qooha jimbi...).*[406]

The war turned into the Manchu favor. The allied forces were
defeated, with loss of four thousand soldiers, three thousand horses and
one thousand armors. The Manchu state enjoyed a glorious reputation
that spreads over ten thousand places (*tere qooha be gidaha de, duin
minggan niyalma waha, ilan minggan morin, emu minggan uksin baha,
tereqi manju gurun i horon tumen bade algika).*[407]

Yulengge, the leader of Juxeri circuit, joined the allies to fight against
Nurgaqi. After the war, Nurgaqi sent an army for retaliation and acquired
the Juxeri circuit into his realm (*tere qooha de, juxeri goloi ejen yulengge
janggin dafi jidere jakade, taizu sure beile juwan biya de, qooha unggifi
juxeri golo be dahabufi gajiha).*[408]

In the sixth month of the year of the green lamb (1595), Nurgaqi sent
his troops to strike the Hoifa tribe. The army took over the Dobi
fortification, which belonged to the leader Baindari (*niohon honin aniya
ninggun biya de, taizu sure beile qooha genefi hoifai baindari beile dobi
hoton be afame gaifi).*[409]

---

[405] Manzhou shilu, p. 77.
[406] Manzhou shilu, pp. 84-88.
[407] Manzhou shilu, p. 99.
[408] Manzhou shilu, p. 99.
[409] Manzhou shilu, p. 102.

In the first month of the year of the yellow dog (1598), Nurgaqi sent his oldest son Quyeng, his youngest brother Bayara, Adviser Gagai, and Adviser Fiongdon, along with one thousand soldiers to attack the Aqulalv circuit that belonged to the Warka tribe. Over twenty villages were taken and the rest surrendered (*suwayan indahvn aniya, taizu sure beile ini ahvngga jui quyeng taiji, fiyanggv deo bayara taiji, gagai jargvqi fiongdon jargvqi de emu qinggan qooha be afabufi, aniya biya de warka aiman i aqulakv golo be dailame... orin funqeme gaxan be gaifi tere goloi ba bai gaxan be gemu dahabufi*).[410]

In the ninth month of the year of the light yellow pig (1599), Nurgaqi subjugated the Hada tribe (*sohon ulgiyan aniya... uyun biya de hadai gurun be dailame... tereqi hadai gurun umesi gukuhe*).[411] However, the Ming Wanli emperor was not happy about this. In the year of the light white ox (1601), Wanli sent a message to Nurgaqi and ordered him to restore Hada. Nurgaqi's military power was insufficient of resisting the Ming, so Nurgaqi obeyed the command and released the Hada leader Urgvdai to his home land (*xahvn ihan aniya... daiming gurun i wan li han taizu sure beile banjire be yebexerakv, si hadai gurun be ainu efulefi gamaha, te biqibe urgvdai be ini bade amasi unggi seme ergelehe manggi, taizu sure beile wan li han i gisun de eterakv ini jui hojihon juxen irgen be hadai bade tebume unggihe manggi*).[412]

Soon, the Yehe leader Narimbulu led some Mongol armies to attack the Hada tribe. Because the Yehe was a subordinate of the Ming empire, Nurgaqi reported this matter to the Wanli emperor but did not receive any response. The Hada people were suffering from famine and went to the Ming's Kaiyuan fortification (kaiyuan shi 開原市) for hunger relief. When being refused by the Han Chinese, cannibalism happened among the Hada people. The refugees had to exchange children, wives, bond-servants and animals to eat. Seizing the moment, Nurgaqi took Hada tribe back under his reign (*yehei gurun i narimbulu beile monggoi qooha be gaifi ududu jergi suqufi gamara jakade, taizu sure beile, daiming gurun i wan li han i baru sini gisun i mini baha hadai gurun be ini bade amasi unggifi tebuhe, hadai gurun be yehei niyalma kemuni suqufi gamambi, mini baha gurun be yehe de ainu salibumbi seme*

---

[410] Manzhou shilu, p. 107.
[411] *Manzhou shilu*, pp. 110-115.
[412] Manzhou shilu, pp. 116.

gisureqi, daiming gurun i wan li han umai donjirakv, tereqi hadai niyalma jeku akv yuyume daiming ni kai yuwan heqen i niyalma de jeku baiqi buhe akv juse sargan booi aha morin ihan be unqafi jeku gaifi jeke tuttu ojoro jakade, taizu sure beile mini baha gurun be ainu faqabumbi seme hadai gurun be gemu bargiyafi hajiha).[413]

Soon Nurgaqi, the Wise Chieftain of the Manchu state, moved his capital fortification from Hvlan Hadai to Hetu Ala, which is between two rivers (*manju gurun i taizu sure beile ini tehe hvlan hadai julergi ala qi gurifi mafai tehe susu suksuhu bira giyaha bira juwe siden i hetu ala de gurifi heqen...*).[414] In the autumn of the same year, Nurgaqi's first wife fell ill and she wanted to visit her mother who lived in Yehe. But Yehe's leader Narimbulu refused to arrange the meeting. After his wife passed away, Nurgaqi poured the anger onto the Yehe tribe. On the eighth day of the first month in the year of the green dragon (1604), Nurgaqi sent the army to attack Yehe and subdued two cities, seven villages and two thousand captives (*taizu sure beile, fujin i eme emhe be jio seme yehe de elqin takvraha manggi, yehei narimbulu beile ini eme be unggihe akv ini booi nantai gebungge niyalma be unggihe... tereqi taizu sure beile haji fujin, eme be aqaki seqi unggihe akv de korsofi, niowanggiyan muduri aniya, aniya biyai iqe jakvn i inenggi, yehe be dailame qooha jurafi, juwan emu de, yehei jang, ankiran gebungge juwe hoton be afame gaifi, tere goloi nadan gaxan be gaiha, juwe minggan olji be bahafi qooha bederehe).*[415]

In the year of the light-red lamb (1607), Qemtehe, an official from the Fio fortification in the Warka tribe of the Eastern Sea, met Nurgaqi and said they lived in a remote place and had to depend on Ula for a living. But Ula's leader Bujantai mistreated them and he thus asked for help to move his people to Nurgaqi's realm. Nurgaqi sent his younger brother, his two sons, and officials to retrieve those people (*fulalvn honin aniya dergi mederi warkai aiman i fio gebungge hoton i qemtehe gebungge amban, taizu kundulen han de hengkileme jifi hendume, be bai goro de dalibufi ulai gurun de dahafi, ulai bujantai beile membe ambula jobobumbi, meni boigon be ganame yabu sehe manggi, taizu kundulen han, ini deo xurgaqi beile, ahvngga jui hong baturu beile, jaqin jui*

---

[413] *Manzhou shilu*, pp. 116-117.
[414] *Manzhou shilu*, pp. 119-120.
[415] *Manzhou shilu*, pp. 120-123.

daixan beile, uju jergi amban fiongdon, hvrhan hiya de ilan minggan qooha be afabufi, fio hoton i boigon be ganame unggihe).[416] Later Ula's Bujantai tried to intercept, but his army was defeated.[417]

On the ninth day of the ninth month in 1607, Nurgaqi led the troops to attack the Hoifa tribe. The army arrived on the fourteenth day, unified the fortification and killed its leader Baindari, his son and all their soldiers. The Hoifa people were taken captive when the Jurchen army returned. Since then the Hoifa tribe perished (*fulahvn honin aniya... taizu kundulen han qooha gaifi, hoifa gurun be dailame uyun biyai iqe uyun de jurafi juwan duin de isinafi, hoifai hoton be kafi afame gaifi, hoton i ejen baindari beile ama jui geren qooha be wafi, irgen be dahabufi qooha bederehe, hoifai gurun tereqi umesi gukuhe).*[418]

In the year of the yellow monkey (1608), Nurgaqi ordered his son and his nephew to besiege Ula's Ihan fortification. The fortification was unified, one thousand Ula soldiers were killed, three hundred armors were obtained and the army returned with captives and animals (*suwayan bonio aniya, ilan biya de taizu kundulen han ini jui argatu tumen beile, deo i jui amin taiji de sunja minggan qooha be afabufi unggifi ulai gurun i ihan alin gebungge hoton be kafi afame gaifi, emu minggan niyalma be waha, ilan tanggv uksin bafafi olji gajime qooha bedereme...).*[419] Up to this point, one can see that the scribes emphasized acquiring people rather than stationing troops to guard the lands. One reason could that Nurgaqi did not have enough human resource to secure those new territories, and another reason would be that he needed to centralize people together for military service.

For this purpose, in the white-dog year (1610), the Jurchen army was sent to the Eastern Sea and unified the Weji tribe (xanggiyan indahvn aniya omxon biyade daizu kundulen han eidu baturu de emu minggan qooha be afabufi unggihi dergi mederi weji i aiman i namdulu, suifun... be gemu dahabufi ...).[420] According to Li Xun 李洵 and Xue Hong 薛 虹, "weji" means "a large forest" (da senlin 大森林), which refers to amounts of people who originally lived in the lower courses of Songhua

---

[416] *Manzhou shilu*, pp. 127-128.
[417] Manzhou shilu, p. 131.
[418] *Manzhou shilu*, pp. 127-137.
[419] Manzhou shilu, p. 138.
[420] *Manzhou shilu*, pp. 142-143.

River (Songhuangjiang 松花江) and Heilong River (Heilongjiang 黑龍
江), being administered by the Ming government through garrisons.[421]

In the seventh month of the next year, two circuits of the Weiji tribe,
Urguqen and Muren, were subdued (*nadan biyade taizu kundulen han ini
jui abatai taiji, fiongdon jargvqi, xongkoro baturu de emu minggan qooha
afabufi unggihe, tere qooha genefi dergi mederi weji i aiman i urguqen,
muren juwe golo be suqufi gemu gajiha*).[422]

In the twelfth month, Nurgaqi sent his son-in-law Hohori and the
Imperial Guards Eidu and Darhan, leading two thousand soldiers to attack
the Hvrha tribe's Jagvtai fortification. After three days of negotiations,
the Hvrha people still refused to surrender. The Jurchen army unified the
fortification, killed one thousand soldiers, and captured two thousand
people and animals. The surrounding circuits all submitted. Five hundred
households were taken back, along with the two circuit leaders, Tulexen
and Erexen (*jorgon biya de, han i hojihon hohori efu, eidu baturu,
darhan hiya ere ilan amban de juwe minggan qooha afabufi, weji i aiman
i hvrhai golo be dailame genefi jagvtai hoton be ilan inenggi kafi, daha
seqi daharakv ofi afame hoton de dosifi emu minggan niyalma be waha,
juwe minggan olji baha, terei xurdeme golo be dahabufi tulexen erexen
gebungge juwe amban, sunja tanggv boigon be dalime gajiha*).[423] Again,
Nurgaqi aimed to acquire more people rather than allotting troops to
guard the lands.

To avoid being subjugated, Ula's leader Bujantai wanted to form an
alliance with the Yehe tribe by sending his daughter and son to Yehe as
hostages. Hearing the news, Nurgaqi started an expedition in the first
month to attack Ula (*bujantai beile ini sahaliyan gebungge sargan jui
qokini gebungge haha jui, jai juwan nadan amban i juse be yehe de
damtun benefi... seme donjifi, sahahvn ihan aniya aniya biyade, manju
gurun i taizu kundulen han geren qooha be gaifi, ulai gurun be
dailame*).[424] The Manchu army's princes, officers and soldiers fought

---

[421] Li Xun 李洵 and Xue Hong 薛紅 (eds.) (1995), *Qingdai quanshi* 清代全史 (A
Complete History of the Qing), vol. 1, Liaoning renmin chubanshe, Shenyang, pp.
16-17.

[422] Manzhou shilu, pp. 144.

[423] *Manzhou shilu*, pp. 145-146.

[424] *Manzhou shilu*, pp. 156-157.

bravely and defeated the Ula army (*manjui qoohai beise ambasa geren qooha hvsutuleme afara jakade, ulai qooha uthai gidabufi*).[425]

In the year of the light black ox (1613), Bujantai escaped to Yehe and since then, every fortification in Ula surrendered to Nurgaqi and the Ula tribe perished (*sahahvn ihan aniya ... bujantai beile ... yehei gurun de genehe... tereqi ulai gurun i babai heqen hoton gemu dahaha... tereqi ulai gurun umesi gukuhe*).[426]

Nurgaqi sent emissaries three times to Yehe for demanding Bujantai back, but Yehe's leader Gintaisi and Buyanggv refused to hand him over. For this reason, on the sixth day of the ninth month, Nurgaqi led his army to attack the Yehe tribe (*bujantai be minde gaji seme ilan jergi takvraqi, yehei gintaisi beile buyangkv beile, bujantai be buhekv oho manggi, taizu kundulen han uyun biyai iqe ninggun de duin tumen qooha be gaifi yehei gurun be dailame juraka*).[427] The army took over the Usu fortification and returned with three hundred households (*usui hoton i dahaha ilan tangv boigon be gajime qooha bederehe*).[428]

At the time, Yehe's leaders, Gintaixi and Buyanggv sent emissaries to the Wanli emperor and accused Nurgaqi of unifying the Hada, Hoifa and Ula tribes; If Nurgaqi acquired the Yehe tribe, the next move would be taking over the Ming's Liaoyang as his capital, and change Kaiyuan and Tieling into his pasture (*tereqi yehei gurun i gintaixi beile, buyanggv beile, manju gurun i taizu kundulen han be ehequme daiming gurun i wan li han de ambasa be unggifi habxame manju gurun, hada, hoifa, ula ilan gurun be dailame efulefi gemu gaiha, te meni yehe be dailame waqihiyafi baba i gurun be baha manggi, suweni daiming gurun be dailafi liyoodung ni heqen be gaifi ini beye dembi, kai yuwan, tiyei ling ni babe gaifi morin i adun ulebumbi seme seme alara jakade...*)[429]

The Wanli emperor intervened. In the green-rabbit year (1615), he ordered Zhang Chengyin (張承廕), the Regional Commander of Guangning (*guangning zongbing* 廣寧總兵), to settle down this territory dispute. Translator Dong was sent to the Jurchen-Manchu state for taking some lands back to the Ming's control (*niohon gvlmahvn aniya ... tere*

---

[425] *Manzhou shilu*, pp. 159-160.
[426] *Manzhou shilu*, pp. 157-162.
[427] *Manzhou shilu*, pp. 164-165.
[428] Manzhou shilu, p. 166.
[429] *Manzhou shilu*, pp. 166-167.

fonde daiming gurun i wan li han guwangning heqen i zung bung guwan hergen i jang qeng yen be jase bitume tuwa seme unggifi jang qeng yen jase bitume tuwafi, amasi bederehe manggi, manju gurun de tungse dung guwe yen be takvrafi hendume meni jasei tulergi suweni tehe babe meni ba obumbi).[430] Furthermore, the Wanli emperor set up a number of stone tablets to occupy many lands beyond his border (*tereqi wan li han babe durime jasei tule ududu bade wehei bithe ilibunjiha).*[431]

Furthermore, the Wanli emperor also sent troops to protect the Yehe tribe. The Yehe leaders, Gintaixi and Buyanggv, took the opportunity and married Buyanggv's sister to the Mongols. The bride had been promised to marry Nurgaqi in the first place. Most of the Jurchen officials suggested a revenge due to the humiliation but Nurgaqi refused (*daming gurun i wan li han qooha unggifi yehe de tuwakiyame tefi, yehei gintaisi, buyanggv, wan li han de ertufi monggo de buhe, te muse nikan be dailaki seme gisureqi, han geli ojorakv ...*).[432] His reasons are that the Jurchens do not have granaries and they cannot support the captives once they were captured. Besides, the old Jurchen people were also dying out of hunger. Therefore, during the time, Nurgaqi ordered to gather the Jurchen people around, consolidate the territories, secure the boundaries, cultivate lands, build granaries and collect grain (*muse de jekui ku akv kai, dailafi baha seme baha niyalma ulha de ulebure anggala, muse fe niyalma hono buqembi kai, ere siden de musei gurun be neneme bargiyaki, babe bekileme jase furdan jafaki, usin weilefi jekui ku gidame gaiki seme hendufi dain deribuhekv*).[433] Thus, one can see that Nurgaqi aimed to accumulate people to build up strength for a greater goal. Instead of attacking the Ming, he sent an army to seize more population from Weji. In the eleventh month, two thousand soldiers were commanded for the assault and obtained some ten thousand people and animals (*omxon biya de taizu kundulen han juwe minggan qooha unggifi dergi mederi weji i aiman qi wesihun... tumen olji baha*).[434]

Shortly after, Nurgaqi was honored by the princes and officials as the Bright Khan (*taizu be geren beise ambasa tukiyeme genggiyen han*

---

[430] Manzhou shilu, p. 172.
[431] Manzhou shilu, p. 174.
[432] Manzhou shilu, pp. 177.
[433] Manzhou shilu, p. 178.
[434] Manzhou shilu, p. 179.

sehe).[435] In the meantime, Nurgaqi unified the surrounding areas and assigned every three hundred men as a company (man. *niru*; chin. *niulu* 牛錄), and every five companies as one regiment (man. *jalan*; chin. *jiala* 甲喇), and every five regiments as one banner (man. *gvsa*; chin. *qi* or *gushan* 旗 或 固 山). Each banner was commanded by a Commander-in-chief (man. *gvsai ejen*; chin. *qizhu* or *dutong* 旗主或都統) and two Vice Commanders-in-chief (man. *meiren i ejen*; chin. *fudutong* 副都統). The previous four banners of yellow, red, blue and white were complemented with four bordered (man. *kubume*; chin. *xiang* 鑲) banners of the same color. In total, eight banners were established (*taizu kundulen han baba be toktobufi ilan tanggv haha de emu nirui ejen sunja niru de emu jalan i ejen, sunja jalan de emu gvsai ejen, gvsai ejen i hashv iqi juwe ashan de emte meiren i ejen sindaha, dade suwayan, fulgiyan, lamun xanggiyan duin boqo tu bihe, duin boqo tu be kubume jakvn boqo tu obufi uheri jakvn gvsa obuha*).[436]

This new military system worked with high efficiency. The scribe described that Nurgaqi commanded the army like a god. Under his leadership, the officers and soldiers all desired to pursue achievements. When hearing news of going to battle, they became excited. They contended with each other to attack cities and charged fearlessly when fighting in fields. Their power was like thunder and lightening. They moved swiftly like wind, crushing enemies in no time (*enduri gese ofi, amban qooha meni meni gung gebu be tuqibuki seme dailambi qoohalambi sehe de urgunjeme. heqen hoton be gaijara de neneme tafara be temxeme talai qooha be afara de juleri dosiki seme fafurxame horon hvsun amban, akjan talkiyan i adali, edun xu i gese dartai andan de etembi*).[437]

On the twenty-first day of the first month in the red-dragon year (1616), when Nurgaqi was fifty-eight years old, the Scholar Erdeni stood on the left side of the throne, announcing the Khan's title as the Bright Khan to Nourish All Lands, and the reigning title as Mandate of Heaven (man. *abkai fulingga*; chin. *tianming* 天命), which dubiously relates to the Confucian teaching of fate (*han i susai jakvn se de fulgiyan muduri aniya aniya biyai iqe de niowanggiyan bonio inenggi... erdeni baksi han i*

---

[435] Manzhou shilu, p. 182.
[436] Manzhou shilu, p. 183.
[437] Manzhou shilu, p. 184.

hashv ergi ashan de ilifi tere bithe be hvlame geren gurun be ujire genggiyen han sefi, aniyai gebu be abkai fulingga sehe).[438] This reign title was not recorded in the "Original Manchu Chronicles", so it must be added in a later time according to the Han Chinese philosophy.

By the end of the year, Nurgaqi sent his two generals and two thousand soldiers to acquire the Sahaliyan tribe in the Eastern Sea. Eleven villages were unified (*manju gurun i taizu genggiyen han, darhan hiya xongkoro baturu juwe amban de juwe minggan qooha be afabufi, dergi mederi sahaliyan i aiman be dailame unggihe... sahaliyan i aiman i juwan emu gaxan be gaifi).*[439] In the following year (1617), four hundred soldiers were sent to the Eastern Sea and collected the people who scattered along the border (*tere aniya duin tanggv qooha be dergi mederi jakarame tefi daharkv samsifi bisire gurun be gaisu seme unggifi, dergi mederi dalin i samsifi tehe irgen be gemu gaifi).*[440]

After unifying the Ming's Fushun and Qinghe, Nurgaqi refocused on Yehe. On the second day of the first month in the fourth year of Abkai Fulingga (1619), the army assaulted Yehe. On the seventh day, the troops penetrated deeply into the Yehe territory, looting from the Niyahan village of Keite fortification to the Yehe fortification's east gate. The Jurchens collected people and animals which were going to enter the fortification, but burned down the villages which located ten *li* (man. *ba*; chin. *li* 里) away from the fortification (*manju gurun i abkai fulingga taizu genggiyen han i sohon honin duiqi aniya aniya biyai iqe juwe de, taizu genggiyen han yehei gurun be dailame genere de... iqe nadan de amba qooha dosifi, keite gebungge hoton, niyaha gebungge gaxan be gidame tabaqin sindafi, yehe gurun i tehe amba heqen i xun dekdere ergi duka de juwan bai dube de isinafi, heqen de dosime genere niyalma ulha be gemu gaifi, heqen qi juwan bai tulergi gaxan i boo be gemu tuwa sindaha).*[441]

After unifying the Ming's Kaiyuan and Tieling, on the nineteen day of the eighth month, Nurgaqi led the officers and soldiers to exterminate Yehe (*taizu genggiyen han bolori dulimbai biyai juwan uyun de, beise*

---

[438] *Manzhou shilu*, pp. 186-187.
[439] *Manzhou shilu*, pp. 190-191.
[440] *Manzhou shilu*, pp. 192-193.
[441] Manzhou shilu, p. 222.

ambasa geren qooha be gaifi yehei gurun be dailame juraka).[442] The Yehe people resisted fiercely, but the Manchus did not retreat. They broke the fortification walls and defeated the defenders (*manju gurun i qooha bedererakv uthai heqen be efuleme uribume tuhebufi ... heqen i duin derei qooha gemu burulafi ...*).[443]

The Yehe tribe perished since then. Up to this year (1619), Nurgaqi expanded his territories from the Eastern Sea to the border of Ming's Liaodong province in the west, stretching from the Nvn River (nenjiang 嫩江) inhabited by the Mongol Khorchin in the north, to the south where the Korean border lies. The scribes remarked that all the Manchu-speaking tribes surrendered and were united into the same state (*yehei gurun tereqi umesi kubuhe, tere aniya manju gurun i taizu genggiyen han dergi mederi qi wasihvn daming gurun i liyoodung ni jase de isitala, amargi monggo gurun i korqin i tehe dube nvn i ula qi julesi solho gurun i jase de niketele, emu manju gisun i gurun be gemu dailame dahabufi uhe obume wajiha)*.[444] Crossley pointed out that Nurgaqi applied his power to reorganize the Jurchen (Manchu) tribes according to their lineage identities as the vessels for war.[445]

In Hong Taiji's reign, Warka, Hvrha, Sahaliyan bira and Sunggari were integrated into the Manchu regime. As we have observed in the previous chapter, the Manchu troops collected households from those remote regions and brought them back to the capital. These new captives were granted with a new identity--Manchu, and together they formed a new community--the Manchu State. Crossley's research affirmed that some Tungusic-speakin groups in remote regions of Northern Asia, such as the Evenks, had been absorbed into the banners by the time of Hong Taiji's death in 1643.[446]

To sum up, three tribes of Weji, Warka and Kvrka are considered as Jurchens in Eastern Sea (Donghai nüzhen 東海女真), which are also named as Wild Jurchens (Yeren nüzhen 野人女真) in the Han Chinese

---

[442] Manzhou shilu, p. 272.

[443] Manzhou shilu, p. 274.

[444] Manzhou shilu, p. 283.

[445] Pamela Kyle Crossley (1999), *A translucent mirror: history and identity in Qing imperial ideology*, University of California Press, Berkeley and Los Angeles, California, pp. 150-151.

[446] Crossley, *A translucent Mirror*, pp. 195-196.

political and academic discourse.[447] The last four tribes in Hvlun Land, Ula, Hada, Yehe and hoifa, are called Haixi Jurchen (海西女真) because they all lived in the valley of Haixi Jiang 海西江, which is today's Songhuajiang (松花江). They are also identified as Four Tribes of Hulun (Hulun sibu 扈倫四部), being adjacent to the Mongols in the west and Ming's Kaiyuan fortification (Kaiyuan shi 開原市) in the South.[448] Furthermore, in Han Chinese documents they also appeared as Haixi Four Tribes (Haixi sibu 海西四部), which were mentioned by the Ming authority as their subordinates. Notably, these titles were not recognized or adopted by the Manchus in their official documents.

4.3 Acquiring Ming Han Chinese Territories

Regarding the Ming's territorial administration, the lowest branches were districts (*xian* 縣), which were supervised by sub-prefectures (*zhou* 州) in some cases, then prefectures (*fu* 府) as a higher authority and finally Provincial Administration Commissions (*buzhenshisi* 布政使司) as the highest.[449] However, Liaodong was a unique territory, which had no institutions of prefectures, sub-prefectures and districts but was governed by the Provincial Administration Commissions in Shandong. Militarily, Liaodong was controlled by a Regional Military Commission (*duzhihuishisi* 都指揮使司), which commanded twenty-five Guards (*wei* 衛) and two sub-prefectures (*zhou* 州).[450] These places were Nurgaqi's targets, which would be taken after he soothed the Jurchen tribes.

---

[447] Yan Chongnian, *Nu'erhachi zhuan*, p. 73.

[448] Yan Chongnian, *Nu'erhachi zhuan*, p. 43.

[449] Charles O. Hucker (1988), *A Dictionary of Official Titles in Imperial China*, Southern Materials Center, Taipei, p. 75.

[450] Yang Yang 楊暘 (1988), *Mingdai liaodong dusi* 明代遼東都司 (The Regional Military Commission of Liaodong in the Ming Dynasty), Zhongzhou guji chubanshe, Zhengzhou, pp. 1-2.

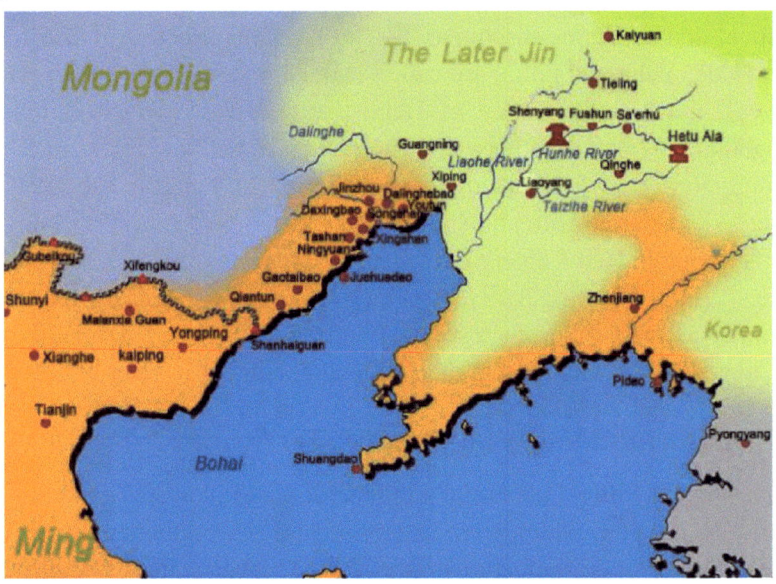

Map 2: Nurgaqi's unification of the Ming's Liaodong region

In the Yellow-monkey year (1608), Nurgaqi wanted to make peace with the Ming's Wanli emperor. Thus he lectured the officials that it takes only a moment to think about evil in a day, but pursuing goodness may take generations and the result is not promised. He wanted to take an oath with the Ming officials in front of the Heaven and Earth for peacemaking, and soon he met the Ming's Vice Regional Commander (man. *fujiyang*; chin. *fujiang* 副將) of Liaodong fortification, which is today's Liaoyang (Liaoyang 遼陽), and the Defence Officer (man. *bei ioi guwan*; chin. *beiyu* 備御), to set up stone tablets. Together they killed a white horse for a sacrifice, pledging that whether Manchus or Han Chinese, whoever crossed the border illegally, must be executed once they are caught. If transgressors were not executed, then the eyewitnesses must be punished. If the Ming Han Chinese broke the covenant, the emperor's Grand Coordinator (man. *dutang*; chin. *dutang* 都堂), Regional Commander (man. *zung bing guwan*; chin. *zongbing guan* 總兵官), the Liaoyang Circuit Intendant (man. *liyoodung ni dooli;* chin. *liaoyangdao* 遼陽道) and its Regional Vice Commander (man. *fujiyang*; chin. *fujiang* 副將), the Kaiyuan Circuit Intendant (man. *kai yuwan i dooli;* chin. *kaiyuandao* 開源道) and its Assistant Regional Commander (man. *canjiyang*; chin. *canjiang* 參將), all these six offices will be penalized. If the Manchus

166

broke the covenant, they would take punishment too. Thereafter, a covenant was made and stone tablets were erected along the border (*suwayan bonio aniya... tere aniya, taizu kundulun han, daiming gurun i wan li han i baru sain banjiki seme geren ambasa i baru hendume, ehe be gvniqi emu inenggi andan de sain doro be udu udu jalin de baiqi baharakv sere muse daiming gurun i emgi, abka na de akdulafi sain banjiki seme gisurefi hodung ni bai liyoodung heqen i fujiyang, fuxun xo hoton i wang bei ioi guwan i emgi aqafi wehe de folome bithe arafi, abka de xanggiyan morin wafi gashvnha tere gashvha bithe i gisun han i jase be nikan manju, yaya hvlhame dabaqi, dabaha niyalma be waha niyalma waki, safi warakvqi, waha akv niyalma de sui isikini, ere gisun be daiming gurun aifuqi, daiming han i guangning ni dutang zung bing guwan, liyoodung ni dooli fujiyang, kai yuwan i dooli canjiyang, ere ninggun amban yamun i hafasa de ehe sui isikini, manju de ehe sui isikini seme wehei bithe be jasei jakarame baba de ilibume gashvha*).[451]

It took Nurgaqi ten years to consolidate his power within the people who speak the same language and to prepare for unification of the Ming's Liaodong province. On the sixteenth day of the first month in the third year of the genggiyen han (1618), two beams of light, one yellow and the other green, charged into the moon. In the early morning Nurgaqi saw those beams and told the princes and officials that he had made up his mind to attack the Ming and nothing can change this decision (*taizu genggyen han i ilaqi aniya, aniya biyai juwan ninggun i qimari tuhere biya i dulin ba be hafu suwayan genggiyen siren goqika bihe... tere siren be safi, han, beise ambasai baru hendume, suwe te ume kenehunjere, mini dolo gvnime wajiha, ere aniya bi ainaha seme nakarakv, daiming gurun be urunakv dailambi seme henduhe*).[452] The reason of going to war, according to Nurgaqi, was that the Ming offended him and caused seven major grudges, besides the uncountable small ones (*han hendume daiming gurun de mini korsohongge nadan amba koro bi, tereqi funqehe buya koro be ya be hedure, daiming gurun be dailaki seme...*).[453]

On the fifteenth day, the army went to besiege Fushun Garrison (man. *fuxun xo*; chin. *fushunsuo* 撫順所) fortification of the Great Ming

---

[451] *Manzhou shilu,* pp. 138-139.
[452] *Manzhou shilu,* pp. 192-193.
[453] Manzhou shilu, p. 195.

(*tofohon i qimari daiming gurun i fuxun xo heqen be kame generede*).[454]
The Manchu soldiers climbed the fortification walls with ladders and
entered the fortification. Li Yongfang, the Mobile Corps Commander,
surrendered immediately (*mangju i qooha heqen de wan sindafi afame
emu erin hono akv heqen de uthai tafaka manggi, li yung fang teni
dahame*).[455]

On the seventeenth day of the fifth month, Nurgaqi led the princes
and officials to attack the Ming. On the nineteenth, the troops entered the
Ming's territory and unified eleven big and small garrisons, including Fu
an pu (Fu'an pu 撫安堡), Hvwa boo qung (Huabaochong 花豹衝) and
San qa el (Sancha'er 三岔兒). On the twentieth, Cui san tun 崔三屯
surrendered, but its neighbouring four garrisons refused to submit, so the
army defeated them (*manju gurun i genggiyen han ini beye geren beise
ambasa be gaifi, daiming gurun be dailame, sunja biyai juwan nadan de,
amba qooha jurafi, juwan uyun de jase dosifi fu an pu, hvwa boo qung,
san qa el pu, amba anjigen uhereme juwan emu pu be afame gaifi orin de
cui san tun pu be dahabuha, tere xurdeme duin pu i niyalma be daha seqi
daharakv ofi, afame gaifi*).[456]

On the twentieth day of the seventh month in 1618, Nurgaqi
commanded the princes, officials and troops to fight the Ming again. The
troops entered the Yahu Pass (Yahuguan 鴉鶻關), besieged and attacked
Qinghe fortification. Regional Vice Commander Zou Chuxian guarded
the fortification with ten thousand soldiers. Circa one thousand
artillerymen fired cannons, and the rest shot arrows, released rollers and
rocks. The Manchu soldiers demolished fortification walls and climbed
up with ladders, without dodging swords and blades. The Han Chinese
soldiers escaped in disorder and the fortification was taken over (*manju
gurun i taizu genggiyen han ini beye geren beise ambasa be gaifi,
daiming gurun be dailame nadan biyai orinde amba qooha jurafi, yahv
guwan furdan be dosifi, qing ho heqen be kafi afara de qing ho heqen be
tuwakiyaha fujiyang hafan zeo qu hiyan tumen qooha be gaifi heqen be
akdulame tuwakiyafi, minggan funqere poo sindame, gabtame wehe
fungkv makdame afara de, manjui qooha uthai heqen be efulefi wan
sindafi tafame, gida jangkv be jailabume bireme fekume dosire jakade,*

---

[454] Manzhou shilu, p. 204.
[455] Manzhou shilu, p. 206.
[456] Manzhou shilu, pp. 214-215.

heqen i duin terei qooha gemu burulafi, manjui qooha heqen be bafafi fujiyang hafan zeo qu hiyan i beye tumen qooha be gemu waha).[457]

The fall of Fushun greatly shocked the Ming court. In the light-yellow lamb year, which is the forty -seventh[458] year of the Ming's Wanli emperor and the fourth year of the Genggiyen han (1619), the Ming's emperor ordered his Regional Commander (man. *zung bing guwan*; chin. *zongbingguan* 總兵官) Du Song 杜松, who is a Yulin person[459] and several commanders for retaliation, with two hundred thousand soldiers to besiege Sarhv (Sa'erhu 薩爾滸) fortification (*sohon honin daiming wan li han i dehi ningguqi aniya, manju taizu genggiyen han i duinqi aniya, wan li han qoohai jiyanggiyun ioi lin i bai zung bing guwan hergen i du sung ... ere geren bithei hafan qoohai jiyanggiyvn sa be manju gurun be urunakv mukiyebu seme orin tumen qooha be afabufi).*[460]

The Ming's army was divided into four routes. Three routes were defeated, and the fourth one, led by Li Rubai and He Shixian, was pulled back by the Grand Minister Commander (man. *jifi bihe dutang*; chin. *jinglüe* 經略) Yang Hao 楊鎬, who resided in Shenyang 瀋陽 for supervision (*tere ilan jugvn i qooha gidabuha be, daiming ni xen yang heqen de jifi bihe dutang yang hao donjifi ambula golofi, qing ho i yahv guwan be tuqike zung bing guwan li ru be, fujiyang ho xi hiyan i qooha be bedere seme niyalma takvrafi li ru be i qooha hvlan i gebungge baqi amasi bedereme genehe be...).*[461]

After the War of Sarhv, the Ming court was no longer able to organize large scales of offense. Ever since, the whole strategic turned into defending the remaining lands and cities. On the opposite, the Later Jin kept attacking. On the tenth day of the sixth month in 1619, Nurgaqi led four hundred thousand soldiers to take Kaiyuan 開原. Before ladders were erected, some Manchu soldiers had already overcome the fortification walls and the Ming soldiers were dispersed (*manju gurun i taizu genggiyen han juwari dubei biyai juwan de, daiming gurun i kai*

---

[457] Manzhou shilu, pp. 216-217.

[458] The Manchu text says "dehi ningguqi aniya" (forty-sixth), which must be a mistake made by the scribes in the first place.

[459] Du Song, one of the Ming's Regional Commander, was a Yulin person, rather than the Regional Commander of Yulin. The scribe must have made a mistake.

[460] Manzhou shilu, pp. 225-226.

[461] Manzhou shilu, p. 252.

yuan heqen be gaime... manju qooha wan sindahakv uthai heqen be dabame dosire jakade, heqen i duin derei qooha gemu burgifi burulaha).[462]

In the same month, Nurgaqi led the princes and officials to unify Tieling 鐵嶺. The Manchu soldiers erected ladders, dismantled fortification walls and entered the fortification. The Ming soldiers scattered *(manju gurun i taizu genggiyen han bolori ujui biya de, beise ambasa geren qooha be gaifi daiming gurun be dailame, tiyei ling heqen be gaime juraka, manju gurun i qooha uthai wan sindafi heqen i keremu be efulefi... heqen i duin dere de iliha qooha gemu burgifi burulaha).*[463]

On the twenty-first day of the eighth month, Nurgaqi led the troops to attack the Ming again. The army entered the territories of Yilu 懿路 and Puhe 蒲河 and the people abandoned their cities. The Manchus stopped to reside *(jakvn biyai orin emu de, manju gurun i taizu genggiyen han beise ambasa geren qooha ber gaifi, daiming gurun be tabqilame, ilu, pu ho i babe dosire de, ilu, pu ho i niyalma heqen waliyafi burulaha bi, tereqi qooha bargiyafi iliha biqi).*[464]

On the tenth day of the third month in 1621, Nurgaqi led his troops to attack Shenyang 瀋陽 fortification (ilan biyai juwan de, taizu genggiyen han, beise ambasa geren qooha be gaifi, daiming gurun be dailame... xen yang heqen be gaime).[465] Three days later, the fortification was unified.

On the eighteenth, Nurgaqi gathered the princes and officials, said that since Shenyang was taken and the enemy was defeated, the troops should take the opportunity to unify Liaoyang (遼陽) fortification as well *(juwan jakvn de, genggiyen han beise ambasai baru hebexeme, ere xen yang ni heqen be afame gaiha, qooha be ambula gidaha, te ere etehe hvsun i uthai amba qooha julesi dosifi liyoo yang heqen be afame gaiki seme hebexeme toktobufi).*[466] The eight banners converged into one, chased and killed the Ming soldiers around the fortification. Meanwhile the Ming's Grand Minister Commander Yuan Yingtai 袁應泰 was supervising the battlefield at the Zhen Yuan Lou 鎮遠樓 in the northeast corner of the fortification. Seeing the fortification was broken, he set fire

---

[462] Manzhou shilu, pp. 259-261.
[463] Manzhou shilu, p. 268.
[464] Manzhou shilu, p. 298.
[465] Manzhou shilu, p. 308.
[466] Manzhou shilu, p. 316.

on the building and burned himself to death. The high officials all died in the disturbance . Zhang Quan 張銓, an Investigating Censor (man. *qa yuwan hergen*; chin. *jiancha yushi* 監察御史), was captured alive. The remaining officials and people all shaved their foreheads and surrendered (*jakvn gvsai qooha aqafi heqen i ninggureme daiming ni qooha be boxome wara de, ging liyoo hergen i iowan ing tai, hergen i xun dekdere amargi hoxoi jen iowan leo sere leosei dele tafufi afara be tuwame bihengge, heqen gaibuha be safi uthai leose be tuwa sindafi buqehe... qa yuwan hergen i jang qiowan weihun jafabuha, tereqi funqehe hafan irgen gemu dahafi*).[467] After Liaoyang was unified, officials and people from circa seventy cities in the east side of the Liaodong river shaved their foreheads and surrendered (*tereqi liyoo yang heqen be baha manggi, liyoodung ni bai birai dergi amba ajigen nadanju funqeme heqen hoton i hafan irgen gemu uju fusifi heqen nisihai waqihiyame dahaha*).[468] This historical even was also recorded in *Qingtaizu wu huangdi shilu* 清太祖 武皇帝實錄 (The Veritable Records of the Forefather Martial Emperor), which specifically identified the cities in the east of the Liao river as Sanhe 三河, Dongsheng 東勝, Changjing 長靜, Changning 長寧, Changding 長定, Chang'an 長安, Chengsheng 長勝, Changyong 長勇, Changying 長營, Jingyuan 靜遠, Shangyulin 上榆林, Shifangsi 十方寺, Dingjiapo 丁家泊, Songjiapo 宋家泊, Zengchizhen 曾遲鎮, Xiyinjiazhuang 西殷家莊, Pingding 平定, Dingyuan 定遠, Qingyun 慶雲, Gucheng 古城, Yongning 永寧, Zhenyi 鎮夷, Qingyang 清陽, Zhenbei 鎮北, Weiyuan 威遠, Jing'an 靜安, Gushan 孤山, Samaji 灑 馬吉, Aiyang 靉陽, Xin'an 新安, Xindian 新甸, Kuandian 寬甸, Dadian 大甸, Yongdian 永甸, Changdian 長甸, Zhenjiang 鎮江, Tangzhan 湯站, Fenghuang 鳳凰, Zhendong 鎮東, Zhenyi 鎮夷, Tianshuizhan 甜水站, Caohe 草河, Weiningying 威寧營, Fengji 奉集, Mujia 穆家, Wujingying 武靖營, Pinglu 平虜, Puhe 蒲河, Yilu 懿路, Xunhe 汛河, Zhonggu 中固, Anshan 鞍山, Haizhou 海州, Dongchang 東昌, Yaozhou 耀州, Gaizhou 蓋州, Xiongyuewushizhai 熊岳五十寨, Fuzhou 復州, Yongningjian 永寧監, Luangu 欒古, Shihe 石河, Jinzhou 金州, Yanchang 鹽場, Wanghaiguo 望海堝, Hongzui 紅嘴, Guifu 歸服, Huanggudao 黃骨島, Xiuyan 岫巖 and Qingtaiyu 青苔

---

[467] *Manzhou shilu*, pp. 325-326.
[468] Manzhou shilu, pp. 328-329.

峪.[469] Many of these names bear good wishes about the life in the frontier, such as east victory, long quietness, long peace, long pacification, long safety, long victory and long bravery, but the final unification belonged to the Jurchens.

After taking Liaoyang, Nurgaqi gathered the princes and officials to discuss whether they should stay or return to their original places. He believed that Liaoyang was a gift from the Heaven but the princes and officials all claimed to go back. Nurgaqi emphasized that if his troops returned, Liaoyang would be recovered and fortified by the Ming Han Chinese; People of the surrounding circuits who had already scattered into mountains and valleys would remain. If the Manchus gave up the acquired lands and returned, they must repeatedly unify these places. Nurgaqi insisted that they should live in the lands given by the Heaven, which is also the intersection where the Ming, Korea and Mongolia connect. The princes and officials all agreed (*taizu genggiyen han geren beise ambasa be isabufi hebexeme hendume, abkai buhe ere liyoo yang heqen de gurime jifi tereo, amasi musei bade bederereo, geren beise ambasa gemu jabume, musei bade amasi bedereki sehe manggi, han hendume, musei bade bedereqi, ere liyoo yang heqen be dasame bekilefi tembi, ere xurdeme golo goloi niyalma alin holo de, samsime ukafi gemu tutambikai, baha bade waliyafi amasi bedereqi, muse jai geli dasame dailambikai, muse abkai buhe bade teki, ere uba daiming, solho, monggo ilan gurun i dulimbai sain ba kai seme henduhe manggi, geren beise ambasa gemu han i gisun mujangga seme jabufi...*)[470]

Nurgaqi's speech marked a crucial change in his understanding of unification. From Sarhv of the Suksuhu tribe, the very first fortification of Nurgaqi's acquisition, to the Ming's Fushun, Qinghe, Kaiyuan, and Tieling, the Jurchen demolished cities, took the captives away,[471] and divided the trophies. Up to this moment, Nurgaqi and his men realized the importance of maintaining their achievements.

---

[469] *Qingtaizu wu huangdi shilu* 清太祖武皇帝實錄 (The Veritable Records of the Forefather Martial Emperor), collected in *Qing ruguanqian shiliao xuanji yi* 清入關前史料選輯 1 (Compilation of Selected Historical Materials before the Qing Entered through Shanhai Pass), vol. 1, compiled by Pan Zhe 潘喆 et al., edtiion Beijing: Zhongguo renmin daxue chubanshe, 1984, p. 369.

[470] Manzhou shilu, p. 331.

[471] Li Xun and Xue Hong ed., *Qingdai Quanshi*, p. 101.

On the first day of the fourth month, Nurgaqi announced that people who lived in the Liaodong province, such as the ones in Dongning Wei 東寧衛, belonged to him in the first place. Now Nurgaqi just took his people and lands back (*ere liyoodung ni bade tehe dung ning wei gurun, mini gurun bihe, mini gurun min ba be bi gaha*).[472] To the people who survived, Nurgaqi said slaughtering them will not bring much benefit and soon all the bounties will be consumed. If they are pardoned to live, many products will be produced from their hands. These products can be used for trade, and all sorts of good fruits and good stuff will be delivered and the benefits would last forever (*wafi gaiha bahangge tere udu, dartai wajimbi kai, ujiqi, suweni gala qi ai jaka gemu tuqimbi, tuqike be dahame, hvda hvdaxara, sain tubihe, sain jaka benjire oqi, tere enteheme tusa kai*).[473]

Nurgaqi was not satisfied with what he had. In 1622, he led the princes and officials to acquire Guangning 廣寧 fortification (*juwan jakvn de, manju gurun i taizu genggiyen han, daiming gurun be dailame guwangning ni heqen be gaime genere de...*).[474] The Ming's Regional Commander Liu Qu 劉渠 resisted with thirty thousand soldiers. The Manchus engaged in the fight before they formed a battle array. The Ming soldiers could not withstand and run away (*daming ni zung bing guwan hergen i lio kioi... ilan tumen qooha gaifi, manjui qooha be naidame jabduburakv uthai afanjiha manggi manju qooha faiwehakv uthai teisu teisu gabtame saqime afame dosire jakade, daiming ni qooha faquhvrafi...*).[475] When it turned dark, Nurgaqi withdrew troops and returned to Xipingpu 西平堡. Ming's defeated soldiers returned to Guangning and reported the situation to the Grand Minister Commander (man. *ging liyoo hergen*; chin. *jinglüe* 經略) Xiong Tingbi 熊廷弼 and Governor (man. *dutang hergen*; chin. *xunfu* 巡撫) Wang Huazhen 王化貞. These two highest officials made a decision to abandon the fortification and run to Shanhaiguan 山海關. The Mobile Corps Commander (man. *iogi hergen*; chin. *youji* 遊擊) Sun Degong 孫得功, who guarded the fortification gate, sent seven people as a delegation to meet Nurgaqi for surrender (*tereqi abka yamjiha manggi, genggiyen han*

---

[472] *Fe dangse*, p. 905.
[473] *Fe dangse*, pp. 907-908.
[474] Manzhou shilu, p. 339.
[475] *Manzhou shilu*, pp. 340-341..

qooha bargiyafi si ping pu de bederefi deduhe. tereqi daiming gurun i burulaha qoohai niyalma guwangning heqen i ging liyoo hergen i hiong ting bi, dutang hergen i wang hvwa jen de... heqen waliyafi burulame genefi, xan hai guwan be dosika, iogi hergen i sun de gung... heqen i duka be jafafi, manju gurun de dahame, nadan niyalma be takvrafi, taizu genggiyen han de dahaki seme jihe manggi...)[476] Afterwards, officials from circa forty cities led their people to yield (*ere uheri dehi funqeme heqen hoton i hafan irgen, meni meni harangga irgen be gaifi gemu dahaha*).[477]

To save the failing situation, the Ming court sent ten thousand troops to Lüshunkou 旅順口, rebuilding the fortification for stationing. Hearing the news, on the fourteen day of the first month in 1625, Nurgaqi ordered three princes to command six thousand soldiers for battling. The army unified and demolished the fortification, slaughtered the soldiers and returned (*daiming gurun i emu tumen qooha quwan i jifi mederi dalin i lioi xun keo i toton be dasafi tehebi seme donjifi, aniya biyai juwan duin de, taizu genggihen han, manggultai beile de ninggun minggan qooha be afabufi unggifi, lioi xun keo hoton be afame gaifi qooha be gemu wafi, hoton be efulefi, tereqi qooha bederehe*).[478]

In the third month, Nurgaqi wanted to move the capital from Dongjing 東京, which is in the east of Liaoyang, to Shenyang. He gathered the princes and officials for a discussion, but they all disagreed based on the ground that Dongjing fortification was recently finished with all sorts of new palaces and offices; besides, dwellings of common people were still under construction, and food may not be sufficient if they move again. Moreover, people were suffering from heavy and frequent labor. But Nurgaqi refused to listen, suggesting that Shenyang's geographical position leads everywhere: to fight the Ming, the army sets off from the place Durbi (du'erbi 都爾弼) and crosses the Liaohe 遼河, they would get on a road that is straight and convenient; To unify the Mongols in the north, it only takes two or three days to reach them; To acquire Korea, the troops can take the Qinghe 清河 road. Furthermore, after moving to Shenyang, from which Hunhe River (man. *hunehe bira*; chin. *hunhe* 渾河) connects Suksuhu River, sufficient woods can float

---

[476] Manzhou shilu, pp. 342-343.
[477] Manzhou shilu, p. 345.
[478] Manzhou shilu, p. 376.

downstream easily for building the palaces and offices. Moreover, for the purpose of traveling and hunting, mountains are nearby with abundant animals. Aquatic animals are easy to access in the rivers. Finally, Nurgaqi made up his mind to move and the rest had to follow. Therefore, on the third day they left Dongjing and stationed in Hupiyi 虎皮驛. On the fourth day they arrived in Shenyang (*manju gurun i taizu genggiyen han dung ging heqen qi, xen yang heqen de guriki seme, beise ambasai baru hebexere jakade, beise ambasa tafualme muse ere dung ging ni heqen be iqe sahafi boo yamun teni araha, irgen i niyalmai boo hono waqihiyame bahara unde kai, te geli ba guriqi irgen jeku ufaraha bi, alaban geli labdu gurun jobombi kai seme tafulara jakade, han marame hendume, xen yang ni ba eiten i arbun i ba, wasihvn daiming gurun be dailafi, durbideri liyooha bira be doofi geneqi jugvn tondo, ba hanqi, amargi monggo gurun be dailaqi, damu juwe ilan inenggi de uthai isinambi, julesi solho gurun be dailaqi, qing ho i jugvn be geneqi, ombi, xen yang ni heqen de teqi, hunehe bira suksuhu birai sekiyen de moo saqifi muke be eyebume gajiqi, boo yamun arara moo duijire moo gemu bahambi, sargara de abalaqi alin hanqi gurgu elgiyen birai butaha inu bahabikai, bi bodofi guriki sembi dere, suwe ainu marambi seme hendufi, ilan biyai iqe ilan de, dung ging heqen qi tuqifi, xen yang heqen de gurime jime hv pi i de dedufi, iqe duin de xen yang heqen de isinjiha*).[479]

Nurgaqi was not satisfied with what he acquired. On the fourteenth day of the first month in the red-tiger year (1626), Nurgaqi commanded the princes and troops to fight the Ming again (*fulgiyan tasha abkai fulinggai genggiyen han i juwan emuqi aniya aniya biyai juwan duin de, taizu genggiyen han gere beise ambasa be gaifi daiming gurun be dailame amba qooha juwafi*)[480] On the twenty third day, the army reached Ningyuan fortification (Ningyuancheng 寧遠城). Nurgaqi released some Han Chinese captives to the fortification, reporting that he led two hundred thousand soldiers to take the fortification, which will be unified inevitably. Nevertheless, if the Ming officials surrendered, they would be granted with high positions. The Circuit Intendant of Ningyuan (man. *heqen i ejen dooli hergen*; chin. *ningyuan dao* 寧遠道) Yuan Chonghuan 袁崇煥 responded that Nurgaqi should not invade this place because these two cities of Ningyuan and Jinzhou 錦州 were despised

---

[479] Manzhou shilu, pp. 377-378.
[480] Manzhou shilu, p. 392.

and abandoned by Nurgaqi in the first place, and later rebuilt by the Han Chinese. Therefore, they would defend to the last moment and will not surrender. Yuan Chonghuan pointed out that Nurgaqi claimed that he had two hundred thousand soldiers, but the estimated figure should be 130,000, which must not be considered as few, though (*orin ilan de amba qooha ning yuwan heqen de isinafi... ning yuwan heqen de jafaha niyalma be takvrame suweni ere heqen be mini orin tumen qoohai afaqi urunakv efujembi kai, heqen i dorgi hafasa suwe dahaqi, bi weisihun obufi ujire, heqen i ejen dooli hergen i yuwan qung hvwan jabume, han ai turgun de uttu holkon de qooha jihe, ginjeo, ning yuwan i babe suwe bahafi waliyaha, be suweni waliyaha babe dasafi tehe, meni meni babe tuwakiyahai buqembi dere, dahaha doro bio, han i qooha orin tumen serengge taxan, aiqi juwan ilan tumen bikai, be inu tere be koso serakv*).[481]

Nurgaqi ordered his soldiers to prepare ladders and armoured vehicles. On the twenty-fourth day, the Jurchen soldiers approached the cities with armoured vehicles. Town walls were broken, big holes appeared, but the walls did not collapse due to the cold weather. The Regional Commander Mangui 滿桂, Circuit Intendant Yuan Chonghuan and the Assistant Regional Commander Zu Dashou 祖大壽 did not fall back but secured the fortification by firing cannons, throwing grenades and rocks. The Jurchens charged without making much advancement. On the following twenty-fifth day, the Jurchen army lost two Mobile Corps Commanders, two Defense Officers and five hundred soldiers (*genggiyen han heqen be afabume qoohai niyalma wan kalka dagilame wajiha manggi, orin duin i inenggi manjui qoohai niyalma heqen de kalka latubufi heqen be efuleme afara de, abka beikuwerefi heqen geqefi, ambula sangga arame efulehe ba urime tuherakv, qoohai niyalma jing afara de, tere heqen i qoohai ejen zung bing guwan hergen i man gui, dooli hergen i yuwan qung hvwan canjiyang zu dai xeo, heqen be bekileme tuwakiyafi buqeme afame emdubei poo sindara, oktoi tuwa maktara wehe fahara afara de manjui qooha afame muterakv bederefi, jai ienggi orin sunja de geli afafi muterakv bederehe, tere juwe inenggi afara de, manju qooha i juwe iogi, juwe bei ioi guwan qoohai niyalma sunja tanggv buqehe*).[482]

[481] Manzhou shilu, p. 394.
[482] Manzhou shilu, pp. 394-395.

Beyond the Shanhai Pass, provisions for the Ming's army were all stored in Juehua Island (Juehuadao 覺華島). On the twenty-sixth day, Nurgaqi ordered Unege to command the Banner Mongol soldiers, combining eight hundred Manchu soldiers, to take the island. The army slaughtered all the residents on the island, burned circa two thousand ships and one thousand stacks of supplies and then returned to the base camp. On the twenty-seventh day, Nurgaqi retreated and set fire to the supplies at Youtunwei 右屯衛. Nurgaqi started this military career since he was twenty-five years old in terms of acquiring lands and cities, but never encountered such a failure, except for Ningyuan. So he returned with great resentment (*orin ninggun de, ning yuwan i heqen i julergi juwan ninggun bai dubede mederi dorgi giyoo hvwa doo gebungge tun de xan hai guwan i tulergi qoohai niyalmai jetere jeku orho be gemu quan i juwefi sindahabi seme donjiqi, taizu genggiyen han jakvn gvsai monggoi qooha i ejen unege de manju qooha jakvn tanggv nonggifi, giyoo hvwa tao be gaisu seme unggifi... juwe minggan funqeme quwan booi gese muhaliyaha minggan funqeme buktan i bele orho be gemu tuwa sindafi, amba qooha de aqanjiha, orin nadan de taizu genggiyen han qooha bedereme, io tun wei jeku be gemu tuwa sindari, juwe biyai iqe uyun de, xen yang heqen de isinjiaha, taizu genggiyen han orin sunja se qi baba be dailame heqen hoton be afaqi bahakv etehekvngge akv, damu ning yuwan heqen be afame bahakv ofi, ambula korsome bederehe*).[483]

On the nineteenth day of the third month in the red-tiger year (1626), a Han Chinese official Liu Xuecheng 劉學成 memorialized that an enterprise starts with man but succeeds with Heaven. Nurgaqi spent less than half a day on seizing Shenyang, and only a day on Liaoyang. The other subdued cities are uncountable. Now two days passed, Ningyuan has not been acquired yet, and the reason is not that, comparatively, people of Liaoyang and Shenyang are fewer and weaker than Ningyuan, or cannons and guns are fewer and powerless. The reason is that since the acquisition of Guangning, cavalries and infantries had not fought for three years. Military officers became indolent and soldiers had no intention for fighting. Moreover, they are unskilled of using chariots, ladders and shields, and weapons were no longer sharp. The Khan considered the unification of Ningyuan as easy so that the Heaven

---

[483] *Manzhou shilu*, pp. 396-397.

agonizes the Khan (*fulgiyan tasha aniya ilan biya juwan uyun de, lio hiyo qeng ni bithe wesimbuhe gisun, weile be deriburengge niyalma, weile muterengge abka kai... jai han, simiyan be inenggi dulin ohakv gaiha, liyoodung be emu inenggi gaiha, liyoodung be emu inenggi gaiha, gvwa heqen ai ton, te ning yuwan be juwe inenggi ainu bahakv, liyoodung, simiyan i niyalma, ning yuwan qi komso budun i haran waka, poo miyooqan, ning yuwan qi komso moyo haran waka, han, guwangning be gaiha qi ebsi, morin yafahan i qooha ilan aniya afahakv, qoohai ejete heolen ohobi, qoohai niyalma afara mujilen akv ohobi, jai sejen wan kalka niyere fangkala, agvra daqun akv, han, ning yuwan be ja tuwara jakade, abka han be suilabuhangge...*).[484] The scribe admitted Nurgaqi's failure, which was attributed to the Heaven's discipline.

Continuously, Liu suggested that it has been an ancient tradition that leaders would employ the guilty people rather than the meritorious. Since the Liaodong people had betrayed the Khan and that makes them guilty, it is better to enlist them for wars than to execute them directly. The strategy of using the Han Chinese to fight the Ming would benefit the Jurchens. Besides, after acquiring lands, it is better to pardon rather than to slaughter them. After taking over Ningyuan, troops should be deployed there, pretending to attack Shanhai Pass (man. *xanaha*; chin. *Shanhai guan* 山海關). Meanwhile the main forces go through Yipianshi 一片石 to attack the capital unexpectedly, striking the enemy when they are not prepared. If so, all the accumulated grains and houses in Tongzhou 通州, and the Tianqi emperor's treasure will be taken over. Otherwise, if attacking Shanhai Pass in usual ways, the army would set fire everywhere from Shanhai Pass to the capital. Jinzhou 錦州, Xingshan 杏山, Tashan 塔山, Lianshan 連山, and Songshan 松山 would burn to ashes, from which no one could benefit. When Liu's memorial entered, Nurgaqi praised it (*julgeqi ebsi, gungge niyalma be takvrarangge, weilengge niyalma be takvrara de isirakv seme henduhebi, liyoodung ni niyalma ukandara ubaxara oqi, weilengge niyalma kai, wafi ainambi, tere be qooha de gamafi, nikan nikan be afaqi, juxen de tusa kai... ba be baha manggi, efulere qi uthai biburengge dele, ning yuwan be baha manggi, ning yuwan de uthai qooha sindafi xanaha be afambi seme yarkiyara, amba qooha i piyan xi deri genehe de, uthai han i heqen de ini gvnihakv*

---

[484] *Fe dangse*, pp. 3281-3288.

de isinambi, jabduhakv be afambi, tuttu oqi, tung jeo i heqen de isabuha jeku, irgen i boo, tiyan ki han i boobei ulin gemu bahambi, tuttu akv xanaha be afafi, emu utu inenggi oho manggi, xanaha qi casi, han i heqen de isitala gemu tuwa sindafi, ginjeo, hing xan, ta xan, liyan xan, sung xan i adali fulenggi ombi, baha seme ai tusa... bithe wesimbure jakade, han saixaha).[485] This memorial must have alerted the Jurchen leaders that they should reevaluate the people and lands that they have unified. Slaughtering the Han Chinese and destroying their cities will cause stronger resistance in the future wars. An effective way of building up an empire is to include different peoples under one regime, so that a higher purpose can be pursued.

After Nurgaqi's death, his son Hong Taiji inherited the throne and continued the warfare for territorial expansion. On the sixth day of the fifth month in 1627, hearing that the Ming Han Chinese were building cities and tilling the lands, Hong Taiji ordered the troops to attack them (*iqe ninggun de, nikan de qooha juraka, waliyaha ginjeo, dalingho, xolingho dasambi, usin tarimbi seme donjifi).*[486] The battle lasted for quite a while. On the eleventh day of the fifth month in 1628, princes Abatai, Yoto, Xoto and the Eight Banner commanders led three thousand cavalries to loot the Han Chinese regions and attack Jinzhou 錦州 under Hong Taiji's command (*juwan emu de, abatai beise, yoto beise, xoto beise, jakvn gvsai ejete de ilan minggan qooha be afabufi, nikan be tabqilabume ginjeo heqen be efulebume unggihe).*[487] On the sixteenth, eight hundred people, horses, oxen and donkeys were captured, Jinzhou, Xingshan and Gaoqiao were attacked, and twenty-one garrisons were destroyed (*juwan ninggun de feksifi, niyalma, morin, ihan, eihen uheri olji ton, jakvn tanggv baha, ginjeo, hing xan, gao kiyoo, ere ilan hoton be efulehe, xi san xan qi ebsi orin emu tai be efulehe).*[488]

During this period, the military operations still concentrated on looting the northern regions of the Ming, including Beijing (*juwan ninggun de, liyang hiyang hiyan qi qooha jurafi, beging heqen i baru jidere de).*[489] Meanwhile, Hong Taiji intended to control the unified

---

[485] *Fe dangse*, pp. 3290-3293.
[486] Fe dangse, p. 3985.
[487] *Fe dangse*, pp. 4185-4186.
[488] *Fe dangse*, pp. 4191-4192.
[489] *Fe dangse*, p. 4636.

lands. On the twenty-first of the fifth month in 1630, eight military men came to report that four cities, Luanzhou 灤州, Yongping 永平, Qian'an 遷安 and Zunhua 遵化 will be discarded (orin emu de, *bebei, songgotu, enggin i emgi jakvn niyalma alanjime, luwan jeo, yung ping, qiyan an, zun hvwa, ere duin heqen be waliyafi jimbi seme alanjiha*).[490] The reason is that prince Amin did not listen to other leaders' advice, and slaughtered all the officials and people in Yongping and Qian'an. Under his command, some troops plundered for treasure, animals and women, and abandoned cities without prioritizing their military duty (*ohakv, marame yung ping, qiyan an i hafan irgen be gemu wafi, ulin, ulha, doholon hehe be dele arafi gaijime, musei qooha be fejile arafi, bargiyafi gaijihakv*).[491] Hong Taiji had to punish Amin in order to earn the support from the Han Chinese. Amin was sentenced to death in the first place, and then was pardoned but imprisoned. All his properties, such as bondservants, treasure, and animals were deprived (... *amba weile de wambihe, wara be nakafi, loo de horiha, ini juxen booi aha, ulin, ulha be gemu gaifi*).[492]

On the twenty-seventh day of the seventh month in 1631, Hong Taiji decided to attack the Ming again. In the following day, he lectured the military generals, "Speaking of palces where we live, such as Shenyang (man. *simiyan*; chin. *Shenyang* 瀋陽) and Liaodong, were they ours? The Heaven gave them to us and then we own them. If we do not fight for the lands, but allow the Han Chinese to build cities and prepare weapons, can we live our life in peace" (*nadan biyai orin nadan de, nikan be dailame ... orin jakvn de, geren qoohai ambasa be isabufi, han hendume, musei tehe simiyan, liyoodung ni ba, musei bao, abka buqi muse baha kai, dailarakv ekisaka biqi, nikan ba na be ibeme hoton heqen arame, qoohai agvra be dasame jabduqi, muse be baibi tebumbio...*)?[493]

On the second day of the eighth month, Hong Taiji ordered his troops to besiege Dalinghe (man. *dalingho*; chin. *dalinghe* 大淩河), which was under construction for half a month according to the words of a Han Chinese captive (*tere inenggi, dalingho i hoton i julergi de, emu nikan be jafafi fonjiqi, dalingho be sahame deribufi hontoho biya oho... tere*

---

[490] *Fe dangse*, pp. 5030-5031.
[491] *Fe dangse*, pp. 5102-5103.
[492] *Fe dangse*, p. 5106.
[493] *Fe dangse*, pp. 5451-5452.

dobori hoton be xurdeme kafi deduhe).[494] After two months of bloodshed, on the twenty-eighth of the tenth month, Zu Dashou 祖大壽, the Ming's Regional Commander, surrendered to Hong Taiji with his remaining soldiers and people in Dalinghe (*daiming gurun i zung bing guwan zu da xeo... se dalingho heqen i geren hafan qooha irgen be gaifi mende dahaha...*). [495] According to Li Xu and Xue Hong's research, the invincible Guan'ning Iron Cavalry (*guan'ning tieqi* 關寧鐵騎), which is the strongest military force of the Ming led by Zu Dashou, now officially joined the Manchus.[496] The loss of the Ming is incalculable because it had taken decades to maintain and develop such a strong army, which finally fell into Hong Taiji's hands. On the twenty-eighth of the sixth month in 1632, the Manchu state made peace with the Ming officials in Xuanfu 宣府 in Shanxi (*orin jakvn de, siowan fu i xen du tang, dung zung bing guwan, doro aqara jalin de beyede alifi manju i emgi doro aqame toktofi*).[497] As Elliott pointed out, the seizure of Dalinghe "served as a springboard" for further acquisition of the remaining Ming cities beyond the Shanhai Pass.[498]

Nevertheless, in the following years, Hong Taiji often sent his army to loot northern frontiers of the Ming, such as Daizhou 代州 in Shanxi.[499] In the second month of 1638 Hong Taiji sent a letter to the Ming officials in Xuanfu 宣府 in Shanxi, declaring that if the Xuanfu officials could open markets for commercial trades, then the Manchus would withdraw from Datong 大同 and Xuanfu to plunder the Liaodong region.[500] In the tenth month, Hong Taiji ordered his troops to attack the Shanhai Pass.[501] A major success did not happen until on the twelfth day of the fourth month in 1642, when the Ming's Tashan fortification 塔山城 crumbled under bombard of Red-coat cannon.[502] Soon Jinzhou 錦州 and Songshan 松山 surrendered. Up to this moment, the Ming's

---

[494] *Fe dangse*, pp. 5464-5465.

[495] *Fe dangse*, pp. 5657-5658.

[496] Li Xun, Xue Hong, *Qingdai quanshi*, p. 300.

[497] *Fe dangse*, p. 6313.

[498] Mark C. Elliott (2001), *The Manchu Way: The Eight Banners and Ethnic Identity in Late Imperial China,* Stanford University Press, Stanford California, p. 93.

[499] Guan Xiaolian et al. (1986), *Qingchu neiguoshiyuan manwen dang'an yibian,* Guangming ribao chubanshe, Beijing, p. 97.

[500] *Qingchu neiguoshiyuan manwen dang'an yibian,* p. 282.

[501] *Qingchu neiguoshiyuan manwen dang'an yibian,* p. 379.

[502] *Qingchu neiguoshiyuan manwen dang'an yibian,* p. 467.

Ningyuan fortification (Ningyuancheng 寧遠城), where Nurgaqi was defeated, stood alone beyond the Shanhai Pass. One year after unifying Songshan, Hong Taiji passed away. The Qing's territorial expansion would restart after the Ming's collapse.

The Manchu Veritable Records concluded Nurgaqi's achievements as subjugating the rebellious with military force, pacifying the obedient with grace, unifying them all, launching punitive expeditions upon the Ming dynasty and acquiring places like Liaodong and Guangning (*taizu genggiyen han fudasihvn ningge be qoohai horon i dailame, ijishvn ningge be erdemui dahabume uhe obufi, daiming gurun be dailame deribufi liyoodung, guwangning ni babe baha*).[503] Most regions in the Liaodong province were subdued by Nurgaqi. Hong Tai pushed the frontier back to Ningyuan, which remained ununified until his demise.

4.4 Allying Mongol Tribes

Regarding the Mongols, Nurgaqi's strategy was to form an alliance. In 1619 Nurgaqi sent a letter to the Khalkha Mongol leaders, accusing them for breaking covenants and looting the amours and other provisions, which Nurgaqi deposited in Kaiyuan fortification (Kaiyuancheng 開原城). Moreover, when Nurgaqi and his soldiers sacrificed their lives to unify Kaiyuan, Tieling and Yehe, the Mongols took the opportunity and snatched their booties away, including grains, population, horses and oxen. "When I took over the cities, did your Mongols join me? Did your Mongols cultivate the lands along with the Han Chinese? You Mongols raise animals, eat meat and wear furs, but my people plow lands and eat grains for a living. We were never one country, but countries with different languages", said Nurgaqi (*suweni monggo geli uttu doro be efuleme mimbe fusihvlame, keyen i hoton de muhaliyafi sindaha uksin, aika jaka be gemu gamahabi, tere jalin de bi umai seme henduhekv, mini beye jobome, mini qoohai niyalma buqeme afafi efuleme gaiha keyen, qilin, yehe i ba i jeku, niyalma, morin, ihan, aika jaka be, gemu suweni monggo ai jalin de gamambi, mini hoton efulere de, suweni monggo mini emgi efulehe biheo, tere usin be suweni monggo emgi aqan weilehe biheo, suweni monggo gurun, ulha be ujime, jali be jeme, sukv be etume banjimbi kai, meni gurun, usin tarime jeku be jeme banjimbi kai, muse*

---

[503] *Manzhou shilu*, pp. 20-21.

juwe, emu gurun geli waka, enqu gisun i gurun kai, suweni monggo gurun uttu doro be efulem, weile arame yabure be, beise suwe sambio, saqi, sambi seme gisun hendufi unggi, sarkv oqi, sain doro be efuleme yabure niyalma be adarame weile arambi, beise suwe sa, bi duin jergi doro jafafi sain banjiki seme bithe unggime niyalma takvraqi).[504]

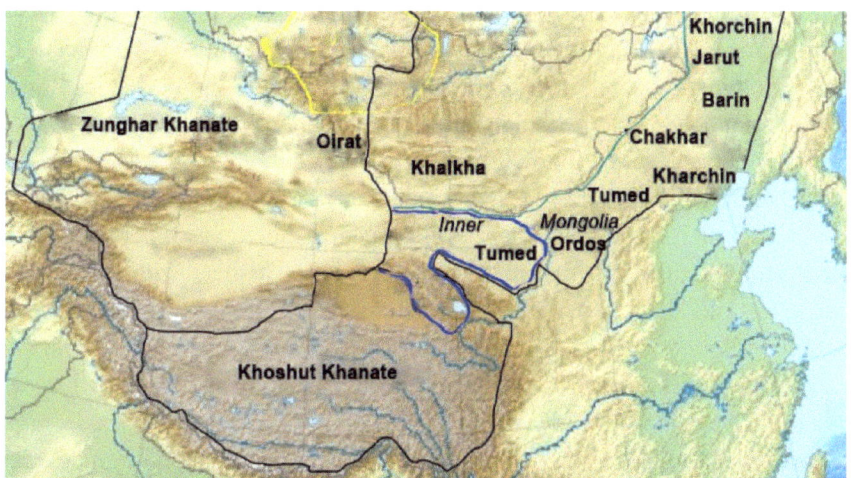

Map 3: Mongol Confederation dated from the seventeenth to the eighteenth century[1]

The conflict with the Mongols dated far back. In the black-rat year (1612), Nurgaqi heard that the Khorchin tribe's leader Minggan has a daughter with exquisite manners, so he sent emissaries for proposal. Minggan sent his daughter to Nurgaqi while declined proposals from other tribes. Nurgaqi held a magnificent wedding to welcome the bride. The scribe interposed a story that his father-in-law, the Mongol prince Minggan, used to join the allies of nine tribes, led by Yehe, to fight Nurgaqi. The allies failed and Minggan escaped on a horse without a saddle. To fix the relationship, now he agreed to marry his daughter to Nurgaqi (*sahaliyan singgeri aniya, taizu kundulen han, monggo gurun i korqin i minggan beilei sargan jui be sain seme donjifi, elqin takvrafi gaiki sere jakade, minggan beile ini sargan jui be da eigen qi hokobufi ini yehe de dafi uyun halai gurun i qooha jihe fonde bontoho morin yalufi burulame tuqike,*

---

[504] *Fe dangse*, pp. 590-593.

*oriqi aniya ini sargan jui be benjire de, taizu kundulen han dorolome
okdofi amba sarin sarilame gaiha).*[505]

unifying Mongols was not an achievable goal in Nurgaqi's time.
Nurgaqi always wanted to ally the Mongols for the unification of Ming
and he always kept a clear mind. In the green-snake year (1605), Engeder,
son of Darhan Baturu from Bayot tribe of Khalkha Mongols, presented
twenty horses as tribute. Nurgaqi considered this tribute as a supplication
for something back because the Mongols had traveled long distance and
went around their enemies. Therefore, he abundantly rewarded Engeder.
In the red-horse year (1606), Engeder guided envoys of five tribes from
the Khalkha Mongols to pay tribute of camels and horses, and honored
Nurgaqi as the Kundulen Khan, which means the Revered Khan. Since
then Mongols from many places come to pay respect (*niohon meihe
aniya,1605 ... tere aniya monggoi kalkai bayot tatan i darhan baturu
belei jui engeder taiji orin morin benjime hengkileme jihe manggi, taizu
sure beile hendume, tain i gurun be duleme bahaki seme jihebidere seme
hendufi, ambula xangname bufi unggihe, fulgiyan morin aniya, jorgon
biyade, ineku enggeder taiji monggo gurun i sunja tatan i kalkai geren
beisei elqin be gajime teme morin benjime hengkileme jifi, taizu sure
beile be tukiyeme kundulen han sehe, tereqi babai monggo lakqahakv
aniya dari hengkileme yabuha).*[506]

An applicable strategy for alliance is marriage and Nurgaqi faithfully
carried it out till the end of his life. In the year of the dark green tiger
(1614), on the fifteenth day of the fourth month, prince Jongnon from the
Jarut Mongol tribe married his daughter to Nurgaqi's second son Guyeng
baturu prince. Guyeng received them with a magnificent banquet and
great manners. On the twentieth day, Neiqi Khan from the Jarut Mongol
tribe married his daughter to Nurgaqi's third son Manggvltai. Soon after,
prince Manggvz from the Khorchin Mongol tribe married his daughter to
Nurgaqi's fourth son Hong Taiji, who received the guests in Hvrki
Mountain fortification of the Hoifa tribe, with great manners and
banquets (*niowanggiyan tasha aniya duin biya tofohon de monggo gurun
i jarut tatan i jongnon beile ini sargan jui be taizu kundulen han i jaqin
jui guyeng baturu beile de sargan benjire de guyeng baturu beile okdome
genefi dorolome amba sarin sarilame gaiha, orin de monggo gurun i*

---

[505] Manzhou shilu, p. 148.
[506] Manzhou shilu, pp. 124-126.

jarut tatan i neiqi han i non be taizu kundulen han i ilaqi jui manggvltai
beile de sargan benjire de manggvltai beile okdome genefi dorolame
amba sarin sarilame gaiha, monggo gurun i korqin i manggvz beilei
sargan jui be taizu kundulen han i duiqi jui beile de sargan benjire de,
(hong taiji) beile okdome genefi hoifai gurun i tehe hvrki hadai hoton i
bade aqafi dorolome amba sarin sarilame gaiha).[507]

In the year of light red snake (1617), in the first month, Nurgaqi took
another daughter of Mongol prince Minggan as his wife. In the second
month, princess Sundai, a daughter of his younger brother Darhan Baturu,
was married into Endeger taiji of the Mongol Khalkha Bayot tribe *(taizu*
genggiyen han i jai aniya fulahvn meihe, aniya biya de monggo gurun i
korqin i minggan beile ini sargan jui be benjihe... juwe biya de, monggo
gurun i kalkai bayot tatan i enggeder taiji de taizu genggiyen han i deo
darhan baturu beilei sargan jui sundai gege be bufi hojihon obuha).[508]

On the twenty-second day of the tenth month in 1619, Lindan Khan
of the Mongol Chakhar tribe sent his emissary Kangkai Baihv to deliver a
letter. In the name of Genghis Khan, the lord of four hundred thousand
Mongols, Lindan Khan greeted Nurgaqi, the lord of thirty thousand
people who live in a riverside. Lindan Khan confirmed that the Ming
used to be an enemy to both of them, but now the situation is different.
Lindan Khan heard that since the year of the horse (1618) the Jurchens
had troubled the Ming; from the summer of the year of the Lamb (1619),
he went to Guangning, summoned the Han Chinese to surrender and
collected tribute. "If you sent soldiers to Guangning," Lindan Khan said,
"I will stop you. We never had grudges, but if you snatch away the
fortification which has surrendered to me, where would my reputation be?
If you do not take my words, then only the Heaven would judge the right
and wrong between you and me" *(juwan biyai orin juwe de, monggo*
gurun i qahar i lindan han i elqin, kalkai sunja tatan i geren beisei elqin
jihe, lindan han i elqin kangkal baihv gebungge amban i gajiha bithei
gisun, dehi tumen monggo gurun i ejen baturu qinggiz han i bithe mukei
ilan tumen manjui ejen genggiyen han jilgan akv sain i tehebio seme
fonjime unggihe, daiming gurun muse juwe gurun de gemu bata kimun
bihe, morin aniya qi ebsi, daiming gurun be sini jobobuha be bi donjiha,
ere honin aniya juwari, mini beye genefi, daiming ni guwangning ni

---

[507] *Manzhou shilu,* pp. 169-171.
[508] *Manzhou shilu,* pp. 192-193.

heqen be dahabufi alban gaifa, te si guwangning ni heqen de qooha genehe de, simbe bi tookabumbi, muse juwe nofi dain akv bihe, mini dahabuha gurun be sinde gaibuha de, mini gebu ai ombi, mini ere gisun be gaijirakv oqi, muse juwe nofi waka uru be abka sambidere).[509]

At the time, Nurgaqi was not strong enough to compete against the Lindan Khan. When the Mongol emissaries returned, he only responded with some harsh words (*unggire fonde muse karu ehe gisun i bithe arafi unggiki seme hendufi*).[510]

Meanwhile the Mongol prince Joriktu Hvng baturu from the Khalkha tribe consulted with the princes from five Khalkha tribes and wrote a letter to Nurgaqi. The Mongols admitted that Jaisai, one of the Khalkha leaders, indeed committed crimes for attacking the Jurchens and he was wrong. However, Nurgaqi's real enemy was the Ming and if Nurgaqi attacks the Ming, the Mongols will join him and directly charge to Shanhai Pass. If they did not keep the words, the Heaven and gods would make a judgement (*kalkai joriktu hvng baturu beile ujulafi geren beisei unggihe bithei gisun genggiyen han de jaisai udu udu jergi weile arahangge waka mujangga, tere be han sa, batangga daiming gurun be dailaqi, emu hebei xan hai de isitala dailaki, ere gisun de isiburakv niyalma be, abka fuqihi sakini).*[511]

On the first day of the eleventh month, Nurgaqi sent five officials, Ekesingge, Qohur, Yahiqan, Kvrqan, and Hife, to consult with the princes of the five Khalkha tribes. In front of Heaven and Earth, a covenant was made between Nurgaqi, Manchu princes of ten banners and the princes of the five Khalkha tribes. If wars broke out between the Ming and either of them, the Manchus and Mongols should make concerted efforts against the Ming (*omson biyai iqe inenggi kalkai sunja tatan i geren beisei elqn i emgi manju gurun i genggiyen han i elqin ekesingge, qohur, yahiqan, kvrqan, hife, ere sunja amban de gasahvre bithe jafabufi, kalkai sunja tatan i geren beisei emgi doro aqafi emu hebei banjiki seme unggihe... genggiyen han i juwan gvsai doro jafaha beise, monggo gurun i sunja tatan i kalkai doro jafaha beise, meni juwe gurun be, abka na gosifi doro jafafi, emu hebei banjikini seme aqabuha dahame, abka na de gashvmbi,*

---

[509] Manzhou shilu, pp. 283-284.
[510] Manzhou shilu, p. 285.
[511] Manzhou shilu, p. 285.

daqi kimungge daiming gurun be emu hebei dailambi, yaya fonde daiming gurun de aqafi, gisurefi emu hebei aqambi).[512]

In the fifth year of the Genggiyen Han's Mandate of Heaven (1620), on the seventh day of the first month, Nurgaqi sent a letter to the Chakhar Lindan Khan, pointing out that his military force is less than thirty thousand people. Furthermore, Nurgaqi proposed that they should work together to fight their common enemy, the Ming (*abkai fulinggan genggiyen han i sunjaqi aniya xanggiyan bonio niyengniyeri ujui biyai juwan nadan de, qahar i lindan han i unggihe bithe karu, unggihe bithei gisun, qahar i han sini unggihe bithe de... ilan tumen gurun akv bime... muse de kimungge daiming gurun be dailaki).*[513] However, after reading the letter, Lindan Khan did not agree and imprisoned Nurgaqi's emissary into Baising fortification (*qahar i lindan han tuwafi, elqin genehe soxe ubasi be jafafi guwangse sangse etubufi, nini baising ni tehe hoton de horiha).*[514]

The Khalkha Mongols did not abide their covenant. In 1621, when Nurgaqi took over Shenyang, four Khalkha princes, Joriktu, Darhan, Bagadarhan, and Sirhvnak, led two thousand cavalries, took the advantage and robbed treasure and grain from Shenyang (*juwan uyun de monggo gurun i kalkai joriktu beilei, darhan baturu, bagadarhan beile, sirhvnak beile, tere duin beilei harangga juwe minggan funqere niyalma, manju gurun i amba qooha dosifi, xen yang heqen be gaiha seme donjifi, xen yang heqen i ulin jeku be gaiki).*[515]

Situation changed a little in the next year, after Nurgaqi had acquired Guangning. Minggan and the other sixteen princes from the Urut Mongol tribe, along with the chieftains of Khalkha tribes, submitted themselves and some three thousand households with animals to Nurgaqi (*juwan ninggun de monggoi urut gurun i minggan... ere juwan nadan beile, kalkai babai taiji meni meni hargangga juxen irgen ilan minggan funqeme boigon adun ulha be yooni gajime ubaxame jihe manggi).*[516] To stabilize the relationship, Nurgaqi lectured the Mongols in his banquet of welcome. He said, "Our Manchu people's custom is to value faithfulness

---

[512] Manzhou shilu, pp. 285-286.
[513] Manzhou shilu, pp. 291-292.
[514] Manzhou shilu, p. 292.
[515] *Manzhou shilu*, pp. 329-330.
[516] Manzhou shilu, p. 347.

and obey the law. You Mongols hold prayer beads, pray to Buddha but constantly rob and cheat. Therefore, the Heaven condemned you and now you surrender to me and your submission earns you some merits. Those who have capabilities will be treated well and those who do not will be taken care of. Do not hold evil intentions..." (*taizu genggiyen han yamun de tuqifi amba sarin sarilaha, han ubaxame jihe monggoi beise be taqibume hendume, meni gurun i banjire doro, tondo akdun xajin i jurgan be jafafi... suweni monggo gurun i niyalma gala de erihe jafafi fuqihi be hvlambime, hvlha holo be nakarakv banjire be, abka wakalafi... suwe mimbe baime jihe dahame erdemungge sain niyalma oqi, erdemui gung de ujire, erdemu akv niyalma oqi, jihe gung de sain ujire, hvlha holo ehe mujilen be ume duribure...*).[517]

Nurgaqi's goal is to form an alliance with the Mongols and he resorted to wars when it was necessary. In the past, prince Angga of the Jarut tribe intercepted the Manchu emissaries and delivered them to Yehe for execution. Moreover, he killed Manchu emissaries who went to other Mongol tribes and captured their animals. Nurgaqi resented and on the fourteenth day of the fourth month in 1623, he ordered chieftain Abatai to command three thousand soldiers for a punitive expedition upon the Jarut. The Manchu soldiers killed Angga and his son, captured their wives, children, soldiers, people and animals and then returned (*dade monggoi kalkai jarut tatan i angga beile, manju gurun i taizu gengiyen han i takvraha elqin be jafafi, batangga yehei gurun de bufi waha, jai amargi monggoi beise de takvraha elqin be jugvn tosofi ududu jergi wafi, adun ulha be durime gaiha, tede taizu genggiyen han korsofi, abatai taiji ... ilan minggan qooha afabufi duin biyai juwan duin de, angga beile be dailame unggifi... tereqi manju gurun i qooha birame dosifi, angga beile ama jui geren qooha be gemu muhaliyame wafi, juse sargan, juxen irgen, adun ulha be gemu gaiha, jai jongnon beilei jui sangtu taiji juse sargan be gemu baha, tereqi duin beile qooha bedereme isinjire de*).[518]

In the war, Sangtu, a leader of Jarut, escaped and left his family behind. Nurgaqi sent emissaries to inform Sangtu that his family was not hurt or insulted and Sangtu came to surrender. Nurgaqi released his wife and children and allowed them to leave for reunion (*han i elqin unggi sehe manggi, tereqi genggiyen han, sangtu sini juse sargan be umai*

---

[517] Manzhou shilu, pp. 383-384.
[518] *Manzhou shilu,*, pp. 355-356.

neiqihekv yooni asarahabi seme elqin takvraha manggi, sangtu henkileme jidere jakade, sangtu i juse sargan be gemu bufi unggihe)[519]

In Nurgaqi's opinion, the Mongol people are like clouds, which join together to form rain. The Mongol tribes gather to form a military force, but they also disperse like clouds and the rain would stop too. "When they disperse," Nurgaqi said, "we shall unify them immediately" (*tere inenggi abka agara de, genggiyen han hendume, monggo gurun i banjirengge, ere agara tuki adali kai, tuki isaqi aga agambi, monggo aiman aqafi qooha ilimbi, monggo aiman aqaha qooha fakqarangge, tuki fakqafi aga galadara adali kai. ini aiman aqaha qooha fakqaha manggi, muse ini songko be dahalame emdubei gaiki seme henduhe, tereqi bedereme*).[520]

Among the Mongol tribes, Khorchin was a faithful alliance. Prince Konggor married his daughter to chieftain Ajige (*juwan nadan de, monggoi korqin i konggor beilei sargan jui be benjime jidere de... ajige taiji de sargan bume amba sarin sarilaha*).[521] For couples of years, the Manchus sent emissaries to Khorchin for maintaining a strong covenant. Both the Manchus and Khorchin Mongols were bullied and humiliated by the Chakhar Mongols, and thus they pledged in front of the Heaven and Earth to form a single mind for retaliation (dade manju gurun i taizu genggiyen han, monggo korqin i beise de elqin takvrame, korqin i beisei elqin kemuni jime ududu aniya oho manggi, taizu genggiyen han elqin takvrafi bithe unggifi korqin i beisei baruakdulame doro aqaki sere jakade... manju korqin meni juwe gurun be qahar fusihvlara de, korsome meni juwe gurun emu hebei banjiki seme akdun gisun be gisureme abka na de gashvmbi).[522]

Regarding the Khalkha Mongols, Nurgaqi allied with the five tribes in order to fight or make peace with the Ming at the same time. Later those Khalkha princes betrayed the covenant and reconciled with the Ming in secret. They also killed the Jurchen frontier guards, chopped their heads off and delivered them to the Ming for rewards. Furthermore, they robbed treasure and animals from the Manchu emissaries. On the fourth day of the fourth month in 1626, Nurgaqi commanded princes,

---

[519] Manzhou shilu, p. 358.
[520] Manzhou shilu, pp. 356-357.
[521] Manzhou shilu, p. 358.
[522] Manzhou shilu, pp. 366-367.

officials and troops to attack some of the Khalkha tribes (*manju gurun i taizu genggiyen han dade, monggo i sunja tatan i kalkai beisei emgi abka na de akdulame, daiming gurun be dailaqi, emu hebei dailambi, aqaqi, emu hebei aqambi seme gashvha bihe, sunja tatan i kalkai beise gashvha gisun be gvwaliyafi, daiming gurun de aqafi emu hebe ofi, manju gurun i taizu genggiyen han i jasei tai niyalma be wafi uju faitafi daiming gurun de benefi, ulin xang ambula gaiha, taizu genggiyen han i takvraha elqin i ulha ulin be ududu jergi durime gaime, taizu genggiyen han de eherere jakade, duin biyai iqe duin de, taizu genggiyen han beise ambasa geren qooha be gaifi, sunja tatan i kalkai monggo be dailame jurafi...*).[523] This military act can be interpreted as the diversion of Nurgaqi's anger upon some Mongols due to Nurgaqi's failure in taking over Ningyuan two months ago.

The army marched in the night of the sixth day and on the seventh, the troops were divided in the eight routes to attack. The vanguards, led by Hong Taiji, Amin, Ajige and Xoto, reached a village owned by Nangnuk, who was the youngest son of Yehe baturu from the Khalkha's Barin tribe. Nangnuk abandoned the village and fled with a few men. The Manchu princes chased after them and Nangnuk fought back on the horse back. Hong Taiji shot Nangnuk to death and the army took over the surrounding villages and their animals. On the ninth day, Nurgaqi ordered the Big Prince, Amin and Hong taiji to command ten thousand cavalries, going to Sira Muren to collect captives (*iqe ninggun i dobofi dulifi, iqe nadan i qimari abka gereme, geren qooha jakvn jurgan i adari fekesime, julergi qoohai (hong taiji) beile, amin beile, ajigen taiji, xoto taiji, neneme kalkai barin i tatan i yehe batutu beilei fiyanggv jui nangnuk beilei gaxan de isinafi, nangnuk beile udu guqu be gaifi booqi tuqifi burulame nukqike, amargi qi manjui qooha i beise amqame jimbi, nangnuk beile jing afaralame burulame genere de, amargi qi emu beile holkon andande isinjifi, nangnuk beilei gala bethe axxame jabdunggala, emu sirdan i gabtame morin qi tuhebuhe tere nangnuk beile be wahangge, taizu genggiyen han i duiqi jui [hong taiji] beile, tereqi amba qooha siran siran i isinjifi, tere xurdeme babai gaxan be gemu gaifi, adun ulha be bargiyame isabufi, iqe uyun de, amba beile, amin beile, [hong taiji]*

---

[523] Manzhou shilu, pp. 400-401.

beile ... emu tumen siliha sain qooha be afabufi, sira muren i ergi de genefi irgen biqi gaisu...).[524]

The three princes crossed Sira Muren river and acquired countless animals before they returned (*sirame manggvltai beile jakvn gvsai qooha ejete de juwe minggan qooha afabume... sira muren i bira be doofi, adun ulha be daliqi wajirakv bahafi...*).[525]

On the second day of the fifth month, Laban Tabunang from the Khalkha's Barin tribe, along with his brother Delger, came to surrender with circa one hundred families. Meantime Nurgaqi rewarded his warriors with the captured people and animals, which numbered 56,500 (*iqe juwe de, monggoi kalkai barin i tatan i gurbusi beilei laban gebungge tabunang ini deo delger be gaifi, emu tanggv boigon be gaijime ukame jime, taizu genggiyen han i qooha de dosinjiha tereqi taizu genggiyen han baha sunja tumen ninggun minggan sunja tanggv olji ulha be geren ambasa qoohai niyalma de jergi bodome xangnaha*).[526]

Up to now, the Khorchin tribe came for alliance on their initiative. On the sixteenth day of the fifth month in 1626, Ooba hvng taiji of the Khorchin tribe came to pay respect. Because Ooba is the prince with the highest rank in the tribe, Nurgaqi ordered Manggvltai and Hong Taiji to receive him. After three days of journey, they met at Jung Gu fortification, which is subordinate to Kai Yuan. After the ceremony, the Manchu hosts held a banquet. On the nineteenth, Ooba repaid the hosts with a banquet at the place named Fan ho. On the next day, the hosts treated the Mongols with another feast. On the twenty-first day, hearing that Ooba was coming, Nurgaqi visited his ancestral temple and traveled ten *li* to meet him (*juwan ninggun de monggoi korqin i ooba hvng taiji, taizu genggiyen han de hengkileme jimbi seme donjifi, genggiyen han ooba hvng taiji be enqu gurun i emu ujulaha beile seme han i jui manggvltai beile, [hvng taiji] beile, geren taijisa be goro okdome unggifi, ilaqi inenggi kai yuan heqen i harangga jung gu qeng heqen de ooba hvng taiji be acafi okdoko beise, ooba hvng taiji ishunde tebeliyeme aqafi, amba sarin sarilaf, juwan uyun de fan ho bigan de isijiha manggi, ooba taiji ini gajiha ihan hvnin wafi okdoko beise de sarilaha, jai inenggi okdoko beise geli karu sarilaha, orin emu de, ooba hvng taiji be isinjimbi seme alajiha manggi, genggiyen*

---

[524] Manzhou shilu, pp. 401-402.
[525] Manzhou shilu, p. 402.
[526] Manzhou shilu, pp. 402-403.

han ooba hvng taiji be okdome tangse de hengkilefi, juwa bai dubede okdofi ...).[527]

Ooba, Hvhodai and Baisgal presented black mink fur, fur coats, horses and camels as gifts and said that tributaries were humble because Chakhar and Khalkha soldiers looted their possessions. Nurgaqi answered, "Those two tribes were greedy and they naturally come to loot. This is an obvious thing. It is fortunate that we could meet today without being killed." Then they attended a great banquet (*ooba hvng taiji, hvhodai taiji baisgal taiji gajiha sahaliyan seke, sekei jibaqa dahv, morin temen be han de alibume hendume, qahar kalka mende dain jifi meni aika jaka be gemu gamaha, han de sain jaka be bahafi gajihakv, genggiyen han hendume, qahar kalka bahaki seme jihe niyalma esi gamaqi, tere be aiseme hendumbi, musei beye sain aqaqi tetendere seme hendufi, amba sain sarilame wajiha manggi).*[528]

On the sixth day of the sixth month in 1626, Nurgaqi ordered to kill a white horse and a black ox and pledged with Ooba. The oath said that they lived a righteous life but were abused by the Ming, the Chakhar and Khalkha tribes. Therefore, they came to the Heaven for indictment. Meanwhile, a horse and ox were killed and the two leaders made a covenant at the riverside of Hunehe, burning incenses and presenting the sacrifice. Nurgaqi led Ooba to kneel three times and kowtow nine times, read two drafts to the audience and burned the drafts (*ninggun biyai iqe ninggun de, korqin i ooba hvng taiji buru, doro jafame abka de xanggiyan morin na de sahaliyan ihan wame, manju gurun i genggiyen han i gashvha gisun, mini tondo banjire be daiming gurun, monggo gurun i qahar kalka gidaxara akabure de, bi dosorakv ofi, abka de habxara jakade... gashvre de hunehe birai dalin de, xanggiyan morin, sahaliyan ihan wafi, hiyan dabufi, yali be gemu dobofi, genggiyen han ooba hvng taiji be gaifi ilan jergi niyakvraha, uyun jergi hengkilehe, juwe bithe be geren de donjibume hvlafi deijihe).*[529]

Because Ooba resisted the enemies alone, Nurgaqi bestowed him with a title of Tuxiyetu Khan (*ooba hvng taiji tuxafi alime gaifi afaha seme tuxiyetu han seme gebu buhe...).*[530] Up to this moment, Nurgaqi

---

[527] Manzhou shilu, pp. 404-405.
[528] Manzhou shilu, pp. 405-406.
[529] Manzhou shilu, pp. 407-409.
[530] Manzhou shilu, p. 409.

attained one of his largest achievements, which is the alliance with the Khorchin Mongols. As a collateral relative of the royal family of the Yuan dynasty, the Khorchin Mongols were subordinate to the Chakhar tribe.[531] Because of the conflicts between these two Mongol tribes, Nurgaqi took the advantage and formed alliance with one of them. Crossley's research confirmed that Nurgaqi's khan rank was closely related to the Khorchins by incorporating them into his regime.[532]

On the twenty-second day of the sixth intercalary month of the red-tiger year (1626), Nurgaqi sent a letter to Vljeitu Daiqing of the Jarut tribe, suggesting that if the Mongols have an honest intention, then the two countries should attack the Ming together, unify and divide the cities for taxation. Or else, the Mongols can deliver captives to the Manchus, who will make them produce silk, satin embroidery, Maoqing cloth (man. *moqin*; chin. *maoqing bu* 毛青布) and blue cloth. This would be a good idea, too. But the Mongols did not think this way but helped the Ming, which was condemned by the Heaven. "Being my enemy is your stupidity", said Nurgaqi. "The Heaven considers me as righteous and thus bestows me with the lands stretching from the Eastern Sea to the west, from Shanhai Pass to the north, including Yehe, Hada, Ula, Hoifa, Guangning and Liaodong. If you do not see it with your eyes, don't you hear with your ears? Now, if the two of us collude, fight the same enemy, and acquire the enemy's wealth, wouldn't it be good? If you do not agree, so we fight against each other, wouldn't we be confined to a small place? It is our stupidity to help strangers but leave our children into conflicts" (*fulgiyan tasha aniya anagan i ninggun biyai orin juwe de, jarut i vljeitu daiqing de unggihe bithei gisun, gengyiyen han hendume, monggo suwe unenggi oqi, muse juwe gurun emu hebei nikan be dailafi, hoton heqen be gaifi nisiha nixihai dendefi alban gaime banjiqi inu ombihe, akvqi, musei bade gajifi, suje, gequheri, moqin samsu jodobume banjiqi, inu sain bihe, suwe ubabe gvnirakv, elemangga abkai wakalaha batangga nikan de dafi, minde dain ohongge, suwe inu farhvn kai, abka mimbe uruxefi, dergi mederi qi wasihvn, xanaha qi ebsi, yehe, hada, ula, hoifa, guwangning, liyoodung ni ba babe siran siran i abkai bure be, suweni yasai sahahvn, xan i donjihakvn, te biqibe, muse juwe gurun hebe aqafi dain gurun be dailame, batangga gurun i ulin be gaime antaka, ere be gvnirakv, musei*

---

[531] Li Xun and Xue Hong, ed., *Qingdai quanshi*, p. 206.
[532] Crossley, A translucent mirror, p. 143.

dolo temxenume dain oqi, emken urhurakv doro bio, weri weile de dafi juse omosi de dain be werirengge, muse inu farhvn kai).[533]

When this letter was sent off, Nurgaqi's life was closer to the end. On the twenty-third day in the seventh month, he fell ill and went to a hot spring in Qinghe (*fulgiyan tasha aniya nadan biyai orin ilan de, han beye nimeme, niowanggiyaha i halhvn muke de genefi).*[534] On the eleventh day of the eighth month in 1626, Nurgaqi passed away in the nominal age of sixty-eight (*abkai fulingga banjiha taizu genggiyen han fulgiyan tasha aniya, juwan biyai juwan emu de, xanggiyan indahvn inenggi honin erin de urihe, soorin de juwan emu aniya tehe, ninju jakvn se bihe).*[535] Before his death, one can see that his ambition was still to ally the Mongols for the unification of the Ming, taking over its land, people, and wealth.

Nurgaqi's efforts were well repaid in the following years. In Hong Taiji's reign, the Manchus successfully integrated the Chakhar Mongols, which is roughly today's Inner Mongolia, into their regime. Hong Taiji spent the first five years (1627-1631) to loot the Ming's northern frontiers and unified the Dalinghe fortification in the Liaodong province. From the sixth year of the Sure Khan (1632), he shifted his focus to subjugate the Mongols. On the first day of the fourth month of the year, Hong Taiji launched large scales of military operations to attack Chakhar (*tere biyai iqe inenggi, qahar be dailame amba qooha axxara de...).*[536] The army traveled long distance across the northern grasslands, and on the tenth day of the fifth month, vanguard Losa sent people to report that Chakhar had fled away and there was no trace detected (*juwan de, juleri genehe loosa songko akv, cahar burulame genehebi seme niyalma takvrafi mejige alanjiha).*[537] On the eleventh day, Hong Taiji met the First Chieftain (man. *amba beile*; chin. *da beile* 大貝勒), prince Manggvltai and other princes. They summoned the Eight Banner officials, Mongol officials, and the Han Chinese officials. Hong Taiji announced that they came to attack Chakhar, which did not resist but escaped. The troops could not catch them. After a group discussion, the officials answered that since the army had entered the Ming territory, they shall attack the

---

[533] *Fe dangse*, pp. 3331-3333.
[534] *Fe dangse*, p. 3334.
[535] Manzhou shilu, pp. 414-415.
[536] *Fe dangse*, p. 6084.
[537] *Fe dangse*, pp. 6191-6192.

Mongol Baising area (man. *baising*; chin. *baixing* 拜興) and then returned to the Ming territory for a bigger success. The final goal is to unify the Ming (*tere inenggi, han i jakade amba beile, manggvltai beile, geren beise aqafi, jakvn gvsai ambasa, monggo i ambasa, nikan i ambasa be gemu isabufi, han hendume, muse qahar be jorime jihe, qahar alihakv burulafi aqahakv... tere geren ambasa hebdefi jabume, emgeri hanqi jihe be dahame, baising de genefi nikan de dosifi umesi amba weile be mutebume yabuqi sain kai seme jabuha, tereqi nikan i baru dosime toktoho*).[538]

On the first day of the sixth month in 1632, Dayaqi Tabunang and the other commanders who went to attack the Shahukou frontier (man. *xurgei duka*; chin. *shahukou* 殺虎口) and Baising reported that the Mongols had fled to the Ming's Shahukou (*dayaqi tabunang, korqin i ukxan, manjusiri be gamame nikan jasei xurgei dukai teisu i baising de tabqin genefi, tere ba i monggo burulafi nikan i jasei xurgei hoton de dosikabi seme alanjiha manggi...*).[539] After negotiations with the Ming officials, the Manchus retrieved the Mongol populations and treasure, which are depicted in the previous chapter.

Now the vast steppe was under the Manchu control. Under Hong Taiji's command, prince Jirgalang and prince Sahaliyan established laws and divided the pasture lands for the outer Mongolian princes who had surrendered (*han i hesei jirgalang beile, sahaliyan beile, tulergi dahaha monggo i beise i nuktere ba be dendeme bume jorime, jai doro xajin be toktobume gisurefi jihe*).[540]

On the twenty-eighth of the eighth intercalary month in 1634, officials of the Chakhar Khan submitted the Khan's wife and people to Hong Taiji. Hong Taiji married the Kahn's wife to reinforce his authority over the Mongol tribes.[541] On the twenty-seventh day of the tenth month in 1634, Hong Taiji offered a sacrifice to Nurgaqi, reporting that Korea had surrendered itself as a younger brother and paid tribute, the five Khalkha and other Mongol tribes, such as Aru, Kalaqin and Tumet, all submitted. Before the Chakhar khan fled away, half of his brothers had surrendered. The Khan himself died on the way to Tibet and all his

---

[538] *Fe dangse*, p. 6193.
[539] *Fe dangse*, p. 6221.
[540] *Fe dangse*, p. 6494.
[541] Qingchu neiguoshiyuan manwen dang'an yibian, p. 107.

195

officials yielded. Now the Ming is the only enemy. [542] Chakhar's submission greatly strengthened the power of the Later Jin state. Based on the *Former Manchurian Chronicles*, Britta-Maria Gruber also analyzed the importance of Mongol role played in Hong Taiji's regime. [543] Nonetheless, in historical course, this is only the beginning of the Manchu unification of the Mongol lands. The Chakhar confederation that lived in the south of Gobi Desert, written as *Mo'nan menggu* 漠南蒙古 in Han Chinese documents, which roughly covers today's Inner Mongolia, was unified by Hong Taiji. The Khalkha confederation, who lived in the north of Gobi Desert, did not submit to the Manchu Qing state until the middle of the Kangxi reign (r. 1654-1722), when the Manchu emperor personally led the army to defeat the Oirat attackers from the Zunghar Khanate. Khoshut Mongols who lived in the Qinghai region yielded in the second year of the Yongzheng reign (r. 1723-1735), after the new Manchu emperor sent Generals Nian Gengyao 年羹堯 and Yue Zhongqi 岳鍾祺 to crash Khoshut's Lobsang Tendzin's uprising. The state of Zunghar Mongols continuously existed till the mid eighteenth century, when the emperor Qianlong (r. 1735-1796) carried out the final unification of the Oirat Khanate on the central Eurasian steppe. If we counted from Nurgaqi's attack on the Khalkha tribes in 1626, down to Qianlong's ultimate subjugation of the Oirats in 1759, the Manchu unification of the Mongol lands took 133 years with the effort of six Jurchen-Manchu monarchs.

As Rawski pointed out, the alliance with Mongol was crucial to the Manchu unification. The Manchus frequently interacted with the Mongols, learning from their culture, language and military organization. [544] The above passages confirmed the Manchu-Mongol relationship was consolidated by marriage exchanges, military unification, and alignment activities.

---

[542] Qingchu neiguoshiyuan manwen dang'an yibian, p. 118.

[543] Britta-Maria Gruber (2006), *Zur Entwicklung der Herrschaft im Aisin-Staat 1616-1636*, Harrassowitz Verlag, Wiesbaden.

[544] Evelyn S. Rawski (1996), "Presidential Address: Reenvisioning the Qing: The Significance of the Qing Period in Chinese History", *The Journal of Asian Studies*, 55. 4: 834.

4.5 Subjugating Korea

Strategically, Nurgaqi chose to ally the Mongols for unification of the Ming, so he intentionally maintained a peaceful relation with Korea. On the eleventh day of the seventh month in 1620, he sent emissaries to Korea for negotiation of refugee issues. In his letter, he humbly referred to his state as "people of a small country" and Korea as a "big country" (*meni ajige gurun i niyalmai hendure anggala, suweni amba gurun ai be sarkv*).[545]

On the twenty-fourth day of the ninth month in 1621, the Korean King sent a Subprefectual Magistrate (man. *ting pan xi hafan*; chin. *ting pan shi guan* 廳判事官) as the emissary to pay tribute. Nurgaqi's three sons-in-law, Urgvdai, Fusi, and Si Uli, along with a Regional Commander Baduri and Scholar Erdeni, to receive the emissary outside the fortification. The emissary presented one hundred *liang* silver, fifty rolls of noil poplin (man. *miyanqeo*; chin. *mianchou* 綿綢), fifty cuts of paper, twenty rolls of grass cloth, fifty rolls of common cloth, fifty knives and ten cuts of oiled paper. Nurgaqi said, "If two countries want to live in peace, they should visit and present gifts to one another. If I took your tribute, my reputation would be ruined. " Nurgaqi refused to accept the gifts and returned them all (*orin duin de, solho han i elqin ting pan xi hafan isinjiha, han i ilan hojihon, urgvdai efu, fusi efu, si uli efu, baduri zung bing guwan, erdeni baksi, sunja amban ukdofi, heqen i tule ebufi aqaha, solho han, ting oan xi sere hafan be takvrafi, tanggv yan menggun, susai miyanqeo, susai kiyan hooxan, orin muxuri, susai boso, susai howesi, juwan iolehe hooxan alban benjihe seme, han de hengkileme jihe, han hendume, juwe gurun sain banjiki seqi, ishunde gungneme beneme yabumbi dere, sini ulin be bi alban gaiqi, gebu ehe seme hendume gaihaikv, gemu bederebuhe*).[546]

During Nurgaqi's time, he did not launch any military campaigns against Korea to unify its lands. In the first month of the green-ox year (1625), Han Run and Han Yi came from Korea to surrender. Han Run's father, Han Minglian, plotted a coup with a Regional Commander (man. *zung bing guwan*; chin. *zong bing guan* 總兵官) Li Guo, to attack the capital fortification Wangjing 王京. The army sent by the Korean King

---

[545] Fe dangse, p. 724.
[546] *Fe dangse*, pp. 1199-1201.

for defense was defeated by Han Minglian, and the capital fortification was abandoned. Han and Li entered the fortification with their troops but both of them were killed by an Commander of Guards (man. *jung giyvn*; chin. *zhongjun* 中軍), who was a subordinate officer of Li Guo. Han Minglian's son, Han Run, and nephew, Han Yi, escaped to Nurgaqi. Nurgaqi granted Han Run as Mobile Corps Commander, Han Yi Defense Officer, with all sorts of rewards, such as wife, bond-servants, houses, lands, oxen, horses, clothes, wealth and other necessities (*abkai fulinggai taizu genggiyen han i juwanqi niohon ihan aniya, aniya biya de solho gurun i han run, han i gebungge juwe niyalma ukame jihe, han run i ama han ming liyan, zung bing guwan i hergen i li guwe gebungge amban i emgi solhoi wang ji doro be faquhvrafi qooha ilifi wang ging heqen be afame dosire de, solhoi wang qooha okdome unggifi gidabure jakade, uthai wang ging heqen be waliayfi burulaha, tereqi han ming liyan, li guwe, tere heqen de dosifi tehe manggi, li guwe i fejergi jung giyvn, li guwe han ming liyan be wara jakade, han ming liyan i jui han run deo i jui han i burulame tuqifi, manju gurun i taizu genggiyen han be baime ukame jidere jakade, taizu genggiyen han, han run be iogi hafan, han i be bei ioi guwan obufi, sargan, aha, boo, usin, morin, ihan, suje, ulin, etuku niyalmai baitalara ai ai jaka be yooni buhe*).[547]

When Hong Taiji took over the throne, the relationship with Korea was changed. In the year of the red rabbit (1627), he ordered a strike upon Korea under the reason that Korea repeatedly offended the Manchu regime (*fulahvn gvlmahvn sure han i suqungga aniya, solho gurun be dailaha, dade solho gurun, manju gurun de jalan jalan i weile bi*).[548] The army set out on the eighth day of the first month (*aniya biyai iqe jakvn de jurafi...*),[549] and unified Yizhou 義州 on the fourteenth day (*solho i i jeo heqen be juwan duin i dobori uthai wan sindafi tafafi gaiha*).[550] On the eighteenth day, the army tried to summon Guoshan 郭山 and Hanshan 漢山 to surrender, but their offer was declined. Those two cities were soon taken over (*juwan jakvn de, go xan, han xan qeng be daha seqi, ojorakv ofi, afame gaiha...*).[551] On the twentieth, the army crossed the

---

[547] Manzhou shilu, pp. 374-375.
[548] *Fe dangse*, p. 3884.
[549] *Fe dangse*, p. 3885.
[550] *Fe dangse*, p. 3886.
[551] *Fe dangse*, p. 3889.

Anzhou River (Anzhoujiang 安州江) and camped near Anzhou 安州. During the night, emissaries were sent to persuade the Koreans to surrender, but the mission was not successful. In the morning of the twenty-first day, the army unified the fortification (*orin de muduri erinde, an jeo i giyang be doofi, heqen i hanqi ing iliha, tere doboni geretele daha seme takvraqi, daharakv ofi, orin emu de qimarilame afafi, uthai emu erin hono ohakv dartai andande afame gaiha*).[552] On the twenty-fifth, the troops departed from Anzhou. On the twenty-sixth, the army reached Pyongyang, which was empty. The fortification's administrator, the Grand Coordinator (man. *du tang*; chin. *du tang* 都堂), the Regional Commander (man. *zung bing guwan*; chin. *zong bing guan* 總兵官), all the officials, military men and common people had fled on their own. The fortification was deserted (*orin sunja de an jeo heqen qi qooha jurafi, orin ninggun de ping rang ni heqen de isinaqi, heqen i ejen du tang, zung bing guwan, heqen hafan qooha irgen ini qisui burgifi, emkeqi kavn gemu heqen waliyafi burulahabi*).[553] The Korean king was forced to pledge loyalty to the Manchu regime, and the Manchu princes were about to report the achievement to Hong Taiji (*neneme solho i wang be gashvbufi beise de medege alanjiha manggi, tere medeke be han de alabume unggifi...*).[554] Nevertheless, prince Amin still decided to loot the Koreans. Under his command, the eight banners split into different routes and robbed for three days. All the treasure, animals, and captives were gathered in Pyongyang for rewards (*jakvn gvsai ambasa be jugvn dendefi tabqin sindaha, ilan dedume tabqilafi, ulin, ulha, niyalma, muterei teile dalime ping rang ni heqen de isinjifi ing iliha, tere heqen de morin teyebume olji dendeme ilifi*).[555] The final achievement was a covenant to ensure Korea's loyalty to the Manchu regime, and then the Manchus returned without further intrusion (*ping rang de gashvha qi amasi, manju i qooha bederere de, solho i umai jaka be neqihekv, amba jugvn be jafafi qooha bederehe*).[556]

In the following years, Korea paid tribute annually but grudges were built up. On the eleventh day of the fourth month in 1636, Hong Taiji led

---

[552] *Fe dangse*, pp. 3890-3891.
[553] *Fe dangse*, pp. 3892-3893.
[554] *Fe dangse*, p. 3947.
[555] *Fe dangse*, p. 3949.
[556] *Fe dangse*, pp. 3953-3954.

the princes and officials to offer a sacrifice to the Heaven and took the throne of Emperor (*juwan emu de, han, geren beise ambasa be gaifi abkai han i soorin de weqehe, weqeme wajiha manggi, han amba soorin de tehe*).[557] When Hong Taiji and his Manchu, Mongol and Han Chinese officials were performing the ritual, the Korean emissaries Luo Dexian and Li Kuo refused to participate. After the ceremony, Hong Taiji believed that the Korean king arranged this incongruousness on purpose in order to provoke a fight (*ineku tere inenggi, enduringge han, manju monggo nikan i geren beise ambasa be gaifi abka de hengkilere de, solho i wang ni elqin lo de hiyan, li ko marame hengkilerakv bifi, hengkilehe manggi enduringge han hendume... tere gemu wang jortai fiktu baime mimbe neneme ehe be deribukini*).[558]

On the twenty-ninth of the eleventh month in 1636, Hong Taiji ordered to attack Joseon by reason that Joseon had violated the covenant (*orin uyun de... uttu gasihvha be hvwaliyaka turgunde dailambi*).[559] On the first day of the twelfth month, Hong Taiji personally led the troops to the war in Joseon (*jorgon biyai iqe de... enduringge han amba qooha be gaifi julesi qoohiyan gurun be dailame genere de*).[560] On the twelfth day, the army arrived in Guoshan fortification (Guoshancheng 郭山城) for camping. The defense force fled, and the remaining soldiers and people all surrendered to Hong Taiji (*juwan juwe de, enduringge han guwang xan hoton de isinafi amba qooha ing iliha... guwang xan hoton be tuwakiyaha hafan burulame genehe manggi, hoton i dorgi qooha irgen gemu dahafi, enduringge han de hengkileme jihe manggi*).[561] On the thirteenth day, the troops passed Dingzhou fortification (Anzhoucheng 定州城) and camped fifteen *li* away from the fortification. On that day, soldiers and people came from Dingzhou to surrender (*juwan ilan de, ding jeo be tofohon ba dulefi deduhe, tere inenggi ding jeo hoton de tehe qooha irgen dahaha manggi*).[562] On the nineteenth, a report said that General Mafuta and the troops had reached Wangjing 王京 on the fourteen day. The Korean king Li Zong 李倧 had run away. Hearing this, General Mafuta pursued and besieged the king at South Hanshan

---

[557] *Fe dangse*, p. 6897.
[558] *Fe dangse*, pp. 6898-6899.
[559] *Fe dangse*, pp. 8376-8378.
[560] *Fe dangse*, pp. 8393-8394.
[561] *Fe dangse*, pp. 8415-8416.
[562] *Fe dangse*, pp. 8417-8418.

fortification (Nan hanshancheng 南漢山城), which is forty *li* away from the Wangjing (*juwan uyun de... mafuta ... se juwan duin de wang ging heqen de isinara inenggi... terei amala wang burulame genehebi, tere mejige be mafuta se donjifi amqame genehei dehi ba i dubei nan han gebungge hodai hoton de amqanafi kaha*).[563]

On the twenty-ninth day of twelfth month, Hong Taiji personally commanded the army to join the siege of Nan Hanshan fortification.[564] After frequent negotiations, on the thirtieth day of the first month in 1637, Li Zong surrendered to Hong Taiji.[565] Due to the current war damage upon Korea's economy, Hong Taiji demanded Korea to pay tribute from 1639, which is two years after the war.[566] The annual tribute include 100 *liang* gold, 1,00 *liang* silver, 200 pairs of buffalo horns, 100 pieces of leopard skin, 100 pieces of softened hairless deer skin, 1,000 bags of tea, 400 pieces of otter skin, and certain amounts of pepper, swords, medicine, paper, sleeping mats, cloth, silk and rice.[567] On the first day of the sixth month in 1638, Hong Taiji granted Li Zong with the title of Korean King, and Li Zong paid tribute as his thankfulness.[568] Since then Korea officially became a dependency of the Qing dynasty, assisting its war against the Ming.

4.6 Conclusion

In conclusion, most of the land acquisition within the Jurchen tribes was completed in Nurgaqi's reign. The new Manchu identity gradually took place between the White Mountain and Black Water. Based on the growing Jurchen populations, resources and territories, the Manchu state increased its power and quickly unified the Ming's Liaodong province.

The Ming's Liyaodong province was Nurgaqi's major goal for territorial expansion due to its rich soils and large agricultural population, which also makes this area an ideal object for taxation. The integration of Liaodong changed Nurgaqi's Jurchen-Manchu regime into an empire that is beyond different ethnic groups.

---

[563] *Fe dangse*, pp. 8436-8439.
[564] Qingchu neiguoshiyuan manwen dang'an yibian, p. 231.
[565] Qingchu neiguoshiyuan manwen dang'an yibian, p. 242.
[566] Qingchu neiguoshiyuan manwen dang'an yibian, p. 245.
[567] Qingchu neiguoshiyuan manwen dang'an yibian, p. 246.
[568] Qingchu neiguoshiyuan manwen dang'an yibian, p. 316.

Meanwhile, the emerging Manchu state kept assimilating Mongol tribes into its governance through marriage and alliance. With the support of the Mongol cavalries and Han Chinese artillerymen, Nurgaqi and Hong Taiji gradually pushed their territory into Shanhai Pass, though the success came at a heavy price.

Compared with Nurgaqi's acquisition of Jurchen lands and Liaodong, Hong Taiji's achievement was the unification of Korea. Two large scales of military campaign thoroughly crushed Korea's resistance. Korea became a dependency and started to pay tribute annually to the Qing. Thus, Hong Taiji secured his home front so that he could better concentrate on the unification of the Ming.

Hong Taiji's another achievement is the defeat of the Chakhar Mongols, whose Khan fled away without a fight. Since then the vast northern steppe was gradually encompassed into the Manchu rule. After Korea's first submission, the Qing started to form a pincer movement, attacking the Ming from the northeast and north frontiers. These geographical advantages resulted in successive military victories, gaining more captives, lands and wealth. The Ming had to defend passively on its far-flung borderlands, until its collapse to Li Zicheng's uprising.

5. Acquisition of Industries

5.1 Introduction

In the previous chapters, we presented the process of Jurchen-Manchu acquisition of currencies, people and lands, which were the basic elements to boost an imperial economy that is pre-industrial by a modern perception. In this chapter, we are going to look at the traditional Manchu economies, in which granary was highlighted as the key to carry out the wars that expanded the empire.

Natural resources in Northeast Asia have been known for a long time. In 1620, Nurgaqi proudly claimed that the Heaven has granted him with lands that produce all sorts of treasure, such as sable furs in three colors, furs of black, white and red foxes, furs of lynx, leopard, sea otter, tiger, otter, red squirrel, ground squirrel, raccoon dog, deer, roe deer, etc., and other products like cotton, silk, cloth, hemp cloth, salt, gold, silver, and iron all come out of the ground, with all kinds of things that provide clothes and food for people to obtain *(abkai salgabufi mini baqi tuqire ulin, ilan haqin i seke, sahaliyan xanggiyan fulgiyan ilan i dobihi, silun, yarga, lekerhi, tasha, hailun, ulhu, solohi, elbihe, buhi, gihi, tenteke furdehe bi, kubun, yohan, boso, jodon, dabsun, jai aisin, menggun, sele gemu na qi tuqimbi, tere gemu bi, eture jeterengge gemu bahabi)*.[569]

The rich natural resources of Northeast Asia attracted the Ming Han Chinese for exploration. In 1616, Nurgaqi complained that the Ming Han Chinese crossed the border and invaded the Jurchen places: every year the Ming Han Chinese came to exploit silver mine, gather ginseng, lumber, search pine nuts, mushroom, jelly fungus, and such intrusion was severe *(ninggun biyade, jase jaka i nikan gemu tuqifi juxen i babe nungnembi seme donjifi, han hendume, anyadari jase tuqifi, menggun feteme, orhoda gurume, moo saqime, hvri, megu, sanqa baime nungnehe ambula oho)*.[570] These lucrative resources represent greater opportunities in trade, as Thomas G. Rawski and Lillian M. Li argued that it was the

---

[569] *Fe dangse*, pp. 673-674.
[570] *Fe dangse*, pp. 202-203.

regional differences in economics that lured the Han Chinese to migrate from North China to Manchuria.[571]

Along with the Han Chinese, the Mongols were also covetous of the Jurchen resources, mainly for grain. In the eighth month of 1619, Nurgaqi had to send a letter to the neighboring Mongol tribes, warning them not to enter his land that stretches eastward to the Yehe tribe. The reason is that Nurgaqi had already unified those lands, and if the Mongols came to plunder grain, Nurgaqi's people would suffer from hunger. If there were no grain, Nurgaqi emphasized, how could he nurture the owners of grain fields? Up to the spring time, all people's life depends on the grain transported from the unified lands *(monggo de unggihe bithei gisun, xun dekdere baru yehe i bade isitala, suweni monggo ume dosire, suwe dosifi mini efuleme gaiha ba i jeku be gamaqi, mimbe jeku akv jobokini seme gvnime gamaha seme gvnimbi, bi tere usin jekui ejen de, bi ai ulebume ujimbi, niyengniyeri otolo, ere efulehe ba i jeku be juweme jembi kai)*.[572]

The conflict between the Jurchens and Mongols, in regard of grain, lies in different modes of life. Besides, scholars have pointed out that the shift of trade route from inner Asia to maritime caused the Mongols to rely on the agricultural economy of their neighbors.[573] On the first day of the eleventh month in 1619, Nurgaqi sent a letter to the Mongol neighbors, pointing out that they were different people who live in different lives: you Mongol people raise animals, eat meat and wear hide; our people make a living by plowing fields and eating grain *(suweni monggo gurun, ulha be ujime, yali be jeme, sukv be etume banjimbikai, meni gurun, usin tarime jeku be jeme banjimbi kai)*.[574] This difference caused the Mongols often to resort to intensive means of getting daily necessities from the Han Chinese and Jurchens. Like the Han Chinese rulers, the Jurchens also gave all sorts of gifts to the Mongol allies for maintaining relationship.

---

[571] Thomas G. Rawski and Lillian M. Li (eds.) (1992), *Chinese History in Economic Perspective*, University of California Press, Berkeley, p. 7.

[572] *Fe dangse*, pp. 555-556.

[573] Lynn Struve, *Shijieshi ji qingchu zhongguode neiya yinsu* 世界史及清初中國的內亞因素-美國學術界的一些觀點和問題 (Elements of Inner Asia in World History and Early-Qing China: some viewpoints and questions in America's academia), collected in *Qingchao de guojia rentong* 清朝的國家認同 (State's Identity of the Qing Dynasty), edited by Liu Fengyun 劉鳳雲 and Liu Wenpeng 劉文鵬, Zhongguo renmin daxue chubanshe, Beijing, 2010. p. 325.

[574] *Fe dangse*, p. 592.

One example is that after being subjugated, some Mongols had to rely on the Jurchens for food. In 1621, Khalkha chieftain Jaisai begged for food by sending one hundred carts. Besides, he also sent three carts and asked for things for his personal use. Nurgaqi and the Eight Chieftains gave him nine chests, three standing trunks, two bottles of distillate spirits, seven hundred pears, four *to*[575] dates, four *to* grapes, one *hule*[576] rice, one *hule* proso millet and one *hule* barnyard millet *(jaisai beile, jeku baime emu tanggv sejen unggihe bihe, emu tanggv sejen de, tanggv hule bele buhe, ini beyede aika unggi seme ilan sejen unggihe bihe, ilan sejen de, han, jakvn beile, uyun guise, juwe horho, juwe malu arki, nadan tanggv sulhe, soro duin to, muqu duin to, hadu bele emu hule, ira bele emu hule, hife bele juwe hule unggihe)*.[577] These were very precious products to the Mongols who returned to the steppe after the Yuan dynasty ended, due to their sole economy pattern of stock raising. Sechin Jagchid and Van Jay Symons argued that wars often broke out in China's northern frontiers when the nomads could not exchange their animal products for food, cloth and manufactured goods through trade.[578] In this Manchu case, the Jurchens had to satisfy the Mongol needs, without trade, in order to sustain a peaceful relationship.

Through the above analysis, the relationship between nature and culture is emerging for the identity of the borderland people is closely tied to the natural environment, in which the economic and military competences take shape, as David A. Bello argued.[579] The above passage also leads to our first topic of this chapter, granary, as one of the most important means to start and promote a great enterprise.

---

[575] The Manchu measure of weight, *to*, must be a loan word from the Chinese *dou* 斗, which is about six kilograms with local variation.

[576] The Manchu measure of weight, *hule*, must be a loan word from the Chinese *hu* 斛, which is about sixty kilograms.

[577] *Fe dangse*, pp. 1287-1288.

[578] Sechin Jagchid and Van Jay Symons (1989), *Peace, War, and Trade Along the Great Wall: Nomadic-Chinese Interactions through Two Millennia*, Indiana University Press, Bloomington and Indianapolis, p. 1.

[579] David A. Bello, Across Forest, Steppe and Mountain: Environment, identity and Empire in Qing China's borderlands, Cambridge: CUP, 2015.

5.2 Agriculture

5.2.1 Granary

In the premodern society, grain was the glue to tie a community together. In 1584, when a thief was caught, Nurgaqi's brothers, assistants and bondservants suggested that it is better to kill the thief rather than beating him. Nurgaqi's response presented a reasonable concern about grain reserve. He said, "if the thief were killed, his owner would take the chance for starting a war and taking our grain away. After plundered, all the subordinate tribes would rebel and disperse due to lack of food" *(buya deote guquse, booi niyalma gemu ere hvlha be tantafi ainambi, wafi dere seqi, taizu sure beile ojorakv hendume, ere be waha de erei ejen ini niyalma be waha seme iletu dain ofi musei jekui eye be gemu fetefi gamambi, jetere jeku akv oqi, musei juxen gemu ubaxambi kai...).*[580]

When enlarging the enterprise, Nurgaqi gradually developed the granary system. In 1613, Nurgaqi started to tax his people by collecting grain, but the people suffered. Accordingly, Nurgaqi requested ten men and four oxen from each company (man. *niru*; chin. *niulu* 牛錄) to plow the waste lands for grain plantation. Since then the Jurchen civilians were exempted from grain taxation and people were no longer worried about this matter. Grain reserve turned to be sufficient and granaries were built up. The Manchu document keeper stressed that in the past there were no granaries *(ineku tere aniya, gurun de jekui alban gaiqi, gurun jobombi seme, emu nirui juwan haha duin nihan be tuqibufi, sula bade usin darime, deribuhe, terei gurun de jekui alban gaijarakv ofi, gurun inu joborakv oho, jeku elgiyen oho, tereqi jekui ku gidaha, terei onggolo jekui ku akv bihe).*[581] Nurgaqi officially established his Jin state in 1616. This evidence demonstrates that grain reserve is one of the key elements that are prioritized in state building.

It took time to develop a mature granary system for sustaining a large human population. In 1615, one of Nurgaqi's speeches confirmed that the Jurchens did not yet have enough granaries and therefore if they kept the war prisoners and animals alive, their own people would have to starve. Nurgaqi's plan was to take some time to integrate the Jurchen people into his governance, secure the borderlands, fix the forts, cultivate the

---

[580] Manzhou shilu, p. 45.
[581] Fe dangse, p. 77.

farmlands, and build up granaries (muse de jekui ku akv kai. dailafi baha seme, baha niyalma ulha de ulebure anggala, musei fe niyalma hono gemu buqembi kai, erei xolo de, musei gurun be neneme bargiyaki, ba na be bekileki, jase furdan be jafaki, usin weilefi jekui ku gidame gaiki seme hendume, tere aniya dain deribuhekv).[582] As Bai Xinliang 白新良 pointed out, this is Nurgaqi's strategy to subjugate the Yehe tribe, unify Manchuria and make war upon the Ming.[583] The tribe of Yehe was an economically developed region that was closely controlled by the Ming empire, and it produced large amounts of grain, which attracted Nurgaqi's attetion. Evidently, building up granaries was an important part of this master plan.

When Nurgaqi was busy building up his state and official granary, most common Jurchens still stored their grain in traditional ways. As Li Minwan 李民寏 observed in a time around 1619, after autumn the Jurchen people dug pits to store grain and then gradually excavate and eat it. Therefore, the grain rots and smells when the weather turns warmer (qiuhou juejiao yicang, jianci chushi, gu rinuan bianyou fuchou 秋後掘窖以藏，漸次出食，故日暖便有腐臭).[584]

Besides reserving their grain, war sometimes rewarded the Jurchens with abundant spoils. On the ninth day of the fourth month in 1621, after taking over the Liaodong city walls, Gao Minghe, the Grand Commandant (man. xeobei; chin. shoubei 守備) of Aihe, reported that in his place, there were 725 hule one to rice, 2,516 hule five to beans, 1,072 hule 4 to 4 sin[585] broom-corn, 391,736 bundles of grass, 862 hule six to rotten soybeans, and finally, 106,104 bundles of rotten grass (aiha i xeobei gao ming ho i bithe, iqe uyun de isinjiha, jeku i ton, bele nadan tanggv orin sunja hule emu to, turi juwe minggan sunja tanggv juwan ninggun hule sunja to, xuxu emu minggan nadanju juwe hule duin to duin sin, orho gvsin uyun tumen emu minggan nadan tanggv gvsin ninggun fulmiyen, niyaha turi jakvn tanggv ninju juwe hule ninggun to, niyaha

---

[582] Fe dangse, p. 139.

[583] Bai Xinliang 白新良 (2006), Qingshi kaobian 清史考辨 (Evidential Research on Qing History), Renmin chubanshe, Beijing, p. 34.

[584] Jianzhou wenjianlu 建州聞見錄 (Records of Hearings and Seeings in Jianzhou), written by Li Minwan 李民寏 (c. 1619), collected in Qingshi ziliao congkan di ba, jiu zhong 清史資料叢刊第八、九種 (The Eighth and Ninth kinds of Qing History Collection), edition Shenyang: Liaoning daxue chubanshe, 1978, p. 43.

[585] The Manchu measure of weight, sin, must be a loan word from the Chinese sheng 升, which is about one kilograms in terms of weighing water.

orho juwan tumen ninggun minggan emu tanggv duin fulmiyen).[586] From the *Qingtaizu wu huangdi shilu* 清太祖武皇帝實錄 (the Veritable Records of the Qing Forefather Martial Emperor), we can know that in 1615, the Eight Banners were established. Originally, there were four banners: Yellow, White, Blue and Red. Eight Banners were created by bordering the four-color flags, which make them into eight (*yuanqi you huang bai lan hong sise, jiang ci sise xiangzhi wei base, cheng bagushan* 原旗有黃白藍紅四色，將此四色鑲之爲八色，成八固山).[587] Throughout Nurgaqi's reign, the Eight Banners assumed full responsibilities for military acts and political administration and accordingly this military unit was in charge of grain economy.

Besides spoils captured in wars, there were also savings accumulated by the Han Chinese commoners. In 1622, officers of Youtunwei 右屯衛 counted their remaining grain: 421,130 *hule* five *to* two *sin* old rice, 15,020 *hule* 7 *to* 1 *sin* millet, 54,320 *hule* 1 *to* 1 *sin* black beans, 13,210 *hule* 5 *to* 3 *sin* broom-corn, and the total number of grain is 503,681 *hule*, 7 *to* and 7 *sin* (*io tun wei de bisire bele i ton, lomi bele dehi juwe tumen emu minggan emu tanggv gvsin hule sunja to juwe sin, je bele emu tumen sunja minggan orin hule nadan to emu sin, sahaliyan tori sunja tumen duin minggan ilan tanggv orin hule emu to emu sin, xuxu emu tumen ilan minggan juwe tanggv juwan hule sunja to ilan sin, uheri susai tumen ilan minggan ninggun tanggv jakvnju emu hule nadan to nadan sin).*[588]

5.2.2 Grain Storage and Transportation

Due to the cold weather in northeast Asia, food was stored underground for long-term consumption. In the eighth month of 1621, reports said that there were 5,000 *hule* grain stored in the cellars, along with 12,000 *hule* as loan which would be collected by each company. "In the old annals," as the document keeper stated, "there were 7,417 *hule* in the old capital city Fe Ala. Regarding this storage, from the eighth month of the monkey year (1620) to the third intercalary month of the chicken year (1621),

---

[586] *Fe dangse*, pp. 935-936.

[587] *Qingtaizu wu huangdi shilu* 清太祖武皇帝實錄 (The Veritable Records of the Qing Forefather Martial Emperor), collected in *Qing ruguanqian shiliao xuanji yi* 清入關前史料選輯 1 (Compilation of Selected Historical Materials before the Qing Entered Shanhai Pass), vol. 1, compiled by Pan Zhe 潘喆 et al., edition Beijing: Zhongguo renmin daxue chubanshe, 1984, p. 334.

[588] *Fe dangse*, pp. 1515-1516.

3,306 *hule* were distributed to the new comers. From the fourth to the eighth month in 1621, 25,056 *hule* and 3 *to* were taken out from the Liaodong storage and distributed to the companies, such as Mongol and Han Chinese. The remaining old official grain is 14,111 *hule*, plus 841 *hule* grain that was loaned to the Liaodong people. The total number is 14,900 *hule*" (*orin jakvn de, araha hvqin de bisire jeku, sunja minggan hule bi, niru de juwe sindame gaijara jeku, emu tumen juwe minggan hule be, fe dangse de fe ala i alban i jeku, emu tumen nadan minggan duin tanggv juwan nadan hule bihe, erebe bonio aniya jakvn biya qi ebsi, qoko aniya anagan i ilan biya qi qasi, iqe anggala de buhengge, ilan minggan ilan tanggv ninggun hule buhe, duin biya qi ebsi, jakvn biya qi qasi, liyoodung ni jeku be, monggo, nikan i anggala nirui, liyoodung ni jeku be, monggo nikan i anggala nirui uksin i niyalma de buhengge, juwe tumen sunja minggan susai ninggu hule ilan sin buhe, fe alban i jeku bisirengge, emu tumen duin minggan emu tanggv juwan emu hule bi, liyoodung ni jeku be juwen sindahangge, jakvn tanggv dehi emu hule, ere uhereme emu tumen duin minggan uyun tanggv*).[589]*

Just three months later, on the first day of the twelfth month in 1621, Nurgaqi declared that the Han Chinese who lived with the Jurchens must honestly report the amount of their grain without concealing. According to their population, each Jurchen will receive four *to* grain each month until the next ninth month, and the remaining grain will be returned to their original Han Chinese owners. The reason of requesting the Han Chinese to help the Jurchens is the difficulties for the Jurchens who had left their home and moved to the newly unified Liaodong region. As for the Han Chinese who had accepted to cohabit with the Jurchens, it was not easy for them to share their houses, grain and lands with their new neighbors. For the Han Chinese who did not cohabit with the Jurchens, they should not stay aloof from such a situation because they also belonged to the same Khan. Therefore, the grain rationed to the Jurchens will be collected from the Han Chinese who did not yet cohabit with the Jurchens as a compensation for the people whose grain was taxed. At last, Nurgaqi stressed that if the Han Chinese did not report the exact amount of their grain, it would not be possible for a full reimbursement later on *(han i bithe, jorgon biyai iqe inenggi wasimbuha, juxen i emgi gamqime*

---

[589] *Fe dangse*, pp. 1131-1133.

tehe nikasa, suweni jeku be ume gidara, udu hule, udu sin, yargiyan ala,
alaha manggi, miyalime tuwafi juxen de anggala tolome, emu angga de,
emu biyade duin sin jeku, uyun biyade isitala bumbi, funqehe jeku be,
jeku i ejen de bumbi, meni juxen goro babe waliyafi, boigon gurime jime
suilaha, juxen be alime gaifi aqan tehe nikan, tehe boo weilehe jeku,
tariha usin bume suilaha, juxen i kamqihakv ba i niyalma, gese emu han i
irgen bime, i umai de darakv, baibi ainu guwembi, juxen de buhe jeku i
jalin de, juxen de kamqihakv ba i nikan i jeku be gaifi, suweni jeku
gaibuha niyalma de toodame bumbi, suweni jeku be yargiyan alarakvqi,
oron toodame baharakv kai).[590]

Granary is also used to support people who moved to other places. On
the second day of the twelfth month in 1621, Nurgaqi sent a letter to the
Mobile Corps Commander (man. *iogi*; chin. *youji* 遊擊) of Shenyang
(man. *simiyan*; chin. *Shenyang* 瀋陽), alerting him that there was no
grain dispatched to the people who moved from Kuandian and Aihe.
Therefore, he ordered Liu Youkuan, the Mobile Corps Commander of
Shenyang, to take three hundred *hule* rice from the Shenyang Granary,
and use oxcarts of his prefecture to transport the rice to the border,
Delishi, where the Fort-keeper Taiju was responsible for further
transportation. The whole process must be strictly guarded and Liu
Youkuan, the Mobile Corps Commander, must travel ten *li* away from the
fortification to supervise, until the tail of the transportation team is out of
sight *(han i bithe, iqe juwe de simiyan i iogi de wasimbuha, kuwan diyan,*
aiha i niyalma, boigon gurime axxafi jimbi, isinaha bade okdome jetere
bele akv, simiyan i iogi lio io kuwan, simiyan i cang ni bele ilan tanggv
hule gaifi, sini simiyan i harangga ba i ihan sejen tuqibufi, tere bele be
jasei tulergi deli wehe de bene, ubaqi unggihe taiju gebungge xeo pu
jorime gamakini, iogi sini beye heqen qi juwan ba i dubede isitala genefi
tuwame, dube lashalafi unggi).[591]

Granaries were mindfully maintained and guarded by the military
force. On the sixth day of the second month in 1622, Nurgaqi sent a letter
to his son-in-law, Donggo, ordering him to carefully dry the grain that
was stored in Youtunwei. The barn must be covered with mats and there
should be open gaps remained in the eaves for ventilation. No grain
should be wasted, the Khan stressed, and the granary must be

---

[590] *Fe dangse*, pp. 1319-1321.
[591] *Fe dangse*, pp. 1325-1326.

appropriately managed with all attention because Youtunwei stores 500,000 *hule* grain, which was produced in the Liaodong region. After organizing the granary, Nurgaqi stationed 500 cavalries for security *(han i bithe, juwe biyai iqe ninggun de donggo efu de wasimbuha, io tun wei i jeku be saikan walgiyafi boo be derhi dasifi, booi sihin jaka be fondolofi sinda, jeku ergen bahakini, jeku be ume mamgiyara, saikan geterembume iqihiya, zo tun wei sunja bujun jeku, musei liyoodung ni ba i jeku kai, jeku be iqihiyame dasame wajiha manggi, morin i qooha sunja tanggv tebu).*[592]

The transportation of grain was treated as a top priority. On the twenty-fourth day of the second month in 1622, Nurgaqi sent an edict to the Grand Coordinators, ordering to stop building the Liaodong fortification and stop cultivating the official lands. The reason is that he needed manpower for transporting the grain stored in Guangning to the other granaries *(han i bithe, juwe biyai juwan duin de du tang de wasimbuha, liyoodung ni heqen saharangge naka, alban i usin weileburengge inu nakaha, terei fonde heqen i wehe juweme jihe niyalma, ihan sejen be, iogi sai fejergi jung giyvn, qiyanzung qi, emte getuken iqiniyame mutebure niyalma be tuqibufi, meni meni ejen arafi unggi, guwangning ni ba i jeku juwefi cang de sindakini...)*[593]

On the twenty-sixth day of the second month in 1622, Nurgaqi issued another decree to summon ten thousand vehicles for depositing grain. The grain stored within the regions of Youtunwei 右屯衛 and Shisanshan 十三山 must not be moved, but the grain of remote sites, such as Baituchang 白土廠, Jing'anpu 靜安堡, Weijialing 魏家嶺, Shihe 石河, Qinghe 清河, Yizhou 義州, Qijiapu 齊家堡, Jinzhou 錦州, Xiaolinghe 小凌河 and Dalinghe 大凌河, etc., must be transported and stocked in the granary of Guangning 廣寧. The early 3,600 vehicles should carry the grain to Sanhepu 三河堡 for storage, and then people would be allowed to return home with their vehicles for farming *(han i bithe, orin inggun de wasimbuha, alban i tumen sejen jeku juwerengge, io tun wei, xi san xan qi ebsi jeku be ume juwere, be tu qang, jing an pu, wei giya ling, xi ho, qing ho, i jeo, qi giya pu, ginjeo, xolingho, dalingho, tere goroki ba i jeku be juweme gajifi, gemu guwangning heqen i cang de sinda, neneme genehe ilan minggan ninggun tanggv sejen i jeku be, sanako pu de gajifi*

---

[592] *Fe dangse*, pp. 1566-1567.
[593] *Fe dangse*, pp. 1617-1618.

211

sindafi, niyalma, ihan, meni meni boode bederefi usin weilekini).[594]
These places were the locations where the previous Ming garrison troops
stationed, along with the Han Chinese commoners who migrated here to
open up the frontiers. Guangning was the most important military base, in
which the Ming's highest military institution in Liaodong region,
Regional Commander's Office (*zongbingfu* 總兵府), resided.

On the seventh day of the third month in 1622, the document keeper
confirmed that those 3,360 vehicles had carried 4,551 *hule* grain to
Niuzhuang 牛莊 *(jeku juweme genere ilan minggan ilan tanggv inju
sejen de, duin minggan sunja tanggv susai emu hule jeku be, nio juwang
de isibuha).*[595] Up to this moment, one can find that the major granaries,
in Nurgaqi's reign, were located at Shenyang, Youtunwei, Guangning,
Sanhepu and Niuzhuang.

In the same period, Nurgaqi requested that all grain that was stored
along the riverbanks of Dalinghe, including the villages near Youtunwei,
must be transported away. Nurgaqi ordered the soldiers of four banners to
feed their horses at Qijiapu and the other four at Jinzhou. Within villages
of Qijiapu and Songshan, the stored grain must be transported to
Guangning. Grain stored in the bordering regions, from Yizhou to Qinghe,
Shihe, Weijialing, Shuangtai, and Baituchang, etc., must be guarded by
the old Mongols and New Mongols who just surrendered *(dalingho i bira
qigin de muhaliyaha bele, io tun wei xurdeme gaxan i juku be gemu
juwebu, duin gvsai qooha, qi giya pu de morin ulebume ili, jai duin gvsai
qooha, ginjeo de morin ulebu ili, qi jia pu, sung xan qi ebsi gaxan gaxan i
jeku be, gemu guwangning ni heqen de juwebu, i jeo qi, qing ho, xi ho,
wei giya ling, xuwang tai, be tu qang ni jase jakai jeku de, musei fe
monggo, iqe jihe monggoso ilikini).*[596] Here one can assume that part of
the stored grain must have been used to feed horses, which were one of
the most valuable assets for Nurgaqi's military regime.

Besides, Nurgaqi also ordered the Mongol soldiers to station at
Baituchang and Shuangtai, feeding their horses with grain stored in
borderlands. If the grain was not enough, they could move to places such
as Weijialing, Shihe, Qinghe and Yizhou for feeding their horses.
However, they were not allowed to touch the transportable grain stored

---

[594] *Fe dangse*, pp. 1673-1676.
[595] *Fe dangse*, pp. 1716-1717.
[596] *Fe dangse*, pp. 1717-1718.

nearby *(monggo i qoohai ejete i sargan iqe jihe alban i jeku jetere niyalmai sargata be, gemu guwangning de tebu, juse hehesi genehe manggi, saikan akdulame asara, hehesi de korafi gamame ukame generahu, monggoso i qooha, be tu qang, xuwang tai de ilifi jase jakai jeku be morin de ulebu, isirakvqi, wei giya ling, xi ho, qing ho, i jeo de isitala ulebu, ebsi gajiqi ojoro hanqi ba i jeku be ume neqire...)*.[597] It is made clear that the stored grain was used to feed horses, which were crucial for military act. The role of state inevitably involves military and economic issues. The storage of grain was prioritized as an important matter. On the twenty-second day of the first month in 1623, Nurgaqi send messengers to Guangning, ordering people to enlarge the walls around his old residence in the fortification. The walls were extended from fifty *da* to one hundred fifty in each side, and the stored grain must be moved into the houses that were measured for building the fortification within one month because the weather will become warmer after the first month. If the grain turns moldy, the ministers who are in charge will be punished *(orin juwe de, guwangning de takvraha bithei gisun, hoton i dorgi, han i tehe yamun i xurdeme heqen sahara babe, emu dere be susaita da dasa seme heduhe bihe, te emu dere be emte tanggvta da dasa, cang ni jeku be, hoton arambi seme futalaha ba i dorgi boode toola, ere jeku be aniya biya be ambume hvdun doolame waqihin, aniya biya be duleke de, halhvn de ambufi jeku wejehe de, genehe amba de weile)*.[598] Here we see the officials, who were also military officers of the Eight Banners, were responsible for grain preservation. The role of the state was closely tied with economic function.

Grain transportation was carried out by the Eight Banners, which combined the functions of the military force and political administration. On the seventh day of the third month in 1622, a report came in that 3,360 carts carried 4,551 *hule* grain to Niuzhuang. The grain was transported by the Eight Banners: the banner of Guard Darhan carried 830 *hule* with 557 carts; the banner of Uncle Abatai carried 820 *hule* with 610 carts; the banner of Age (man. *age*; chin. *age* 阿哥) Tanggvdai carried 490 *hule* with 372 carts; the banner of Guard Borjin carried 505 *hule* with 380 carts; the banner of Muhaliyan carried 400 *hule* with 302 carts; the banner of Age Subahai carried 380 *hule* with 265 carts; the

---

[597] *Fe dangse*, pp. 1719-1720.
[598] *Fe dangse*, pp. 1940-1941.

banner of Imperial Son-in-law Donggo carried 311 carts with 260 carts; the banner of Age Abatai carried 815 *hule* with 615 *(iqe nadan de, darhan hiya i gvsa, sunja tanggv susai nadan sejen, jeku jakvn tanggv gvsin hule, abatai nakqu i gvsa, ninggun tanggv juwan sejen, jeku jakvn tanggv orin hule, tanggvdai age i gvsa, ilan tanggv nadanju jwe sejen, jeku duin tanggv uyunju hule, borjin hiya i gvsa, ilan tanggv jakvnju sejen, jeku sunja tanggv sunja hule, muhaliyan i gvsa, ilan tanggv juwe sejen, jeku duin tanggv hule, subahai i gvsa, juwe tanggv ninju sunja sejen, jeku ilan tanggv jakvnju hule, donggo efu i gvsa, juwe tanggv ninju sejen, jeku ilan tanggv juwan emu hule, abatai age i gvsa, ninggun tanggv tofohon sejen, jeku jakvn tanggv tofohon hule, uhereme ilan minggan ilan tanggv ninju sejen, jeku duin minggan sunja tanggv susai emu hule, nio juwang de isinjiha seme boolaha).*[599] Hence we see a strong hand of the state upon the grain transportation, being executed by the Eight Banners that performed multiple functions regarding military, political and economic affairs.

Nonetheless, the situation of grain storage changed dramatically due to the difficulties of maintaining the vast unified regions. In 1622, Nurgaqi recruited the Han Chinese people to live and cultivate crops in Guangning but later the Jurchens did not defeat the Han Chinese military force to further their frontiers.[600] On the twenty-fourth day of the third month in 1623, Nurgaqi sent an edict to Guangning, ordering the army to inspect the fortification, destroy all the solid places, and burn all the houses down. Those houses that were not burned thoroughly in the previous days must be burned completely in the next day. "Peel the iron sheets off the fortification gates and then burn the gates," Nurgaqi commanded, "take all grain away and retreat to Shenyang," *(han i bithe, guwangning de unggihe, heqen i dorgi akdun babe gemu doigonde baiqame efule, boo gemu tuwa sinda, nenehe inenggi tuwa sindafi tuleme wajihakv boo be, jai inenggi dasame waqihaiyme sindame gilgabu, heqen dukai sele be hvwakiyame gaifi tuwa sinda, jeku juweme wajime jakade gemu jio).*[601] In Nurgaqi's understanding, grain is a strategic resource that must be strictly controlled by the state. The Manchu-language

---

[599] *Fe dangse*, pp. 1720-1722.

[600] Li Xun 李洵 and Xue Hong 薛虹, (eds.) (1995), *Qingdai quanshi* 清代全史 (A Complete History of the Qing), vol. 1, Liaoning renmin chubanshe, Shenyang, p. 158.

[601] *Fe dangse*, pp. 2164-2165.

documents presented researchers with a command economy when the Jurchens encountered with the Han Chinese intensely in the early seventeenth century.

5.2.3 Importance of Grain Storage

Grain market was closed after the Jurchen army entered the Liaodong region, except in some difficult times when people did not have enough to eat. In 1621, Nurgaqi stressed previously some rich Han Chinese people owned expansive lands and hired labor to grow crops, which were not for consumption but for sale. The poor people had no lands and food, and they had to buy grain for a living. When their money ran out, they ended up as beggars. In Nurgaqi's opinion, the rich people will only hoard the grain and let it become rotten, or collect the valuables for storage. It is better to take the grain to nurture the poor people and beggars, and thus the Khan's beautiful name will pass on and benefit the future generations. Besides, the Han Chinese commoners were allowed to harvest the crops which were planted within this year *(... julge suweni nikan gurun bayan niyalma, ba ambula gaifi usin be niyalma turifi weilebume, jeke seme wajirakv jeku unqambihe, yadara niyalma, usin jeku akv ofi udame jembihe, udame ulin wajiha manggi, giohambihe, bayan niyalma, jeku isabufi niyara, ulin isabufi baibi asarara anggala, tenteke giohara akv yadara niyalma be ujiqina, donjire de inu gemu sain, amaga jalan de hvturi kai, ere aniya tariha jeku be, meni meni gaisu, bi te usin be tolofi, emu haha de, jeku tarire sunja qimari, kubun tarire emu qimari usin be neigen dendefi bumbi, suwe haha ume gidara, haha gidaqi, usin baharakv kai...).*[602] Here one can see that the state acted as the guardian of the welfare of people regardless of society as a diversified whole, as Helen Dunstan pointed out in her studies on the economy of the Qing in a later time.[603] Grain merchants' pursuit of profit would definitely conflict with some groups of the society in an intense way, nonetheless, Nurgaqi's regime undoubtedly intervened the grain market, which was nearly put to a stop.

---

[602] *Fe dangse*, pp. 1072-1074.
[603] Helen Dunstan (1996), Conflicting Counsels to Confuse the Age: A Documentary Study of Political Economy in Qing China, 1644-1840, University of Michigan Center for Chinese Studies, Ann Arbor, p. 247.

Within the banner system, even animals get to eat the stored official grain. In order to stabilize the ally relationship, in 1621 Nurgaqi instructed one Mobile Corps Commander (man. *iogi hergen i hafan*; chin. *youji* 遊擊) to take the old rice from the Shenyang granary and distributed it to the Mongols who just surrendered to him. The ration is two *sin* for each person, each ox, each horse per month, and one *sin* for each sheep per month. For the Mongols who wanted to settle down, each lineage can make their own selection. For those who want to move, if their newly born sheep cannot be taken away, they can be left to the Eight-Banner Nomadic Mongols (man. *gusai nuktere monggoso*; chin. *baqi youmu menggu* 八旗遊牧蒙古) for nurture *(han, orin juwe de simiyan i iogi lio io kuwan de wasimbuha, simiyan i cang ni lomi bele be, monggo i ukame jihe niyalma de, emu biyade anggala tolome jewete sin bu, ihan morin, emke de juwete sin bu, honin emke de emu sin bu... boode tembi sere qihangga niyalma oqi, mukvn mukvn i simnefi tenju, qihangga genere, gamaqi ojorakv deberen banjiha durga ulha be, gvsai nuktere monggoso de ejen arame afabufi weri.*[604] Naturally, these baby animals would also enjoy the rationed grain as they grow bigger.

Granary was also used for famine relief, especially to the Mongol allies. In 1623, Nurgaqi sent a letter to the Imperial son-in-law Si Uli, who is also known as Tong Yangxing 佟養性, and General Aita, instructing them to take the grain which they had obtained, along with salt selected from Gaizhou and Fuzhou, and delivered them to Guard Naqibu and Fulata for relieving the Mongols who had no food *(han i bithe, sunja biyai orin ninggun de wasimbuha, si uli efu, aita, suweni bahai teile jeku be, jai gai jeo, fu jeo de dabsun simneme gaifi, naqibu hiya, fulata de bu, jeku akv monggo de salakini).*[605] This passage clearly points out that famine relief was carried by the state, which was embodied by the Eight Banner system.

Grain reserve is one of the most important matters for the Han Chinese, too. One example is that the frontier fortification Dalinghe 大凌 河 fell into the Jurchen hands due to grain shortage. On the twentieth day of the ninth month in 1631, When Hong Taiji besieged the fortification, the army captured a Han Chinese person who said that there was only half heap of grain left in the fortification, which was about one hundred

---

[604] *Fe dangse*, pp. 1384-1387.
[605] *Fe dangse*, p. 2387.

hule in Han Chinese measurement. Originally, there were 7,000 horses, but most of them died. Among the remaining two hundred horses, about seventy can be ridden. Half of the conscripted labors were dead and the survivors fed on horse meat. There was no firewood and therefore saddles were burned for fuel *(jai orin de, talingho hoton i niyalma be jafafi fonjiqi, jeku emu hontoho bulun, ainqi nikan hule i emu tanggv hule be sembi, nadan minggan morin buqeme wajifi, ergen bisirengge juwe tanggv, yaluqi ojorongge nadanju isime bi sere, erei majige tafi bisirengge, ainqi morin i yali de tahabi, duijirengge wajifi, enggemu gemu deijime wajiaha sere...).* [606] The Han Chinese sources even recorded cannibalism: during the Dalinghe Battle, people in the fortification ate one another, but the Ming loyalists still defended until they died *(qing dalinghe zhi yi, chengzhong ren xiangshi, mingren you sishou* 頃大淩河之役，城中人相食，明人猶死守).[607] With formidable cannons cast by the Han Chinese artisans, which will also be specified in later passages, Hong Taiji besieged Dalinghe for nearly three months, which caused severe food scarcity among the Han Chinese garrison troops.

However, granary system was sufficiently constructed and well maintained in Nurgaqi's time, famine still stroke the whole country when Hong Taiji officially became the Khan in 1627. After taking the throne, Hong Taiji launched wars to invade Korea and to attack the Ming's Jinzhou 錦州. The invasion of Korea was successful but the siege of Jinzhou ended up with great loss. Lots of Manchu soldiers died and Hong Taiji had to retreat to Shenyang on the fifth day of the sixth month in 1627 *(iqe duin de, ginjeo heqen i julergi dere de afame... tere afaha de, qoohai niyalma ambula buqehe, amba qooha amasi bedereme, iqe sunja de ginjeo qi jurafi, juwan juwe de bonio orinde, han, simiyan i heqen de isinjiha).* [608]

Just ten days later, the document keepers wrote that at that time people were hungry and one *sin* grain was worth eight *yan* silver. There were commoners who ate human flesh. During the time, plenty of silver

---

[606] *Fe dangse,* pp. 5569-5571.

[607] *Qingshigao* 清史稿 (The Draft of Qing History), vol. 2, compiled by Zhao Erxun 趙爾巽 (1844-1927) et al., 1928, edition Beijing, Zhonghua shuju, 1976, p. 37.

[608] *Fe dangse,* pp. 4036-4037.

remained in the country, but there were no markets for transaction. The silver's price was low, but the price of anything else, including treasure, was high. A good horse cost three hundred *yan* silver, a strong cattle cost one hundred yan, a roll of satin embroidery cost two hundred fifty *yan* and a roll of deep-green cloth (man. *moqin*; chin. *maoqing bu* 毛青布) cost nine *yan* silver. Thieves and bandits rose up, stealing oxen and horses. People also killed each other, leaving the country into chaos. The officials reported to the throne, suggesting that if the bandits were not severely punished, nothing else can be done to change the situation. Hong Taiji replied, "The harvest of crops was a failure across the country, and people are about to die of hunger. Therefore, they steal. Whip and then release those who were caught, and pardon those who are at large. I should be blamed for the failure of crops, not people." In this year, laws were reinforced on easy terms, and silver reserve was used for famine relief *(gurun yuyume ofi, emu sin jekukvn yan menggun salimbihe, irgen niyalmai yali be inu jeke, tere uquri gurun de menggun elgiyen, hvdaxara ba akv ofi, menggun i hvda ja, ulin yaya jaka i hvda mangga, emu yebken morin de, ilan tanggv yan menggun, emu sain ihan de, emu tanggv yan, emu gequheri de, emu tanggv susai yan, emu moqin de, uyun yan salimbihe, holo hvlaha dekdefi, morin ihan hvlhara, niyalma wanure faquhvn oho manggi, ambasa dosifi han i baru wesimbume hendume, hvlha be wame iseburakvqi kai, han hendume, ere aniya gurun jeku ufarafi, irgen yuyume buqere isifi hvlhambi kai, nambuhangge be tantafi sindaki, namburakvngge guwekini, jeku ufaraha weile muse de bi, irgen de akv seme hendufi, dere aniya xajin be sulukan obufi, ku i menggun tuqibufi irgen der salaha).*[609] Cannibalism was a serious issue throughout China's history. Research has noted that when Hong Taiji besieged the Han Chinese garrison troops in 1630s and 1640s, including the Dalinghe Battle in the previous paragraph, the Han Chinese soldiers ate human meat due to food shortages in wars.[610] Nonetheless, earlier than these Han Chinese events the same tragedy had already happened among the Manchus. When Hong Taiji made it to Khan, his authority was severely challenged by his brothers and cousins, who were appointed by Nurgaqi as chieftains to lead the banner troops. To consolidate his authority, Hong

---

[609] *Fe dangse*, pp. 4045-4047.

[610] Wang Sizhi 王思治(1978), *Qingshi lungao* 清史論稿 (Drafts of Research on Qing History), Bashu shushe, Chengdu, p. 113.

Taiji had to win wars for demonstrating his superiority over the competitors. Most of the male adults were sent to battlefields and few were left to tend the crops. Meanwhile, global crises also struck China and affected the agrarian economies.[611] Historical research believes that a cooling climate, being similar to the Little Ice Age in Europe, also happened in China in the seventeenth century and intrigued political turmoil.[612]

In our Manchu case, it must be the Little Ice Age, or something alike, that caused appalling climate changes. The early Manchu documents said that on the tenth day of the seventh month in 1632, when the Manchu army crossed the top of the Xing'an Ling (man. *hinggan*; chin. *xing'an ling* 興安嶺), the army camped at Niqugun Durbin. On that day, due to coldness, two to three hundred captives who wore thin clothes were frozen to death. There was still ice that remained on the mountaintop and in the valleys (*manju i qooha, nadan biyai juwan de hinggan i ninggu be dabafi, niqugun durbin gebungge bade ing iliha, tere inenggi asuru beiguwen ofi, etuku nekeliyen olji niyalma juwe alin tanggv bebereme buqehe, alin i ninggu i hafirahvn golo de juhe kemuni bihe*).[613] The unusual cold weather also appeared sixteen years ago, in Nurgaqi's reign. The early Manchu documents also said that the Amur River annually freezes between the fifteenth to the twentieth day in the eleventh month, but in 1616 when Nurgaqi attacked the Sahalian and Hvrha tribes, the Amur River froze in the beginning of the tenth month, which was forty days earlier than before (... *julge sahalian ula, omxon biyai tofohon de orin de amala juhe jafambihe... amba genggiyen han i qooha genehe niyalma aniya, juwan biyai iqereme juhe jafara jakade...*).[614] Geoffrey Parker attested usually cold weather in Japan, Europe and Middle East ranging from 1616 to 1620, along with general crisis across the globe caused the Little Ice Age in the seventeenth century.[615] Thus, it is reasonable to postulate a drastic climate change that had resulted in

---

[611] Peter C. Perdue (2005), *China Marches West: The Qing unification of Central Eurasia*, The Belknap Press of Harvard University Press, Massachusetts, Cambridge, p. 120.

[612] Lillian M. Li (2007), Fighting Famine in North China: State, Market, and Environmental Decline, 1690s-1990s, Stanford University Press, Stanford, p. 27.

[613] *Fe dangse*, p. 6379.

[614] *Fe dangse*, pp. 214-220.

[615] Geoffrey Parker (2012), Global Crisis: War, Climate Change and Catastrophe in the Seventeenth Century, Yale University Press, New Haven, pp. xx-xxii.

agrarian failure, which caused a grave famine in the first year of Hong Taiji's reign (1627).

Hong Taiji did not blame the common people for the failure of harvesting crops, and one can infer that the grain reserve was not strong enough to sustain the frequent wars and the state had to dispense silver to the famine victims, who would buy food from markets. Market is the last resort for the state to solve a crisis. In 1636, Hong Taiji issued a decree to emphasize that rice and millet are reserved for eating and market is open for circulation. All the subordinate officials and civilians should calculate their family members and save enough grain for self-consumption, but the rest should go to market for selling. One must not stockpile grain like before in case of causing the grain price expensive (*migu suoyi beishi, shitiao suoyi liutong... jin dang ge ji erdeng jiakou zuyong wai, youyouzhe ji wang shi dimai, wude reng qian yongji, zhiyou gugui zhiyu* 米穀所以備食，市糴所以流通...今當各計爾等家口足用外，有餘者即往市糴賣，勿得仍前壅積，致有穀貴之虞).[616] In 1637, it turned to be another hungry year. Hong Taiji heard that most of those great clans and wealthy families who had hoarded grain were expecting the price would soar high so that they could seize the moment to attain profits. Nonetheless, Hong Taiji declared that the affluent officials and civilians must sell their surplus if they have accumulations (*zhen wen jujiafushi, you jichu zhe, duo qiwang gujia tenggui, yibian chengshi sheli... guanmin furaozhe, fanyou canggu, juzhuo famai* 朕聞巨家富室，有積儲者，多期望谷價騰貴，以便乘時射利...官民富饒者，凡有藏谷，俱著發賣).[617] Furthermore, Hong Taiji ordered that the banner-men who had savings should have some compassion, selling extra grain to the poor ones within a company, by which one can get a fair price for it (*jinsui ouzhi nianji, fan jigu zhijia, yi cun renxu zhixin, yu ben niulu nei you kunfazhe, jiang gu tiaomai, keyi quzhi* 今歲偶值年飢，凡積穀之家，宜存任恤之心，遇本牛錄內有困乏者，將谷糴賣可以取值).[618] This is official arrangement for marketed grain, which admits state's reliance on commercial transaction in regard of famine relief. The state has to

---

[616] *Qingshilu* 清實錄 (The Qing Veritable Records), vol. 2, edition Beijing: Zhonghua shuju, 1985, p. 399.

[617] *Qingshilu*, vol. 2, p. 439.

[618] *Qingshilu*, vol. 2, p. 444.

balance between private pursuit of profit and the survival of the poor.[619] Hence, we conclude that the state exerted its great influence on grain market during the early Manchu regime.

5.2.4 Farming Official Lands

During the pre-unification era, the Eight Banners and the Han Chinese commoners cultivated lands. After Liaodong was taken over, the Eight Banners for supporting the military force confiscated large quantities of lands. Some researchers named these lands as Enclosure (*quandi* 圈地), which was the forerunner of enclosing the Han Chinese lands into the banner's ownership after the Manchu unification in 1644.[620]

On the fourteenth day of the seventh month in 1621, Nurgaqi informed every village under his governance regarding the land distribution: 100,000 *inenggi*[621] from Haizhou, 200,000 *inenggi* from Liaodong, and together it will be 300,000 *inenggi* lands allocated for cultivating grain to support the troops that were stationed in the area. According to estimation of Wang Zhonghan 王鍾翰, if one inenggi converts to five Han Chinese *mu* 畝, these 300,000 *inenggi* lands equal 1,500,000 Han Chinese *mu*.[622]

As for the commoners, they can still farm their lands in the original places. The large amounts of deserted lands owned by the chieftains, officials and affluent families should be enlisted into the 300,000 *inenggi* as part of Nurgaqi's requisition to support the military force. If there is further need, the troops can take lands from Songshanpu to Tieling, Yilu, Puhe, Fanhe, Hontoho, Shenyang, Fushun, Dongzhou, Magendan, Qinghe and Gushan, etc., for cultivation. If the lands were still not enough, the army can take those lands which are beyond the border (*juwan duin de, usin dendeme genembi seme, gaxan gaxan de neneme medege alanaha gisun ere inu, hai jeo bade juwan tumen inenggi, uhereme gvsin tumen inenggi usin be gaifi, meni ubade tehe qoohai*

---

[619] Dunstan, Conflicting Counsels to Confuse the Age, p. 247.

[620] Zhang Yan 張研 (1998), *Qingdai jingji jianshi* 清代經濟簡史 (A Brief History of Qing's Economy), Zhongzhou guji chubanshe, Zhengzhou, p. 29.

[621] The Manchu square measure, *inenggi*, was used for land measurement, which roughly correspond with the Chinese unit *Shang* 坰, which roughly equals to 10,000 square meters, with local variation.

[622] Wang Zhonghan 王鍾翰 (1957), *Qingshi zakao* 清史雜考 (Miscellaneous Research on Qing History), Renmin chubanshe, Beijing, p. 8.

niyalma morin de buki, jai meni geren baisin niyalmai usin, meni bade tarikini, suweni liyoodung ni ba i beise ambasa, bayasai usin faliayha ambula kai. tere usin be dosimbume, meni gaire gvsin tumen usin be, ere xurdeme bahaqi wajiha, isirakvqi, sung xan pu qi ebsi, qilin, ilu, puho, fan ho, hontoho, simiyan, fusi, dungjeo, magendan, niowanggiyaha, gu xan de isitala tari, tede isirakvqi, jase tuqime tari...).[623] Now one neutral observation is that the state encouraged the expansion of land cultivation during the time.

Speaking of the lands distributed for the Han Chinese subjects, Calculating Men for Distributing Lands (*jidingshoutian* 計丁授田) is the term coined by some scholars to describe this historical event.[624] After unifying the Ming's Liaodong region, Nurgaqi commanded that from now on, all lands must be sorted and counted, and each man will be granted with five *inenggi* grain fields, plus one *inenggi* cotton field *(... ereqi julesi, giohoto niyalma be giohaburakv, giohoo de, hvwaxan de, gemu usin bumbi, meni meni usin be kiqeme weile, ilan haha de, emu qimari alban usin weilebumbi).*[625]

Some Han Chinese commoners were also granted with quantities of farmlands for revenue purpose. On the first day of the tenth month in 1621, Nurgaqi sent an edict to the Han Chinese: from the next year, there will be taxation in grain to support the military, in fodder to raise horses, and upon the lands, they are farming. People of the five garrisons in Liaodong can farm those 200,000 *inenggi* fields, which did not have owners. Furthermore, 100,000 *inenggi* fields will be separated from the owner-less lands and assigned to the people in Haizhou, Gaizhou, Fuzhou and Jinzhou *(iqe inenggi, nikasa de wasimbuha gisun, ishun aniya qoohai niyalmai jetere jeku, morin ulebure orho liyoo, tarire usin gaimbi, liyoodung ni sunja wei niyalma, ejen akv usin be tebume, orin tumen inenggi, hai jeo, gai jeo, fu jeo, kinjeo duin wei niyalma de, ineku ejen akv usin be tebume, juwan tumen inenggi usin be tuqibufi bu).*[626]

---

[623] *Fe dangse*, pp. 1070-1072.

[624] Guo Chengkang 郭成康 and Liu Jianxin 劉建新 (1982), *Nu'erhachi jidingshoutian yu kaoshi* 努爾哈赤"計丁授田"諭考實 (Evidence on Nurgaqi's Decree of Calculating Men for Distributing Lands), collected in *Qingshi yanjiuji* 清史研究集 (Collection of Research on Qing History), vol. 2, compiled by Qing Institute of Renmin University of China, Zhongguo renmin daxue chubanshe, Beijing, pp. 88-114.

[625] *Fe dangse*, p. 1074.

[626] *Fe dangse*, pp. 1205-1206.

The Jurchen authority also sponsored people to move to other places, where labor was scarce but resource is plenty after the wars. On the twenty-third day of the eleventh month in 1621, Nurgaqi sent a document to the people in Zhengjiang, Tangshan, Fenghuang, Zhengdongpu and Zhenyipu, reminding that from Qinghe northward and from Sancha'r southward, there are Jurchens who live along the borders, with seven or eight *ba* as the farthest sites and one or two *ba* as the nearest. There are houses for living, seeds for farming, beautiful grass, trees and fertile soil. "Why don't you move to those places," suggested the Khan, "to enjoy their food, plentiful grain, grass, trees and everything else? In spring, the lands beyond the borders can also be farmed. If you want to farm the lands within the borders, you can select all fields from Sancha'er, Hui'anpu, Fushun, Dongzhou, Mahadan, and Shanyangyu, for farming as you wish." If they do not want to move, then people of Zhengjiang and Tangshan should move to Weiningying, while people of Fenghuang, Zhendongpu and Zhenyipu can move to Fengjipu. They can share houses and food. If the grain is insufficient, there will be support from the Khan's granary. Presumably, there will be enough grain to eat and enough lands for farming and there is no need to pay *(orin ilan de, jeng giyang, tang xan, fung hvwang, jeng dung pu, jeng yi pu, sunja ba i niyalma de wasimbuha, niowanggiyaha qi amasi, sanqar qi julesi, jase jakarame juxen i tehengge, goro ba nadan jakvn ba bi, hanqi ba emu ba juwe ba bi, tehe boo weilehe jeku yooni bi, orho moo elgiyen, usin huweki, ba sain, suwe tede genehe de, weilehe jeku be tehei jembi, jeku orho moo elgiyen, ai jaka de umai joborakv, niyengniyeri usin tarire erinde, jasei tulegi ba tariqi inu tari, jasei dorgi ba tariki seqi, sanqar, hvi an pu, fusi, dung jeo, mahadan, xan yang ioi i babe qihai tari, tubade genere qihakv oqi, jeng giyang, tang xan i niyalma, wei ning ing de guri, fung hvwang, jeng dung pu, jeng i pu i niyalma, fung ji pu de guri, boo be aqan te, jeku be aqan jefu, isirakvqi, han i cang ni jeku buf ulebumbi, jeku be inu jeqi isimbi, usin be inu tariqi tesumbi seme bodohobi, suwembe hvda tuqibume udaburakv).*[627] It is outspoken that the state offered farming lands as an incentive to expand territory after the war.

Sometimes, farming tools and seeds were provided to the Han Chinese people who cultivate official lands. On the fourteenth day of the

---

[627] *Fe dangse*, pp. 1283-1286.

third month in 1622, the Grand Coordinators sent a document to the Commander of Guards (man. *jung giyvn*; chin. *zhongjun* 中軍) of Sarhv, declaring that among the neighboring eight cities, most of the new Han Chinese comers had already been equipped with farm tools and soybean seeds according to the number of oxen they possessed. Those who have claimed such equipment should not claim again, otherwise, they would be punished. Those who have nothing can claim farm tools molded by the administration and if they need more, they can claim at Qinghe 清河. Each household should claim enough soybean seeds and if not, they can be granted with lima-beans *(du tang ni bithe, juwan duin de sarhv i jung giyvn de wasimbuha, sini jakvn heqen i gurime jihe iqe boigon i nikan, ihan de halhan ofoho turi bi sere, akv niyalma komso sere, bisire niyalma ume gaijara, bisire niyalma doosidame gaiqi weile, akv niyalma be tuwame bu, musei hunggerehe halhan ofoho bu, halhan isirakvqi, niowanggiyaha de gana, turi use isiqi wajiha, isirakvqi, afiya turi be tufi gaikini).* [628] Such passages confirm that the Manchu state overly intervened the land distribution and food production, performing a role of guardian for the economic development.

The Jurchen way of farming remained different from the Han Chinese. On the twenty-third day of the fifth month in 1623, the Grand Coordinator sent documents to remind the Jurchens not to imitate the Han Chinese farmers who hoe their lands twice. According to our old custom, the official document said, farmers should pull up the weeds and then hoe the lands. If the Jurchens follow, the Han Chinese way to hoe their lands twice, then saltpetre will emerge in field ditches and grass cannot be completely removed from the area of crop's root. Company officers who are in charge of farming must urge people to work faster *(du tang ni bithe, sunja biyai orin ilan de wasimbuha, usin be nikan be alhvdame juwe jergi ume yangsara, musei fe kooli dabgifi dahame hukxen, nikan be alhvdame juwe jergi yangsaha de, usin i holo de siyoo dekdembi, jekui da i orho be hafafi waqihiyame yangsaburahv, usin boxoro janggin hvdun boxome weilebu).* [629] Pei Huang argued that the Jurchen have learned the Han Chinese way of farming which encouraged the sinicization of the

---

[628] *Fe dangse*, pp. 1752-1753.
[629] *Fe dangse*, pp. 2368-2369.

Manchus,[630] nonetheless, the above passage clearly tells that there has been traditional way of farming among the Jurchen society, at least in Nurgaqi's reign. Both Jurchen and Han Chinese farmers have their unique way of cultivation, and the Jurchen way worked efficiently in the particular environment of northeast Asia.

5.2.5 Subsidiary Food Production

In the early stage of unifying the Han Chinese cities, many civilians were executed by the Jurchen army. Later Nurgaqi realized that it is better to keep those commoners, and in return, they can produce stuff to benefit the Jurchen rulers. One of the benefits is fruit planted by the Han Chinese people. On the first day of the fourth month in 1621, the Khan said, "when unifying Liaodong fortification (man. *liyoodung ni heqen*; chin. *liaodong cheng* 遼東城),[631] many of my Jurchen soldiers died. It took a heavy price to obtain the Liaodong people, who were not killed after the war but treated with kindness. They lived peacefully as before. People in Haizhou, Fuzhou and Jinzhou did not resist as the Liaodong people did and therefore, you should not worry about being slaughtered. It only takes one day to kill and a moment to eat. Slaughter can be done instantly but there is no benefit from doing so. If I pardon you and take care of your life, your hands will produce all sorts of products, which can be used for commerce. Furthermore, you will contribute delicious fruit and other stuff, which is forever beneficial. If so, I will treat you well" *(han hendume, liyoodung ni heqen be afara de, mini qoohai niyalma inu kejine buqehe kai, tuttu buqeme afafi baha liyoodung ni heqen i niyalma be, hono wahakv gemu ujifi, fe kemuni banjimbi kai, suweni hai jeo, fu jeo, ginjeo i niyalma, liyoodung ni gese afahabio, suwe ume olhoro, waqi emu inenggi, jeqi emu erin kai, wafi gaiha bahangge tere udu, dartai wajimbi kai, ujiqi, suweni gala qi ai jaka gemu tuqimbi, tuqike be dahame, hvda hvdaxara, sain tubihe, sain jaka benjire oqi, tere enteheme tusa kai, tuttu oqi, suwembe bi geli gosimbi).*[632]

As for the daily needs, such as fish, vegetable and fruit, the document keeper recorded the contributions made by some military officers,

---

[630] Pei Huang (2011), *Reorienting the Manchus: A Study of Sinicization, 1583-1795*, Cornell East Asia Series 152, Ithaca New York, p. 101.
[631] In the early Manchu documents, Liaodong City refers to Liaoyang 遼陽.
[632] *Fe dangse*, pp. 907-908.

bondservants and civilians. On the seventeenth day of the fifth month in 1621, Aita, the Mobile Corps Commander of Gaizhou, contributed with two large fish, 2,400 small fish and one basket of cherry *(juwan nadan de, ginjeo heqen i aita iogi, amba nimaha juwe, ajige nimaha juwe minggan duin tanggv, ingtori emu kuwangse benjihe).*[633] On the eighteenth day, the bond-servant gardeners delivered melons and cherries; Li Xiuyi delivered one plate of apricots, two plates of cherries and two plates of King Snake-gourds from Xiangyangsi *(juwan jakvn de, yafan i booi niyalma, hengki, ingtori benjihe, hiyang yang si i li sio i, guilehe emu fan, ingtori juwe fan, nasan hengke juwe fan benjihe).*[634] On the nineteenth day, Mobile Corps Commander Zhang contributed one plate of King Snake-gourds, one plate of cherries, and two plates of apricots; Mobile Corps Commander Liu delivered two plates of King Snake-gourds, and two plates of cherries; Wang Ying delivered one plate of cherries from Jinglitun *(juwan uyun de, jang iogi, nasan hengke emu fan, ingtori emu fan, guilehe juwe fan benjihe, lio iogi, nasan hengke juwe fan, ingtori juwe fan benjihe, jing li tun i wang ing, ingtori emu fan benjihe).*[635] On the twentieth day, Cultivated Talent (man. *xusai*; chin. *xiucai* 秀才) Zhang contributed two *to* cherries *(orin de, jang xusai ingtori juwe to benjihe).*[636] On the twenty-first day, Su Youbin, who belonged to the Sunjai Village owned by Chieftain Amin, delivered two plates of apricots, two plates of melons, and one *to* peas *(orin emu de, amin beile i sunjai tun i su io bin, guilehe juwe fan, hengke juwe fan, bohori emu to benjihe).*[637] On the twenty-second day, Li Jinhou delivered one plate of eggplants from Ei Meizhuang *(orin juwe de, o mi juwang gaxan i li jin heo, hansi emu fan benjihe).*[638]

Besides contributions made by commoners, orchards were nurtured by professionals to meet the Khan's need. In the first month of 1622, Nurgaqi ordered farmers and monks, who are good at cultivating fruit trees, to move into Guangning and plant fruit trees for the Khan's use *(jai*

---

[633] *Fe dangse*, p. 982.
[634] *Fe dangse*, p. 983.
[635] *Fe dangse*, p. 984.
[636] *Fe dangse*, p. 985.
[637] *Fe dangse*, p. 985.
[638] *Fe dangse*, p. 988.

tubihe moo ujime bahanara niyalma, hvwaxasa, guwangning de jifi, han i jetere tubihe moo be ujime te).[639]

In the second month of 1623, the Fusi Imperial Son-in-law, Li Yongfang 李永芳, sent a memorial from Jinzhou 金州, reporting that within ten *li* around Jinzhou fortification, there are two hundred fifty-six pear trees, one hundred fourteen apple trees, two hundred forty-six apricot trees, 2,818 jujube trees, 58 peach trees and the total number is 3,792, allocated in eighty orchard gardens. In Muchangyipu, there are 84 pear trees, 50 peach trees, 17 apricot trees, 600 jujube trees, 4 plum trees, 4 callery pear trees and the total number is 800 in two locations. Three hundred men have been assigned to watch those trees. Furthermore, there are twenty salt producers, ten fishermen, and ten bird catchers, who have been left behind inside Jinzhou fortification *(fusi efu i ginjeo qi wesimbuhe bithei gisun, ginjeo i hoton i jurdeme juwan ba i dolo bisire sulhe moo juwe tanggv susai ninggun, pinggu moo emu tanggv juwan duin, guilehe moo juwe tanggv dehi ninggun, soro moo juwe minggan jakvn tanggv juwan jakvn, toro moo susai jakvn, uhereme tubihe moo ton, ilan minggan nadan tanggv uyunju juwe, ere moo yafan i ton jakvnju, mu qeng i pu i xulhe moo jakvnju duin, toro moo susai, guilehe moo juwan nadan, soro moo ninggun tanggv, foyoro moo duin, uli moo duin, uhereme mooi ton, jakvn tanggv, mooi yafan juwe, ere moo be tuwakiyabume ilan tanggv haha werihe, jai dabsun fuifure niyalma orin, nimaha butara niyalma juwan, gasha butara niyalma juwan, ere niyalma be gemu ginjeo i hoton de werihe).*[640]

Besides the contribution made by civilians and professionals to satisfy the need of supreme leaders, the Manchu document does support that fruit plants were also grown for economic purpose. On the seventeenth day of the seventh month in 1621, Nurgaqi warned that within or outside the fortification, if people tie their horses and oxen on the fruit trees of the Jurchen residence, the trees will die out. He commanded all the tree owners and the Han Chinese people must attentively take care of the trees and sell the fruits in time *(han i bithe, juwan nadan de wasimbuha, heqen i dorgi, heqen i tulergi juxen i tehe boode bisire tubihe moo de, morin ihan hvwaitafi ijume buqembi, meni*

---

[639] *Fe dangse*, p. 1552.
[640] *Fe dangse*, pp. 1992-1994.

meni mooi ejen nikasa de hendufi, saikan tuwakiyame jujibu, ujifi hvda gaime unqakini).[641]

5.2.6 Tobacco

Among the agricultural economies, there should be tobacco plantation. Tobacco as a plant was not mentioned in the Manchu documents written in Nurgaqi's time. Comparatively, poppy flowers occurred as Rice-Sack Flower (*mi'nanghua* 米囊花) from time to time in Han Chinese literature since the Tang dynasty (618-907). A Tang poet Yong Tao 雍陶 (ca. 834) depicted that Rice-Sack Flowers first appeared in front of his horse (*maqian chuxian mi'nanghua* 馬前初見米囊花); Fang Yue 方岳 (1199-1262), a Southern Song poet, wrote that one time he faced Rice-Sack Flowers with an empty stomach in the morning (*zhaoji ceng dui mi'nanghua* 朝飢曾對米囊花); Shen Zhongyan 沈鍾彥 (ca. 1608-1668) pictured the blossom of Rice-Sack flowers on his fence (*litou yifang mi'nanghua* 籬頭已放米囊花) in his poem named as Poppy Flowers (*yingsuhua* 罌粟花); last but not least, Cao Yin 曹寅 (1658-1712), who was the grandfather of Cao Xueqin 曹雪芹 (ca. 1715-ca. 1763), described that the Rice-Sack flowers are glittering the courtyard (*manting cuican mi'nanghua* 滿庭璀璨米囊花), also in his poem dedicated to a painting Poppy Flowers (*tihua yingsu* 題畫罌粟). However, whether these poppy plants were suitable for smoking is unknown. Scholar Han Dacheng 韓大成 believed that tobacco was grown for commercial purpose after the middle period of Ming and tobacco plants spread from Fujian and Guangdong provinces.[642]

Tan Qian 談遷 (1594-1658) mentioned the Gold-Silk-Smoke (*jinsiyan* 金絲菸), named as tobacco (*danbagu* 淡巴菰) that came from oversea-foreign countries, flooded into Fujian and Guangdong provinces. The nature of tobacco is dry and poisonous, which can kill people. In the second year of Tianqi (1622), the plantation of tobacco spread through Guangxi due to the obstruction in Guizhou. In the sixteenth year of Chongzhen (1643), the imperial orders banned tobacco, even by

---

[641] *Fe dangse*, p. 1078.

[642] Han Dacheng 韓大成 (1957), *Mingdai shangpin jingji de fazhan* 明代商品經濟的發展 (The Development of Commercial Economy in the Ming Dynasty), collected in *Mingqing shehui jingji xingtai de yanjiu* 明清社會經濟形態的研究 (Research on Patterns of Social Economy in the Ming and Qing Dynasties), Shanghai remin chubanshe, Shanghai, p. 11.

sentencing the private sellers to death. However, the situation could not be changed (*jinsiyan, chu haiwai fanguo, yue danbagu, liuru minyue, ming jinsiyan... chongzhen shiliunian chijin, sifan zhi lunsi, erbuneng ge ye* 金絲菸，出海外番國，曰淡巴菰，流入閩粵，名金絲菸。性燥有毒，能殺人。天啓二年，貴州道梗，借徑廣西，始移其種...崇禎十六年敕禁，私販至論死，而不能革也).[643]

The Manchu-language documents gave details of what the Han Chinese people planted in the Liaodong region and what they paid as taxation to Nurgaqi's court, but there were few records of tobacco plantation and consumption. Suddenly, tobacco appeared frequently in Hong Taiji's reign. The reason, according to Goodrich's research, could be the Manchus adopted tobacco from Koreans after the first quarter of the seventeenth century.[644] Goodrich's assumption can be confirmed by writings of Liu Tingji 劉廷璣, who recorded that the smokable grass is called tobacco, and by word of mouth, tobacco beyond the pass originated in Korea (*yancao ming danbagu... guangwai xiangchuan benyu gaoli* 煙草名淡巴菰...關外相傳本於高麗國).[645] A Korean source also recorded that in 1638 Koreans smuggled tobacco, which was named as South-Miraculous Grass, into Shenyang. However, the Qing military leaders, who interrogated the Koreans rampantly, discovered this secret business. The Korean source also commented that the South-Miraculous Grass originated in Japan (*jiawu wo guoren qianyi nanlingcao rusong shenyang, wei qingjiang suojue, dasi jieze. nanlingcao, ribenguo suochan zi cao ye* 甲午我國人潛以南靈草入送瀋陽，爲清將所覺，大肆詰責。南靈草，日本國所產之草也).[646] Thus, we can assume Japan-Korea as one route of importing tobacco into Manchuria in the first half of the seventeenth century.

---

[643] *Zaolin zazu* 棗林雜俎 (Miscellany of Jujube Forest), written by Tan Qian 談遷 (1594-1658) and edited by Luo Zhonghui 羅仲輝 and Hu Mingxiao 胡明校, edition Beijing: Zhonghua shuju, 2006, pp. 478-479.

[644] L. Carrington Goodrich (1938), Early Prohibitions of Tobacco in China and Manchuria, *Journal of the American Oriental Society*, Yale University Press, 58.4: 684.

[645] *Zaiyuan zazhi* 在園雜誌 (Miscellaneous Records of Zaiyuan), written by Liu Tingji 劉廷璣 (1654-?), edited by Zhang Shouqian 張守謙, edition Beijing: Zhonghua shuju, 2005, p. 117.

[646] *Mingdai Man Meng shiliao* 明代滿蒙史料 (Manchu-Mongol Historical Materials of the Ming Dynasty), *Lichao shilu chao* 李朝實錄抄 (Selected Compilation from the Veritable Records of the Chosŏn Court), vol. 14, edition Tokyo: 文海出版社有限公司印行 (Wenhai Publishing Co., Ltd.), 1953, p. 412.

Accordingly, in Hong Taiji's reign, the early Manchu documents detailed that in many occasions, the Khan gave tobacco to his elders as a gift. For example, on the twenty-eighth day of the intercalary eleventh month in 1631, Hong Taiji gave twenty kiyan tobacco to his big grandma and small grandma *(orin jakvn de, amba mama, ajige mama de han i unggihengge, seke mahala emte, orita kiyan dambagu...)*.[647] Lots of tobacco was also given to the Mongols as gifts. On the fifth day of the twelfth month in 1631, when the emissaries of Aru tribe was going to return, twenty *kiyan* tobacco were given as gifts *(iqe sunja de, aru i arna nomqi i elqin genehe, arna nomqi de unggihengge... dambagu orin kiyan...)*[648] On the seventh day, when the Mongol Lama from Arut was going to return, Hong Taiji did not accept his horses as a gift, but gave him ten *kiyan* tobacco on the contrary *(iqe nadan de, arut i monggo lama gehehe, gajiha morin be gaihakv, lama de ... dambagu juwan kiyan...)*[649] On the fourteenth day, in total there were sixty-five *kiyan* tobacco given to the Arut tribe *(juwan duin de, aru i jaisang hvwang taiji... dambagu juwan kiyan buhe... dambagu dehi kiyan... dambagu tofohon kiyan buhe...)*[650] On the seventeenth day, twenty *kiyan* tobacco were given to Uncle Sanggarjai of the Khorchin tribe *(tere inenggi, korqin i sanggarjai nakqu... orin kiyan dambagu...)*.[651]

The above passages suggest that tobacco circulated among the nobles in the upper Manchu and Mongol societies. The plantation of tobacco can be confirmed by Goodrich's research, which was based on a translation of Manchu-Han Chinese bilingual decree, stating that the Manchu court evidently and repeatedly prohibited the consumption, sale and plantation of tobacco in 1639.[652] Now we can conclude that within five years, the Manchus and the Han Chinese central governments prohibited tobacco successively. However, in the second month of the six year of Chongde (1641), Hong Taiji instructed the Ministry of Revenue (*hubu* 戶部) and said that the previous order of prohibiting tobacco repeatedly rebuked the planters and consumers and recently the Khan himself saw the ministers

---

[647] *Fe dangse*, p. 5695.
[648] *Fe dangse*, p. 5707.
[649] *Fe dangse*, p. 5708.
[650] *Fe dangse*, pp. 5714-5719.
[651] *Fe dangse*, pp. 5726-5727.
[652] Goodrich (1938), Early Prohibitions of Tobacco in China and Manchuria, *Journal of the American Oriental Society*, Yale University Press, 58: 651-652.

were still consuming it, which caused the civilians to follow their bad example. Therefore, the ban is lifted. For anyone who consumes tobacco, they should plant and consume by themselves. Those who travel beyond borders and buy tobacco must be executed (*qian suoding jinyan zhi ling, qi zhongzhe yongzhe, lü xing shenchi. jinjian dachen deng youran yongzhi, yizhi xiaomin xiaoyoubuzhi, guxing kaijin. fan yuyong yanzhe, wei xuren zizhong er yongzhi. ruo chubian huomaizhe chusi* 前所定禁煙之令，其種者用者，屢行申飭。近見大臣等猶然用之，以致小民效尤不止，故行開禁。凡欲用煙者，惟許人自種而用之。若出邊貨買者處死).[653] As we specified earlier, the Chongzhen Emperor banned tobacco in 1643, but soon Hong Chengchou 洪承疇, the Supreme Commander of Jiliao (*jiliao zongdu* 薊遼總督), petitioned that soldiers of Liaodong were deeply addicted to tobacco, which was considered as their own life (*liaodong shuzu, shici ruoming* 遼東戍卒，嗜此若命), and consequently the ban was lifted.[654] This historical event can also be verified by Wang Bu 王逋, a Qing scholar, who wrote that tobacco, came from the middle of Fujian and people on the frontiers needed tobacco exclusively for curing the cold illness, so therefore, people beyond the pass even exchanged a horse for one *jin* tobacco. In the *guiwei* year of Chongzhen (1643), a restraining order was given and illegal planters were imprisoned. Nonetheless, the punishment of law was minor in comparison with the generous profits and therefore people ignored the imperial edict. Soon the court sentenced the offenders to death. Shortly after, however, because the cold illness of frontier force cannot be cured without tobacco, the prohibition was stopped (*yancao, chuzi minzhong. bianshangren hanji, feici buzhi. guanwairen zhi yi pima yi yan yijin. chongzhen guiwei, xia jinyan zhiling, minjian sizhongzhe wentu. faqing lizhong, min bu fengzhao. xun ling fanzhe zhan. ran bujiu yin bianjun binghan wuzhi, suiting shijin* 烟草，出自閩中。邊上人寒疾，非此不治。關外人至以匹馬易烟一觔。崇禎癸未，下禁煙之令，民間私種者問徒。法輕利重，

---

[653] *Donghualu* 東華錄 (Record of Donghua Gate), compiled by Wang Xianqian 王先謙 (1842-1917), self-collected documents, publisher was not indicated, block-printed edition in 1884, volume of Chongde liunian 崇德六年卷, p. 59.

[654] *Zhongguo yancao shihua* 中國煙草史話 (Historical Narrative of Tobacco in China), edited by Zhang Daming 張大明, edition Beijing: Zhongguo qinggongye chubanshe, 1993, p. 7.

民不奉詔。尋令犯者斬。然不久因邊軍病寒無治，遂停是禁).[655] Hence, the Manchus may have come to contact with the Han Chinese tobacco consumers, either soldiers or merchants, in the Liaodong region.

It is sensible to suggest that tobacco consumption was an important part of daily life of people in northeast Asia, including both Han Chinese and Manchus. Solid evidence proves that Koreans purposefully brought tobacco into Manchuria, and another possible route is that the Han Chinese also brought tobacco into the Liaodong region, where the Manchus were exposed to this product through wars and commercial exchanges.

5.3 Animal Husbandry

In the pre-industrial world, horse was prioritized as one of the most efficient means for transportation and war. When Zhu Yuanzhang started his enterprise against the Mongols at the east of Yangtze River, horse was his most urgent need and therefore, he sent messengers to buy horses everywhere (*chu, taizu qi jiangzuo, suoji weima, lü qianshi shiyu sifang* 初，太祖起江左，所急惟馬，屢遣使市與四方).[656] Nearly three hundred years later, Nurgaqi, the Manchu forefather (Taizu), launched a new enterprise with horses, too.

In this book, animal husbandry is treated differently than the agricultural economies because the Jurchens raised horses mainly for military purpose. Albert Feuerwerker stated that "the Ming government's role in the horse trade with Manchuria and Mongolia remained significant,"[657] however, the early Manchu documents recorded few messages about horse-trading between the Jurchens and Han Chinese. According to the Han Chinese source, three horse markets were set up in the Liaodong region since the Yongle reign (r. 1403-1424), exchanging for horses with rice, cloth and silk (*mashizhe, shi yonglejian, liaodong*

---

[655] *Yin'an suoyu* 蚓庵瑣語 (Trivial Words of Earthworm Hut), written by Wang Bu 王逋 (?-?), collected in
　　Congshu jicheng xubian 叢書集成續編 (Continuation of Collected Series), vol. 216, edition Taipei: Xinwenfeng
　　chuban gongsi, 1988, p. 204.
[656] *Mingshi* 明史 (History of Ming), vol. 92, Beijing edition: Zhonghua shuju, 1980, p. 2277.
[657] Albert Feuerwerker, The State and the Economy in Late Imperial China, p. 305.

she shi san, liaodong yi mi bu juan 馬市者，始永樂間，遼東設市三…
遼東以米布絹…).[658] Based on this source, it is reasonable to suppose
that both the Jurchens and Mongols raised and sold horses to the Han
Chinese in Liaodong.

According to a Korean source written circa 1619, among the six
domestic animals, the Jurchen exclusively raised horses in large numbers;
households of the Jurchen officers owned hundreds of thousands of
horses, and even the soldiers owned no less than tens of them (*liuchu wei
ma zuisheng, jianghu zhijia, qianbai chengqun, zuhujia yibuxia shishupi*
六畜惟馬最盛，將胡之家，千百成羣，卒胡家亦不下十數匹).[659] One
particular example is that the third day of the fourth month in 1619, the
document keeper recorded that because the military horses and all the
other horses captured in wars were weak, they must be fed with green
grass so that they would be fat and strong. Along with the horse matter,
Nurgaqi ordered the garrison troops to cultivate the wastelands at the
borders, build up cities, and station frontier guards to protect the lands
(*duin biyai iqe ilan de, qoohai morin turgalhabi, olji morin maquhabi,
niowanggiyan oho de morin tarhvbiki, jeqen i usin tarikini, jaifiyan de
hoton sahafi usin weilere be tuwakiyara anafu qooha ilikini seme*).[660]

State's animals were well fed with fodder collected from the
commoners. On the seventeenth day of the eighth month in 1621,
Nurgaqi ordered the officials to quickly collect grain and grass for
feeding the animals (*juwan nadan de, fe an i gaijara alban i jeku orho be,
hvdun hafirame boxofi ulebu*).[661]

Besides fodder, animals also directly fed on grass during the
wintertime. On the seventh day of the ninth month in 1621, Nurgaqi sent
a document to Gaizhou, commanding that the garrison soldiers must take
the right amount of grain from granary. People who live in Jinzhou and
Fuzhou are governed by the district of Gaizhou and they can borrow
granary grain, firewood, grass and fodder for horses. The seawater will
freeze soon, and reliable people should be commissioned to goad the
redundant animals to the grassy places for feeding (*iqe nadan de, gai jeo
de unggihe gisun, musei anafu tehe qoohai niyalma, cang ni juku be*

---

[658] *Mingshi*, vol. 92, p. 2277.
[659] Li Minwan, *Jianzhou wenjianlu*, p. 42.
[660] *Fe dangse*, pp. 413-414.
[661] *Fe dangse*, pp. 1120-1121.

miyalime gaifi jefu, ginjeo, fu jeo i boigon niyalma be, gai jeo i niyalma de kamqibufi, duijire orho, morin i jetere liyoo be juwen bufi ulebu, niyalmai jeterengge cang ni jeku be juwen bu, mederi dogon juhe jafara isika kai, sain akdun niyalma be tuqibufi, fulu ulha be qasi orho bisire bade ulebume unggi).[662]

Due to the constant wars, large amounts of grain and fodder became owner-less. The Eight Banners, as military force and political administration, were in charge of registering and collecting fodder as levy. On the sixteenth day of the ninth month in 1621, Nurgaqi ordered his son-in-law, Tong, along with the eight Mobile Corps Commanders and Regional Military Commissioner (man. *dusi*; chin. *dusi* 都司) Li, to rapidly investigate the owner-less grain and grass, which should be delivered for the horse keepers who do not have grass. This matter must be handled immediately, otherwise, those disobedient bond-servants would sell them soon. Moreover, fodder must be collected along with the official grain, which should be delivered with the carts alternatively used for building the fortification *(tung fuma, si jakvn iogi, li dusi de hendufi, ejen akv jeku orho be hvdun geterembume baiqafi iqihiyame gaifi benju, morin de uleburengge akv ulefukini, tere be hvdun iqihiyarakvqi, ejen akv aha, balai unqame waqihiyambi kai, jai alban i gaijara jeku de orho dahabume gaisu, tere jeku orho be, heqen weileme hvlaxame jidere sejen de tebufi gajikini).*[663]

Horse raising was considered as an official duty to the banner-men, which must not be avoided. On the seventh day of the first month in 1622, Nurgaqi urged the Han Chinese to pay their taxation according to the regulation of the chicken year (1621). Those who possess the official horses must report to the administration. No horses should be concealed, otherwise, the concealers will be killed. Those who do not own horses must pay five *jiha* silver within this dog year *(han i bithe, nikasa de iqe nadan de wasimbuha, qooko aniya i fe an i gaijara alban i aika jaka be hvdun, waqihiyame bu, alban i morin bisire niyalma, minde alban i morin bi seme wesimbu, bisire morin be ume gidara, gidaha niyalma be wambi, morin akv niyalma, ere indahvn aniya emu haha de sunjata jiha menggun).*[664]

---

[662] *Fe dangse*, pp. 1152-1153.
[663] *Fe dangse*, pp. 1181-1182.
[664] *Fe dangse*, pp. 1443-1444.

The Jurchens kept high expectations upon horse raising. On the fifteenth day of the second month in 1622, after unifying Guanging, Nurgaqi ordered his daughters to return to the Mongol tribes and fatten their horses as soon as possible. According to the Jurchen standard, the fat Mongol horses are actually lean. Therefore, horses must be fattened up according to the Jurchen standards. Lean horses should not be sent for mission and they should wait to be fattened. Nurgaqi emphasized that other things can be given as gifts, but not horses. No one should expect a horse from him (*tofohon de,han hendume, boode isiname jaka de, gege be hvdun jurambumbi, yalufi genere morin be hvdun tarhvbu, suweni monggo i durun i tarhvn sere morin turga kai, meni durun i ambula tarhvbu, morin turga ohode unggirakv, morin tarhvhai teile unggimbi, suwende morin akv sehe seme gvwa jaka bure gojime, mini morin suwende burakv, mende ume erere*).[665]

Even for the horses of different breeds, such as Korean horses, must be fattened up. On the twenty-seventh day of the second month in 1622, the Khan ordered the banner-men to select the undersized Korean horses, which will be assigned to each company for feeding. No one should ride those Korean horses, except for the emergency, so they could be fattened up with buttocks in shape of a quail's back and necks in shape of axe-handle (*han i bithe, juwe biyai orin nadan de wasimbuha, beye ajige solho alaxan be sonjofi, emu nirui niyalma tofohon, morin be umai bade ume yalubure, karhama be muxu i huru gese, dalan be suhe fesin i gese tarhvbu*).[666] Good horse keepers were selected for professional employment. In the third month of 1622, the Grand Coordinators sent a document to the Defense Officer of Pinglupu, selecting fifteen people who own fat horses to feed other horses. As the reward, an official camel will be allocated to these fifteen horse keepers for carrying their food and other stuff (*du tang ni bithe, ping lu pu i beiguwan de wasimbuha, tarhvn morin i tofohon niyalma be tuqibufi, morin be boxome ulebu, jakvn gvsai siden i emu temen bu, tofohon niyalmai jetere aika jaka aqikini*).[667]

Within the banner system, the Han Chinese military men must raise their military horses according to the Jurchen standard. Specific regulations were set up to raise, protect and take care of horses. Either

---

[665] *Fe dangse*, pp. 1626-1623.
[666] *Fe dangse*, pp. 1682-1683.
[667] *Fe dangse*, pp. 1726-1727.

riders, teammates, or the Khan's treasury, depending on different situation, must supplement dead horses right away. On the twenty-fifth day of the fifth month in 1623, the Khan sent an edict to urge the Han Chinese to fatten their horses, which will be inspected on the fifteenth day of the eighth month. If the horses are lean, the owners and their superior Company Commander will receive punishment of flogging, and the commander must pay one *yan* silver for each lean horse as penalty. Within the districts, all horses owned by the Han Chinese can herd with the horses of Jurchens, with their saddles, bridles and weapons kept in the house of their commanders. If the horses of the Han Chinese army are lean, suffering from boils, or die of fatigue, the riders must pay compensation. If all people agree that the horses have died of plague, then the loss must be compensated by twenty men. Afterwards, if horses died of plague again, then the loss will be compensated by the Khan's treasury *(han i bithe, sunja biyai orin sunja de wasimbuha... nikan i qoohai morin be hvdun boxome tarhvbu, jakvn biyai tofohon de tuwambi, morin turga oqi, morin i ejen be, qiyanzung be tantambi, kadalara ejen de, turgan morin tome emte yan menggun gaimbi, meni meni harangga nikan i morin be, musei juxen i morin i emgi adula, enggemu, hadala, ai ai qoohai agvra be, gemu kadalara ejen i boode bargiyame gaifi asara, nikan i qoohai morin turgalara, darin tuqire, qalire buqeqi, tere morin be yaluha ejen toodakini, gere seme nimeku de buqeqi, neneme buqehe morin be orin haha aqan udafi bukini, amala nimeku de geli buqeqi, han i ku i menggun i udafi bu).*[668]

In short, one can see that horse-raising was strictly governed for military usage. Furthermore, the Jurchens also raised pigs for food. One passage points out that pigs were also kept by the Han Chinese who cohabited with the Jurchens. On the seventh day of the sixth month in 1622, a Regional Vice Commander (man. *fujiyang*; chin. *fujiang* 副將) Liu reported to Nurgaqi that in the Bolopu, which is thirty *ba* away in the north of Gaizhou, a bond-servant Xose of Hvsita's Company (man. *niru*; chin. *niulu* 牛錄) lived there. A cohabiting Han Chinese man came to Commander Liu and sued that his cattle was used by the Jurchens for plowing, he himself served the Jurchens and his wife also cooked for the Jurchens, but the Jurchens robbed, killed his pigs and only threw one or

---

[668] *Fe dangse*, pp. 2381-2383.

two *jiha* as payment *(iqe nadan de, lio fujiyang bithe wesimbume, gai jeo i amala gvsin ba i dubede, bo lo pu i jakade hvsita nirui aha xose tehebi, aqafi tehe nikan, gai jeo de lio fujiyang de habxanafi, amala mini ihan be juxen tarimbi, mini beyebe inu juxen takvrambi, mini sargan inu buda bujubumbi, mini ujihe ulgiyan be, amba ulgiyan de emu juwe jiha maktame bufi, gidame jafafi wambi seme uttu habxara jakade)*.[669]

This passage at least points out that the looted pigs were undervalued than a regular market price. Another passage confirmed that the Han Chinese people raised pigs and the Jurchen authority protected their properties. Three Jurchens who were under the company of Yanjuhv robbed three pigs from the Han Chinese. They killed the pigs and ate them. Two of the robbers were punished and the other one received death penalty *(yanjuhv nirui ilan niyalma, nikan i ulgiyan be durime wafi jeke seme, juwe niyalma be erulehe, emu niyalma be waha)*.[670]

Through the banner system, state also sponsored pig raising. On the twenty-seventh day of the third month in 1622, the Grand Coordinators declared that anyone who wants to raise pigs can submit a liability statement to their Company Commanders (man. *nirui ejen*; chin. *niulu ezhen* 牛錄額真) or Deputy Secretaries (man. *janggin*; chin. *zhangjing* 章京), who will help them buy sows. If the sows were killed under the cover of pig keeping, the commanders and secretaries will be flogged by one hundred. The buyers will also be flogged, and their ears and noses will be pierced as extra punishment. No one is allowed to kill sows under the cover of buying pigs *(du tang ni bithe, orin nadan de wasimbuha, ulgiyan ujiki sere niyalma, nirui ejen, daise janggin de akdulafi, mehe ulgiyan udafi uji, ujimbi seme udafi waha de, nirui ejen, daise janggin de tanggv xusiha i weile, udaha niyalma de tanggv suxiha, oforo xan i wele, erei elgin de balai ulgiyan udafi ume wara)*.[671]

Nonetheless, pigs were also considered as state's property in some circumstances. On the twenty-seventh day of the first month in 1623, Mobile Corps Commander Quan discharged one thousand households in Jianzhou, from which he took two hundred forty pigs and delivered them to the Defense Officer Wang in Fuzhou *(kiowan iogi ginjeo ba i emu minggan boigon i niyalma be faqabufi, juwe tanggv orin ulgiyan gajifi, fu*

---

[669] *Fe dangse*, pp. 1868-1867.
[670] *Fe dangse*, p. 1150.
[671] *Fe dangse*, pp. 1802-1803.

jeo i wang beiguwan de afabuha).[672] It is evident that the state was behind the horse raising and pig farming, which were critical for military act and welfare of the nobles.

5.4 Hunting, Fishing and Gathering

5.4.1 Hunting

Hunting was a traditional profession among the Jurchen-Manchu societies. In the third month of 1615, when Nurgaqi established a regulation for the chieftains and officials to hold feasts, he mentioned that there were people who were outside hunting in the wilderness, searching ginseng, sable and silver squirrel for months (*orhoda seke ulhu butara biganrame juwe ilan biya yabure niyalma* ...).[673] This passage tells that some Jurchen people were gathering and hunting as a profession. Besides, from a state's perspective, hunting was also military manoeuvre under strict organization.

In the eleventh month of 1615, the document keeper stated that whenever Nurgaqi mobilized the troops or went hunting, he upheld the rule of law, which forbids the soldiers to make any sound. It has been said that if the troops make noises, the enemy will notice; in case of hunting, the mountain will echo if there were noises and animals will flee. No matter where the soldiers go, they must remember this rule. Five companies are assigned to one team and they must move or stop at one location. Accordingly, they should attack one target: soldiers who wear thick armors and hold long spears must fight in the front and soldiers in light armors shoot arrows from behind. The selected soldiers will ride horses and watch the battle from afar, helping the troops who are going to fail. Therefore, the army has won every war. Up to today every Company (man. *niru*; chin. *niulu* 牛錄) will receive one arrow as an order for hunting. The Khan said that if one company moves in one route, sometimes the soldiers could not reach the hunting site even up to the moment when they go home. Now ten companies receive one arrow as the order to hunt, and in this way, each company can enter the hunting ground two or three times. If soldiers of ten companies do not travel in one route, or, if some of them run away and join the other company for

---

[672] *Fe dangse*, p. 1963.
[673] Fe dangse, p. 121.

hunting in the ground, they should be punished *(sure kundulen han, daqi dain dailara de, aba abalara de fafun qira, jamaraburakv, jilgan tuqiburakv, dain de jamarame jilgan tuqiqi, bata serembi, abade jamarme jilgan tuqiqi, alin urambi, gurgu genembi seme, ai ai bade yabure de, geren qoohai niyalma de gemu doigon i taqibume ejebume hendufi, sunja niru be emu baksan arafi, yabuqi, emu babe yabume, ebuqi, emu bade ilhi ilhi ebume, afara bade emu babe afame, golmin jiramin uksin etuhe niyalma, hida jangkv jafafi juleri afame, weihuken sirata uksin etuhe niyalma, beri sirdan jafafi amargiqi gabtame, sonjoho mangga qoohai niyalma, morin yalufi enqu tuwame ilifi, eterakv bade aisilame afafi, yaya dain be eteme muteme yabuha, tede aba abalara de, emu nirui niyalma , emu niru bufi yabumbihe, han hendume, emu nirui niyalma, emu babe yabuqi, ememu nirui niyalma, amasi boode isinjitele fere de bahafi yaburakv seme, juwan niru be aqabufi emu niru bufi yabume deribuhe, tereqi emu abade, emu nirui niyalma, juwe ilan jergi fere de bahafi dasime yabuha, tere juwan nirui niyalma, emu babe yaburakv, emu juwe niyalma bulqame ukame, gvwa emgi fere de yabuha de, tere yabuha niyalma de inu weile)*.[674]

Hunting as an economy was highly competitive between the Eight Chieftains (man. *jakvn beile*; chin. *babeile* 八貝勒), who were appointed by Nurgaqi to run the state. Chaos was created since they hunted individually for themselves, while ignoring Nurgaqi as the highest representative of the state. Nurgaqi's solution is to divide the prey evenly under his supervision. On the third day of the second month in 1623, soldiers who were stationed in Guangning chased away the Mongols who came to steal grain. As spoils, the soldiers captured two hundred oxen from the Mongols. One hundred fifty oxen were delivered to Nurgaqi, and fifty were given to the soldiers. Immediately, the document keeper recorded, in the past the Eight Chieftains sent one hundred hunters individually to hunt animals, hunting marten for its fur, or collecting pearls. Each chieftain kept their own harvest. To avoid chaos, from the black-dog year (1622) all the harvested pearls, and furs of sable, lynx, tiger, wolves, otter and red squirrel, etc., were divided into eight shares evenly *(iqe ilan de, guwangning de tehe qoohai niyalma, hvlhame jeku gaijiha monggo be boxufi, juwe tanggv ihan baha, emu tanggv susai ihan*

---

[674] *Fe dangse*, pp. 145-148.

benjihe, jai susai ihan be qoohai niyalma de buhe, ai ai furdehe tana seke butaha, butarangge, taqi jakvn beile boo emte tanggv haha sindafi, baha jaka be meni meni gaimbihe, tuttu faquhvn ojorahv seme, sahaliyan indahvn aniyai butaha tana seke silun tasha niohe hailun ulhu, tenteke ai ai butaha jaka be gemu jakvn ubui neigen dendehe).[675] The individual ownership of hunting earnings created tensions between the Khan and the chieftains, so that Nurgaqi started to claim the power of distributing wealth.

This new edict has strengthened Nurgaqi's power of controlling the resources, and since then, all the harvest must be distributed under his permission. On the fifth day of the second month in 1623, the Specially-Appointed Ministers of the Eight Banners (man. *jakvn gvsai enqulehe ambasa*; chin. *baqi zhuanguan dachen* 八旗專管大臣) harvested furs of 1,493 sables, one hundred and two otters, 936 red squirrels, 281 raccoon dogs, 4 tigers, 20 ground squirrels, 8 foxes and captured 104 eagles, which were brought to the Khan *(jakvn gvsai enqulehe ambasai budaha seke uhereme ton, emu minggan duin tanggv uyunju ilan, emu tanggv juwe hailun, ulhu uyun tanggv gvsin ninggun, elbihe juwe tanggv jakvnju emu, silun juwan ninggun, damin emu tanggv duin, tasha duin, solohi orin, dobihe jakvn).* [676] In the section of Acquisition of Currencies we noted an silver treasury that was owned by Nurgaqi, and here we can posit that, in the first place, the income generated by hunting was possessed by the chieftains individually, until the late Nurgaqi's reign.

The relevant distribution was no longer determined by the participation of hunting, but according to military ranks. On the sixth day of the second month in 1623, the Khan ordered to abolish the regulation that allowed Specially-appointed Ministers to send their own hunters to hunt for themselves. From now on all the hunted animals, such as furs of tiger, lynx, fox, raccoon dog, red squirrel, ect., along with eagle plumes, will be distributed to the military officers according to their ranks, ranging from the Regional Commander (man. *zung bing guwan*; chin. *zongbingguan* 總兵官) to the Defense Officers (man. *beiguwan*; chin. *beiyu* 備御), whether they went hunting or no. Twenty-eight furs are granted to the first rank, twenty-three to the second, eighteen to the third,

---

[675] *Fe dangse*, pp. 1975-1977.
[676] *Fe dangse*, p. 1980.

fifteen to the fourth, thirteen to the fifth, eleven to the sixth, nine to the seventh, fifth to the eighth, four to the ninth *(enqulehe ambasa hergen i bodome haha sindafi butaha jaka be meni meni gaimbihe, tere be nakafi, butafi baha tasha silun seke dobihi hailun elbihe ulhu, damin i dethe, ai ai furdehe be, butaha sindaha sindahakv niyalma de, iqe ninggun i inenggi, zung bing guwan qi fusihvn, beiguwan qi wesihun, ilhi ilhi hergen i bodome buhe, uju jergi de orin jakvta, jai jergi de orin ilata, ilaqi jergi de juwan jakvta, duiqi jergi de tofohoto, sunjaqi jergi de juwan ilata, ninggqi jergi de juwan emte, nadaqi jergi de uyute, jakvqi jergi de junjata, uyuqi jergi de duinte buhe).*[677]

Throughout his life, Nurgaqi kept hunting as a hobby and a practical profession that benefits the state's institutions. On the fifteenth of the fourth month in 1623, the Khan traveled beyond the borders to inspect the farming lands and encircled animals for hunting. Ten deer and roe deer were killed and distributed to the functioning officials. The team camped at the landing place of Barga river *(tofohon de, jase tuqifi usin tarire babe tuwame aba abalafi, buhv gio juwan isime wafi, hergengge ambasa de salame buhe, barga i dogon de deduhe).*[678]

Soldiers were also able to share the achievement of hunting. On the sixteenth dya, the Khan departed the place named as Jang i jan to inspect the farming lands and encircled the animals for hunting again. This time they killed twenty deer and roe deer, which were not given to the functioning officials but distributed to the soldiers for cooking soup to eat. Later the Khan cast net on the Liao river. He traveled by boat and caught ten fish by a steel fork. That night, they camped at the landing place of Liao river *(juwan ninggun de, jang i jan qi wasihvn, usin tarire be tuwame aba sindafi, buhv gio orin isime wafi, hergengge ambasa de buhekv, geren qoohai niyalma de sile jekini seme salame bufi, liyooha de asu hvrhan sindafi, han i beye weihu de tefi, xaka jafafi juwan isime nimaha wafi, liyoha dogon de deduhe).*[679]

The ownership of properties, including booty from war and preys from hunting, was emerging along with the expansion of the state. The section of Acquisition of Currencies tells that Nurgaqi strictly controlled the distribution of precious metals, and this chapter shows that Nurgaqi

[677] *Fe dangse*, pp. 1981-1982.
[678] *Fe dangse*, p. 2221.
[679] *Fe dangse*, pp. 2222-2223.

was aware of the relationship between the hunting income and his authority. State starts to step further in the distribution of wealth.

Furthermore, in a broader view of Qing history, one must note that hunting is more than an mere economic activity, but a tradition that maintains a Manchu identity which is culturally distinct than the other ethnic peoples. [680] Through the above analysis, one can know that Nurgaqi had well maintained hunting as a military exercise and personal hobby. However, hunting as a custom declined in Hong Taiji's time. In the seventh month of 1636, Hong Taiji mentioned that in Nurgaqi's time, when people heard about hunting, they would prepare eagles and play football for a celebration; people cried out if they were not permitted to participate. However, Hong Taiji criticized his subordinates, today the youngsters only indulged themselves in travelling, leisure and entertainment (*taizushi, wodeng wen mingri chulie, ji yu wei tiaoying cuqiu. ruobu ling wang, qi qing suixing. jin zhi zidi, wei wu chuwai youxing, xianju xile* 太祖時，我等聞明日出獵，即豫爲調鷹蹴毬。若不令往，泣請隨行。今之子弟，惟務出外遊行，閒居戲樂). [681] For remedy, he personally led the officials to hunt and punished those who performed inadequately by forfeiting their horses (*shang xinglie, yi weichang zhongduan shouyi fa … angbang siren suocheng zhima* 上行獵，以圍場中斷獸逸罰…昂邦四人所乘之馬). [682] Hong Taiji repeatedly declared that the Qing state was based on the profession of riding and shooting, and if people did not practice arrows and bows, but got addicted to banquets and entertainment, then hunting and battle array would be unfamiliar to them. Consequently military manoeuvre would be out of practice (*wo guojia yi qishe weiye, jinruo bu shiqin gongshi, weidan yanle, ze tianlie xingzhen zhishi bi zhi shukuang, wubei heyou er de xi hu* 我國家以騎射爲業，今若不時親弓矢，惟耽宴樂，則田獵行陣之事必致疎曠，武備何由而得習乎). [683] Thus, one can see that in the pre-industrial era, hunting was embedded with multiple functions rather than merely increasing financial income.

---

[680] Nicolas K. Menzies (1994), *Forest and Land Management in Imperial China*, Macmillan Publishers St. Martin's Press, New York, p. 58.

[681] *Qingshilu*, vol. p. 386.

[682] *Qingshilu*, vol. 2, p. 441.

[683] *Qingshyilu*, vol. 2, p. 446.

5.4.2 Fishing

Fishing was another traditional profession among the Jurchen-Manchu societies. Elliott pointed out that the Yeren Jurchens depended more on fishing while the Jianzhou and Haixi were more of hunters.[684] The documents written on the twenty-fourth day of the fifth month in 1620 mentioned that Nurgaqi had his own bond-servants, named as Hanquha, Gvnaqin, Lodori, and Ahadai, whose profession was fishing for the Khan *(orin duin de... han i booi nimaha baire hanquha, gvnaqin, lodori, ahadai duin niyalma).*[685]

Besides personal hobby displayed in the previous passages, fishing was also considered as a collective practice, which was carried out by the Eight Banners. After inspecting the farming lands, on the following seventeenth day of the fourth month in 1623, Nurgaqi ordered the Eight-Banner troops to cast nets on the Liao river. The Khan took a boat to search fish but caught nothing. Later the army moved boats and nets to a large pond, caught nothing but broke the fishnets. The Khan raged and requested to find out which banners had brought all their nets and which had not. He would punish those banners that did a poor job. The inspection confirmed that the Bordered White Banner brought their big net which is longer than eight *da*,[686] the net of Bordered Red Banner is seventeen *da*, Plain White Banner nineteen *da*, Plain Yellow Banner seven and half *da*, Bordered Yellow Banner twenty-one and half *da*, Plain Red Banner eighteen *da*, Plain Blue Banner's net is fifteen *da*, which was too broken for fishing, and Bordered Blue Banner seventeen *da*. The Khan ordered to discuss the matter at home. According to his command, all nets must be brought back and the punishment upon their neglect of duty will be severe. The army camped at the bank of the pool *(juwan nadan de, qimari erde liyoha de hvrhan asu sindafi, han i beye weihu de tefi, nimaha baiqi bahakv ofi, tereqi weihu hvrhan be amba omo de gamafi, nimaha baiqi inu bahakv, hvrhan hvwajara jakade, han jili banjifi, wei gvsai hvrhan yooni gajihabi, wei gvsai hvrhan yooni gajihakvbi, hasa baiqa, weile araki seme baiqaqi, kubuhe xanggiyan i*

---

[684] Elliott, *the Manchu Way*, p. 49.

[685] *Fe dangse*, p. 995.

[686] The Manchu measure of length, *da*, corresponds with *tuo* 庹 in official document. One *da* is about five *chi* 尺, which is the distance between the ends of middle fingers of two stretching arms (of an adult person) in two opposite directions.

gvsai hvrhan jakvn da, emu kooji, kubuhe fulgiyan i gvsai juwan nadan
da, gulu xanggiyan i gvsai juwan uyun da, gulu suwayan i gvsai nadan
da emu gala, kubuhe suwayan i gvsai orin emu da emu gala, gulu
fulgiyan i gvsai juwan jakvn da, gulu lamun i gvsai tofohon da niyahabi
ehe, kubuhe lamun i gvsai juwan nadan da, ere weile be boode genefi
gisureki, ambula weile maktaki seme gajiha, tere omo i dalin de
deduhe).[687]

Fishing also had an entertainment purpose. In the seventh month of
1623, the Khan, leading the chieftains and officials, left the town for
fishing. They returned after a big banquet *(ineku tere inenggi, han, geren*
beise ambasa be gaifi, heqen qi tuqime nimaha hvrhadame genefi, amba
sarin sarilafi jihe).[688]

The Eight Chieftains also had their own fishermen. In a warm season
of 1624, the Khan ordered Bada and Tuhei to inform the fishermen of the
Eight Chieftains to gather at Durbi for fishing on the fifteenth day of the
month, regardless of their current locations. The Khan will take his wives
to watch the activity. The Gvwalqa tribe will also fish at the fishing
location *(han hendume, bada, tuhei, suwe jakvn beise i booi nimaha beire*
niyalma be, dergi wargi de bisirengge be, gemu ere biyai tofohon de
durbi de isabufi nimaha baime aliya, han, fujisa be gamame genembi,
gvwalqa sa ini baire bade baikini).[689] Compared with hunting, fishing
was less intervened by the supreme leader who represented the state.
Nonetheless, the Manchu documents still highlighted the superior role of
Nurgaqi in the fishing profession over the chieftains.

5.4.3 Gathering

Gathering was a profitable economy. In the ancient societies, civilians
harvested bee honey for personal use and for sale. The document keeper
recorded that on the fifth day of the eleventh month in 1621, Mobile
Corps Commander (man. *iogi*; chin. *youji* 遊擊) Zhao of New
fortification contributed seven buckets of honey, which is four hundred
gin to the Khan *(iqe heqen i jao iogi, nadan sihan duin tanggv gin hibsu*

---

[687] *Fe dangse*, pp. 2223-2225.
[688] *Fe dangse*, p. 2575.
[689] *Fe dangse*, pp. 2770-2771.

benjihe).[690] This honey must have been collected by his soldiers or bond-servants.

Both the Han Chinese and Jurchens harvested ginseng, pine nuts, mushroom, jelly fungus, honey and cut woods. In the Han Chinese culture, ginseng was highly rated as a herb for nourishing their bodies and extending lifespan. As the most prominent product of nature that represents a Manchu identity in the Qing dynasty, ginseng grows in Changbaishan, which borders today China's three northeast provinces, part of Russia and all over Korean peninsula.[691] The document keeper recorded that in 1604 the Jurchens sold ginseng to the Han Chinese. Because the ginseng was water-bathed, so the Han Chinese refused to buy such wet goods. The Jurchens were afraid that the water-bathed ginseng could not last and thus sold them immediately with a cheap price. Nurgaqi wanted to boil ginseng and dry them under the sun, but his subordinates did not agree. Nurgaqi did not listen to his subordinates, but boiled the ginseng, sold in a slow pace and made a fortune abundantly out of it *(julke daqi daiming gurun de orhoda unqambihe de madabufi usihin unqame daiming gurun i hvdai niyalma jortai gaijarakv ohode, orhoda niyambi seme ebxeme unqame ofi, hvda ambula baharakv bihe, taizu sure beile bujufi walgiyafi unqaki seqi, beise ambasa marame bujufi adarame walkiyambi seqi, taizu sure beile emhun marame orhoda be bujufi walgiyafi olhoho manggi, elhei unqame deribufi hvda ulin ambula bahame oho).*[692] Wang Zhonghan 王鍾翰 pointed out that ginseng gathering was also highly regarded by Hong Taiji as one of the essential ways for people to make a living and he also encouraged the Manchus, Han Chinese and Mongols to gather ginseng for trading with the Ming merchants.[693] Furthermore, Feng Jia argued that the ginseng business, together with furs, was monopolized by Nurgaqi for greater profits.[694] As we ascertained in the section of hunting, the prey distribution was not

---

[690] *Fe dangse*, p. 1228.

[691] Seonmin Kim (2017), Ginseng and Borderland: Territorial Boundaries and Political Relations between Qing China and Chosŏn Korea, 1636-1912, University of California Press, California, pp. 1-38.

[692] Manzhou shilu, p.124.

[693] Wang Zhonghan, *Qingshi zakao*, p. 47.

[694] Feng Jia (2017), Emperor's Coffer: The Qing Imperial Fiscal Separation Between Privy Purse and State Treasury, PhD book, University of California, Los Angeles, pp. 78-79.

controlled by Nurgaqi until 1623, which indicated that fur business was not monopolized by the state in the early Manchu regime.

In Hong Taiji's time, the harvested ginseng was also an important means for the Jin state to pay off their trade deficit. Due to the long-lasting wars between the Later Jin and Ming China, Korea, presumably became the intermediate of commercial transaction. According to the early Manchu annals, the Korean government made decent profits by reselling the Jurchen ginseng to the Ming Han Chinese. On the twentieth day of the twelfth month in 1635, Hong Taiji sent emissaries to Korea, accusing the Korean king for manipulating the ginseng price. In the beginning, the price was fixed on sixteen *liang* silver for one *jin*, but later the Korean king lied that the Ming Han Chinese merchants did not come to buy and accordingly the price had to be lowered to nine *liang* per *jin*. However, according to the confession of the Han Chinese war prisoners from Tieshan 鐵山, ginseng was sold the Han Chinese who lived on Pidao 皮島, at the price of twenty *liang* silver per *jin*.[695]

On the nineteenth day of the sixth month in 1636, due to the previous trade deficit with Korea, Hong Taiji sent Mafuta and Muhu, along with a Deputy Company Commander (man. *funde boxokv*; chin. *daizi* 代子) and a soldier from each company, to deliver ginseng to Korea's Yizhou for balancing the deficit *(juwan uyun de, mafuta, muhu de emu gvsai emte funde boxokv, emu nirui emte uksin be adabufi, solho de neneme hvdaxaha eden i jalan de i jeo de orhoda benebume unggihe)*.[696] On the twenty-ninth day of the eighth month in 1636, Mafuta and Hasitan delivered seven hundred *gin* ginseng to Yizhou, as one way to pay off some overdue Korean debt *(orin nadan de, mafuta, hasitan,fe eden i nandan tanggv gin orhoda be i jeo de benefi jio seme unggihe...)*.[697] Besides, large amounts of ginseng was also used as a leverage, along with pearls and furs, to exchange with the Ming empire for its gold, silver, silk and cloth, as truce condition. Though the agreement was not reached between the two parties, as Wang Zhonghan 王鍾翰 indicated, ginseng was not treated as living products, but commercial goods, which reflect

---

[695] Qingchu neiguoshiyuan manwen dangan yibian, p. 217.
[696] *Fe dangse*, pp. 7342-7343.
[697] *Fe dangse*, p. 7673.

gathering as an existed economic factor.[698] Moreover, as Lin Sun proclaims, wild ginseng, along with sable fur, brought abundant incomes into state's treasury and played crucial roles in the empire building of the early Qing dynasty.[699]

In Nurgaqi's reign, products of hunting and gathering brought significant income to the state. As we found out in the section of Acquisition of Lands, the Jurchens traded with the Han Chinese at the four markets in Fushun, Qinghe, Kuandian and Aiyang, where they gained large quantities of currencies and treasure that enriched the Manchus state remarkably (... *fuxun xo, qing ho, kuwan diyan, ai yang duin duka de hvda hvdaxame ulin nadan gaime, manju gurun bayan wesihun oho*).[700] In Hong Taiji's reign, the Manchu state had to rely on Korea for commercial exchange due to the frequent wars with the Ming empire. Nonetheless, these traditional professions were the basic driving forces to increase the economic power for greater achievements.

According to Van Jay Symons, after 1644 the profession of ginseng gathering was monopolized by the Qing state through banners and government, except for a short time period when merchants managed it.[701] In this light, we can argue that before 1644, ginseng gathering and trade was gradually dominated by the state, first through the banners in Nurgaqi's reign and then via the Ministry of Revenue when Hong Taiji reformed the polity.

5.5 Mining

Metals were an important matter for the ancient government to maintain dominance over its people. For a long time, salt and iron were the substitute word for economy in some Han Chinese dynasties. Furthermore, precious metals, such as gold and silver, are always reliable medium for people to exchange their labor of different forms. Wang Zhonghan 王鍾翰 found that in the second half of the sixteenth century,

---

[698] Wang Zhonghan, *Qingshi zakao*, p. 49.

[699] Lin Sun (2018), The Economy of Empire Building: Wild Ginseng, Sable Fur, and the Multiple Trade Networks of the Early Qing Dynasty, 1583-1644. PhD thesis, University of Oxford.

[700] Manzhou shilu, p. 73.

[701] Van Jay Symons (1981), *Ch'ing Ginseng Management: Ch'ing Monopolies in Microcosm* (Occasional Papers No 13), Arizona Sate University Center for Asian Studies, Tempe, p. 10.

the Jurchen societies already had their own artisans for recasting their iron tools which were exchanged from the Ming and Korea.[702] However, the mining of iron was rather late. The Manchu document keeper recorded that in the light-yellow-pig year (1599), the Jurchen authority under Nurgaqi's leadership started to mine gold, silver and iron *(sohon ulgiyan aniya... ilan biya de aisin menggun feteme urebume sele wereme urebume deribuhe).*[703]

After taking over the Liaodong region, on the tenth day of the twelfth month in 1621, Nurgaqi ordered one of his Regional Vice Commanders (man. *fujiyang*; chin. *fujiang* 副將) to continuously collect grain, silver, charcoal, iron and salt as usual taxation from the people of Gaizhou, Fuzhou and Jinzhou who had not yet cohabited with the Jurchens *(sini gai jeo, fu jeo, ginjeo, de juxen kamqihakv kai, fe an i gaijara jeku, menggun, yaha, sele, dabsun i alban be ainu hvdun boxofi unggirakv).*[704] This passage proves that iron was smelted in these regions in a considerable amounts, and thus Nurgaqi enlisted their product, iron, as tax.

Nurgaqi's regime highly valued the iron producers, who enjoyed certain privilege of staying where they were after being unified. On the thirteenth day of the twelfth month in 1621, the Khan ordered the people who are manufacturing iron in Shajing not to move to other places, but still live in the current place *(han i bithe, juwan ilan de wasimbuha, sele urebure xa jing ni ba i niyalma be, ume guribure, kemuni tekini).*[705] The reason could be that the iron product was considered as one of the top important strategic materials for state management.

Besides, the Jurchen authority always paid attention to obtain new artisans for developing their iron-manufacturing economy. On the twenty-ninth day of the second month in 1623, Nurgaqi heard that the Han Chinese iron-manufacturers live in a place, which is thirty ba beyond the new borders, and he ordered Lenggeri to catch them, tie them up with ropes and bring them back. *(sele urebure nikan, iqe jase i tule gvsin ba i*

---

[702] Wang Zhonghan, *Qingshi zakao*, p. 8.
[703] Manzhou shilu, p. 112.
[704] *Fe dangse*, p. 1341.
[705] *Fe dangse*, p. 1348.

dubede tehebi sere, tere be jafame menggeri si, susai niyalma be gamafi, jafafi saikan akduleme huthufi unggi).[706]

Shicheng 石城 was also an iron-manufacturing site in Nurgaqi' time. On the fourth day of the third month in 1623, the document keeper mentioned the place Shicheng, where iron is manufactured *(iqe duin de, sele urebure xi qeng ni ba i beiguwan wang zi deng ...).*[707]

The early Manchu document also mentioned gold and silver mining, which was secondary to farming regarding its importance in traditional societies. On the first day of the third month in 1623, the Grand Coordinators informed the Han Chinese, saying that those who work in places where gold and silver are manufactured should not dig and wash during the farming time in case of delaying farm work. Apart from farming seasons, those gold and silver miners must work under permission, otherwise, they will be punished for illegal mining. If they do not have enough lands for farming, they can cultivate lands within and beyond borders as they wish. Those who live in fortresses can plow along the borders and garrison at the side of Korean border *(ineku tere inenggi, du tang ni bithe, nikan de wasimbuha, aisin menggun tuqire ba i niyalma, usin weilere erinde ume fetere, usin i weile tookaburahv, usin weilere xolo tuqike erinde, aisin wereki menggun feteki sere niyalma bithe wesimbufi, were fete sehe manggi, were, fete, tele bithe weisimburakv, dergi gisun akv, suweni qisui werehe de fetehe de weile, usin isirakv niyalma, jasei jakarame tulegi dorgi be qihai tari, tai niyalma, ere aniya tai jakarame usin tari, ishun aniya jeku akv seme burakv. emu gvsai emte kiru i ejen, emu nirui emte xanggiyan bayara be gaifi, solho i ergide anafu teme genehe).*[708]

Furthermore, the work of mining gold and silver was also controlled by the Eight Chieftains (man. *jakvn boo*; chin. *bajia* 八家). On the third day of the fourth month in 1623, the Khan received nine hundred thirty *liang* silver and six *liang* seven *qian* gold, which were exploited by the official institution. Nurgaqi asked if the miners had already paid their grain taxes twice a year. Hearing the positive answer, Nurgaqi received the gold but refused the silver, which was distributed to the miners. Besides, sixty *liang* was granted to Shi Guozhu, the supervisor, and five

---

[706] *Fe dangse*, p. 2075.
[707] *Fe dangse*, p. 2090.
[708] *Fe dangse*, pp. 2085-2087.

liang was given to each of the eight supervisors from the Eight Chieftains *(alban i fetehe menggun uyun tanggv gvsin yan, aisin ninggun yan nadan jiha benjire jakade, ere menggun fetehe niyalma juwe jergi bure jeku buheo seme fonjifi, juwe jergi jeku gemu buhe sere jakade, aisin be gaiha, menggun gemu amasi bederebume fetehe niyalma de buhe, boxome felebuhe xi guwe ju de ninju yan buhe, jakvn booi tuwame weilebuhe jakvn niyalma de sunjata yan buhe, alban i jeku be fonjihangge, jeku buhekv biqi, tere be nakabufi weile araki sehebi).*[709]

Mining generated considerable revenue for the state and provided materials for the state to equip its military force for greater territorial expansion. Here one observes the state's authority of dominating this industry over the illegal mining probably because the latter was less mentioned by the scribes of the early Manchu documents. The state may have purchased metals through the available markets.

5.6 Salt

5.6.1 Significance of Salt

Few people would consider salt as an important factor in modern life. Some people eat less in order to stay healthy. In ancient China, salt industry was a special business that concerned people's well-being, impacted state's revenue and functioned as a fountain of fortune for salt merchants, whose power of monopoly was granted by the state.[710] In the late Ming period, commercial economy developed exponentially, and yet the Han Chinese merchants did not gain certain level of autonomy that can protect their own economic and political interest. Kwan Man Bun depicted a vivid culture of salt merchants of Tianjin that played a considerable role in realms of the state, public and private in late imperial China.[711] In our Manchu case, little trace of salt merchants, whether Han Chinese or Jurchen-Manchu, is detected in the process of state building.

In the time of Nurgaqi (1559-1626), salt was an indispensable substance to nourish people's lives, to maintain a strong tie with allies,

---

[709] *Fe dangse*, pp. 2183-2184.

[710] Chen Ran 陳然 et al., (eds) (1987), *Zhongguo yanyeshi luncong* 中國鹽業史論叢 (General Essays on Salt History of China), Zhongguo shehui kexue chubanshe, Beijing, p. 1.

[711] Kwan Man Bun (2001), The Salt Merchants of Tianjin: State-Making and Civil Society in Late Imperial of China, University of Hawai'i Press, Honolulu, pp. 6-7.

and to embark upon a great enterprise of unifying the neighboring lands. Being different than the unification era, when salt monopoly was handled by the merchants and "the state merely collected an excise levy,"[712] the Jin regime secured every section of the salt production by its military force, a.k.a., the Eight Banners, which acquired the salt production sites from the Ming, carried out and closely monitored its production, transportation, and distribution.

Some Jurchen chieftains made a report to Nurgaqi, indicating that the shortage of salt had severely affected the state's expansion. Though we lacked a concrete date for when this passage was penned, it is still significant in as much as salt was as important as cereals, thus directly affecting the imperial administration.

duiqi beile, abatai beile, jirgalang beile, yoto beile, xoto beile, sahaliyen age, hoton tai arame genehe be henuneme ganafi isinjiha, isinjifi han de alame, musei guribuhe gurun, qilin qi qasi dung qi ebsi, tariha jeku fangkala, yangsame tutahabi, jetere jeku isirakv, dabsun akv, simiyan i dogon de weihu komso seme...[713]

The fourth Beile [*Hong Taiji* 皇太極], Abatai Beile, Jirgalang Beile, Yoto Beile, Xoto Beile and Sahaliyen Age, who went to build fortification walls and fortresses, were called to come back. After returning, they told the Khan that our country people who moved out [experiencing that] from Qilin [Tieling 鐵嶺] onward to Dung [Dong 洞] crops they grew were short, cultivation was delayed, food for eating could not be obtained, and there was no salt. Few boats were at the ford of Simiyan [Shenyang 瀋陽]...

A Korean source, "Records of Hearings and Seeings in Jianzhou" (*Jianzhou wenjian lu* 建州聞見錄), also confirms a severe shortage of salt supply due to wars between Ming and Later Jin. Nurgaqi accumulated salt for years beforehand but the common people still had a hard time accessing the market later on. Thus, salt became extremely expensive because supplies were cut off.

盐酱极贵，闻五、六年前，奴酋专令贸盐，盖将为背畔之计也。今则将胡家尚有所储，而闾阎则绝乏已久云。[714]

---

[712] Richard von Glahn (2016), The Economic History of China: From the Antiquity to the Nineteenth Century, Cambridge University Press, Cambridge, p. 316.

[713] *Fe dangse*, pp. 3399-3400.

[714] Li Minwan, *Jianzhou wenjian lu*, p. 43.

Salt and soy sauce were extremely expensive. [I] hear that five or six years ago, the Chief Nu [Nu *qiu* 奴酋]⁷¹⁵ specifically ordered to purchase salt and presumably, this was because of plans for rebellion. Nowadays the barbarian households still have some reserves, but [the commoners in] the villages [*lüyan* 闾阎] have been in scarcity for a long time.

The author of this source is Li Minwan 李民寏, who was captured by the Jurchens in the war of Sarhv (Sarhu 萨尔浒) that took place in 1619. He lived as a captive for a year (*gu chen jing nian xian zei* 顾臣经年陷贼)⁷¹⁶ and reported his observations to the Korean King after his return. Nonetheless, only three years later, the situation of lacking salt was completely reversed. Not only had the Jurchens enough salt for self-consumption, they were also able to provide salt for their new subjects.

han, juwan emu de yamun de tuqifi, beise be isabufi... musei gurun i booi ahasi ukakangge, gemu dabsun bahafi jeterakv ofi ukambi kai, te dabsun bahafi jembi, liyooha qi ebsi, gubqi golo gemu dahahabi... liyoodung ni hoton de teme toktoho.⁷¹⁷

The Khan, on the eleventh [of the fourth month], sat in his yamen and gathered the princes... regarding the matter of bondservants fleeing from our country, it is all because they could not get salt to eat. Now they have salt to eat, and from the Liao River to our side, every district has surrendered to us... [The Khan] decided to live in Liaodong fortification.

This passage was a speech given by Nurgaqi to his princes on the eleventh of the fourth month in the sixth year of Genggiyen Han (1621), when he took over Ming's Liaodong region and moved his capital to Liaodong fortification. He admitted that in the past bondservants would give up their loyalty and flee into other places due to lack of salt. Nowadays Nurgaqi's administration could provide salt for people in his neighboring lands, and they surrendered to him. Nurgaqi made a clear point that salt has to some extentd a deep influence on the future of his empire.

---

⁷¹⁵ According to the annotations of *Jianzhou wenjian lu*, p. 27, 奴酋 refers to 努爾哈赤.

⁷¹⁶ Jianzhou wenjian lu, p. 54.

⁷¹⁷ *Fe dangse*, p. 937.

5.6.2 Production of Salt

The following Korean source points out that Nurqaqi managed to buy salt from a Korean locality Manpu to ease the shortage. However, the Ming officials often interrupted this business.

庚申正月二十一日，小農耳回來，言於奴酋曰："滿浦厚接差胡，有倍於前，更不助兵，真的無疑。"且言河瑞國載來苧紙、鹽之事。奴酋深喜曰："朝鮮之厚待汝者，不過看我而然也。鹽則滿浦多有之乎？若許則可以載來矣。"小農耳又言："差人則以唐官方來，未及入送，正二月間，更為出來，則入送云矣。"[718]

On the twenty-first day of the first month of the year *gengshen* [1620], Sonongyi [Xiaononger 小农耳][719] returned and told the Chief Nu that "[The place of] Manpu received the Jurchen emissaries [*chaihu* 差胡] generously, in a way many times better than before. Furthermore, [Korea] will not send army to help [the Ming], and there is truly no doubt. " Moreover, Sonongyi reported on the matter that He Ruiguo shipped ramie paper and salt here. The Chief rejoiced deeply and said, "The reason that Korea treated you generously is nothing but [because of] looking up to me. Is there much salt in Manpu? If so, one can ship more here." Sonongyi again said, "Because the Ming officials just arrived, the emissaries could not make a shipment. Between the first and second months, they will ship out when the Ming officials leave for a shift."

This Korean source can be verified by a Manchu source in the *Fe dangse*:

orin emu de, solho de takvraha xolonggo amasi isinjifi alame, solho han i hendurengge, ai ai weile be fe yabuha mampu i heqen de jio, meni gisun i hafan takvraqi, inu mampu deri unggimbi seme alanjiha.[720]

On the twenty-first day [of the sixth month in the sixth year of the Genggiyen Han, 1621], Xolonggo, who was dispatched to Korea, returned and reported, "The Korean King's word is that everything will be conducted in the old way when coming to the Manpu fortification. If

---

[718] *Zhazhong rilu* 柵中日錄 (Dairies in Prison), Li Minwan 李民寏 (c. 1619), collected in *Qingshi ziliao congkan di ba, jiu zhong* 清史資料叢刊第八、九種 (The Eighth and Ninth kinds of Collections of Qing History Material), edition Shenyang: Liaoning daxue chubanshe, 1978, p. 20.

[719] According to the annotations of *Zhazhong rilu*, p. 28, 小农耳 pronounces as "Sonongyi" in Korean language. Its corresponding Manchu name should be xolonggo.

[720] *Fe dangse*, pp. 1045-1046.

we send our translator [man. *gisun i hafan*], [we shall] also send [him] to Manpu."

The events recorded in these two sources happened sequentially and confirmed that Nurgaqi indeed tried to procure salt and other sources from the Manpu fortification of Korea. Nonetheless, due to the difficulties caused by the Ming officials, Nurgaqi decided to make his own salt. The earliest salt production was recorded in the sixth month of the fifth year of Genggiyen Han (1620), when Nurgaqi sent people to boil salt at the Eastern Sea, which is close to today's Hunchun 琿春 where fuel from forests was abundant.

ninggu biyade, xun dekdere ergi mederi de, deribume dabsun fuifume unggihe.[721]

In the sixth month, at the seaside where the sun is rising, [the Khan] sent people there and started to boil salt.

This passage testifies that from the very beginning salt was produced by military men that were commissioned by the state. The following text reveals that three months later, Nurgaqi selected four men from every battalion (man. *niru*; chin. *niulu* 牛錄) and sent them to the Eastern Sea for salt production.

juwan biyai tofohon de, arbuni canjiyang, emu nirui duite niyalma be gaifi, dergi mederi de dabsun fuifume ganafi, juwe biyai orin jakvn de isinjifi...[722]

On the fifteenth of the tenth month [in the last year], Arbun, an Assistant Regional Commander [man. *canjiyang*; chin. *canjiang* 參將], led four people from every battalion to boil and fetch salt at the Eastern Sea. [He] returned on the twenty-eighth of the second month [in this year]...

The yield must be enormous, because one of the previous passages tells that in the fourth month of the next year (1621), they were able to provide salt for the subjugated people in Liaodong. Besides producing salt, the Jurchens were able to obtain substantive salt from the Han Chinese saltworks after the wars.

juwan ilan de, gai jeo i tung iogi, alban i dabsun emu tumen gin benjihe.[723]

---

[721] *Fe dangse*, p. 715.
[722] *Fe dangse*, pp. 771-772.
[723] *Fe dangse*, p. 1166.

On the thirteenth [of the ninth month in 1621], Mobile Corps Commander [man. *iogi*; chin. *youji* 遊擊] Tung of Gai Jeo [Gaizhou 蓋 州] sent ten thousand *jin* official salt here.

The Jurchens did not lower salt yield after taking over the Han Chinese saltworks. A letter from the Grand Coordinator (Man. *du tang*; chin. *dutang* 都堂), on the fourteenth of the second month in 1622, was sent down to Aita, a Regional Vice Commander (man. *fujiyang*; chin. *fujiang* 副將), commanding that the official salt must be boiled abundantly and diligently (*du tang ni bithe, juwe biyai juwan duin de, aita fujiyang de wasimbuha, alban i dabsun be ambula kiqeme fuifubu).*[724]

In the coming years, the empire acquired more and more Han Chinese workers to boil salt. On the seventh of the second month in the eighth year of Genggiyen Han (1623), the State captured twenty salt workers after subduing Gin Jeo, which is the modern Jinzhou district of Dalian. The "Records of Liaodong" (*Liaodong zhi* 遼東志) confirms that Jinzhou Garrison had thirty-three soldiers who were in charge of boiling salt (*Jinzhouwei jianyanjun sanshisan ming* 金州衛煎鹽軍三十三名)[725] during the Jiajing empeor's reign (r. 1522-1566).

fusi efu i ginjeo qi wesimbuhe bithei gisun... jai dabsun fuifure niyalma orin, nimaha budara niyalma juwan, gasha budara niyalma juwan, ere niyalma be gemu ginjeo i hoton de werihe.[726]

Fusi Efu [a son-in-law of the Khan] from Ginjeo reported [to the throne] and the following: ... furthermore, there are twenty salt-boiling people, ten fish-catching people, ten bird-catching people, [and they are] all left behind in Ginjeo fortification.

In the same year, on the twenty-sixth of the sixth month, the Jurchens took Yoojeo (Yaozhou 耀州), which is close to the modern Yingkou City (Yingkou Shi 营口市). The salt workers were allowed to live in their hometowns and the honest ones could live in Yoojeo fortification.

... *jai dabsun fuifure niyalma, meni meni gasan de kemuni tekini, akdun akdun be gajifi, yoo jeo de tebu* ...[727]

---

[724] *Fe dangse*, p. 1615.
[725] *Liaodong zhi* 遼東志 (Records of Liaodong), edited by Ren Luo 任洛 (1485-1544) et al. in 1537, vol. 3, included by Jin Yufu 金毓绂 (?-?) in his *Liaohai congshu* 遼海叢書 (Liaohai Series), printed in Shenyang from 1933-1936, p. 389.
[726] *Fe dangse*, pp. 1193-1994.
[727] *Fe dangse*, p. 2522.

Furthermore, regarding the salt-boiling people, they can still live in each village of their own [as they] wish. [We can] select the honest ones and [allow them] to live in Yoojeo.

The Han Chinese salt producers under the Eight Banners enjoyed certain privileges of being exempted from harvesting crops and building fortification walls. The Grand Coordinator wrote to the Mobile Corps Commander of Gai Jeo for a specific regulation:

du tang ni bithe, orin emu de gai jeo i iogi jao i ho de unggihe, jakvn gvsai dabsun fuifure nikan be, jeku handure, heqen sahara alban de ume dabure...[728]

Grand Coordinator's letter, on the twenty-first [of the seventh month in 1623], was sent to Gaizhou's Mobile Corps Commander Jeo i ho [chin. *Zhao Yihe* 趙義和], [ordering him] not to include the Han Chinese salt workers, who are under the Eight Banners, as official workers for harvesting crops and building cities...

More than ten years later, the empire still obtained more salt workers from the Ming empire for salt production. The following passage indicates that in the first year of Respectable Virtue (*wesihun erdemungga,* 1636) the Manchus seized some Han Chinese salt workers in Dung Jing (Dongjing 東京), An Xan (Anshan 鞍山) and Hai Jeo (Haizhou 海州), warning that those workers might escape along with enemy boats. The "Records of Liaodong" also confirm that there were forty-four soldiers who boiled salt in Haizhou Guard (*Haizhouwei jianyanjun sishisi ming* 海州衛煎鹽軍四十四名).[729] Such Han Chinese documents show that the Ming state decisively monopolized the salt production in the Liaodong region, with little reference of the involvement of civil merchants. The Manchu-language chronicles exhibit a similar case:

dung jing, an xan, hai jeo, ere jergi hoton i emu hoton emte ambasa beyei teile bedereme meni meni hoton de jikini, gvwa ambasa qoohai niyalma gemu irexen i jakade tubade bikini, nikan i quwan gemu biqi, bederere be tuwame bisu, quwan bederere onggolo dabsun i niyalma be ume sindara, ukame generahv quwan bederehe manggi, dabsun i niyalma be sindafi fuifubu.[730]

---

[728] *Fe dangse*, pp. 2624-2625.
[729] *Liaodong zhi*, vol. 3, p. 388.
[730] *Fe dangse*, pp. 7841-7842.

[Regarding] the cities of Dung Jing [Dongjing 東京], An Xan [Anshan 鞍山], Hai Jeo [Haizhou 海州], only one official is allowed to return to their own fortification. The other officials and soldiers must stay at such places as Irexen. If the Han Chinese boats are still there, [our soldiers should] return and watch them. Before the Han Chinese boats leave, do not release the salt workers, in case they run away. After [the Han Chinese] boats will have left, salt workers can be released for boiling salt.

These passages clearly tell that the Jurchen-Manchu state produced its own salt by its military force in the beginning and commissioned the Han Chinese workers to do the job. The early Manchu annals show that in Hong Taiji's reign, salt industry was committed to three state-owned production sites, which were managed by the Eight Banners. Each site had produced 15,000 *jin* salt and in total, the three sites had submitted 45,000 *jin* salt to the state, by the eighth day of the fifth month in 1638, when the document was written.[731] When Nurgaqi unified Liaodong, his army also acquired the Ming's salt production sites along the seashore. Plus the production provided by the state-owned sites, the Jurchens were able to expand their empire by taking over Korea, the remaining Ming's Liaodong region and the neighboring Mongol tribes.

5.6.3 Distribution of Salt

The Manchu annals show that salt was mainly bestowed to people. Arbun, an Assistant Regional Commander, distributed salt according to the Jurchen male adults in the country. The Han Chinese also boiled salt, which was distributed according to the number of their male adults.

juwan biyai tofohon de, arbun canjiyang, emu nirui duite niyalma be gaifi, dergi mederi de dabsun fuifume ganafi, juwe biyai orin jakvn de isinjifi, gurun i haha budome salame buhe, jai jakvn pu i nikasai fuifuha dabsun be qende bufi haha tolome dendehe.[732]

On the fifteenth of the tenth month [in the last year], Arbun, an Assistant Regional Commander, led four people from every battalion to boil and fetch salt at the Eastern Sea. [He] returned on the twenty-eighth of the second month [in this year], counting the country's men to distribute salt. As for salt boiled by the Han Chinese people at the Eight

---

[731] Qingchu neiguoshiyuan manwen dang'an yibian, pp. 309-310.
[732] *Fe dangse*, pp. 771-772.

Fortresses [Bapu 八堡], it was divided and distributed to them by counting their men.

Among the people who received salt, the annals emphasize that construction workers who built fortification walls were abundantly awarded with salt, with twenty-five *jin* for each of them, along with a piece of cattle.

juwan jakvn de, heqen weilehe niru nirui niyalma de, emte ihan, orin sunja gin dabsun xangname buhe.[733]

On the twenty-eighth, to the battalions that built fortification walls, each battalion-man was awarded with a piece of cattle and twenty-five *jin* salt.

Soon thereafter, on the twenty-seventh day, to every two of the [same] people who were building the fortification walls, one *jin* salt was given again *(orin nadan de, hoton weilere niyalma de, geli juwe niyalma de emu gin dabsun buhe)*.[734]

Nurgaqi even issued an edict to highlight his purpose of rewarding people building fortification walls, manifesting his care and sympathy for those men working hard for him.

hoton weilere niyalma de, neneme emu jergi buhe dabsun jeme wajire unde kai, wajinggala geli dabsun buhengge, gurun i niyalma wehe moo unufi suilara be safi gosime buhe kai.[735] Regarding the people building fortification walls, [even though] the salt previously given has not yet been eaten up, more salt is to be given. I am aware and remember that our country's people endure hardships for carrying stone and wood [and therefore], I have [them salt] given.

As for transferring salt, one passage particularly points out that there is a straight road for transporting salt at the place of Xuwang Xan (Shuangshan 雙山), from which one can see that salt transportation was a highly important matter that deserved a special road.

orin juwe de, iqe heqen, aiha be guribu seme unggihe bithe, fung hvwang ni iogi, jeng giyang, tang xan, jeng dung pu, jeng i pu i harangga buya gaxan i pu heqen i niyalma be, gemu sarhv de gamame gene

---

[733] *Fe dangse*, p. 796.
[734] *Fe dangse*, p. 821.
[735] *Fe dangse*, pp. 823-824.

niowanggiyaha i niyalma be, xuwang xan de dabsun juwehe tondo jugvn bisire, dere jugvn be fonjifi unggi.[736]

On the twenty-second [of the eleventh month in the sixth year of Genggiyen Han], a letter was sent to move people to New Town [Xincheng 新城] and Aiha [Aihe 靉河], [saying that] the Mobile Corps Commander of Fung Hvwang [Fenghuang 鳳凰] must move all the people from Jeng Giyang [Zhenjiang 鎮江], Tang Xan [Tangshan 湯山], Jeng Dung Pu [Zhengdongpu 鎮東堡], Jeng i Pu [Zhenyipu 鎮夷堡] and its affiliated Small-Village Pu [Xiaotunpu 小屯堡], to Sarhv [Sarhu 薩爾滸]. As for sending people from Limpid River [man. niowanggiyaha; chin. Qinghe 清河], [there is] a straight road for transporting salt at Xuwang Xan [Shuangshan 雙山], from which [one can] ask for directions.

Moreover, transportation of salt was strictly supervised by military force. Nurgaqi adopted Ming's military ranks to be granted to his subordinates, i.e., such high titles as Grand Coordinator (man. du tang; chin. dutang 都堂), Regional Commander (man. zung bing guwan; chin. zongbing guan 總兵官), Regional Vice Commander (man. fujiyang; chin. fujiang 副将), Mobile Corps Commander (man. iogi; chin. youji 遊擊) as , and Defense Officer (man. beigwuan; chin. beiyu 備御). The following passage tells that Defense Officers were assigned to transport salt, and one can see that salt was highly prioritized in the state's administration.

alaha manggi, tutu oqi, jetere dabsun be geren alban i niyalma be ume dabure, du tang, zung bing guwan, fujiyang, canjiyang, iogi, beiguwan i bodome, nadan tanggv ninggun beiguwan de, emte tanggv gin dabsun be salame bufi, emu gvsai emte beiguwan be gaifi xajin canjiyang benehe …[737]

After reporting, if so, do not count all the official tax-contributors [to distribute] salt for consumption. Count the number of Grand Coordinators, Regional Commanders, Regional Vice Commanders, Assistant Regional Commanders, Mobile Corps Commanders and Defense Officers [to distribute salt]. [There are] seven hundred and six Defense Officers and each is assigned with one hundred jin salt. One Defense Officer from

---

[736] *Fe dangse*, p. 1278.
[737] *Fe dangse*, pp. 2397-2398.

each banner, being led by the Assistant Regional Commander Xajin, escorted it.

This passage was documented in the eighth year of Nurgaqi's reign (1623), revealing that the Later Jin state adopted a new way of distributing salt through the military leaders rather than counting the male adults in its country. This new system must have been considered to as a more effective way for distribution. There is no doubt that salt was circulated as a strategic material in these northeast regions, where its production and transportation were closely involved with military affairs. Moreover, to the Jurchen-Manchus and some Han Chinese who were under their rule, salt was distributed as a reward to those who contributed significantly to the empire. Nonetheless, little proof of the existence of salt merchants and their participation of distribution appeared in the official documents kept by the Jurchen-Manchu scribes.

5.6.4　Consumption of Salt

In the previous section, it became obvious that the salt consumed by the Jurchens and Han Chinese was either distributed by the Banner men or bestowed by Nurgaqi. Furthermore, the annals also tell that the Mongols consumed large quantities of salt, which was given to them by Nurgaqi as disaster-relief supply or gift. In the eighth year of Genggiyen Han (1623), Nurgaqi ordered his men to transfer salt produced in Gai Jeo (Gaizhou 蓋州) and Fu Jeo (Fuzhou 復州), along with grains as a relief to the Mongols who had no food. The "Records of Liaodong" also confirm that Gaizhou Garrison had sixty-eight soldiers for boiling salt (*Gaizhouwei jianyanjun liushiba ming* 蓋州衛煎鹽軍六十八名) and Fuzhou sixty-two (*Fuzhouwei jianyanyun liushier ming* 復州衛煎鹽軍六十二名).[738]

han i bithe, sunja biyai orin ninggun de wasimbuha, si uli efu, aita, suweni bahai teile jeku be, jai gai jeo, fu jeo de dabsun simneme gaifi, naqibu hiya, fulata de bu. juku akv monggo de salakini.[739]

The Khan's letter, on the twenty-sixth of the fifth month, is sent to Si Uli Efu [Imperial Son-in-law] and Aita [a Regional Vice Commander], [ordering] "to give the grains you have gathered, along with salt selected

---

[738] *Liaodong zhi*, vol. 3, p. 389.
[739] *Fe dangse*, p. 2387.

from Gai Jeo and Fu Jeo, to Naqibu Guard and Fulata, for relieving the Mongols who have no food."

Days later, another large amount of salt was given to thousands of Mongols who lacked salt. This passage tells that ten thousand *jin* salt were taken from salt fields and successively sent to the Mongols for consumption.

… jai monggo i nadan minggan ninggun tanggv jakvnju jakvn niyalma de, dabsun buqi isirakv ofi, fuifure ba i dabsun be gaifi, nenehe amaga uheri emu tumen gin dabsun buhe, …[740]

Furthermore, 7,688 Mongol people were not provided with enough salt. Procuring salt from the salt-boiling places, [the Jurchens] gave ten thousand *jin* salt in total [to the Mongols] from beginning to end.

In Hong Taiji's reign (r. 1626-1643), salt was also used as a special gift to maintain relationships with some eminent Mongol leaders. On the nineteenth of the fifth month in the fifth year of Sure Han (1631), Hong Taiji (1592-1643) sent a basket of salt to Tusiyetu Efu and Gege *(han, tusiyetu efu gege de unggihengge... dabsun emu xoro).*[741]

On the third day of the twelfth month in the fifth year of Sure Han (1630), envoys from Dalai Qvhur were leaving. Through them, one *sin* (man. *sin*; chin. *dou* 斗) salt was bestowed to the place of Dalai Qvhur *(iqe ilan de, dalai qvhur elqin genehe, dalai qvhur bade unggihengge... dabsun emu sin).*[742] Just three days later, on the seventh, a Mongol Lama from Aru was going to return. The horses he brought were declined, but one *sin* salt was given to him *(iqe nadan de. aru i monggo lama genehe, gajiha morin be gaihakv... dabsun emu sin buhe).*[743]

One month later, in the beginning of a new year, Hong Taiji gave one *sin* salt to a Mongol women, who lost her husband and lived alone ever since *(juwan juwe de, karaqin i subudai dureng ni sargan be eigen akv anggasi seme, han i gvsime unggihengge... dabusun emu sin).*[744] The woman's late husband was named as Subudai Dureng, who belonged to the Karaqin (Kelaqin 克拉沁) tribe in Mongolia.

---

[740] *Fe dangse*, p. 2468.
[741] *Fe dangse*, pp. 5667-5678.
[742] *Fe dangse*, p. 5705.
[743] *Fe dangse*, p. 5708.
[744] *Fe dangse*, pp. 5776-5777.

Besides, for sustaining a strong tie with the Mongols, salt was also bestowed to Hong Taiji's older generations for maintaining relationships. Just a few days after bestowing the Mongol widow, Hong Taiji gave one *sin* salt to his Big Grandma and on the same day, he gave another *sin* salt to his grandmother (man. *mama*; chin. *zumu* 祖母) when Small Grandma's messenger returned *(tere inenggi, amba mama de unggihengge... dabsun emu sin... tere inenggi, ajige mama i elqin genehe, mama de unggihengge... dabsun emu sin).*[745]

The above passages demonstrate that salt mainly circulated as a special gift for building up and endorsing relationships. Nurgaqi took over the Ming's salt-producing sites and used their product to provide for the Mongols. Hong Taiji continued this policy and nurtured his connections with his ally leaders and the elders in the royal family.

Throughout the Manchu annals and other relevant sources, one can tell that salt was a strategic material owned by the Jurchen-Manchu empire, being monopolized by the state in sections of production, transportation and consumption. Evidence has not yet been found in the *Fe dangse* which shows that the ruling elite circulated salt as a commercial commodity. Kwan Man Bun suggested that market exerted great impact on the formation of modern society in Europe,[746] but in the Manchu case, state maintained an absolute control in salt industry, with little role played by the market. The concept of salt merchant was not even mentioned in the Manchu chronicles and the reasons probably is not because of the contempt of merchants. Nurgaqi himself was a merchant in his young age, travelling between the Jurchen and Han Chinese regions for sales of ginseng and other native products. His stories of conducting commercial business were recorded in the Han Chinese-language "Veritable Records of the Forefather Martial Emperor" (*Qing taizu wu huangdi shilu* 清太祖武皇帝實錄), as glorious achievements in the early stage of his great enterprise. Being different than the Han Chinese, the Manchu culture highly valued commerce and industries, which will be analyzed with more evidence in the following chapters.

Nurgaqi accumulated salt while prepared wars against the Ming. The supply was, however, not sufficient after wars broke out, and his procurement from Korea was impeded by the Ming officials. Therefore,

---

[745] *Fe dangse,* pp. 5721-5723.
[746] Kwan Man Bun, The Salt Merchants of Tianjin, pp. 2-7.

Nurgaqi started to produce his own salt, which successfully met people's need and fueled his acquisition of Liaodong. Besides self-consumption, Nurgaqi was able to supply and relieve some Mongols with salt when they were in need. Furthermore, his successor, Hong Taiji, also bestowed salt as a means to maintain strong ties with his Mongol allies. Thus, it is fair to conclude that salt played a substantial role in the state's administration and expansion during the reigns of Nurgaqi and Hong Taiji, sustaining their governance over people who lived in Northeast Asia. Finally yet importantly, state's exclusive dominance of salt industry was clearly observed in the early Manchu documents.

5.7 Military Industries

5.7.1 Firearms

Compared with conventional economies, the military economies, in the aspect of firearm manufacturing, were established rather late in the Jurchan-Manchu state. In the early stage of the empire-building, firearms were mainly acquired through wars, along with cold weapons. On the thirteenth day of the seventh month in 1621, people of Niuzhuang delivered weapons which they captured in war: two hundred armors, two hundred bows, 1,000 poisoned arrows, 3,000 large cannon balls, 5 *to* small cannon balls, and 50 *gin*[747] steel *(juwan ilan de, nio juwang ni niyalma, juwe tanggv uksin, juwe tanggv beri niru, okto sirdan emu minggan, poo i muhaliyan, ambasa muhaliyan ilan minggan, buya muhaliyan sunja to, gan sele susai gin gajihabi).*[748] This is just a tiny fraction of Nurgaqi's acquisition of firearms. Just three months ago, when his army took over Liaoyang, large quantities of Ming's guns fell into Nurgaqi's hands. This event can be confirmed by Xu Guangqi, who was the Left Vice Minister of Rites *(libu zuoshilang* 禮部左侍郎). When counselling state's affairs in 1629, Xu told the Emperor Chongzheng that years ago when defending Liaoyang, he wrote to Xiong Tingbi again, warning him definitely not to display battalions and guns outside the fortification and it would be enough to defeat the enemy by fortification walls and cannons. Nevertheless, Xiong Tingbi did not listen. Neither did

---

[747] The Manchu measure of weight, *gin*, must be a loan word from the Chinese word *jin* 斤, which is about five hundred grams with local variation.

[748] *Fe dangse*, p. 1077.

his successor Yuan Yingtai. Later the army got out of the fortification, defensing along the river. The army collapsed and escaped when the enemy was in sight. The enemy obtained all firearms and there were no so soldiers left to guard the fortification (*xi liaoyang zhishou, chen zai yishu Xiong Tingbi, wei chengwai lieying zhipao, wanfenbuke. zhi pingcheng yongpao, zizu jinzei. Tingbi buting, Yuan Yingtai ji zhi, yiran. hou dabing chucheng, juhe ershou, wangdi kuisan, huoqi jiwei diyou, shoupizhe sui zhi wuren* 昔遼陽之守，臣再遺書熊廷弼，謂城外列營置砲，萬分不可。只憑城用砲，自足盡賊。廷弼不聽，袁應泰繼之，亦然。後大兵出城，拒河而守，望敵潰散，火器皆爲敵有，守陣者遂致無人).[749]

Regarding the cold weapons, the Jurchen administration employed its own craftsmen for manufacturing and repairing. On the sixteenth day of the ninth month in 1621, Nurgaqi ordered Yegude to manage the bow-making business: two *jiha* silver to make armors for a Company-Commanding Defense Officer (man. *nirui ejen beiguwan*; chin. *niulu ezhen beiyu* 牛錄額真備御); one *jiha* silver to make armors for a Deputy Company-Commanding Defense Officer (man. *dase beiguwan*; chin. *dazi beiyu* 代子備御); one *yan* silver, paid by chieftains, to make ten official armors, one *jiha* silver to make a bow, and five *fun*[750] silver to fix a broken bow (*yegude de beri faksi be iqihiya seme afabuha, nirui ejen beiguwan i uksin hadaha de, juwe jiha menggun bu, daise beiguwan, qiyanzung ni uksin hadaqi, emte jiha menggun be aqan bu, alban i juwan uksin hadaha de, beise emu yan menggun bumbi, emu beri arabufi, emu jiha bu, bijaha beri be dasabure de, sunja fun bu*).[751] Notably, the development of handicraft economies was insufficient and disorganized, as Wang Zhonghan 王鍾翰 argued, and they were strictly controlled by the Manchu aristocrats for military usage, rather than commercial purpose.[752]

The Han Chinese equipment captured in war, such as armors, was also repaired for further usage. On the seventh day of the third month in

---

[749] *Xu Guangqi quanji* 徐光啓全集 (The Complete Work of Xu Guangqi), edited by Zhu Weizheng 朱維錚 and Li Tiangang 李天綱, edition Shanghai: Shanghai guji chubanshe, 2010, p. 103.

[750] The Manchu measure of weight, *fun*, must be a loan word from the Chinese word *fen* 分, which is one percent of one Chinese ounce *liang* 两.

[751] *Fe dangse*, pp. 1184-1185.

[752] Wang Zhonghan, *Qingshi zakao*, pp. 11-12.

1622, as for the Mongol comers, Nurgaqi ordered to equip good soldiers with good armors and bad soldiers with bad armors. According to the Jurchen soldiers' convention, words are marked at the end of their helmets and on the back of their armors. Furthermore, Nurgaqi sent people to Guangning for fixing the Han Chinese armors which will be given to the Mongols *(ukame jihe monggo de, sain niyalma de sain uksin, ehe niyalma de ehe uksin be etubu, musei adali saqa i iberi, uksin fisa de bithe hada... guangning de takvrafi, monggoso de, nikan i uksin be gemu dasafi buki).*[753]

Both firearms and cold weapons were equipped to the army in Nurgaqi's reign. On the fourth day of the eleventh month in 1621, Nurgaqi sent an edict to order three Mobile Corps Commanders (man. *iogi*; chin. *youji* 遊擊) from each banner to prepare military equipment: one Mobile Corps Commander prepares large cannons for one banner, with two horses allocated to each cannon. Specific personnel is appointed to manage the cannons and horses. As for the remaining soldiers, the strong ones are selected to use bow and arrows; those who are not able to pull the bows should use three-barrel guns and matchlocks *(han i bithe, iqe duin de wesimbuha, gvsa gvsai ilata iogi de hendufi, emu iogi be gvsade amba poo dagilabu, emu poo de morin juwete, niyalma afabu, tereqi funqehe niyalma be sonjofi beri ashaqi ojoro sain niyalma be beri ashabu, beri ashaqi ojorakv niyalma be, gemu ilan sangga i poo miyooqan jafabu seme henduhe).*[754]

The captured firearms reached a considerable number, which was sufficient to build independent artillery teams. On the sixth day of the first month in 1622, large artillery troops were established in the banners which were commanded by either Han Chinese or Jurchen officers. Nurgaqi informed that the Han Chinese official who is in charge of four thousand people must select two hundred men to be soldiers, being equipped with ten large cannons, eighty matchlocks and with another one hundred men at his disposal; the Han Chinese official who is in charge of three thousand people must select one hundred fifty men to be soldiers, being equipped with eight large cannons, fifty-four matchlocks and with another seventy-five men at his disposal; the Han Chinese official who is in charge of two thousand people must select one hundred men to be

---

[753] *Fe dangse*, pp. 1715-1716.
[754] *Fe dangse*, pp. 1226-1227.

soldiers, being equipped with five large cannons, forty matchlocks and with another fifty men at his disposal. The Jurchen official who is in charge of 2,700 people must select one hundred thirty-five men to be soldiers, among which sixty-seven are equipped with six large cannons, forty-five matchlocks and another sixty-seven men are at his disposal; the Jurchen official who is in charge of 1,700 people must select eighty-five men to be soldiers, among which forty-four men are equipped with five large cannons, thirty-six matchlocks and another forty-one men are at his disposal; the Jurchen official who is in charge of one thousand people must select fifty men to be soldiers, among which twenty-five men are equipped with two large cannons, twenty matchlocks and another twenty-five men are at his disposal; the Jurchen official who is in charge of five hundred people must select twenty-five men to be soldiers, among which ten men are equipped with one large cannon, eight matchlocks, and with another fifteen men are at his disposal *(han i bithe, iqe ninggun de wasimbuha, nikan i hafan duin minggan kadalara niyalma, juwe tanggv qooha tuqibu, emu tanggv qooha de, amba poo Juwan, qang poo jakvnju dagila, jai emu tanggv qooha be sini qihai sula takvra, ilan minggan kadalara niyalma, emu tanggv susai qooha, ilibu, jakvn amba poo, susai duin qang poo dagila, jai nadanju sunja niyalma be sini qihai sula takvra, juwe minggan kadalara niyalma, emu tanggv qooha ilibu, sunja amba poo, dehi qang poo dagila, jai susai niyalma be sini qihai sula takvra, juxen i hafan juwe minggan nadan tanggv kadalara niyalma, emu tanggv gvsin sunja qooha ilibu, ninju nadan niyalma de ninggun amba poo, dehi sunja qang poo jafabu, jai ninju nadan niyalma be sini qihai sula takvra, emu minggan nadan tanggv kadalara niyalma, jakvnju sunja qooha ilibu, dehi duin niyalma de duin amba poo, gvsin ninggun qang poo jafabu jai dehi emu niyalma be sini qihai sula takvra, emu minggan kadalara niyalma, susai qooha ilibu, orin sunja niyalma de juwe amba poo, orin qang poo dakila, jai orin sunja niyalma be sini qihai sula takvra, sunja tanggv kadalara niyalma, orin sunja qooha ilibu, juwan niyalma de emu amba poo, jakvn qang poo dagila, jai tofohon niyalma be sini qihai sula takvra)*.[755] The equipment of firearms looks impressive according to the descriptions in these early Manchu annals; however, the application of firearms was rarely detectable during the time.

---

[755] *Fe dangse*, pp. 1440-1443.

The previous passages confirm that Nurgaqi equipped both Han Chinese and Jurchen troops with firearms, and the Han Chinese troops just owned slightly more firearms than the Jurchen troops. Speaking of the troops stationed across the unified regions, they were also required to practice cannon firing. In the third month of 1622, among every twenty people in Jinzhou and Fuzhou, one man is selected to serve in the army. Since the current month, they are trained to fire cannons until the tenth day of the coming month *(ginjeo, fu jeo... orin haha de emu haha qooha ilihangge, ere biyaqi poo sindame taqibu, iqe biyai juwan de naka).*[756]

There was no record of cannon manufacturing in Nurgaqi's reign and thus one can infer that all their firearms were acquired from the wars. Few evidence shows that these captured weapons were deployed to attack the Ming troops. A reason could be that the technology of guns was not advanced enough to compete against the cavalries and therefore, the Jurchen-Manchus did not pay much attention to employing firearms in wars, until the Battle of Ningyuan (Ningyuanzhizhan 寧遠之戰) in 1626. Some Han Chinese sources suggest that Nurgaqi was injured by cannon balls and died in a few months. One proof is based on Gaodi, the Grand Minister Commander, who reported to the court on the thirteenth day of the second month in 1626, said that the Jurchen enemy attacked Ningyuan, but the defenders cannon-killed one chieftain, who was wrapped with red cloth and carried away by the enemy soldiers while they cried loudly *(bingzi, jinglüe gaodi bao nuzei gong ningyuan, paobi yi datoumu, yong hongbu baoguo, zhongzei taizu, fangsheng daku* 丙子，經略高第報奴賊攻寧遠，砲斃一大頭目，用紅布包裹，眾賊擡去，放聲大哭).[757] According to Gu Yingta 谷應泰, who was a scholar lived in the late Ming and early Qing, the dead chieftain bombarded by Yuan Chonghuan was Hatu 哈兔, the oldest grandson of the Jurchen Marshal *(yuanchonghuan... bi qi shuai zhangsun tatu* 袁崇煥…斃其帥長孫哈兔).[758] The Manchu-language annals did not mention the injury of

---

[756] *Fe dangse*, pp. 1745-1746.

757 *Xizong shilu* 熹宗實錄 (The Veritable Records of Xizong), edition Taipei: photo-printed according to the copy of Guoli beiping tushuguan 國立北平圖書館 (National Library in Beiping), 1962, p. 3218.

[758] *Mingshi jishi benmo* 明史紀事本末 (Entire Historical Events of the Ming), written by Gu Yingtai 谷應泰 (1620-1690), edition Beijing: Zhonghua shuju, 1977, p. 1473.

Nurgaqi, but said that he retreated with great resentment (*ambula korsome bederehe*).[759] Later he blamed some Khalkha Mongol tribes for betraying the oath of alliance and did not assist his attack upon Ningyuan, and therefore, Nurgaqi personally led the troops to strike some Mongol tribes.[760] This is evidence that could prove that the cannon may not injure Nurgaqi, at least not badly. Nonetheless, scholars argue that the Jurchens began to realize the power of cannons since then, though they may not have the knowledge that the cannons were manufactured by European standard of technology.[761]

The Jurchen-Manchu state did not make any firearms until the fifth year of Sure Han (1631). Checking Hong Taiji's *Veritable Records* written in the Han Chinese language, it says that,

造紅衣大將軍礮成，鎸曰天佑助威大將軍，天聰五年孟春吉旦造。督造官、總兵官佟養性，監造官遊擊丁啓明、備御祝世蔭，鑄匠王天相、竇守位，鐵匠劉計平。先是我國未備火器，造礮自此始。[762]

Red-Coat-General-in-Chief Cannon [763] was successfully manufactured, and on its body it is engraved with Heaven-Blessing-Helping-Powerful General-in-chief and it was cast in a good day of the early spring in the fifth year of Tiancong (1631). Supervising-Manufacture Official is Regional Commander Tong Yangxing, Quality-Control Officials are Mobile Corps Commander Ding Qiming and Defense Officer Zhu Shiyin, manufacturers are Wang Tianxiang and Dou Shouwei, and blacksmith is Liu Jiping. In the past firearms were not equipped in our country and this is the beginning of cannon making.

Another passage from the documents kept by the Eight-Banner secretaries on monthly duty says that,

是日，始鑄大將軍炮成。炮文曰：天佑助威大將軍。金國天聰汗五年孟春吉日創造。督造婿總兵官佟養性，監造遊擊丁啓明、備御祝

---

[759] Manzhou shilu, p. 397.

[760] Manzhou shilu, pp. 400-401.

[761] Tonio Andrade, The Gunpowder Age: China, Military Innovation, and the Rise of the West in World History, Princeton University Press, Princeton, 2016, p. 199.

[762] Qing shilu 清實錄 (The Qing Veritable Records), vol. 2, edition Beijing: Zhonghua shuju, 1985, p. 109.

[763] Because the Jurchens were considered as barbarians in traditional Chinese view, the Chinese expression of Red-Barbarian Cannon (*hong yi pao* 紅夷炮) was modified as Red-Coat Cannon (man. *hvng i poo*; chin. *hong yi pao* 紅衣炮) under the Manchu governance.

世蔭，鑄匠王天相、竇守位，鐵匠劉計平。先是連鳥槍尚未造，造炮自此始。[764]

In this day (the eighth day of the first month), General-in-chief Cannon was first manufactured. The text on the body of the cannon says, Heaven-Blessing-Helping-Powerful General-in-chief, made in a good day of the early spring in the fifth year of Jin State's Tiancong Khan. Supervisor is Imperial Son-in-law, Regional Commander Tong Yangxing, Quality-Control Officials are Mobile Corps Commander Ding Qiming and Defense Officer Zhu Shiyin, manufacturers are Wang Tianxiang and Dou Shouwei, and blacksmith is Liu Jiping. In the past, even matchlocks were not manufactured and this is the beginning of cannon making.

This passage further confirms that no firearms were produced before the eighth day of the first month in 1631. Moreover, the Manchu secretaries recorded that on the twenty-fifth day of the first month in 1631 Hong Taiji continuously recruited craftsmen for making the General-in-chief Cannons (*ershiwu ri, shouqu zao dajiangjunpao jiangyi* 二十五日，收取造大將軍炮匠役).[765]

On the thirteenth day of the third month in 1631, when Hong Taiji inspected the newly recruited troops, he ordered the Field Army (*xingyingbing* 行營兵) and Garrison Army (*zhushoubing* 駐守兵) to spread into two wings for firing cannons (man. *poo*; chin. *pao* 砲 or 炮) and matchlocks (man. *qang poo* or *miyooqan*; chin. *niaoqiang* 鳥槍). After seeing a good performance, he rewarded them with silver from his treasury. Hong Taiji also inspected twenty-four Han Chinese artillerymen and two gunpowder producers who were Han Chinese (*shisanri... shiri, han chuyue xinbian, ling xingyingbing, zhushoubing fenlie liangyi, yan fang huopao, niaoqiang xianshu, chu kutang dashang... yan fang huopao hanren ershisi ming, zhizao paoyao hanren erming* 十三日，…是日，汗出閱新編，令行營兵、駐守兵分列兩翼，驗放火炮、鳥槍嫻熟，出庫帑大賞…驗放火炮漢人二十四名，製造炮藥漢人二名).[766]

---

[764] *Tiancong wunian baqi zhiyuedang*, 天聰五年八旗值月檔 (annals Kept by the Eight Banners on Monthly Duty in the Fifth Year of Tiancong), vol. 1, complied and translated by Guan Xiaolian 關孝廉, edition Beijing: Diyi lishi dang'an'guan, 2014, p. 4.

[765] *Tiancong wunian baqi zhiyuedang*, vol. 1, complied and translated by Guan Xiaolian 關孝廉, p. 6.

[766] *Tiancong wunian baqi zhiyuedang*, 天聰五年八旗值月檔 (annals Kept by the Eight Banners on Monthly Duty in the Fifth Year of Tiancong), vol. 2, complied and

Regarding cannon-manufacturing, all contributors were abundantly rewarded by the state. On the fifteenth day of the third month in 1631, Hong Taiji promoted a Mobile Corps Commander Ding Qiming to a Regional Vice Commander because he discovered the craftsmen who can make Red-Coat Cannons and supervised the manufacture of Red-Coat Cannon since then (*shiwuri, yi dingyouji wei fujiang, zhuosheng yuanyou, chachu hongyipao zhujiang, yi jiangzao hongyipao zici shi* 十五日，以丁遊擊爲副將，擢升緣由：查出紅衣炮鑄匠，以監造紅衣炮自此始···).[767] Besides, the cannon manufacturer Wang Tianxiang, two of his assistants and one artilleryman were also abundantly rewarded. The four of them used to be war captives and were assigned to the Jurchens as bondservants. For the capability of casting Red-Coat Cannons, Wang Tianxiang was promoted to a Company Commander (*qianzong* 千總), being granted with five couples of bond-servants, two oxen, one horse, one donkey, satin clothes and green clothes for him and his wife. Ten rolls of deep-green cloth were rewarded to his assistants and the artilleryman (*zhujiang wangtianxiang, zhuzaojiang er'ren, hui fangpaoren yiming, gai siren yuanxi fulu, gei zhushenjia weinu. yi hongyipao gu... wang tianxiang zhuowei qianzong, shanggei nupu wudui, niu ertou, ma yipi, lü yitou, fuqi duanyi ge yixi, maoqingbuyi geyixi. zhuzaojiang erming, fang hongyipao zhe yiming, ge shang maoqingbu shipi* 鑄匠王天相、助造匠二人、會放炮人一名，該四人原係俘虜，給諸申家爲奴。以紅衣炮故···王天相擢爲千總，賞給奴僕五對、牛二頭、馬一匹、驢一頭、夫妻緞衣各一襲、毛青布衣各一襲。助造匠二名，放紅衣炮者一名，各賞毛青布十匹).[768]

The self-manufactured weapons greatly improved Hong Taiji's confidence for further military operation. On the twenty-seventh day of the seventh month in 1631, Hong Taiji ordered to attack the Ming empire and the army set off in the early morning (*nadan biyai orin nadan de, nikan be dailame muturi erin de qooha juraka*).[769] The document keeper recorded that on the twelfth day of the eighth month; the Jurchen army used the Red Coat Cannons to bombard a terrace in the southwest side of

---

translated by Guan Xiaolian 關孝廉, edition Beijing: Diyi lishi dang'an'guan, 2014, p. 5.

[767] Tiancong wunian baqi zhiyuedang, vol. 2, p. 5.
[768] Tiancong wunian baqi zhiyuedang, vol. 2, p. 6.
[769] *Fe dangse*, p. 5451.

the Dalinghe fortification, penetrated a wall and killed one person. Later, the Jurchen army used the Red-Coat Cannons and General-in-chief Cannons to attack the south side of the fortification, destroyed four walls and two boards on the fortification wall *(hoton i julergi xun tuhere hoxoi tai be, hvng i poo sindara jakade, emu keremu fondo emu niyalma goifi buqehe... hvng i poo, amba jiyanggiyvn be, hoton i julergi dere be sindaha, duin kereme, juwe matun efujehe...).*[770] On the thirteenth day of the ninth month in 1631, the document keeper wrote that "our Han Chinese army used cannons to bombard the terrace in the east of the fortification, which was totally destroyed. Six people on the terrace were killed and the rest escaped during the night" *(heqen i xun dekdere derei tai be, musei nikan qooha poo sindafi tai gemu efujehe, tai i ninggude ninggun niyalma buqehe...).*[771]

matchlocks were also put into actual usage during the war. In the first month of 1632, Hojiger was promoted into a Defense Officer (man. *beiguwan*; chin. *beiyu* 備御) due to his good performance of charging in the front when the army besieged Dalinghe town (Dalinghe Cheng 大淩河城) and attacked Jinzhou 錦州 under Hong Taiji's command. When striking the terrace of Yuzizhang, he led ten musketeers and shot three enemies. Later his ten musketeers killed a woodcutter of Dalinghe *(hojiger be wesibuhe turgun, dalingho hoton be kaha de, ginjeo de han i genefi gidaha qooha de, juleri niyalma wame yabuha, ioi zi jang tai afara de, moyooqan sindara juwan niyalma be gamafi ilan niyalma be goibuha, miyooqan sindara juwan niyalma be gaifi, dalingho hoton i orho gaijara niyalma be miyooqan sindame emke waha... tuttu ofi wesibufi beiguwan obuha).*[772]

Cannon manufacturing has not only changed the course of history, but also the military career of some individual person. In the first month of 1632, Hong Taiji rewarded Li Ming of the Bordered Yellow Banner, who was good at firing Red-Coat Cannons and General-in-chief Cannons. When the enemies departed from the Dalinghe town and attacked a terrace, which was under the Jurchen control, Li killed many enemies by the cannons. When attacking the Obondoi Gate, he continuously fired the cannons for two months *(kubuhe suwayan i li ming be wesibufi beiguwan*

---

[770] *Fe dangse*, pp. 5487-5499.
[771] *Fe dangse*, p. 5496.
[772] *Fe dangse*, pp. 5839-5842.

obuha, obuha turgun, dalingho i qooha tuqifi tai be gaijara de, hvng i poo, amba jiyanggiyvn gamafi sindaha manggi, niyalma ambula goifi buqehe... obondoi duka de juwe biya poo sindaha).[773]

Another example is that in the second month of 1632, Defense Officer Zu was promoted to Mobile Corps Commander because he supervised the manufacture of the cannonballs for the Eight Banners to attack Dalinghe: 8,500 large cannonballs for Redcoat and General's Cannon, along with 85,000 bullets. All the manufactured cannonballs and bullets were provided to the six Regiments of Han Chinese Army (man. *jalan i nikan*; chin. *jiala hanjun* 甲喇漢軍), the army of Eight Chieftains (man. *jakvn beise*; chin. *ba beile* 八貝勒) and soldiers in the other battle fields, and there was still remaining. He urged workers to cast cannonballs and bullets in daytime and inspected the military camps during the night. Last year, he cast three Red-Coat Cannons, and this year four *(zu beiguwan be wesimbufi iogi obuha, obuha turgun, dalingho de jakvn gvsai hvng i muhaliyan, jiyanggiyvn i muhaliyan, uheri jakvn minggan sunja tanggv, ajige muhaliyan jakvn tumen sunja minggan, mini boxome hungkerehe muhaliyan be, ninggun jalan i nikan jakvn beise i booi poo sindara niyalma de, ba bade afara de jalukiyame bufi geli funqehe, inenggi oqi, muhaliyan arara be boxoho, dobori oqi, ing be giyarime yabuha, duleke aniya ilan hvng i hungkerehe, ere aniya duin hung i hungkerehe...).*[774]

This passage was written in the second month of the sixth year of Sure Han (1632). In comparison with the previous Han Chinese version of *Veritable Records*, this Defense officer Zu should be Zhu Shiyin 祝世蔭. The Manchu document keeper must have made a mistake of transcribing the Han Chinese surname Zhu into Zu,[775] which should be indicated as Ju in our transcribing.

The newly produced firearms could also have encouraged the state for holding regular military manoeuvre. As Peer Vries asserted that compared to feelings of common identity, training, drills and harsh

---

[773] *Fe dangse*, pp. 6004-6005.

[774] *Fe dangse*, pp. 6000-6001.

[775] Huang Yi'nong 黃一農 (2004), *Hongyi dapao yu huang taiji chuangli de baqi hanjun* 紅夷大炮與皇太極創立的八旗漢軍 (The Red-Barbarian Cannon and the Eight-Banner Chinese Army Established by Hong Taiji), *Lishi yanjiu* 歷史研究 (Historical Research) 2004.4: 83.

discipline can mobilize the masses more efficiently for specific tasks.[776] On the twenty-second day of the first month in 1632, Hong Taiji led the First Chieftain, all the secondary chieftains and officials to the North-drill Ground for inspecting the Han Chinese army, who were under the command of Imperial Son-in-law Si Uli (Tong Yangxing 佟養性) to practice the usage of armors, shields, flags and fire Red-Coat Cannons. Later they came to the West Drill Ground to inspect the Jurchen soldiers, who fired guns and cannons. Furthermore, the Han Chinese soldiers under Si Uli's leadership loaded gunpowder into the Red-Coat Cannons, Falcon Cannons (man. *fa gung poo*; chin. *fa gong pao* 發貢炮) and General's Cannons, and practiced to shoot targets. Then small cannons were displayed and fired for drill. Afterwards, Hong Taiji and the other leaders watched the newly surrendered officials to shoot arrows *(orin juwe de, han, amba beile, geren taijisa, ambasa, si uli efu i geren nikan qooha uksin saqa etufi, tu kalka faidafi, hvng i poo sindara be tuwame amargi giyooqan de tuqike, tuqifi neneme wargi giyooqan de faidaha juxen i dagilaha poo miyooqan sindaha, jai si uli efu i nikan qoohai hvng i poo, fa gung poo, jiyanggiyvn poo de gemu muhaliyan sindafi, aigan ilibufi sindame tuwaha, jai buya poo be faidafi sasa sindaha, sindame wajiha manggi, dalingho qi gajiha iqe hafasa be gabtabume tuwaha...).*[777] The Imperial Son-in-law, Si Uli, has a Han Chinese origin. The Manchu word *giyooqan* derived from the Han Chinese word *jiaochang* 校場, which means drill ground. This passage could indicate that the Jurchen-Manchus adopted the Han Chinese method of training their firearm units. Tonio Andrade researched on the Han Chinese and Korean musketry volley technique roughly from 1639 to 1649,[778] and we have reasons to believe that the Jurchens were quickly catching up in this respect.

On the same day, Tong Yangxing 佟養性, who was also a Banner-Han Chinese Regional Commander, memorialized to Hong Taiji for request of producing more firearms. Tong mentioned that the Red-Barbarian Cannons (*hongyi dapao* 紅夷大炮) and General's Cannons are indispensable weapons for attacking cities, but the

---

[776] Peer Vries (2015), State, Economy and the Great Divergence: Great Britain and China, 1680s-1850s, Bloomsbury, London, p. 420.

[777] *Fe dangse*, pp. 5931-5933.

[778] Tonio Andrade, *The Gunpowder Age,* pp. 183-186.

Three-barrel guns, Breech-loading swivel guns (eng. *The Frankish Cannon*; chin. *folangji* 佛郎機) and matchlocks were specially deployed for defending cities. Furthermore, he pointed out that even one hundred big cannons were not enough and hundreds of thousands of *jin* gunpowder was little (*gongda chengchi biyong hongyidajiangjun, jinyao biyong. qi biehao jiangjunpao cizhi. zhiyu sanyangqiang, folangji, niaoqiang dengxiang, te chengshou zhiju er... dapao baiwei buduo, huoyao shushiwan youshao* 攻打城池必用紅夷大將軍，緊要必用。其別號將軍炮次之。至於三眼槍、佛郎機、鳥槍等項，特城守之具爾…大炮百位不多，火藥數十萬猶少).[779] In accordance with "Records of Firearms",[780] Yin Xiaodong 尹曉冬 claimed that the late Ming army divided guns into three categories such as *zhanchong* 戰銃 "field gun", *gongchong* 攻銃 "siege gun" and *shouchong* 守銃 "defense gun".[781] The above passage tells that the Later Jin army, under the leadership of Han Chinese officers, also had the knowledge of classifying guns for different military purpose.

According to Lin Wenzhao 林文照 and Guo Yongfang 郭永芳, the Frankish Cannon was introduced to China in 1517, which is the twelfth year of Zhengde when the Portuguese people first arrived in Canton.[782] The word *folangji* 佛郎機 (*farang* or *faranj*) was originally used by the Middle Easterners to address the Franks,[783] but in the Ming dynasty, it referred to both the Portugal country and the weapon produced by the Portuguese. The deployment of the Frankish Cannon for defending

---

[779] *Tiancongchao chengong zouyi* 天聰朝臣工奏議 (Memorials of Ministers in the Tiancong Reign), collected in *Qing ruguanqian shiliao xuanji* 清入關前史料選輯 (Collected Historical Materials before the Qing Entered Shanhai Pass), edition Beijing: Zhongguo renmin daxue chubanshe, 1989, p. 9.

[780] Bing lu 兵錄 (Records of Firearms), series of military books, was composed by He Rubin 何汝賓 in 1606. Its new print in 1630 contains fourteen volumes, which are a comprehensive description about art of war.

[781] Yin Xiaodong 尹曉冬 (2014), *16-17 shiji xifang huoqi jishu xiang zhongguo de zhuanyi* 16-17 世紀西方火器技術向中國的轉移 (Transmission of Firearm Technology from the West to China from the Sixteenth to Seventeenth Century), Shandong Jiaoyu chubanshe, Ji'nan, pp. 215-217.

[782] Lin Wenzhao 林文照 and Guo Yongfang 郭永芳 (1984), folangji huochong zuizao chuanru zhongguo de shijian kao 佛郎機火銃最早傳入中國的時間考 (Evidence about the Earliest Time When The Frankish Cannon was Introduced to China), *Ziran kexueshi yanjiu* 自然科學史研究 (Studies in the History of Natural Sciences), 3. 4: 372-377.

[783] Daniel G. Konig (2015), Arabic-Islamic Views of the Latin West: Tracing the Emergence of Medieval Europe, Oxford University Press, Oxford, pp. 289-330.

against the nomads along the Great Wall can be dated in 1530, the ninth year of Jiajing,[784] when Wang Hong 汪鋐, the Right Censor-in-chief (youduyushi 右都御使), proposed to the Ming court for using the Frankish Cannons he had submitted: among the small ones, those weigh less than twenty jin and reach the targets of six hundred paces, can be deployed on the lookout platforms; the larger ones that weight more than seventy jin and can shoot as far as five or six li, can be deployed on the forts. By using these weapons, the army can achieve victories by sitting without attacking (jiunian qiu, hong leiguan you duyushi, shangyan... dang yong chen suo jin folangji, qi xiao zhi ershijin yixia, yuan ke liubaibu zhe, ze yongzhi duntai... qi da zhi qishijin yishang, yuan ke wuliuli zhe, ze yongzhi chengpu 九年秋，鋐累官右都御使，上言…當用臣所進佛郎機，其小止二十斤以下，遠可六百步者，則用墩臺...其大至七十斤以上，遠可五六里者，則用之城堡...可坐收不戰之功).[785] The description of firing range was exaggerated. Scientific experiments show that muzzle-loading guns all range circa 500 to 1,500 meters. Even though the Frankish guns were breech-loading, physically it was impossible for the large ones to reach five or six li, which is about 2500 and 3000 meters, due to the limitation of cannon making by traditional technology. Nonetheless, The Ming emperor was happy and adopted this strategy.

The writers of the Ming's official history considered this event as the beginning of deploying the Frankish Cannons but the Ming army never could defeat the enemy because the officers and soldiers were not good at operating the firearms (di yue, ji congzhi. huopao zhi you folangji zici shi. ran jiangshi bu shan yong, qi moneng zhikou ye 帝悅，即從之。火礮之有佛郎機自此始。然將士不善用，迄莫能制寇也).[786] In this case, the Frankish Cannons designed by the Portuguese and improved by the Han Chinese were applied to defend rather than attack.

In comparison, Red-Barbarian Cannons were specially used for dismantling the fortification walls. Shen Dingping 沈定平 pointed out that in the early 1700s the Portuguese captured Red-Hair Large Weapons (hongmao daqi 红毛大器) from the Dutch ships in Macao Harbour and

---

[784] Tonio Andrade, *The Gunpowder Age*, p. 136.
[785] *Mingshi*, book 28, vol. 325, pp. 8431-8432.
[786] *Mingshi*, book 28, vol. 325, p. 8432.

then the Macao people started to manufacture this weapon.[787] Hearing the news, the Ming government officials privately purchased a few from Macao and applied them in the war of Ningyuan in 1626. After being defeated, the Later Jin rulers tried to obtain these daunting cannons for reversing the war situation. Tong Yangxing, as an officer of Han Chinese origin who surrendered to the Later Jin, had a good knowledge about different functions of different firearms. To assist the Khan for accelerating the enterprise, he requested for a large number of cannons to attack the forts. Thus, we can see the urgent need for developing military economies that were commanded by the state during the war period. On the nineteenth day of the third month in 1633, a craftsman Jin Shichang 金世昌 was promoted to a Defense Officer because he successfully cast cannons without using wax,[788] which must be the technique of Clay-mode for metal casting. The previous technology should be Lost-wax casting, which usually takes place in winter rather than summer, for the reason of condensing wax quickly in a cold weather. Huang Yi'nong contended that the clay mode produces weapons in a similar quality compared to Lost-wax, but the process of manufacture is not confined to changes of seasons,[789] and therefore, more guns can be made within certain periods of time. Nevertheless, Red-Barbarian Cannon, as the most formidable weapon, could not be easily produced due to the limited sources of the time. Even with the improved casting technique, consumption of metal was enormous during wartime. Sheng Dingping 沈 定平 argued that, before the surrender of the Ming Commanders Kong Youde 孔有德 and Geng Zhongming 耿仲明 in the fifth month of the seventh year Tiancong (1633), the number of Red-Barbarian Cannons owned by the Later Jin was around six, which can be calculated according to the "*Veritable Records of Qing Taizong.*"[790] But just merely two months later, a court memorial pointed out that the number of Red-Barbarian Cannons had reached some thirty, consisting of

---

[787] Shen Dingping 沈定平 (2012), *Ming Qing zhi ji zhongx iwenhua jiaoliushi-mingji: qutong yu bianyi* 明清之際中西文化交流史-明季：趨同與辨異 History of China-West Cultural Communication during the Ming Qing Transition-the End of Ming: Convergence and Differentiation, The Commercial Press, Beijing, p. 548.

[788] Qingchu neiguoshiyuan manwen dang'an yibian, p. 9.

[789] Huang Yi'nong, Hongyi dapao yu huang taiji chuangli de baqi hanjun, pp. 79-80.

[790] Shen Dingping, Ming Qing zhi ji zhongxiwenhua jiaoliushi, p. 581.

newly-manufactured cannons and old cannons obtained from ships of Lüshun 旅順, which were brought by Kong Youde and Geng Zhongming.[791] As we found out in the previous passages, Red-Barbarian Cannons were specially designed for bombarding the fortification walls, and the Ming's military advantage was neutralized because the Jurchen-Manchus also deployed powerful weapons in the same class. Quantities of firearms helped the Later Jin army gradually gain upper hand when laying siege to the Han Chinese cities, besides victories achieved by cavalries in fields .

Falcon cannons and Frankish guns were recorded in the Compilation of Coast Defence Strategies with Illustrations (*chouhaitubian* 籌海圖編) which was first printed in 1562. [792] As muzzle-loading and breech-loading weapons, they were effectively deployed for fighting wars with formidable power, often in exaggerated ways, against invaders. Nevertheless, one shall notice that the Red-Barbarian Cannons, Falcon cannons and Frankish guns, were all European-designed weapons, which later were adopted by the Han Chinese and Manchus in the first half of the seventeenth century. As Nicola Di Cosmo argued that firearms manufactured according to European military technology continuously played a vital role in the Qing state building of mid seventeenth century.[793] Since the Jurchen-Manchu army employed barrel guns and cannons, we can assure that their gunpowder was used as forward propellant, which suits the fifth stage of gunpowder weapons.[794] Thus, we go to our next topic of gunpowder, which originally was a Han Chinese invention but gradually turned into the Manchu favor.

5.7.2 Gunpowder

A few Manchu passages of the early Manchu documents have proved the existence of gunpowder-making production. On the eleventh day of the second month in 1623, Nurgaqi asked his subordinates to recommend

---

[791] Shen Dingping, Ming Qing zhi ji zhongxiwenhua jiaoliushi, p. 581.

[792] *Chouhaitubian* 籌海圖編 (Compilation of Coast Defence Strategies with Illustration), by Zheng Ruoceng 鄭若曾, punctuated and checked by Li Zhizhong 李致忠, edition Beijing: Zhonghua shuju, 2007.

[793] Nicola Di Cosmo (2004), Did Guns Matter? Firearms and the Qing Formation, in *The Qing Formation in World-Historical Time*, 1st ed., vol. 234, Lynn A Struve (2004), ed., Harvard University Asia Center, Massachusetts.

[794] Joseph Needham (1974), *Science and Civilisation in China: Chemistry and Chemical Technology*, vol. 5, Cambridge University Press, London, p. 147.

people who can produce sulfur, which is a key element for manufacturing gunpowder. The sulfur craftsmen are treated wells as the satin-silk producers, being exempted from all sorts of official errands *(juwan emu de..., lio hvwang arara niyalma biqi tuqinu, tere niyalma inu boobai kai, gequheri suje jodoro uju jergi niyalmai jergi de obure, te gequheri suje jodoro niyalma biqi tuqinu, ai ai alban waliyara).*[795]

Another passage clearly pointed out that sulfur-making aims at military usages and rewards for sulfur artisans were significant. On the fifth day of the sixth month in 1623, Yan Manzi and Xie Manzi, who were in charge of official coal, delivered sulfur that they had produced for making gunpowder. The authority granted them with the posts of a Company Commander (man. *qiyanzung*; chin. *qianzong* 千總) along with one set of clothes, boots, hat and ten *yan* silver for each of them as financial rewards *(iqe sunja de, jakvn gvsai siden i wehe yaha deijire yan man zi, siye man zi, poo sindara suwayan okto be urebufi benjihe seme, juwe niyalma de qiyanzung ni hergen bufi, emte etuku gvlha mahala, juwanta yan menggun xangname buhe).*[796]

According to the Manchu-language documents, most sulfur producers were Han Chinese. On the eighteenth day of the sixth month in 1623, a Han Chinese person, Ji Dase, contributed sulfur that was produced by himself. Accordingly, the authority granted him with a post of a Company Commander (man. *qiyanzung*; chin. *qianzong* 千總) along with three rolls of satin, five rolls of deep-green cloth, ten *yan* silver and other stuff such as satin embroidery, clothes, hats and boots *(juwan jakvn de, ji dase gebungge nikan, lio hvwang urebufi benjire jakade, wesibufi qiyanzung ni hergen bufi, ilan suje, moqin samsu sunja, menggun juwan yan, gequheri etuku, mahala gvlha xangnaha).*[797]

Besides military purpose, gunpowder was also used for entertainment. On the second day of first month in 1624, in the early evening the Khan led all the chieftains to ascend the Gate of Conciliating Afar (man. *goroki be gosire duka*; chin. *huaiyuanmen* 懷遠門) in the west part of the fortification and ordered to play fireworks (man. *pojan*; chin. *pozhang* 炮 仗). Usually fireworks are displayed on the fifteenth and sixteenth day. Because of the presence of the Mongol chieftains, the Khan wanted them

---

[795] *Fe dangse*, pp. 2011-2013.
[796] *Fe dangse*, pp. 2407-2408.
[797] *Fe dangse*, pp. 2489-2490.

to see the fireworks before they returned home and thus arranged this display *(han, iqe juwe i yamji, geren beise be gaifi indahvn erinde tuqifi, heqen i wargi fajiran i goroki be gosire dukai dele tefi, pojan qargilakv efibuhe, efime wajiha manggi, ulgiyan erinde dosika, pojan qargilakv be, dekdeni tofohon juwan ninggun de efibumbihe, ba ba i monggo beise jihebi, tuwafi genekini seme tuttu jortai efibuhe).*[798]

The consumption of gunpowder during wartime was enormous. On the sixteenth day of the ninth month in 1631, Hong Taiji ordered the First Chieftain, Secondary Chieftain Jirgalang, and Erke Quhur to command four banners' Defense Army (man. *bayara*; chin. *hujun* 護軍), two armored soldiers from the current companies, and one official from each banner, with one Red-Coat Cannon, twenty General-in-chief Cannons and General's Cannons, to attack the Ming's terrace, in which the Han Chinese soldiers had captured horses and camels from the Jurchens before. The army surrounded the terrace and fired cannons. Later the siege troops requested for ten thousand *jin* gunpowder and sixty mules for transporting the gunpowder to the front *(tere inenggi, amba beile, jirgalang taiji, erke quhur duin gvsai bayara yooni, ing ni emu nirui juwete uksin, gvsade emte amban, hvng i poo emke, amba jiyanggiyvn ilhi jiyanggiyvn orin gamame, morin temen gaiha, tai be afame genefi, tai be kafi poo sindaha... poo i okto emu tumen gin unggi, aqire losa ninju...).*[799]

The firearms demonstrated great power in the wars of invading Korea. On the twenty-sixth day of the twelfth month in 1636, after hearing his troops were pursuing the Korean king, Hong Taiji sent a command to Dudu, who was entitled as Doroi Elehun Chieftain (chin. *duoluo anping beile* 多羅安平貝勒), urging him to arrive soon with Red-Coat Cannons, General-in-chief Cannons and other firearms. The cannons, matchlocks, bullets and gunpowder can be carried by the Eight-Banner Han Chinese Artillery Troops (man. *ujen qooha*; chin. *baqihanjun* 八旗漢軍) and the military horses and mules owned by the Three Kings (man. *ilan wang*; chin. *sanwang* 三王). As for the artillery carriers owned by the three Han Chinese kings, they must be transported by their good officials with cooperation of the Manchu officials*(enduringge han i hese, doroi elehun beile de wasimbuha... bi tere medege be donjifi, suweni gajire hvng i, amba jiyanggiyvn poo, tuwai agvra be hvdun isinjire be ebseme gvnimbi,*

---

[798] *Fe dangse*, pp. 2718-2719.
[799] *Fe dangse*, pp. 5518-5523.

ujen qooha, ilan wang ni qoohai morin losa de aqiqi ojoro poo, miyooqan, terei muhaliyan, okto gajime... nikan ilan wang ni hvng i, amba jiyanggiyvn i sejen de qeni mutere sain hafasa be afabufi suweni emgi gajikini...).[800]

Military industry was a special profession that involves innovative technologies and substantive funds for quantitative manufacture. Here the role of the state was exclusively dominant and the Manchu scribes, except for those Han Chinese artisans who contributed their technique, recorded few private enterprises.

5.8 Commerce and Revenue and Other Manufacturing Industries

5.8.1 Regulations on Commerce

Commerce was closely supervised by the Jurchen-Manchu state during the wartime. On the fifth day of the fifth month in 1621, a new edict was released to regulate the trade. The administration was afraid that bandits would rob people from the Khan's fortification if they traded in small cities and villages. Furthermore, all traders who travel alone without a permit must be arrested. People form small cities and fortresses of other places are allowed to take mass commodities to the Khan's fortification for trade, and as for daily necessities, which can be traded among villages *(han i heqen i niyalma, tulergi buya heqen, buya gaxan de unqame udame hvda generahv, han i heqen i niyalma, tulergi buya heqen, buya gaxan de hvdaxame yabumbihede, hvlha kiyangdu mujilengge niyalma, xolo bahafi durime quwangname yabumbi, tuttu emteli doron akv hvdaxame yabure niyalma be saha de, jafafi benju, tulergi buya heqen, buya gaxan i niyalma, amba hvda be gemu han i heqen de hvdaxa, buya hvda be meni meni gaxan i dolo hvdaxa).*[801]

Grain transaction for commercial purpose was permitted in emergent situations. On the twenty-fourth day of the second month in 1622, Nurgaqi sent a document to the Grand Coordinators and declared that after moving the people of Guangning away into other regions, the new residents will consume grain from the cohabited people. If there is a grain shortage, more grain should be brought there collaboratively. The

---

[800] *Fe dangse*, pp. 8453-8455.
[801] *Fe dangse*, pp. 967-968.

administration should transport more grain to the commoners who have no food to eat. If there is available grain which can be transported for sale, it would be allowed to do so *(han i bithe, juwe biyai juwan duin de du tang de wasimbuha... jai guwangning ni ba i niyalma gurime genefi, kamqiha ba i niyalma bisire juku be aqan jefu, isirakv oqi aqan juwe, baisin niyalma jeku akvqi juweme jefu, jeku bifi juweme unqaqi, inu suweni qiha).*[802]

Regular commercial transactions were severely affected by the ongoing war between the Jin state and the Ming China because some business can be used as a tool to hurt the enemy. But real business, no matter owned by the Jurchens or Han Chinese, was strictly protected by law. On the fifteenth day of the sixth month in 1622, the Grand Coordinators sent a decree that requires all Jurchen and Han Chinese shop owners to carve their names on stone tablets or woods, which should stand in front of shops. Those who do not declare their names will be punished. The peddlers who do not have their own shops are prohibited from conducting their business because they could sell poisoned goods. The Jurchen women and children should be alerted that if they buy food, they must remember the names of shop owners. Otherwise, if they die of poison, no authority could make judgement but only suspicion. As for the Jurchen and Han Chinese businesspersons, they are all Khan's people and no one should rob their goods. The Jurchen and Han Chinese people should arrest the robbers, whenever they witness the crime. If the robbers run away, all Jurchen and Han Chinese people should assist the arresting and there will be a reward for those who arrest robbers successfully *(du tang ni bithe, ninggun biyai tofohon de wasimbuha, juxen nikan puseli sindara niyalma, puseli ejen i hala gebu be, wehe de, moo de folome bithe arafi, puseli jakade ilibu, ejen i gebu hala be bithe arame temgetulerakv oqi weile, puseli akv gala jafafi unqame yabure niyalma be gemu nakabu, jafafi unqame yabure niyalma, imbe baiqibe baharakv seme oktolorongge gemu tere kai, musei juxen juse hehesi de aname ulhibume hendu, ya udame jetere niyalma, jeke puseli ejen be ejeme gaisu, ejeme gaijarakv oqi, si oktolobufi buqeqi, buhiyeme wei baru gisurembi, juxen nikan gemu emu han i gurun kai, yaya niyalma unqera jaka biqibe, ai ai jaka be ainu durimbi, durime niyalma be juxen saqi, juxen jafa,*

---

[802] *Fe dangse*, pp. 1617-1619.

nikan saqi, nikan jafa, jafaburakv burulame sujure be, juxen nikan yaya uqaraha niyalma dafi aisilame jafa, jafaha niyalma de xangnambi).[803]

The Jurchen administration also intervened commerce due to security reasons. On the third day of the first month in 1624, Nurgaqi ordered to close all the pawnshops. The reason is that items can be pawned for silver, which will encourage thieves to steal people's property, such as clothes, to exchange for silver and then flee. This is not what the pawnshop owners want. Furthermore, money lending in silver must be stopped and all debts must be collected before the tenth of the first month. Moneylenders can sue the debtors if they cannot pay off. After the tenth day, debts can be collected by people who know the inside situation. Moreover, only the animal keepers can sell horses, oxen, mules, donkeys, sheep, goats, geese, ducks and chicken by themselves. Selling other people's stuff for profit is forbidden. Anyone who detected the illegal sellers can sue them and keep whatever they sell. Regulating commerce in such way is because there were thieves who stole animals and sold them on the streets. Bandits are rising in the country *(iqe ilan de wasimbuha bithei gisun, han hendume, juxen, nikan damtun i puseli be gemu naka, damtun jafafi menggun buqi, hvlha ehe niyalma weri etuku be hvlhafi, damtun jafabufi menggun gaifi ukambi, damtun i puseli ejen si mujakv buyembi kai, jai menggun juwen sindara be inu gemu naka, juwen sindaha niyalma, aniya biyai juwan qi ebsi gaime waqihiya, purakvqi jafafi habxa, juwan be tulike de, hetu saha niyalma gaisu, jai morin, ihan, losa, eihen, honin, niman, niongniyaha, niyehe, qoko unqara niyalma, meni meni ujihengge be unqa, aisi bahaki seme weringge be udafi unqara be saha niyalma, unqara niyalma be jafafi, dele alanjifi, unqara jaka be jafaha niyalma gaisu... erebe ai turgun seqi, giyai de bisire ulha be hvlhafi unqambi, gurun de hvlha dekdembi seme wasimbuha gisun ere inu...).*[804]

In Hong Taiji's time, market economy, in the aspect of pig transaction, was fully recognized by the state, which set up laws to protect markets. The law also prohibited the privileged people, such as bondservants of the Khan and chieftains, from interfering the markets. The goal of establishing such laws is to ensure that market operates on its own terms. On the first day of the ninth month in 1727, Hong Taiji

---

[803] *Fe dangse*, pp. 1882-1884.
[804] *Fe dangse*, pp. 2719-2723.

declared that in the past, when the Khan and chieftains purchased pigs from the banner-men, they would announce a price on their own and took the pigs by force. Such behaviors were prohibited since now. According to their wishes, pig sellers were also allowed to negotiate prices and sell their pigs beyond banners. If the bondservants of the chieftains purchased pigs by force, law will punish them. Hong Taiji's edict emphasized that no one should buy pigs from the bond-servants of the Khan and chieftains, otherwise, the buyers and sellers would be punished according to the law *(iqe uyun de, han, joo bithe wasimbume hendume... han, beise ulgiyan udara de, nenehe adali gvsai niyalma de hvda maktame bufi ergeleme udara be enteheme naka, ulgiyan i ejen ini qihalahai gvsa doome hvda bahara be tuwame unqakini, beise i booi ulgiyan udara niyalma hvda maktame bufi ergeleme gaiha de, tuhere an i weile, han, beise i booi aha de ulgiyan ume udara, udaha niyalma de unqaha aha de gemu tuhere an i weile gaimbi, nikan, solho, monggo ulha de kiqebe ujire faksi ofi, ulha elgiyen kai, musei gurun i niyalma ulha ujirakv jing waqi, ai ulha bimbi, ereqi amasi, saikan kiqeme uji seme fafulaha).*[805] The market finally gained upper hands against the state. Without considerable profits and property safety, no one would conduct business for nothing, which consequently hurts the state.

Purchasing grain was one of the top priorities in Hong Taiji's reign due to the insufficient grain reserve. Shortly after Hong Taiji invaded Joseon and converted it into an ally, the state had to buy grain from Joseon. On the twenty-eighth day of the first month in 1628, the Joseon king's reply arrived and said that due to grain shortage, the Jin state decided to buy gain from Joseon. As a neighboring country, Korea should not ignore. However, in the previous invasion, the eight circuits were disturbed and the granaries were empty. Furthermore, the Korean letter said that last year the spring rain was too much and the summer drought was too severe. Accordingly, people lost good timing to cultivate and thus they were very much worried about food, too. As for the western circuits, the remaining people were few. After the Jurchen troops withdrew from Yi Zhou, refugees from the Liaodong region came to occupy the places, burning and raiding every household without leaving any chicken or dog behind. Westward from Qing Chuan, grass grows

---

[805] *Fe dangse*, pp. 4093-4098.

thickly and this is not just a personal perception but was witnessed by the emissaries from both countries. Consequently, as the Korean king indicated, regarding the rice transaction, even though the Koreans had thought of everything and exhausted every effort, it is still like seeking fish by following a tree branch and there was not much that one can do. Even so, out of moral principle, Korea still would like to help with three thousand *hule* rice. As for the commercial intercourse between the countries at Yi Zhou, the Korean government had already informed its people. Those businesspersons who are inside and outside the country, and the survivors of the two western circuits who wanted to redeem their parents, wives and children, should prepare grain and some valuables for the trip. The Korean king stressed that this was all they can do regarding the Jurchens' request for purchasing grain. Furthermore, the Korean king offered a piece of advice to maintain the commercial relationship between the two countries: mutual transactions should be conducted according to willingness of both sides, who both will benefit from the transactions without being forced to do so. If the Jurchen authority wanted to attract more rice and goods to its markets, the prices must be evaluated fairly so that people long to come. If the goal is not to achieve sufficiency of one day but to nourish the market in slow and peaceful pace, then the Korean merchants will carry their goods on their back or by carts to join the markets. The Korean authority had repeatedly ordered the frontier officials to notify their people for participating in the markets. If Korea only talked apparently without real efforts to open the markets, the Heavenly will judge. If the Jurchen state suppressed transactions and robbed goods, which made people unhappy and refused to join markets, and on the contrary, the Jin state blamed Joseon for violating the rules, the Heaven will judge, too. *(orin jakvn de, qoohiyan gurun i wang ni bithe isinjiha, wesihun gurun, jeku isirakv ofi, mende jeku udaki seqi, hanqiki gurun i doro be herserakv tuwaqi ojorakv, damu mini gurun qooha iliha fonde, jakvn golo axxafi, cang ku gemu untuhulehebi, tere dade, tuleke aniya niyengniyeri aga muke amba, juwari hiyariha ambula, usin i erin ufarafi, irgen jetere jalin dembei jobombi, jai xun tuhere ergi golo de funqehe irgen ambula akv, wesihun gurun i jeo de qooha bargiyaha amala, buqere de jialame ukaka liyoodung ni irgen ba bade isafi, boo hvwa be tuwa sindame talame, qooko yendahvn be sulabuhakv, qing quwan qi wasihvn gemu orho suiha ubaliyakabi, tere be mini gisurere anggala, jihe juwe amban i yasai tuwaha, meni gurun, wesihun gurun de hvsun teile faxxaki serakvngge akv, olhon moo de nimaha baiqi ai arga tuqire, tuttu sehe seme, mini doro be bi waqihiyarakvqi ojorakv seme, arkan ilan minggan hule bele bahafi, wesihun gurun i gvnin de aqabumbi, jai i jeo i giyang de juwe gurun hvdaxambi seme, dorgi tulergi hvdai niyalma, wargi juwe golo i funqehe irgen, ama eme juse sargan be joliki sere niyalma, meni meni bele jeku ulin tuwafi gene sehe, wesihun gurun i jeku udaki serengge, ede wajiha kai, jai emu gisurere babi, ishunde hvdaxarangge, meni meni buyere qiha, juwe yaya aisi be gvnimbi, argeleqi ojorongge waka, wesihun gurun, bele ulin ambula jikini seqi, hvda be neqin salibuqi, niyalma ini qihai urgun i genere, emu inenggi tesure be bairakv, elheken i gamame ohode, meni gurun i hvdai niyalma, unun fiyana i bulun de heru hadaha gese isanambi kai, irgen de dahvn dahvn i hendu, boljohon be ume jurqebure seme jeqen i hafasa de afabuhabi, meni gurun oilo uttu gisurefi, yargiyan i hvsun waqihiyame hvda neirakv oqi, abka sakini, wesihun gurun gidaxame hvdaxame ulin be durime gaime, irgen be urgun i hvda jiburakv oso manggi, meni gurun be jurqehe seqi, inu abka sakini).*[806] This is a long statement made by the Korean government, lecturing the Jurchens about the importance of free and fair market. It is a warming sign that the Korean state was sensible of respecting the market and let the 'invisible hand' do its job, if we are allowed to borrow a modern term from the Smithians.

Regarding the Jurchen request for market opening, the Korean government responded positively, in both commercial and political ways. In a few days, on the second day of the second month in 1628, the Korean emissaries delivered another letter, which said that some Korean officials had taken orders to collect three thousand *hule* rice, within which one thousand would be carried to markets for sale and the rest would be given as a present. This is just a heartfelt intention, which is not a common practice. Nonetheless, the Korean king wished that the Jurchen state should accept this gift. According to the Korean conventions, two states maintain good relations out of trustworthiness and principles, rather than wealth. If the amount of wealth determines the depth of relationship, this is shame for a man of principle and the two countries should be alerted not to go that direction. Such a lecture was embedded with another

---

[806] *Fe dangse*, pp. 4139-4145.

intention: Korea wanted to have its war prisoners back without further cost. Immediately, the letter mentioned that other documents had discussed of returning Korean refugees and since the two countries had negotiated peace, it would be good to see some effects of releasing the old and young prisoners and reuniting the fathers, sons, husbands and wives *(iqe juwe de, solho i elqin isinjiha, jihe bithei gisun, takvraha niyalma, jidere elqin i emgi isinjifi... jai hafasa de hendufi, arkan ilan minggan hule bele iqihiyafi, emu minggan be hvda de unggifi hvdaxambi, juwe minggan be bai benembi, ere mujilen okini sehengge, an i beherengge waka, wesihun gurun alime gaijara be buyere, juwe gurun i ishunde sain banjire ujen, akdun jurgan de bi, ulin de akv, ulin bisire akv i jalin hajilara xumin miqihiyan ojorongge, tere ambasa saisai giruqun, musei juwe gurun i targaqi aqarangge kai, geli bithe de henduhengge, ukaka irgen be jafafi amasi genju sere weile be... juwe gurun gisurendufi doro aqaha, aqaha amala sakda asihan be sindafi, ama jui, eigen sargan dahvme bahafi aqaqi, yala sain weile kai...)*.[807] Thus, one can note that in terms of economic decisions, the role of the state is activist as E-tu Zen Sun specified about the relationship between government and private economy in Qing times,[808] which also fits into both Manchu and Korean cases before the Manchus entered the passes.

It is obvious that the Korean state tried to manipulate the situation in favor of Korea, paying a smaller price to get its war prisoners back. Regarding the establishment of two markets at Huining and Yizhou, the Korean government stalled the progress due to the previous political turmoils and war damages. On the eighth day of the third month in1628, Korean emissaries brought a document, which says that since the two countries had reached peaceful terms, there would have been no doubt to open a market at Huining. In the past, there were many Warka people who were living in six circuits near the border, and many Korean businesspersons would travel there fore trading. It has been a long time since the Warka people stopped trading, whose situation cannot be known by the Manchu state. As for the market in Yizhou, though it had been agreed for opening, people were still suffering from wars and therefore,

---

[807] *Fe dangse*, pp. 4150-4158.
[808] Jane Kate Leonard and John R. Watt (eds.) (1992),*To Achieve Security and Wealth: The Qing Imperial State and the Economy, 1644-1911*, East Asia Program Cornell University, New York , p. 18.

merchants may not be able to arrive in time even under the government's order. Furthermore, it was beyond Korea's capacity to open two markets at two cities. Otherwise, there is no such a reason to allow a market that exists there but not here. One has to begin with a good ending in mind, and thus can see the positive effects *(iqe jakvn de, solho i elqin isinjiha, bithe de henduhe gisun, hvi ning de hvdaxara weile, juwe gurun sain oqi tetendere, hoksondure ba akv, damu neneme warka sa, ninggun golo de tehengge ambula ofi, tuttu gurun i hvda tubade isinafi hvdaxambihe, te warka lakqafi hvdaxarakv goidaha kai, wesihun gurun tubabe ainahai bahafi waqihiyame sambini, i jeo de hvdaxara be udu angga aljaqibe, dain qooha de irgen kokirafi, goroki hanqiki hvdai niyalma be gene seme henduqi, hono boljohon de bahafi generakv ojorahv sembi, juwe bade hvda neire anggala, fusihvn gurun i weile hvsun akvmbume muterakv yargiyan, tuttu akvqi, ubade hvdaxambime, tubade hvdaxarakv doro bio, weile deriburei tuktan de, duberei jalin bodoho de, amala yargiyan ombi, seoleki).*[809] This passage sounds like an excuse of the Korea state to postpone the opening of markets, but a good philosophy was embedded: market needs to function wells on a free and fair term, with less arbitrary intervention from the state.

Another official document declared Korea's unwillingness to open a market at Yizhou, saying that it would be a fine thing and there would be no regret for the Korean authority to support it. However, the site is far in the north with few people and scarce goods. Besides, merchants from hinterland would not want to go due to the separation of numerous passes and high mountains. Even though the market can be opened, there would be no goods for transaction, and the Manchu people would make a futile journey. Therefore, discussions should be made by exchanging letters of the two states. According to the previous letter, the Manchu state hoped that all Korean inhabitants in the north should travel freely without obstacles for exchanging what they have, and this must be good for them. Nevertheless, if all the dispatched officials and commoners conduct trade according to the Yizhou rule, it would go beyond the capacities of the northern people. All the previous words are truth and the relevant doubts will resolve themselves if the Manchu state thinks repeatedly with a fair mindset *(i jeo de hvda neifi hvwaliyan i teile, be ainu hairambi, damu*

---

[809] *Fe dangse*, pp. 4170-4172.

amargi jase lakqame goro, irgen komso ulin akv, tere dade jugvn geli haksan goro, dabkvri furdan kamqime dabagan de dalibufi, dorgi ba i hvdai niyalma ainaha seme generakv, udu hvda neiki sehe seme hvdaxara ulin akv, wesihun gurun i niyalma untehuri jifi untuhun generahu seme, tutu nenehe bithe hebdenehe bihe kai, jihe bithei gisun uttu, wesihun gurun amargi jeqen i tehe irgen be, qeni qisui genere jidere bisire akv be ishunde hvdaxakini seqi, tede hvwanggiyarakv, jai takvrara hafan niyalma i jeo i hvdai adali ohode, amargi irgen i hvsun muterakv ombi, erele alara gisun, gemu weile dursun i inu ba, wesihun gurun neqin mujilen i urebume gvniha de, ini qihai sume kenehunjerakv ombi kai).[810]

A free and fair market that operates on its own terms was highlighted again by the Korean government, though it seems reluctant for the Korean merchants to join the market due to harsh conditions. Commercial transaction must be conducted on free will, which is the message we can learn from these diplomatic communications between the Manchu and Korean states.

Commercial transactions between the Later Jin and Korea was not soothing. Market functioned on its own rules, but both governments wanted to interfere for their own benefits. Sometimes, the reasons of intervening market have little to do with market itself and market can be used as an advantage to enforce political bargain.

5.8.2 Revenue

As we discussed in the section of currencies, both Nurgaqi and Hong Taiji launched successive wars to fight the Ming and acquired substantive precious metals for filling up the state's treasury. Still, taxation on the Han Chinese subjects became an important matter after the Jurchen army took over the Ming's Liaodong region. The Ming empire heavily depended on direct taxation for revenue, like most preindustrial societies,[811] so did the Jurchen-Manchu state. Throughout most of the Qing period, tax on salt remained as the second largest source for state's revenue after agriculture.[812] Nonetheless, few Manchu sources point out that the Later Jin and early Qing state imposed heavy tax on the

---

[810] *Fe dangse*, pp. 4322-4325.

[811] Madeleine Zelin (1984), The Magistrate's Tael: Rationalizing Fiscal Reform in Eighteenth-Century Ch'ing China, University of California Press, California, p. 5.

[812] Zhongguo yanyeshi luncong, p. 2.

production, distribution and consumption of salt. The reason could be that the state owns every section of salt industry, including its supply for banner people and allies. Tax on salt circulated in the Han Chinese market of Liaodong region could still be weighty, especially in Nurgaqi's reign when commercial tax became an important channel to enrich the state.

In light of the Manchu documents that were produced before the unification of China, tax collection under the Jurchen rule mainly was conducted according to the Ming's convention. However, some private levies being charged by the previous Han Chinese officials were abolished by the Jurchen regime. On the third day of the sixth month in 1621, the administration declared to open the market at the suburbs in the west of Liaodong town. The price of goods and tax rates will be charged according to the Ming's regulation *(ninggun biyai iqe ilan de, liyoodung ni heqen i wargi guwali de, ejen sindafi hvda ilibuha, ai ai nunqara udara hvda be, qifun be, gemu nikan i songkoi obuha).*[813] It is impossible to say that the role of the early Manchu state is to facilitate the market and let the price do its job for greater economic development. However, no one can deny that market was an important source for state's revenue and the Manchu authority was fully aware of that.

In Nurgaqi's reign, the Jurchen officers must obey the law to conduct business and pay tax accordingly. On the sixth day of the tenth month in 1621, the administration examined a case, in which Kvwataiji, a Mobile Corps Commander, indulged his bondservants to trade with some Han Chinese people in private and refused to pay tax. As a punishment, he was removed from the post due to conducting business that had violated the law *(iqe ninggun de beidehe gisun, kvwataiji, ini booi niyalma be sindafi, hvlhame nikan de hvdaxame, qifun burakv, xajin be efuleme hvdaxaha seme weile afafi, iogi hergen be nakabuha).*[814] It is outspoken that the Manchu state exerted its influence upon commercial transactions due to the ongoing wars. Besides, the government officials, who were also military officers under the banner system, had to submit to their higher authority in the aspect of commercial transaction.

During the wartime, tax collection can arouse strong resistance from the Han Chinese people. On the tenth day of the twelfth month in 1621,

---

[813] *Fe dangse*, pp. 1020-1021.
[814] *Fe dangse*, pp. 1209-1210.

Nurgaqi urged Aita, a Regional Vice Commander, to collect official taxation, such as grain, silver, charcoal, iron and salt, from the Han Chinese people who lived in Gaizhou, Fuzhou, and Jinzhou, where the Jurchens did not cohabit with the Han Chinese. Nurgaqi also ordered a Defense Officer Tong to charge the official taxation as usual, with one hundred soldiers under his command in case of being attacked by the Han Chinese *(han i bithe, aita fujiyang de juwan de wasimbuha... sini gai jeo, fu jeo, ginjeo de juxen kamqihakvbi kai, fe an i gaijara jeku, menggun, yaha, sele, dabsun i alban be ainu hvdun boxofi unggirakv, tung beiguwan de tanggv qooha adabufi unggi, fe an i gaijara alban be boxome gaikini, qooha akvqi yaka langtuxarahv).*[815] This passage shows that the banner system, as a military force to underpin the state, also functioned as the administrative force for tax collection.

Grain taxation was always important to the administration, which facilitated the Jurchen people to move into the Han Chinese residential regions. On the twenty-ninth day of the eleventh month in 1621, Nurgaqi sent a document to Li Yongfang, the Imperial Son-in-law of Fusi (man. *fusi efu*; chin. *fuxi efu* 撫西額駙), stating that when the relocated Jurchen households run out of food, he must collect grain from the villages along the way to support them *(han i bithe, orin uyun de fusi efu de wasimbuha, gurime genere boigon i niyalma jetere jeku wajiqi, jugvn i gaxan gaxan de jeku gaifi ulebume gama).*[816]

Regarding the tax rate, the Jurchen authority inherited the Ming's convention, but exterminated some exorbitant taxes and levies. On the eighth day of the twelfth month in 1621, Nurgaqi declared that taxation for his treasury would be charged according to the old regulations, no more no less. Furthermore, all the rice, wheat, beans, sesame, grain, vegetable, indigo, brushes, paper and other miscellaneous levies collected by the Han Chinese officials in private had already been stopped. If the Jurchen and Han Chinese officials still charge those irregular taxes, people should sue them *(han i ku de sindara iletu alban gaijara jaka be ekiyemburakv madaburakv, fe kemuni gaimbi, terei tulkiyen nikan i hafasai beye, ini qisui enquleme gaijara hadu, maise, turi, malanggv, jeku, sogi, giyen, fi, hooxan, ai ai buyarame gaijara alban be nakabuha, mini nakabuha jaka be, juxen nikan hafasa qeni qisui hvlhame gaji*

---

[815] *Fe dangse*, pp. 1340-1341.
[816] *Fe dangse*, p. 1313.

sehede, geqileme alanju).[817] It is reasonable to assume that the Jurchen regime enacted new policies for pacifying their Han Chinese subjects by cutting off the unnecessary charges while maintaining the Ming's taxation system. Market could benefit from these agricultural products that are under the farmers' disposal.

Collecting taxes according to the Ming rule was repeatedly emphasized. On the fourteenth day of the twelfth month in 1621, Nurgaqi sent an edict to urge tax collection according to the old way with nonstop *(han takvrafi, fe an i gaijara alban boxome unggihe, ume ilibure seme, juwan duin de wasimbuha)*.[818] Collecting official fodder for military horses was highlighted in the new regime. On the same day, Nurgaqi sent a document to Aita, a Regional Vice Commander, to bring the taxed fodder collected from Gaizhou and Fuzhou. Those who did not deliver their fodder must pay in silver *(han i bithe, aita fujiyang de wasimbuha, gai jeo, fu jeo de alban i orho be gaijiqi, isiburakv ba i niyalma de menggun gaisu)*.[819] Again, due to military purpose, Nurgaqi frequently urged his subordinate officers to collect fodder. On the eighteenth day of the twelfth month in 1621, the Khan sent a document to Aita, the Regional Vice Commander, to collect the official fodder. However, regarding the exorbitant tax levies, which were privately collected by the Han Chinese officials, such as grain, grass, wheat, sesame, indigo, brushes, paper and so on, must be stopped. For this reason, the Khan will reimburse silver from his treasury as compensation for the decreasing income of Han Chinese officials *(han i bithe, juwan jakvn de aita fujiyang de wasimbuha, sini wesimbuhe bithe be gemu tuwaha, fe an i han i iletu gaijara ai ai alban be ume nunggire, ume ekiyeniyere, fe kemuni gaisu, liyoodung ni xurdeme juxen i kamqiha ba i niyalma, orho wajihabi, jeku amqarakv, juxen i ijinahakv ba i jeku orho be gaifi jalgiyarakvqi, qoohai morin de ai ulebumbi, nikan hafasai qeni qisui enquleme gaijara jeku orho, maise, malanggv, olo giyen, fi, hooxan ai ai gaijara be gemu nakabuha, tere jalin de, han, ku i menggun bumbi)*.[820] Here, one can see that tobacco did not appear as a crop in the Liaodong

---

[817] *Fe dangse*, p. 1336.
[818] *Fe dangse*, p. 1349.
[819] *Fe dangse*, p. 1349.
[820] *Fe dangse*, pp. 1361-1362.

region, and hence we can assume that it was not popular enough to arouse the state's attention, or it had not yet arrived in Northeast Asia.

For the Han Chinese people who cohabited with the Jurchens, they enjoyed certain privilege of being exempted from being charged with grain ration. On the first day of the first month in 1622, the Khan sent an edict to stop collecting grain ration from the Han Chinese people who cohabited with the Jurchens. The Han Chinese who mingled with the Jurchens were permitted to eat grain ration as their Jurchen neighbors, according to their population of each household. If the grain ration was not enough, the administration should collect more from the Han Chinese who do not cohabit with the Jurchens and then distribute the collected grain with oxcarts that are used for constructing the fortification walls *(han i bithe, iqe juwe de wasimbuha, juxen i emgi kamqiha nikan I jeku be, juxen i angga tolome miyalime gaijara be nakaha, kamqifi tehe nikan juxen i gese angga tolome miyalime jefu, isirakvqi, juxen I kamqihakv ba i niyalmai jeku be, heqen weileme jidere ihan sejen de gajifi bukini)*.[821] It is obvious that the cooperative Han Chinese were treated differently in the respect of taxation.

Under the Jurchen governance, taxation was usually classified into three categories: grain, silver and fodder. The gold and silver miners should pay with their products. On the tenth day of the second month in 1623, the Grand Coordinators reported that every year each man must submit official grain, official silver and fodder for military horses as their taxation, which is valued as three *yan* silver. According to this rate, the six hundred gold miners should pay three hundred *yan* gold each year, and the ten thousand silver miners should pay thirty thousand *yan* silver *(juwan de, du tang ni bodofi wesimbuhe bithe, emu aniya, emu hahai alban i tuqirengge, alban i jeku, alban i menggun, morin de ulebure liyoo, uhereme ilan yan, ilan yan menggun be bodofi, aisin werere ninggun tanggv haha de, emu aniya ilan tanggv yan aisin gaimbi, menggun urebure emu tumen haha de, ilan tumen yan menggun gaimbi)*.[822] Here we can conclude that mining had become an important source of state revenue before the Manchus entered the passes.

Military force was also required to cultivate crops and pay taxation. On the sixteenth day of the second month in 1623, the Grand

---

[821] *Fe dangse*, pp. 1413-1414.
[822] *Fe dangse*, pp. 2010-2011.

Coordinators ordered to tax two hundred *hule* grain upon every three hundred men in each Company (man. *niru*; chin. *niulu* 牛錄). As for the two hundred *hule* taxation, one hundred will be transported to Shenyang and the other half will be stored in the grain-producing area. For example, if the grain is collected in Haizhou, then the other half of taxation will be stored in Haizhou. So is Shenyang and so on. One hundred *hule* grain must be transported to Shenyang before the tenth of March with paperwork submitted to the Grand Coordinators. All officers, from the Regional Commander to the Defense Officer, will be severely punished and discharged if they violated this decree. As for the Han Chinese who were governed by the Jurchen officials, two *hule* grain are imposed upon every three men. Regarding the imposed grain, one *hule* goes to Shenyang Granary, the other *hule* deposits in each grain-producing site, such as Liaodong, Fuzhou, Gaizhou and Haizhou, etc. People who live within the region of Gaizhou must deliver their grain to Shenyang before the twentieth of March, with paperwork submitted to the Grand Coordinators; people who live beyond the region of Gaizhou but within Fuzhou must deliver their grain to Shenyang before the thirtieth of March, with paperwork submitted to the Grand Coordinators *(du tang ni bithe, juwan ninggun de wasimbuha, emu nirui ilan tanggv haha de, juwe tanggv hule jeku gaimbi, emu tanggv hule be simiyan de benembi, jai emu tanggv hule be hai jeo i iqi niyalma hai jeo i cang de sinda, liyoodung ni iqi niyalma liyoodung ni cang de sinda, simiyan de benere emu tanggv hule be, ilan biyai juwan de wajiha seme bithe arafi du tang de benju, zung bing guwan qi fusihvn, beiguan qi wesihun, ere gisun be jurqeqi, amba weile arafi hergen efulembi, juxen i hafasai kadalara nikasa de henduhe gisun, ilan haha de gaijara juwe hule jeku be, emu hule be simiyan i cang de bene, emu hule be liyoodung ni iqi niyalma liyoodung ni cang de sinda, fu jeo, gai jeo, hai jeo iqi niyalma hai jeo i cang de sinda, simiyan de benere jeku be, gai jeo qi ebsi niyalma, ilan biyai orin de wajiha seme du tang de bithe weisibu, gai jeo qi qasi, fu jeo qi ebsi niyalma, ilan biyai gvsin de wajiaha seme du tang de wesibu)*.[823] We must admit that during Nurgaqi's reign, the military force was also performing the political administration upon the people. The Eight Banners were the government, representing the state to rule people. But

---

[823] *Fe dangse*, pp. 2024-2027.

the banner-men also paid taxes to the highest supreme leader, who is the state himself.

Grain taxation was highlighted in terms of collecting grain in preference to silver. The reason probably is that the state needed grain to support the fast-growing population, which sometimes required the administration to disseminate grain promptly without storing in granary. On the twenty-sixth day of the third month in 1623, Nurgaqi sent an edict to order the officials who took over the granaries in Haizhou and Shenyang for collecting grain in righteous manners. All the imposed grain must not be stored but distributed away immediately. If officials taxed more in silver but less in grain, which caused insufficient grain distribution, they will be punished *(orin ninggun de unggihe bithei gisun, hai jeo i cang, simiyan i cang de jeku alime gaiha hafasa, suwe gaijara jeku be tondoi gaisu, gaiha jeku be asararakv, te bumbi kai, suwe menggun basa gaifi, jeku be ekiyehun gaifi buqi, isirakv ohode ainambi).*[824] Given the situation of war, the state adjusted the means of tax collection. Comparatively, grain is an urgent need for sustaining the war and appeasing people.

Commercial tax was collected at vital communication lines under the new regime. On the thirteenth day of the third month in 1623, under the leadership of the Grand Coordinators, the administrators of the Eight Banners are responsible for accommodating visitors by seeing them off and receiving the new ones, registering the captured animals and collecting business tax at on the bridges *(genere be fudere, jidere be okdoro, baha ulha be asarara, kiyoo de hvdaxabure qifu...).*[825] Here, we see the military force carried out the administrative work.

In Nurgaqi's reign, the rate of commercial tax was high due to state security reasons. Since the third day of the first month in 1624, the Jurchen authority regulated that all the legal animal traders must pay tax in silver, and the tax rate is one *jiha* for each *yan*. Regarding the collected tax from the Jurchen businessmen, collectors keep twenty percent and ten percent is given to the relevant Company Commanders (man. *niru ejen*; chin. *niulu ezhen* 牛錄額真) and Deputy Commanders (man. *daise janggin*; chin. *daizi zhangjing* 代子章京). As for the collected tax from the Han Chinese traders, ten percent can be kept by the Defence Officers

---

[824] *Fe dangse*, p. 2168.
[825] *Fe dangse*, p. 2119.

(man. *beiguwan*; chin. *beiyu* 備御) and Company Commanders (man. *qiyanzung*; chin. *qianzong* 千總). Speaking of the animals brought by the Mongols, they cannot be resold by other shop owners but only by the Mongols themselves. Twenty percent of the tax collected from the Mongols goes to the tax collectors, and ten percent goes to the shop owners. The reason for regulating commercial transaction in such a way is that there were thieves who stole animals and sold them on the streets. Bandits are rising in the country. This is the decree, which has imposed a heavy tax on the traders. Therefore, the tax rate was reduced to three *fun* for each *yan*, since the year Hong Taiji ascended the throne *(iqe ilan de wasimbuha bithei gisun... yaya unqara niyalma ulha de yan i bodome, emu yan de qifun emu jiha gaisu, juwe ubu be qifun gaijara niyalma gaisu, emu ubu be nirui ejen, daise janggin gaikini, nikan i qifun i emu ubu be, kadalara beiguwan, nikan qiyanzung gaikini, monggo i gajiha ulha be monggo unqakini, tataha booi ejen ulame gaifi ume unqara, qifun juwe ubu be qifun i niyalma gaisu, emu ubu be tafaha booi ejen gaikini, erebe ai turgun seqi, giyai de bisire ulha be hvlhafi unqambi, gurun de hvlha dekdembi seme wasimbuha gisun ere inu, tere qifun gaiha be ambula seme, amala sure han, tehe aniya qi qifun ekiyeniyefi, emu yan de ilan fun obuha)*. [826] The high tax rate imposed by Nurgaqi's administration was markedly different than the Confucian idea of benevolent government that advocates storing wealth within the people *(cangfuyumin* 藏富於民)*.[827] The early Manchu government shows less mercy to the merchants, who might be thieves in disguise and brought insecurity to the state.

The above passages confirm that the state's revenue was managed by the Eight Banners, which was also a military unit. Another passage also confirms that during Nurgaqi's reign, state administration was carried out by the Eight Banners, being supervised by the Grand Coordinators (man. *du tang*; chin. *dutang* 都堂). On the seventh day of the second month in 1623, Nurgaqi officially confirmed the Grand Coordinators of the Eight Banners as the constitution to administrate the country: Eight Grand Coordinators were appointed to govern the Eight Banners, and in every banner, there are two Judges (man. *beidesi*; chin. *shenshiguan* 審事官), who lead eight Mongol judges and eight Han Chinese judges, along with

---

[826] *Fe dangse*, pp. 2719-2723.
[827] Dunstan, Conflicting Counsels to Confuse the Age, p. 151.

four clerks who are in charge of the announcements made by chieftains (*iqe nadan de, jakvn gvsade jakvn du tang, emu gvsade juwede beidesi, monggo beidesi jakvn, nikan beidesi jakvn, beise i bithe monggolifi gisun tuwakiyara niyalma duite sindaha*).[828] It has little doubt that revenue was ultimately being controlled by the Grand Coordinators. However, the Eight Chieftains still exerted great influence upon the state's income.

On the twenty-fourth day of the sixth month in 1627, about two months before Nurgaqi died, he left some final words to the chieftains and officials, mentioning that in the past, his six ancestors, along with tribes of Donggo, Wanggiyan, Hada, Yehe, Ula, Hoifa and Monggo, all lusted for wealth, and aspired for crooked selfishness but not collective fairness. Consequently, brothers fought against and killed one another, so that they perished one by one. Other than my words, the Khan emphasized, you all have ears and eyes and you have seen and heard about it. "In consideration of these lessons," Nurgaqi said, "I predetermine that anything obtained by one of the Eight Chieftains must be fairly divided by the Eight Chieftains for fair use. No one is allowed to take an improper share for private purpose" (*ershisi ri, di xun zhuwangchen yue, xi wozu liuren ji dongguo, wangjia, hada, yehei, wula, huifa, menggu, ju tan caihuo, shang siqu, bushang gongzhi. kundi zhong zixiang zhengduo shahai, nai zhiyu baiwang. budai woyan, rúdeng qiwu ermu, yi chang jianwenzhi yi. wu yi bi wei qianjian, yuding bajia dan de yiwu, bajia junfen gongyong, wude fenwai siqu* 二十四日，帝訓諸王臣曰，昔我祖六人及東郭、王佳、哈達、夜黑、兀喇、輝發、蒙古，俱貪財貨，尚私曲，不尚公直。昆弟中自相爭奪殺害，乃至於敗亡。不待我言，汝等豈無耳目，亦嘗見聞之矣。吾以彼爲前鑒，預定八家但得一物，八家均分公用，勿得分外私取).[829] This policy directly led to the collective ownership of the state's property, which undermines Hong Taiji's authority that represents the state. Thus Hu Gongming 胡貢明, a Han Chinese official, memorialized to Hong Taiji, specifying that under the current system, competent personnel were divided and employed by the Eight Chieftains, and lands were also divided and occupied by the Eight Chieftains. Accordingly, when fighting for one personnel or one piece of land, the chieftains do not yield to the Emperor and the Emperor cannot make the chieftains yield, either. "Every policy meets its

---

[828] *Fe dangse*, p. 1997.
[829] Qingtaizu wu huangdi shilu, p. 391.

hindrance," Hu said bluntly, "though enjoying the empty fame of Khan, your majesty is no different than a chieftain of Plain Yellow Banner" (*youren bi bajia fenyangzhi, ditu bi bajia fenjuzhi, ji yiren chitu, beile burongyu huangshang, huangshang yi burongyu beile. shishichezhou, suiyou yi yan zhi xuming, shi wuyu zhenghuangqi yi beile* 有人必八家分養之，地土必八家分據之，即一人尺土，貝勒不容於皇上，皇上亦不容貝勒。事事掣肘，雖有一汗之虛名，實無異整黃旗一貝勒).[830] According to Bai Xinliang 白新良, after Hong Taiji gained the throne, he reformed the two white banners into the yellow ones, which were commanded by himself.[831] In any case, comparison of the Khan with a chieftain of Plain Yellow Banner (man. *gulu suwayan gvsa*; chin. *zhenghuangqi* 正 or 整黃旗), in Hu's memorial, underlines that Hong Taiji's supremacy was confined and threatened by the other chieftains in every aspect, especially over the issues of personnel and properties. According to Feng Jia, Hong Taiji successfully tamed the Eight Chieftains and restricted their power over banner affairs and correspondingly, the state's bureaucratic power was increased, with the regard of revenue included.[832]

When Hong Taiji changed the name of the state from Jin to DaQing in 1636, Hooge was put in charge of the Ministry of Revenue (*haoge guan hubu shi* 豪格管戶部事).[833] Since then, the duty of tax collection was gradually transferred into a department of the government, whose profession is to handle taxes. One must note that this is a result of fierce political struggles between the Khan and chieftains. In 1632, a Han Chinese official Hu Gongming 胡貢明 advised Hong Taiji to collect one third of the spoils into the official treasury, rather than evenly distributed all of them to the chieftains. In Hu's calculation, after plundering, if the army acquired eighty thousand *liang* silver, the eight chieftains can divide it with seven thousand *liang* for each, the remaining twenty-four thousand goes to the official treasury; if the emperor wants to reward someone, he can ordered the Ministry of Revenue to draw from the treasury and give it to the person (*jiaru xiaci bingma chuqu, ruo deyin*

---

[830] Tiancongchao chengong zouyi, p. 34.

[831] Qingshi kaobian, pp. 56-113.

[832] Feng Jia, *Emperor's Coffer*, pp. 114-115.

[833] *Qingshigao*, vol. 2, compiled by Zhao Erxun (1844-1927) et al., edition Beijing: Zhonghua shuju, 1977, p. 58.

*bawan liang, bajia pingfen qiqian liang, liu sanba erwan siqian liang shouru guanku... ruoyao shangren, ji ming hubu xiang guanku quge*i 假如下次兵馬出去，若得銀八萬兩，八家平分七千兩，留三八二萬四千兩收入官庫...若要賞人，即命戶部向官庫取給).[834] Since Hong Taiji was ultimately in charge of the official treasury, this strategy elevated the Khan's superiority over the chieftains in the political respect, and earned the state with surplus in financial control. Scholar Lai Huimin 賴惠敏 contended that since the implementation of twice-a-year tax policy (*liangshuifa* 兩稅法) in the Tang dynasty, land tax became an important item of state's revenue and down to the Qianlong period in the Qing dynasty, commercial tax became the major source for the royal family.[835] In our Jurchen-Manchu case, nonetheless, it is reasonable to postulate that wars still brought a considerable income to the Khan and the state in Hong Taiji's reign, besides land and commercial taxes. The state made wars and caused its economy to grow.

5.8.3 Other Manufacturing Industries

All sorts of artisans were highly valued by the Jurchen authority. After unifying the Liaodong town, Nurgaqi immediately ordered the officers to report the exact number of Han Chinese soldiers, fortresses, commoners, and craftsmen such as carpenters, painters and so on, who lived in the Liaodong town (*liyoodung ni ba i qoohai ton udu, heqen pu i ton udu, baisin ton udu, mujan, hvwajan, ai ai faksisa be gemu bithe afafi wesimbu*).[836]

Even artisans who make daily necessities were highly cherished by Nurgaqi. On the seventh day of the sixth month in 1621, Haizhou people who lived in Ximu fortification contributed 3,510 green bowls and jars. For this matter, the Khan said, "It has been said that pearls, gold and silver are called treasure. How could we consider them as treasure? Can we wear them when it is cold? Can we eat them when we are hungry? The sages of this country know what people do not know and artisans can do what people cannot do, and such people actually are the real treasure. Today people of Ximu fortification dedicated their green bowls, pots and

---

[834] Tiancongchao chengong zouyi, p. 12.

[835] Lai Huimin 賴惠敏, *Qianlong huangdi de hebao* 乾隆皇帝的荷包 (Emperor Qianlong's Purse), Zhonghua shuju, 2016, p. 1-3.

[836] *Fe dangse*, p. 916.

jars, and indeed, they are the useful ones among the numerous country people. Is it appropriate to grant official titles and gifts to such capable people? The Grand Coordinators, Regional Commanders, Circuit Intendants (man. *dooli*; chin. *daoyuan* 道員), Regional Vice Commanders, and Mobile Corps Commanders should discuss and report to me" *(iqe nadan de, hai jeo heqen i harangga ba i si mu qeng ni gaxan i niyalma, ilan minggan sunja tanggv juwan niowanggiyan moro, tamse afafi benjihe, tere inenggi, han hendume, tana aisin menggun be boobei serengge, tere ai boobei, beikuwen de etuqi embio, urunere de jeqi ombio, gurun ujire mergen sain niyalma, gurun i bahanarakv jaka be bahanara, ararakv jaka be arara faksi niyalma, tere mene unenggi boobei dere, te si mu qeng ni baqi niowanggiyan io noho moro, fengse, malu arafi benjihebi, tere geren gurun de baitangga weile kai. tere arafa de, faksi be hergen bumbio, ulin xangnambio, du tang, zung bing guwan, dooli, fujiyang, iogi suwe hebexefi arara babe, amasi fesimbu seme bithe arafi wasimbuha).*[837] After court discussion, on the eighth day, after discussion, a title of Grand Commandant (man. *seobei*; chin. *shoubei* 守備) and twenty *yan* silver were rewarded to the person of Ximu fortification who contributed green bowls, pots and jars, which are very useful to the country *(si mu qeng ni baqi, niowanggiyan moro, tamse, pengse arafi benjihe niyalma de, gurun i baitangga jaka be tuqibuhe seme seobei hergen buhe, orin yan menggun xangnaha).*[838]

As for the indicative items used by the military officers, the high-rank officers can make themselves and the low-rank officers must submit gold to the chieftains, whose artisans can produce accordingly. On the twenty-sixth day of the eleventh month in 1621, the Khan informed that Regional Commanders and Regional Vice Commanders can make their own Official Cap Buttons (man. *jingse*; chin. *dingzi* 頂子) with gold bestowed by the Khan. Regarding the other officers, from the Assistant Regional Commanders, Mobile Corps Commanders down to the Defense Officers, they can wrap gold with paper and deliver it to the Chieftains with proper documents, and the Chieftains' craftsmen will manufacture for them *(han i bithe, orin ninggun de wasimbuha, zung bing guwan, fujiyang de sangnaha aisin be, suweni qisui jingse tvbu, jai canjiyang,*

---

[837] *Fe dangse*, pp. 1023-1025.
[838] *Fe dangse*, p. 1032.

iogi, beiguwan qi wesihun, meni meni aisin be hooxan de uhefi bithe arafi
meni men beise de benju, beise i faksi tvfi bukini).[839]

Summer hat was an important dress code to the banner leaders. On
the thirtieth day of the first month in 1622, Nurgaqi informed Xajin and
Monggotu to summon the Korean artisans for making summer hats and
armors for the chieftains of the Eight Banners. In every banner, a
Superintendent (man. *ejen*; chin. *zhuguan* 主管) was appointed to
supervise more production of summer hats *(gvsin de, xajin, monggotu de*
unggihe bithe, suweni juwe nofi, jakvn gvsai beise i boro uksin arara
solho faksisa be gemu baiqame isabufi, emu gvsade emte ejen sindafi,
boro ambula arabu).[840]

Textile production did not begin until the time when Nurgaqi
officially established his regime to fight against the Ming openly. In 1616,
the authority started to popularize silkworm breeding and growing cotton
in the country *(tere aniya, suje jodoro subeliyen bahara umiyaha ujime*
teribuhe. boso jodoro kubun tarime gurun de de selgiyehe).[841] The
species of cotton could be American, *Gossypium hirsutum*, which was
introduced to Manchuria via Korean.[842] Sven Beckert believes that
cotton was widely grown by the Han Chinese during the Yuan dynasty
and cotton production was introduced to the Ming's unification
throughout the Ming dynasty.[843] Thus, the plantation of cotton could also
be influenced by the people who lived in the Liaodong region. Even so,
according to observations of a Korean official staff Li Minwan 李民寏,
who was a war prisoner of Battle Sarhv in 1619, the Jurchen women
could only weave linen, and all damask and embroidery were made by
the Han Chinese. Therefore, the Jurchens stripped all clothes off the dead
bodies in battlefield, from which one can know how much they value
clothes *(nvgong suozhi, zhiyou mafu, zhijin cixiu ze tangren suoweiye...*
zhanchang jiangshi, wubu chituo, qi gui yifu kezhi 女工所織，只有麻布，
織錦刺繡則唐人所爲也...戰場殭屍，無不赤脫，其貴衣服可知).*[844]

---

[839] *Fe dangse*, pp. 1193-1194.

[840] *Fe dangse*, pp. 1535-1536.

[841] *Fe dangse*, p. 198.

[842] Gang Deng (1999), The Premodern Chinese Economy: Structural Equilibrium
and Capitalist Sterility, Routledge, London, p. 377.

[843] Sven Beckert (2014), *Empire of Cotton: A Global History*, Penguin Books,
London, p. 30.

[844] Li Minwan, Jianzhou wenjianlu, p. 42.

Meanwhile, the Ming's silk production was well developed in the southern provinces, such as Hu Silk (*husi* 湖絲) in Zhejiang and Lang Silk (langsi 閬絲) in Sichuan, as famous brands and also with silk trade centers, such as Linghu 菱湖, Baoning 保寧 and Shimen 石門. As for cotton and cloth, the Ming's Yanzhou 兗州, Taicang 太倉 and Zhengyang 鎮洋 were well known for cotton plantation, selling their harvest to southern China. Meanwhile, places such as Songjiang 松江, produce cloth out of Bombax ceiba (*jibei* 吉貝 or *mumian* 木棉), which sold across the country.[845] Comparatively, the silk and cloth economies in Nurgaqi's reign were at an early stage.

For this reason, the artisans who produce satin and silk were particularly rewarded because their production concerns the official dress code of the state. On the eleventh day of the second month in 1623, seventy-three people were commanded to produce satin embroidery, silk fabric and Rank Badges (man. *puse*; chin. *buzi* 補子). Nurgaqi praised, "The craftsmen can produce such satin embroidery, silk fabric and rank badges in the place that is not the original manufacturing location, and they are the most valuable treasure." Nurgaqi bestowed wives, bondservants, clothes, and food to the artisans who are not married, exempted them from all sorts of public errands and military duty, and moved their houses nearby for better attention. There is a requirement for the artisans to produce certain amount of satin embroidery and silk fabric, and there will be reward for extra work. More pay comes with more products and less pay comes with less products. All artisans are rewarded according to the amount of their products and they are exempted from public errands and military service. Moreover, Nurgaqi encouraged officials to recommend artisans who can make gold thread and sulfur, considering these workers also as valuable treasure. These artisans were also well treated as the artisans who produce satin embroidery and silk fabric. Finally, Nurgaqi emphasized that if there were people who can produce satin embroidery and silk fabric, they should be recommended right away and are exempted from all sorts of public errands *(juwan emu de, gequheri suje puse jodombi seme, nadanju ilan niyalma tuqifi jodoho gequheri suje puse be han tuwafi, jodorakv bade gequheri suje puse jodoqi, boobai kai seme saixame hendufi, sargan akv niyalma de, sargan,*

---

[845] Han Dacheng, Mingdai shangpin jingji de fazhan, pp. 20-22.

aha, eture jetere be yooni bufi, alban qooha aia ai de daburakv, hanqi hoqifi ujimbi, emu aniya gequheri suje udu jodombi, ambula jodoqi ambula xangnara, komso jodoqi komso xangnara, weilefi bahara be tuwame xangnara, ai ai alban de daburakv, qooha iliburakv, jai sese, lio hvwang arara niyalma biqi tuqinu, tere niyalma inu boobai kai, gequheri suje jodoro uju jergi niyalmai jergi de obure, te gequheri suje jodoro niyalma biqi tuqinu, ai ai alban waliyara).[846]

Moreover, the textile production achieved significant progress in Hong Taiji's reign. Wang Zhonghan confirmed that since the second year of Tiancong (1628), the court had been promoting the textile production, and up to the seventh year (1633), different kinds of textile can be sufficiently produced with the native cotton of Liaodong for domestic usage.[847] Nevertheless, few traces of cotton production can be found as incentives that gave birth to industrial capitalism. Unlike the cotton industry that resulted in global capitalism,[848] the Jurchen-Manchu statesmen and commoners focused on acquisition of money, lands, people and industries for the purpose of building the state, rather than expanding the market across the globe. Up to now, one can conclude that from cotton culture to manufacture, the state played a key role in promotion, production and consumption, and thus this popular handicraft industry was not entirely a private enterprise in the preunification era of the Qing period.[849]

Besides satin and silk makers of the textile production, artisans who produce useful stuff, such as gold thread, paper, bowls and plates, were also generously awarded. On the twenty-fifth of the third month in 1623, the Grand Coordinator declared that Gao Jiazhong was employed due to his capability of producing satin embroidery, silk fabric and gold thread. The authority granted him with wife, bondservants, clothes and food. Now, anyone who can make satin embroidery, silk fabric, gold thread, paper, fine colorful satin, bowls and plates, must recommend themselves to the authority. After test, the real capable ones, such as Gao Jiazhong, will be employed and well supported *(orin sunja de, du tang hendume,*

---

[846] *Fe dangse*, pp. 2011-2013.

[847] Wang Zhonghan, *Qingshi zakao*, p. 50.

[848] Beckert, *Empire of Cotton*, pp. 1-78.

[849] Albert Feuerwerker, The State and the Economy in Late Imperial China, p. 305.

gao giya jung sebe gequheri suje jodombi, sese arambi seme tukiyefi, sargan, aha, eture jeterengge yooni buhe... te yaya niyalma gequheri suje jodoro, sese arara, hooxan hergere, sain narhvn alha moro fila arara, tenteke ai ai baitangga niyalma biqi, tuqike manggi tuwafi bahanara yargiyan oqi, gao giya jung sei adali tukiyefi ujimbi).[850]

Artisans of other manufacturing industries, such as lathing molds, making welding agent and mercury, were also demanded by the state. In the fourth month of 1623, the authority granted an ox to the artisan who lathes mold for making summer hats. Nurgaqi also emphasized that if there are people who can produce welding agent for gold and silver, they should be recommended and employed *(buru i durun xurure faksi de emu ihan buhe. aisin menggun i hangnara okto be arame bahanara niyalma biqi tuqinu weisimbure).*[851] In the ninth month of 1623, Gembulu led fifty people to search artisans who can produce mercury *(gembulu, susai niyalma be gaifi toholon muke arara juxen baime genefi...).*[852]

As for pigments, there was no direct Manchu-language evidence that confirms their manufacture. On the fifteenth day of the third month in an undated year, Haksaha and Engke brought an edict, which says that Kurqan received the allocated silver, which was delivered to the Regional Vice Commander Gao, who would buy some fine silk fabric. Regarding the five hundred *yan* silver as allocated funds, twenty *yan* will be used to purchase pigments, such as powder of mercury sulfide red (man. *okto qinuhvn*; chin. *yinzhu* 銀朱), Plumbum Rubrum (man. *hvwang dan*; chin. *huangdan* 黃丹), brass powder (man. *aisin okto*; chin. *jinfen* 金粉), azurite (man. *xi qing*; chin. *shiqing* 石青), basic copper carbonate (man. *tung lu*; chin. *tonglü* 銅綠), gamboge (man. *teng hvwang*; chin. *tenghuang* 藤黃), orpiment (man. *xi hvwang*; chin. *shihuang* 石黃), and pigment green (man. *da lu*; chin. *da lü* 大綠). Such pigments must be purchased frequently *(ilan biyai tofohon de, haksaha, engke i gajiha bithe, ere unggihe menggun be kvrqan si alime gaifi, gao fujiyang de afabufi baitangga sin suje udabu, menggun i ton sunja tanggv yan, orin yan de nirure okto uda, udara okto qinuhvn, hvwang dan, aisin okto, xi qing,*

---

[850] *Fe dangse*, pp. 2165-2167.
[851] *Fe dangse*, pp. 2263-2264.
[852] *Fe dangse*, p. 2665.

tung lu, teng hvwang, xi hvwang, da lu, ere haqin i okto be kiqeme udabu).[853]

According to the convictions of the Jurchen-Manchu authority, economies were a system in which each manufacture entails one another and ultimately, all economies belonged to the supreme leader. On the sixth day of the second month in 1632, Hong Taiji told a story, which may help us understand the ownership of the Manchu authority about economies: In the past, Qagandai, a son of Genghis Khan, sharpened a willow branch into a whip by a saw blade (man. *fufungge huwesi*; chin. *judao* 鋸刀). Then he bragged that all the people are gathered by Father Genghis Khan, but this willow whip was totally made by myself. Oqir Sure replied, "this saw blade was made by the craftsmen who were gathered by Father Khan. Otherwise, could you make a whip by pinching with fingers and biting with teeth? The great enterprise, all people and all sorts of stuff, were all created by Father Khan himself. Anyone who thinks wrongly of this but considered himself as smart will be laughed by all the future generations" *(julge qinggis han i jui qagandai, fufungge huwesi i suhai moo be meileme susiha arame hendume, ere sahahvn iliqaha irgen, ama qinggis han isabuha dere, ere suhai moo i xusiha be bi mutebuhe sehe manggi, oqir sure hendume, ere xusiha araha huwesi, han ama i ilibuha faksi tvrakv biqi, si hitahvn i fatambiheo, weihe i kajambiheo seme jabuha sere, ere utala doro gurun irgen ai jaka gemu han ama i emhun beye fukjin ilibuhangge, tere be te geli waka arame, musei beyebe mergen sain arame gisureqi, tumen jalan de wakalaburengge kai, suwe saikan eje, ishunde mujilen bahabuki seme henduhe).*[854]

Accordingly, we see a Manchu perspective, which was highly influenced by their previous Mongol rulers and current allies, emphasizing the role of the state that patronizes industries. The ancient people may not have the knowledge of modern economics, but the relationship between the state and economy has a long historical standing. Economy had taken place long before the first existence of state, however, the state intervened economy as soon as it was born. The early Manchu documents provide vivid records about the rise of the Manchu empire, which was founded by Nurgaqi's personal endeavor that includes his

---

[853] *Fe dangse*, pp. 3359-3360.
[854] *Fe dangse*, pp. 5963-5964.

economic achievements. From this view, one can say that private economy can finally bring forth state, which on the contrary regulates and interferes the numerous private economies. These Manchu-language annals tell that the state exercises a sturdy hand on economy, which should alert people that live at the moment.

5.9 Conclusion

In the above analysis, one can see that the Jurchen-Manchus fought for resources and economies against the Han Chinese and Mongols. After unifying the Ming's Liaodong region, the Jurchen authority took over the Han Chinese economies, such as farming, granary, orchards and salt producing. Granary was the most important production of the Jurchen state. The common Han Chinese farmers contributed large amounts of grain as taxation to the authority. Regarding the grain produced by the military force, half was stored in the capital and half in the regional sites where the grain was harvested. Large granaries were allocated in Shenyang, Youtunwei, Guangning, Sanhepu and Niuzhuang, etc. Though grain reserve was heavily intervened by the state, more evidence is needed to confirm that Nurgaqi's regime was operating in a different form than Confucian convictions of political economy.

Along with the cultivatable lands, orchards were also taken over by the Jurchens. The harvested fruits went to market for sale besides the contribution for the Khan's personal use. Animal husbandry, especially horse-raising, was carefully managed to fuel the military expansion. As traditional Jurchen professions, hunting, fishing and gathering were maintained throughout the pre-unification era. Iron mining was extremely important to the war machines and farming, but mining gold and silver was secondary after farming due to plausible reason that the Jurchen army had acquired quantities of precious metals from the Ming people.

Salt has been a fundamental component of traditional economy. The early Manchu documents support that the Jurchen authority, through the banner system, dominated the salt production, transportation, distribution and consumption. Furthermore, salt was one of the principal means to maintain the ally relationship with the neighboring Mongol tribes. In the pre-unification period, the salt production was comprehensively controlled by the state through the military force of the Eight Banners, rather than commissioned to the franchise system.

Though Nurgaqi founded considerable firearm troops, the firearms were not self-produced but acquired from the Han Chinese. The Manchu documents indicate that Nurgaqi's administration had techniques and artisans for making gunpowder. The firearm economies were officially established in Hong Taiji's reign. The Han Chinese war prisoners successfully manufactured qualified cannons and bullets that equipped the banner troops to win the battles of Dalinghe and invaded Korea. Besides, it is also reasonable to conclude that the military production was set up due to the high demand of the ongoing wars, which were started by political institutions.

Commerce was strictly controlled due to the existing wars between the Jin and Ming states. Free markets did exist from time to time, even for grain transaction as a strategic material. Besides grain levy from the military force, taxation mainly targeted the Han Chinese subjects with grain, silver and fodder. Being different from their Han Chinese rivals, Nurgaqi's administration imposed heavy taxes upon commercial transactions. Along with the banner officers, tax collectors were able to glean from the markets and vital communication sites, such as bridges. The high tax rate did not change until Hong Taiji took over the Khan-ship and the importance of charging commercial tax deserves further research.

Textile production was well established with the recruited Han Chinese artisans, who were also amply awarded for their qualified work. Nurgaqi, Hong Taiji and the other Jurchen visionaries eagerly searched the previous artisans in the unified lands, with generous compensation, to produce all sorts of daily necessities for boosting the operation of a rising empire. Satin, silk, bowls, plates, paper, gold thread, welding agent, mercury and such products fueled a great enterprise for massive development. Relatively, these economies were developing slowly due to the ongoing wars with the Han Chinese and Mongols, and lack of knowledge and technologies.

6. Epilogue

History records the existence of the past, which consists of all sorts of economic phenomena that deserve analysis by different academic disciplines. In this research, the thematic question would be what Manchu economy is, based on evidence gleaned from Manchu, Han Chinese and Korean sources. The major source is the early Manchu documents, which were composed before 1644, after which the Eight-Banner military force entered China Proper under the Manchu leadership. The Jurchen-Manchu acquisition of precious metals, human population, lands, and economies frequently appears in the primary sources, which catch our attention to postulate these events as basic components of Manchu economy. Due to the constant wars with the Ming, commerce within the newly unified lands was strictly controlled, intervened and heavily taxed by the Jurchen state during Nurgaqi's reign. However, when Hong Taiji seized the throne, the state exercised a relatively light hand on commerce, which is similar to its Ming opponent.

Throughout the pre-unification era, one can see that the Manchu economy was a mixture that consists of multiple traditional economies. Before the unification of Liaodong, the Jurchens maintained their traditional modes of economy, such as hunting, fishing and gathering, while raised animals like the Mongols, cultivated crops like the Han Chinese, and engaged in trade with the regional authorities of the Ming's Liaodong region. After taking over Liaodong, the Jurchen-Manchu state benefited from the plenteous Han Chinese labor, fertile lands, specialized professions and substantial silver as the major currency for developing their economy. Agriculture provided major direct tax for the state's revenue to pay its officials and support its military force. The granary systems was highly centralized into the control of Nurgaqi and his Eight Banners. Nurgaqi, who was discontented due to grain hoarding in market, banned Liaodong's grain market. However, this command-based granary system did not function well in the early Tiancong reign (r. 1627-1636). As a final resort, Hong Taiji had to implement policies more flexibly and gave out silver to the famine refugees in order to buy grain from markets. Market is the ultimate solution to ease the state's catastrophe.

The Jurchen-Manchu state's monetary polices were markedly different from its Han Chinese rival, such as the remarkable amount of gold for circulation. The Ming state monetary system encompassed multiple currencies, such as silver, brass coin and paper notes. Since the early Ming period, the paper notes had already been corrupted by over-issuing while neglecting the correspondent reserve of precious metals. Throughout the Ming dynasty, fewer brass coins were cast in comparison with the Song due to the Ming's limited resource of copper ore. Another sensible speculation is that large quantities of copper was used for casting weaponry. To the end of the dynasty, the quality of brass coins was jeopardized severely, and in some regions, low-quality coins were no longer physically fit to sustain commercial transactions. Unlike the Ming, the Manchu authority mainly adopted silver for fiscal and commercial management and the Manchu documents do support that even small-scale business was conducted in silver, which was a reliable medium of exchange. Correspondingly, the Manchu state did not experience fiscal chaos caused by over-issued paper notes or coins with poor fineness. It is reasonable to assume that the Manchu leaders learned valuable lessons from its neighboring Ming state and its predecessor Mongol empire.

Moreover, massive amounts of silver currency circulated in the Later Jin and early Qing state was the result of commercial transactions with its neighboring lands and war trophy from the Ming. Scholarly research proves that the Ming empire was low in silver production from mining and mainly obtained its silver currency through business with Portuguese and Spanish traders, who shipped this precious metal from Japan and the New World in Age of Discovery, especially South America. Thus, we shall have a global view of looking at the silver that circulated in Manchuria, which finally fueled the Manchu unification of the Ming China.

The Jurchen-Manchu demographic growth was realized through unifying the other tribes who spoke the same Jurchen language, acquiring the Mongol confederations, especially Chakhar, and capturing the Ming Han Chinese by unifying their lands. These acquired populations significantly fueled the army and cavalry with labor and provided sufficiently for the state to sustain specialized professions, such as farming, mining, smelting, and weaving, salt producing, and so on. The fledgling Jin state eagerly recruited and employed the Han Chinese artisans and other professionals, whose skills greatly benefited people's life, the empire's operation and expansion.

Territories expanded exponentially during the pre-unification era. Nurgaqi acquired the lands from his neighboring Jurchen tribes and soon dominated their rich sources, labors, and products of hunting, gathering and mining. The Manchu nation became prosperous for trading with the Ming. After years of preparation, Nurgaqi unified the Ming's Liaodong region, which remarkably strengthened his empire with a larger population, stronger economies, and sufficient currencies. After gaining the throne, Hong Taiji immediately attacked Korea and turned Korea into an ally for securing his home front. In the following years, Hong Taiji repeatedly dispatched troops to subdue Chakhar, and successfully occupied the vast steppe beyond the Great Wall. The unified northern lands provided the Jurchen-Manchu state with richer sources, broader markets, and more workforce for realizing a greater enterprise.

Traditional economies are the foundation on which the state runs. Traditional economies produce goods for people to exchange with, and generate multiple sources of revenue to enrich the state. Traditional economies of the Jin state, such as farming, herding, fishing and gathering, were well maintained throughout Nurgaqi's reign, especially in the regard of granary. In Hong Taiji's time, the state experienced a great famine, and had to purchase grain from Korea. Other than this, the manufacturing economies, such as cannon making, were well established in Hong Taiji's reign. The cast weapons performed well in the wars against the Ming Han Chinese, who lost the fortification of Dalinghe after strong resistance. Such an instance proves that a great demand can be created by the state, which stimulates the growth of economy to some extent. As for the relationship between economy and state, in this Jurchen-Manchu case, one can see that Nurgaqi built up his own regime on a growing economy under his management, from which we can include that a stronger state depends on a stronger economy. The relationship between economy and state is somehow different from the relationship between industry and empire, which can exist with one another.[855]

---

[855] Vries, State, Economy and the Great Divergence: Great Britain and China, 1680s-1850s, pp. 295-296.

As von Glahn stated, the constituents of "... land, labor, capital and new productive resources, and rising public and private demand provided the impetus for sustained economic growth". [856] The sophisticated markets in Liaodong region were ravaged by wars. The Jurchen state was able to reopen the markets and then imposed heavy tax levies upon commerce. The aggressive state activism was changed when Hong Taiji ascended to the khan-ship, who lessened the burden on commercial transactions and nurtured the development of market economy, especially in the respect of pig-selling business where market was fully respected. Furthermore, the highly productive agriculture of the Liaodong region profited the Jurchen-Manchu war machines by providing sufficient grain and fodder, which well fed the fast-growing army and large amounts of military horses. On the other hand, the Jurchen-Manchu state stopped the Han Chinese officials from charging private exaction, which protected the common people' well-being and the growth of market economy.

Thus, one can conclude that the Jurchen-Manchu state effectively acquired the basic elements of developing its economy for a greater purpose: sufficient silver as the major currency, large quantities of human population as labor, and extensive lands for sustainable resources, revenue and multiple economies such as agriculture, stock-raising, mining, smelting and so on. The economies were also acquired through wars, in which prisoners were taken and recommended for contributing with their professions. In a modern society, wealth was mainly created manifold by the production of a revolutionary industry, or the increased output within industries according to sufficient market demand. A growing modern economy is being boosted by growing debt, which secures all functions of a society by pre-investment. Before the Industrial Revolution, when wealth was mostly manifested by the amount of precious metals, human population, lands and traditional economies, an increasing ownership of these components would almost equal to a growing economy, which was acquired by successive military achievements in the Manchu case.

---

[856] von Glahn, The Economic History of China, p. 252.

Bibliography

Pre-modern Sources:

Baqi manzhou shizu tongpu 八旗滿洲氏族通譜 (The Common Genealogy of Eight Banner Manchu Clans), edition Shenyang: Liaoshen shushe, 1989.

China in the Sixteenth Century: The Journals of Mathew Ricci (1583-1610), written by Matteo Ricci and Nicolas Trigault, translated from the Latin by Louis J. Gallagher, S. J. Random House, New York, 1953.

Chouhaitubian 籌海圖編 (Compilation of Coast Defence Strategies with Illustration), by Zheng Ruoceng 鄭若曾, punctuated and checked by Li Zhizhong 李致忠, edition Beijing: Zhonghua shuju, 2007.

Donghualu 東華錄(Record of Donghua Gate), compiled by Wang Xianqian 王先謙 (1842-1917), self-collected documents, publisher was not indicated, block-printed edition in 1884, volume of Chongde liunian 崇德六年卷.

Dorgi yamun asaraha manju hergen i fe dangse; Neige cangben Manwen laodang 內閣藏本滿文老檔 (The Version of Manchu Old Chronicles Stored by the Grand Secretariat), compiled by Wu Yuanfeng 吳元豐 (b. 1956) et al., edition Shenyang: Liaoning minzu chubanshe, 2009.

Feng menglong quanji 馮夢龍全集 (The Complete Works of Feng Menglong),* Book 15,* Feng Menglong 馮夢龍, edition Nanjing: Fenghuang chubanshe, 2007.

Houjin hanguo (Huangtaiji) tiancongchao gao bu zou shu 後金汗國(皇太極)天聰朝稿簿奏疏 (The Drafts, Accounts, Memorials and Statements in the Tiancong Reign (Hong Taiji) of the Later Jin Khanate), complied by Chen Zhanqi 陳湛綺, edition Beijing: Quanguo tushuguan wenxian weisuo fuzhi zhongxin, 2010.

Hu Gongming chenyan tubaozou 胡貢明陳言圖報奏 (Hu Gongming's Memorial of Reporting and Returning the Imperial Kindness),* Hu Gongming 胡貢明, exerpted from *Qingchu shiliao congkan disizhong* 清初史料叢刊第一種 (The First Collection of Historical Materials for the Early Qing), *tiancongchao chengong zouyi*

天聰朝臣工奏議 (Official Memorials of the Tiancong's Reign), liaoning daxue lishixi, edition Shenyang: Liaoning daxue chubanshe, 1980.

Jianzhou wenjianlu 建州聞見錄 (Records of Hearings and Seeings in Jianzhou), written by Li Minwan 李民寏 (c. 1619), *collected in Qingshi ziliao congkan di ba, jiu zhong* 清史資料叢 刊第八、九種 (The Eighth and Ninth kinds of Qing History Collection), edition Shenyang: Liaoning daxue chubanshe, 1978.

Jiu Manzhou dang 舊滿洲檔 (The Former Manchurian Chronicles), edition Taipei: Taibei gugong bowuyuan, 1969.

Liangchao congxin lu 兩朝從信錄 (The Narration and Records of the Two Reigns), Shen Guoyuan 沈國元, excerpted from *Qing ruguanqian shiliao xuanji* 清入關前史料選輯 (The Selected Historical Materials before the Qing Entered through Shanhai Pass), vol. 2, compiled by Pan Zhe (潘喆), et al., edition Beijing: Zhongguo renmin daxue chubanshe, 1989.

Liaodong zhi 遼東志 (Records of Liaodong), edited by Ren Luo 任洛 (1485-1544) et al. in 1537, vol. 3, included by Jin Yufu 金毓绂 (?-?) in his *Liaohai congshu* 遼海叢書 (Liaohai Series), printed in Shenyang from 1933-1936.

Manwen taizu gao huangdi benji shu 滿文太祖高皇帝本紀書 (The Manchu-language Biography of the Founding-father Lofty Emperor), author unknown, collected by The Kyoto University Research Centre for the Cultural Sciences, a copy in 1819.

Manwen yuandang 滿文原檔 (The Original Manchu Chronicles), edition Taipei: Taibei gugong bowuyuan, 2005.

Manzhou shilu 滿洲實錄 (The Manchu Veritable Records), collected in *Qing shilu* 清實錄 (The Qing Veritable Records), edition Beijing: Zhonghua shuju, 1986.

Mingdai Man Meng shiliao 明代滿蒙史料 (Manchu-Mongol Historical Materials of the Ming Dynasty), *Lichao shilu chao* 李朝實錄 抄 (Selected Compilation from the Veritable Records of the Chosŏn Court), vol. 14, edition Tokyo: 文海出版社有限公司印行 (Wenhai Publishing Co., Ltd.), 1953.

Ming jingshi wenbian 明經世文編 (Compilations of Statecraft in the Ming Dynasty), vol. 408, compiled by Chen Zilong 陳子龍 (1608-1647), edition Beijing: Zhonghuashuju, 1962.

Ming Shi 明史 (History of Ming), vol. 7, compiled by Zhang Tingyu 張廷玉 et al., edition Beijing: Zhonghua shuju, 1974.

Mingshilu 明實錄 (The Ming Veritable Records), vol. 1, *Ming taizu shilu* 明太祖實錄, Zhongyang yanjiuyuan lishi yuyansuo jiaoyin 中央研究院歷史語言研究所校印, vol. 142, Taibei, 1962.

Mingshi jishi benmo 明史紀事本末 (Entire Historical Events of the Ming), written by Gu Yingtai 谷應泰 (1620-1690), edition Beijing: Zhonghua shuju, 1977.

Qingchu shiliao congkan diqi zhong 清初史料叢刊第七種 (The Seventh Compilation of Early Qing Historical Materials)*, chaoxian lichao shilu zhong de nüzhen shiliao xuanbian* 朝鮮李朝 實錄中的女真史料選編 (Selected Compilation of Jurchen Historical Materials in Veritable Records of Korea's Chosŏn Court), Wang Zhonghan jilu 王鍾翰輯錄, edition Shenyang: Liaoning daxue chubanshe, 1978.

Qing ruguanqian shiliao xuanji, yi, 清入關前史料選輯 1 (Selected Historical Materials before the Qing Entered through Shanhai Pass), *Qing taizu wu huangdi shilu* 清太祖武皇帝實錄 (The Qing Veritable Records of Martial Emperor Taizu), edition Beijing: Gugong bowuyuan paiyinben, 1989.

Qing shilu 清實錄 (The Qing Veritable Records), edition Beijing: Zhonghua shuju, 1986.

Qingchu neiguoshiyuan manwen dang'an yibian 清初内国史院满文档案译编 (Compiled Translation of Manchu Chronicles Kept by the Early Qing Palace Historiographic Academy)*,* translated and compiled by Guan Xiaolian 關孝廉 et al., edition Beijing: Guangming ribao chubanshe, 1986.

Qingshigao 清史稿 (The Draft of Qing History), compiled by Zhao Erxun 趙爾巽 (1844-1927) et al., 1928, edition Beijing: Zhonghua shuju, 1976 & 1977.

Qingtaizong shilu gaoben 清太宗實錄稿本 (The Draft of Veritable Records of Qingtaizong), collected in *Qingchu shiliao congkan* 清初史料叢刊 (Historical Materials for the Early Qing), vol.3, liaoning daxue lishixi, edition Shenyang: Liaoning daxue chubanshe, 1980.

Qingtaizu wu huangdi shilu 清太祖武皇帝實錄 (The Veritable Records of the Forefather Martial Emperor), selected from *Qing ruguanqian shiliao xuanji yi* 清入關前史料選輯 1 (Compilation of Selected Historical Materials before the Qing Entered through Shanhai

Passes), vol. 1, compiled by Pan Zhe 潘喆 et al., edition Beijing: Zhongguo renmin daxue chubanshe, 1984.

Qingwen zhiyao jiedu 清文指要解讀 (Guidance of Essential Elements of Manchu Language), edited by Zhang Huake 張華克, edition Taipei: Wenshizhe chubanshe, 2005.

Taizong wen huangdi shilu 太宗文皇帝實錄 (The Veritable Records of Taizong Wen Emperor), excerpted from *Qingshilu* 清實錄 (The Qing Veritable Records)*,* vol. 2, edition Beijing: Zhonghua shuju, 1986.

Tiancongchao chengong zouyi 天聰朝臣工奏議 (Memorials of Ministers in the Tiancong Reign), collected in *Qing ruguanqian shiliao xuanji* 清入關前史料選輯 (Collected Historical Materials before the Qing Entered through Shanhai Pass), vol. 2, edition Beijing: Zhongguo renmin daxue chubanshe, 1989.

Tiancong wunian baqi zhiyuedang, 天聰五年八旗值月檔 (annals Kept by the Eight Banners on Monthly Duty in the Fifth Year of Tiancong), vol. 1 & 2, complied and translated by Guan Xiaolian 關孝廉, edition Beijing: Diyi lishi dang'an'guan, 2014.

Jin Shi 金史 (The History of Jin), Tuotuo 脫脫 and et al., edition Beijing: Zhonghua shuju, 1975.

Xizong shilu 熹宗實錄 (The Veritable Records of Xizong), edition Taipei: photo-printed according to the copy of Guoli beiping tushuguan 國立北平圖書館 (National Library in Beiping), 1962.

Xu Guangqi quanji 徐光啓全集 (The Complete Work of Xu Guangqi), edited by Zhu Weizheng 朱維錚 and Li Tiangang 李天綱, edition Shanghai: Shanghai guji chubanshe, 2010.

Yin'an suoyu 蚓庵瑣語 (Trivial Words of Earthworm Hut), written by Wang Bu 王逋 (?-?), collected in *Congshu jicheng xubian* 叢書集成續編 (Continuation of Collected Series), vol. 216, edition Taipei: Xinwenfeng chuban gongsi, 1988.

Zaiyuan zazhi 在園雜誌 (Miscellaneous Records of Zaiyuan), written by Liu Tingji 劉廷璣 (1654-?), edited by Zhang Shouqian 張守謙, edition Beijing: Zhonghua shuju, 2005.

Zaolin zazu 棗林雜俎 (Miscellany of Jujube Forest), written by Tan Qian 談遷 (1594-1658), and edited by Luo Zhonghui 羅仲輝 and Hu Mingxiao 胡明校, edition Beijing: Zhonghua shuju, 2006.

Zhazhong rilu 柵中日錄 (Dairies in Prison), Li Minwan 李民寏 (c. 1619), collected in *Qingshi ziliao congkan di ba, jiu zhong* 清史資料叢

刊第八、九種 (The Eighth and Ninth kinds of Collections of Qing History Material), edition Shenyang: Liaoning daxue chubanshe, 1978.

Zhongguo yancao shihua 中國煙草史話 (Historical Narrative of Tobacco in China), edited by Zhang Daming 張大明, edition Beijing: Zhongguo qinggongye chubanshe, 1993.

Secondary Sources in Western and Eastern Languages:

Andrade, Tonio (2016), The Gunpowder Age: China, Military Innovation, and the Rise of the West in World History, Princeton University Press, Princeton.

An Shuangcheng 安雙成 (1983), "Shun Kang Yong sanchao baqi ding'e qianxi" 順康雍三朝八旗 丁額淺析 (A Preliminary Analysis of the Eight Banners Active Registration in the Shunzhi, Kangxi and Yongzheng Periods), *Lishi dang'an* 歷史檔案 (Historical Archives), 1.2:101-102.

Bai Xinliang 白新良 (2006), *Qingshi kaobian* 清史考辨 (Evidential Research on Qing History), Renmin chubanshe, Beijing.

Barakatullo Ashurov (2018), "Coins Convey a Message: Numismatic Evidence for Sogdian Christianity", *Central Asiatic Journal*, 61.2: 257-295.

Beckert, Sven (2014), *Empire of Cotton: A Global History,* Penguin Books, London.

Bello, David A. (2015), Across Forest, Steppe and Mountain: Environment, identity and Empire in Qing China's borderlands, Cambridge: CUP.

So, Billy K. L. (ed.) (2013), The Economy of Lower Yangzi Delta in late Imperial China：Connecting Money, Markets, and Institutions, Routledge, London.

Cai Linshan 蔡林杉 (2013), *Qing Taizong Huangtaiji zhuan* 清太宗皇太極傳 (Biography of Qing Taizong Hong Taiji), Sanqin chubanshe, Xi'an.

Chen Bo (2016), "The Making of 'China' out of 'Zhongguo'", *Journal of Asian History*, 50.1: 73-116.

Chen Jiexian 陳捷先 (2011), *Huangtaiji xiezhen* 皇太極寫真 (A Profile of Hong Taiji), Shuangwu yinshuguan, Beijing.

Chen Ran 陳然 et al., (eds.) (1987), *Zhongguo yanyeshi luncong* 中國鹽業史論叢 (General Essays on Salt History of China), Zhongguo shehui kexue chubanshe, Beijing.

Chen Shengxi 陳生璽 (2018), *Daming diguo de yunluo: Huangtaiji gaige yu jiashen fengyun jubian* 大明帝國的隕落：皇太極改革與甲申風雲巨變 (The Fall of the Great Ming Empire: Hong Taiji's Reform and the Tremendous Change in 1644), Zhongxi shuju, Shanghai.

Crossley, Pamela Kyle (1987), Manzhou Yuanliu Kao and the Formalization of the Manchu Heritage, *The Journal of Asian Studies,* 46.4: 761-790.

Crossley, Pamela Kyle (1999), *A translucent mirror: history and identity in Qing imperial ideology,* University of California Press, Berkeley and Los Angeles, California.

Dai Jianbing 戴建兵 (2011), *Zhongguo huobi wenhuashi* 中國貨幣文化史 (History of China's Currency Culture), Shandong huabao chubanshe, Ji'nan.

Deng, Gang (1999), The Premodern Chinese Economy: Structural Equilibrium and Capitalist Sterility, Routledge, London.

Di Cosmo, Nicola (2004), Did Guns Matter? Firearms and the Qing Formation, in *The Qing Formation in World-Historical Time*, 1st ed., vol. 234, Lynn A Struve (2004), ed., Harvard University Asia Center, Massachusetts.

Dunstan, Helen (1996), Conflicting Counsels to Confuse the Age: A Documentary Study of Political Economy in Qing China, 1644-1840, University of Michigan Center for Chinese Studies, Ann Arbor.

Du Jiayi 杜家驥 (2005), *Huangtaiji shidian* 皇太極事典 (A Dictionary of Hong Taiji's Events), Yuanliu press, Taipei.

Elliott, Mark C.(2001), The Manchu Way: The Eight Banners and Ethnic Identity in Late Imperial China, Stanford University Press, Stanford, California.

Elliott, Mark C.(2005), *Ethnicity in the Qing Eight Banners,* collected in *Empire at the Margins: Culture, Ethnicity, and Frontier in Early Modern China,* edited by Pamela Kyle Crossley, Helen F. Siu, and Donald S. Sutton, University of California Press, California.

Feng Jia (2017), Emperor's Coffer: The Qing Imperial Fiscal Separation Between Privy Purse and State Treasury, PhD book, University of California, Los Angeles.

Feuerwerker, Albert (1984), The State and the Economy in Late Imperial China, *Theory and Society,* Elsevier Science Publishers, Amsterdam, 13.3: 297-326.

Franke, Herbert and Twitchett, Denis (eds.) (1994), *The Cambridge History of China: Alien Regimes and Border States, 907-1368,* vol. 6, the Press Syndicate of the University of Cambridge, Cambridge.

Frederic Wakeman, Jr. (1985), The Great Enterprise: The Manchu Reconstruction of Imperial Order in Seventeenth-Century China, University of California Press, London.

Goodrich, L. Carrington (1938), Early Prohibitions of Tobacco in China and Manchuria, *Journal of the American Oriental Society,* Yale University Press, 58.4: 651-652.

Gruber, Britta-Maria (2006), *Zur Entwicklung der Herrschaft im Aisin-Staat 1616-1636,* Harrassowitz Verlag, Wiesbaden.

Guo Chengkang 郭成康 and Liu Jianxin 劉建新 (1982), *Nu'erhachi jidingshoutian yu kaoshi* 努爾哈赤"計丁授田"諭考實 (Evidence on Nurgaqi's Decree of Calculating Men for Distributing Lands), collected in *Qingshi yanjiuji* 清史研究集 (Collection of Research on Qing History), vol. 2, compiled by Qing Institute of Renmin University of China, Zhongguo renmin daxue chubanshe, Beijing.

Gu Xiaoqing 顧曉清 (2009), *Huangtaiji: kaichuang DaQing jiangshan de Tiancong han* 皇太極：開創大清帝國的天聰汗 (Hong Taiji: The Heavenly Bright Khan who founded the Great Qing Country), Zhongguo huaqiao chubanshe, Beijing.

Han Chunyan 韓春艷 (2010), *Huangtaiji de shengjing chunqiu* 皇太極的盛京春秋 (Hong Taiji's Time in Shengjing), Harbin chubanshe, Harbin.

Han Dacheng 韓大成 (1957), *Mingdai shangpin jingji de fazhan* 明代商品經濟的發展 (The Development of Commercial Economy in the Ming Dynasty), collected in *Mingqing shehui jingji xingtai de yanjiu* 明清社會經濟形態的研究 (Research on Patterns of Social Economy in the Ming and Qing Dynasties), Shanghai remin chubanshe, Shanghai.

Huang, Pei (2011), *Reorienting the Manchus: A Study of Sinicization, 1583-1795,* Cornell East Asia Series 152, Ithaca New York.

Huang Yi'nong 黃一農 (2004), *Hongyi dapao yu huangtaiji chuangli de baqi hanjun* 紅夷大炮與 皇太極創立的八旗漢軍 (The Red-Barbarian Cannon and the Eight-Banner Han Chinese Army Established by Hong Taiji), *Lishi yanjiu* 歷史研究 (Historical Research) 2004.4: 83.

Hucker, Charles O. (1988), *a Dictionary of Official Titles in Imperial China,* Southern Materials Center, Taipei.

Jagchid, Sechin and Van Jay Symons (1989), *Peace, War, and Trade along the Great Wall: Nomadic-Chinese Interactions through Two Millennia,* Indiana University Press, Bloomington and Indianapolis.

Jiang Zhengcheng 姜正成 (2012), *Tiancong Chongde: Huangtaiji* 天聰崇德：皇太極 (From the Tiancong khan to the Chongde emperor: Hong Taiji), Zhongguo yanshi chubanshe, Beijing.

Jin Zecan 金澤燦 (2013), *Nu'erhachi quanzhuan* 努爾哈赤全傳 (A Full Biography of Nurgaqi), Huazhong keji daxue chubanshe, Wuhan.

Kim, Seonmin (2017), Ginseng and Borderland: Territorial Boundaries and Political Relations between Qing China and Chosŏn Korea, 1636-1912, University of California Press, California.

Kwan Man Bun (2001), The Salt Merchants of Tianjin: State-Making and Civil Society in Late Imperial of China, University of Hawai'i Press, Honolulu.

Lai Huimin 賴惠敏 (2016), *Qianlong huangdi de hebao* 乾隆皇帝 的荷包 (Emperor Qianlong's Purse), Zhonghua shuju.

Lan Yong 藍勇 et al. (2003), *"Qihoubianqian he zhongguo lishi"* 氣候變遷和中國歷史 (Climate Change and History of China), *Zhongguo lishi dili luncong* 中國歷史地理論叢 (Collections of Essays on Chinese Historical Geography), 18.1: 63.

Leonard, Jane Kate and John R. Watt, (eds.) (1992), *To Achieve Security and Wealth: The Qing Imperial State and the Economy, 1644-1911,* East Asia Program Cornell University, New York.

Li, Lillian M. (2007), Fighting Famine in North China: State, Market, and Environmental Decline, 1690s-1990s, Stanford University Press, Stanford.

Li Guangfu 李光福 and Su Weiyu 蘇偉宇 (2013), *Qingtaizu Nu'erhachi Manqing de dianjizhe* 清太祖努爾哈赤滿清的奠基者 (Nurhaci: The Founder of the Qing Dynasty), Haitun chubanshe, Beijing.

Li Jingping 李景屏 (1993), *Shuangxiong zhidou: Huangtaiji yu Yuan Chonghuan juezhu ji*, 雙雄 智斗：皇太極與袁崇煥角逐記 (A Battle of Wisdom between Two Heroes: A Record of Competition between Hong Taiji and Yuan Chonghuan), Zhongguo renmin daxue chubanshe, Beijing.

Li Xun 李洵 and Xue Hong 薛虹, (eds.) (1995), *Qingdai quanshi* 清代全史 (A Complete History of the Qing), vol. 1, Liaoning renmin chubanshe, Shenyang.

Li Yin 李寅 (2017), *Zhihui zhi wang: Li Yin pingshuo Huangtaiji* 智慧之王：李寅評說皇太極 (The Lord of Wisdom: Li Yin's Comments on Hong Taiji), Zhongguo gongren chubanshe, Beijing.

Lin Man-houng (2006), *China upside Down: Currency, Society and Ideologies, 1808-1856,* Harvard University Asia Center, Cambridge Massachusetts.

Lin Shixuan 林士鉉 (2009), *Qingdai Menggu yu Manzhou zhengzhi wenhua* 清代蒙古與滿洲政 治文化 (Political Culture of Mongol and Manchu in Qing Dynasty), Guoli zhengzhi daxue lishixuexi, Taipei.

Meng Sen 孟森 (1934), *Minguan Qingxi tongji* 明元清系通紀 (Comprehensive Chronicles of Narrating the Qing's Genealogy according to the Ming's Notation System) zhengbian juan 6, the Jingtai reign, Guoli beijing daxue chubanshe, Beijing.

Meng Sen 孟森 (1959), *Baiqi zhidu kaoshi* 八旗制度考實 (Evidential Research on the Eight Banners System), collected in *Ming Qing shi lunzhu jikan* 明清史論著集刊 (Collected Papers on the Treatise of Ming-Qing History), Zhonghua shuju, Beijing.

Meng Sen 孟森(1992), *Manzhou kaiguo shi* 滿洲開國史 (History of the Manchu State-Founding), Shanghai guji chubanshe, Shanghai.

Michael, Franz (1942), The Origin of Manchu Rule in China: Frontier and Bureaucracy as Interacting Forces in the Chinese Empire, John Hopkins Press, Baltimore.

Mio Kishimoto 岸本美緒 (2010), *Hou shiliushiji wenti yu Qingchao* "後十六世紀問題" 與清朝 (The Problems of the Post-sixteenth Century and the Qing Dynasty), collected in *Qingchao de guojia rentong* 清朝的國家認同 (State's Identity of the Qing Dynasty), edited by Liu Fengyun 劉鳳雲 and Liu Wenpeng 劉文鵬, Zhongguo renmin daxue chubanshe, Beijing.

Needham, Joseph (1974), Science and Civilisation in China: Chemistry and Chemical Technology, vol. 5, Cambridge University Press, London.

Pang, Tatjana A. and Stary, Giovanni (2010), Manchu Versus Ming: Qing Taizu Nurhaci's 'Proclamation' to the Ming Dynasty, *Aetas Manjurica 14,* Otto Harrassowitz, Wiesbaden.

Parker, Geoffrey (2012), Global Crisis: War, Climate Change and Catastrophe in the Seventeenth Century, Yale University Press, New Haven.

Peng Xinwei 彭信威 (1958), *Zhongguo huobishi* 中國貨幣史 (History of Currencies in China), Shanghai renmin chubanshe, Shanghai.

Perdue, Peter C. (2005), *China Marches West: The Qing conquest of Central Eurasia*, The Belknap Press of Harvard University Press, Massachusetts, Cambridge.

Pozzi, Alessandra, Juha Antero Janhunen and Michael Weiers (eds.) (2006), Tumen jalafun jecen akū: Manchu Studies in Honour of Giovanni Stary, *Tunguso Sibirica 20,* Harrassowitz Verlag, Wiesbaden.

Quan Hansheng 全漢昇 (2012), *Zhongguo jingjishi luncong* 中國經濟史論叢 (Collection of essays on China's Economic History), vol. 1, Zhonghua shuju, Beijing.

Rawski, Evelyn S. (1996), "Presidential Address: Reenvisioning the Qing: The Significance of the Qing Period in Chinese History", *The Journal of Asian Studies,* 55.4: 834.

Rawski, Thomas G. and Lillian M. Li (eds.) (1992), *Chinese History in Economic Perspective,* University of California Press, Berkeley.

Roth Li, Gertraude (2002), State Building before 1644, in *The Cambridge history of China: vol. 9 Part I: The Ch'ing Empire to 1800,* ed. Willard Peterson, Cambridge University Press, Cambridge.

Rowe, William (2009), *China's Last Empire: The Great Qing,* the Belknap Press of Harvard University Press, Massachusetts.

Shan Shikui 單士魁 (1978), *Qingdai dang'an congtan* 清代檔案叢談 (Collected Talks about the Archives of the Qing Dynasty), Zijincheng chubanshe, Beijing.

Shen Dingping 沈定平 (2012), *Ming Qing zhi ji zhongxiwenhua jiaoliushi-Mingji: qutong yu bianyi* 明清之際中西文化交流史-明季：趨同與辨異 History of China-West Cultural Communication during the

Ming Qing Transition-the End of Ming: Convergence and Differentiation, The Commercial Press, Beijing.

Sheng Ye 聖燁 (2005), *Mashang diwang: Huangtaiji simi dang'an quan jiemi* 馬上帝王：皇太極 私密檔案全揭秘 (Emperor on the Horseback: A Complete Exposure of Hong Taiji's Private Chronicles), Beifang wenyi chubanshe, Harbin.

Smith, Richard J. (1974), Chinese Military Institutions in the Mid-Nineteenth Century, 1850-1860, *Journal of Asian History,* 8. 2: 136.

Song Naiqiu 宋乃秋 (ed.) (2007), *Huangtaiji zhuan* 皇太極傳 (Biography of Hong Taiji), Zhongguo xiju chubanshe, Beijing.

Spence, Jonathan D. (1966), *Ts'ao Yin and the K'ang-hsi Emperor: Bondservant and Master,* Yale University Press, New Haven.

Stary Giovanni (1984), The Manchu Emperor "Abahai": Analysis of an Historiographic Mistake, *Central Asiatic Journal,* 28. 3: 296-299.

Stary, Giovanni and Walravens, Hartmut (2013), Selected Manchu Studies: contributions to history, literature, and shamanism of the Manchus, Klaus Schwarz Verlag, Berlin.

Struve, Lynn (2010), *Shijieshi ji qingchu zhongguode neiya yinsu* 世界史及清初中國的內亞因素 - 美國學術界的一些觀點和問題 (Elements of Inner Asia in World History and Early-Qing China: some viewpoints and questions in America's academia), collected in *Qingchao de guojia rentong* 清朝的國家認同 (State's Identity of the Qing Dynasty), edited by Liu Fengyun 劉鳳雲 and Liu Wenpeng 劉文鵬, Zhongguo renmin daxue chubanshe, Beijing.

Sun, Lin (2018), The Economy of Empire Building: Wild Ginseng, Sable Fur, and the Multiple Trade Networks of the Early Qing Dynasty, 1583-1644. PhD thesis, University of Oxford.

Sun Wensheng (2005), *Huangtaiji dadi* 皇太極大帝 (The Great Emperor of Hong Taiji), Beifang wenyi chubanshe, Harbin.

Swope, Kenneth (ed.) (2005), *Warfare in China since 1600,* The Cromwell Press, Trowbridge, Wiltshire.

Symons, Van Jay (1981), *Ch'ing Ginseng Management: Ch'ing Monopolies in Microcosm* (Occasional Papers No 13), Arizona Sate University Center for Asian Studies, Tempe.

Tibet and Manchu: An Assessment of Tibet-Manchu Relations in Five Phases of Historical Development, DIIR publications, Dharamsala, 2008.

Von Glahn, Richard (1996), Fountain of Fortune, Money and Monetary Policy in China, 1000-1700. University of California Press, Berkeley.

Von Glahn, Richard (2016), The Economic History of China: From Antiquity to the Nineteenth Century, Cambridge University Press, Cambridge.

Von Glahn, Richard (2019), Modalities of the Fiscal State in Imperial China, *Journal of Chinese History,* 29.4: 1.

Vries, Peer (2015), State, Economy and the Great Divergence, Great Britain and China, 1680s-1850s,

Bloomsbury, London.

Wakeman, Frederic Jr. (1985), *The Great Enterprise*, The Manchu Reconstruction of Imperial Order in Seventeenth-Century China, University of California Press, London.

Wang Sizhi 王思治 (1978), *Qingshi lungao* 清史論稿 (Drafts of Research on Qing History), Bashu shushe, Chengdu.

Wang Zhanjun 王占君 (2013), *Huangtaiji* 皇太極 (Biography of Hong Taiji), Huaxia chubanshe, Beijing.

Wang Zhonghan 王鍾翰 (1997), *Qingshi xinkao* 清史新考 (New Evidential Research on Qing History), Liaoning daxue chubanshe, Shenyang.

Wang Zhonghan 王鍾翰 (1957), *Qingshi zakao* 清史雜考 (Miscellaneous Research on Qing History), Renmin chubanshe, Beijing.

Xu Che 徐徹 and Dong Xiansheng 董顯聲 (2011), *Huangtaiji* 皇太極 (Biography of Hong Taiji), Zhongguo wenshi chubanshe, Beijing.

Xu Chen 徐徹 and Zhang Shu 張樹 (2017), *Qingchu erdi* 清初二帝 (The Two Emperors of the Early Qing), Shenyang Chubanshe, Shenyang.

Yan Chongnian 閻崇年 (1983), *Nu'erhachi zhuan* 努爾哈赤傳 (The Life of Nurgaqi), Beijing chubanshe, Beijing.

Yan Chongnian 閻崇年 (1983), *Qingchao kaiguoshi* 清朝開國史 (History of the Qing Dynasty's State-founding), Lianjing chuban gongsi, Taipei.

Yan Guangliang 閆光亮 (2004), *Kaiguo huangdi Huangtaiji* 開國皇帝皇太極 (The State-Founding Emperor Hong Taiji), Shenyang chubanshe, Shenyang.

Yang Yang 楊暘 (1988), *Mingdai liaodong dusi* 明代遼東都司 (The Regional Military Commission of Liaodong in the Ming Dynasty), Zhongzhou guji chubanshe, Zhengzhou.

Yin Xiaodong 尹曉冬 (2014), *16-17 shiji xifang huoqi jishu xiang zhongguo de zhuanyi* 16-17 世 紀西方火器技術向中國的轉移 (Transmission of Firearm Technology from the West to China from the Sixteenth to Seventeenth Century), Shandong Jiaoyu chubanshe, Ji'nan.

Yu Yingshi 余英時 (2010), *Zhongguo jinshi zongjiao lunli yu shangren* 中國近世宗教倫理與商 人 (China's Early Modern Religious Ethic and Merchants), Lianjing chuban shiye gufen youxian gongsi 聯經 出版事業股份有限公司 (Linking Publishing Company), Taipei.

Zelin, Madeleine (1984), The Magistrate's Tael: Rationalizing Fiscal Reform in Eighteenth-Century Ch'ing China, University of California Press, California.

Zhao Lingzhi 趙令志 (2001), *Qing qianqi baqi tudi zhidu yanjiu* 清前期八旗土地制度研究 (Research on the Land System of the Eight Banners in the Early Qing), Minzu chubanshe, Beijing.

Zhang Bo 張波 (2014), *Tiancong Chongde Wangchao* 天聰崇德王朝 (The Reigns of Tiancong and Chongde), Zhongguo qingnian chubanshe, Beijing.

Zhang Minglin 張明林 (2011), *Kaiguo yingzhu: Qing Taizong Huangtaiji* 開國英主：清太宗皇太 極 (The Outstanding Monarch of Founding the State), Xiyuan chubanshe, Beijing.

Zhang Yan 張研 (1993), *Jianrixing: Huangtaiji chuanqi* 踐日行：皇太極傳奇 (Travels of Trampling on the Sun: The Legend of Hong Taiji), Zhongguo renmin daxue chubanshe, Beijing.

Zhang Yan 張研 (1998), *Qingdai jingji jianshi* 清代經濟簡史 (A Brief History of Qing's Economy), Zhongzhou guji chubanshe, Zhengzhou.

Zhao Duo 趙鐸 (1992), *Qing kaiguo jingji fazhanshi* 清開國經濟發展史 (The Economic History of Qing's Empire-Building), Liaoning renmin chubanshe, Shenyang.

Zhao Gang (2006), "Reinventing China: Imperial Qing Ideology and the Rise of Modern Chinese National Identity in the Early Twentieth Century", *Modern China,* 32. 1: 3-30.

Zhuang Jifa 莊吉發 (1997), *Qingshi lunji (er)* 清史論集 （二） (Collection of Treatise on the Qing History, 2), Wenshizhe chubanshen.

Glossary

Assistant Regional Commander (man. *canjiyang*; chin. *canjiang* 參將)

Azurite (man. *xi qing*; chin. *shiqing* 石青)

Basic copper carbonate (man. *tung lu*; chin. *tonglü* 銅綠)

Banner (man. *gvsa*; chin. *qi* or *gushan* 旗 or 固山)

Battalion Commander (man. *nirui ejen*; chin. *niulu ezhen* 牛錄額真)

Battalion Commander of Dongjing (man. *dung ging ni emu bezung* ; chin. *dongjing bazong* 東京把總)

Battalion-Company (*meng'an mouke* 猛安謀克)

Battle of Sarhv (*Sa'er'hu zhi zhan* 薩爾滸之戰)

Black River (man. *sahaliyan ula*; chin. *heilongjiang* 黑龍江)

Bombax ceiba (*jibei* 吉貝 or *mumian* 木棉)

Bordered Red Banner (man. *kubuhe fulgiyan gvsa*; chin. *xianghongqi* 鑲紅旗 or 廂紅旗)

Brass (*huangtong* 黃銅)

Brass powder (man. *aisin okto*; chin. *jinfen* 金粉)

Breech-loading swivel gun (eng. *The Frankish Cannon*; chin. *folangji* 佛郎機)

Bronze (*qingtong* 青銅)

Calculating Men for Distributing Lands (*jidingshoutian* 計丁授田)

Cannon (man. *poo*; chin. *pao* 砲 or 炮)

Chieftain (man. *beile* or *beise* as a plural form; chin. *beile* 貝勒)

China Numismatic Museum (*zhongguo qianbi bowuguan* 中國錢幣博物館)

Chinese Banners (*hanjun baqi* 漢軍八旗)

Circuit Intendant (man. *dooli*; chin. *daoyuan* 道員)

Circuit Intendant of Ningyuan (man. *heqen i ejen dooli hergen*; chin. *ningyuan dao* 寧遠道)

Civilians (man. *irgen*; chin. *minren* 民人)

Clan (man. *hala*; chin. *xingshi* 姓氏 or *zongzu* 宗族)

Coin (man. *jiha*; chin. *qian* 錢)

Commander-in-chief (man. *gvsai ejen*; chin. *qizhu* or *dutong* 旗主或都統)

Commander of Guards (man. *jung giyvn*; chin. *zhongjun* 中軍)

Company (man. *niru*; chin. *niulu* 牛錄)

Company Commander (man. *nirui janggin*; chin. *zuoling* 佐領 or *niulu zhangjing* 牛錄章京 or *qianzong* 千總)

Copper (*hongtong* 紅銅)

Councillor (man. *jargvqi;* chin. *zha'er guqi* 扎爾固齊)

Court of Colonial Affairs (man. *tulergi golo be dasara jurgan*; chin. *lifanyuan* 理藩院)

Cultivated Talents (*xiucai* 秀才)

Dahvr (man. *dahvr*; chin. *dahu'er* 達瑚爾)

Daily Accumulation of Knowledge (*ri zhi lu* 日知錄)

Defence Officer (man. *bei ioi guwan*; chin. *beiyu* 備御)

Defense Officer of Yongningjian (man. *yung ning giyan*; chin. *Yongningjian* 永寧監)

Defensive Army (man. *bayara*; chin. *hujun* 護軍)

Deputy Secretaries (man. *janggin*; chin. *zhangjing* 章京)

Deputy Company-Commanding Defense Officer (man. *dase beiguwan*; chin. *dazi beiyu* 代子備御)

Director in Ministry of Rites (*libulangzhong* 禮部郎中)

Dragon-Tiger General (*Long hu jiang jun* 龍虎將軍)

Eastern Pearls (man. *tana*; chin. *dongzhu* 東珠)

Eight Banners (man. *jakvn gvsa;* chin. *baqi* 八旗)

Eight-Banner Han Chinese Artillery Troops (man. *ujen qooha*; chin. *baqihanjun* 八旗漢軍)

Eight-Banner Manchus (man. *gvsai manju*; chin. *baqi manzhou* 八旗滿洲)

Eight-Banner Mongols (man. *gvsai mongol*; chin. *baqi menggu* 八旗蒙古)

Eight Chieftains (man. *jakvn boo* or *jakvn beise*; chin. *bajia* 八家 or *ba beile* 八貝勒)

Emperor (man. *hvwangdi*; chin. *huangdi* 皇帝)

Enclosure (*quandi* 圈地)

Falcon Cannon (man. *fa gung poo*; chin. *fa gong pao* 發貢炮)

Field Army (*xingyingbing* 行營兵)

Fireworks (man. *pojan*; chin. *pozhang* 炮仗)

First Chieftain (man. *amba beile*; chin. *dabeile* 大貝勒)

First-rank-lord officials (man. *geren i ejen ambasa*; chin. *zong ezhen dachen* 總額真大臣)

Fushun Garrison (man. *fuxun xo*; chin. *fushunsuo* 撫順所)

Gamboge (man. *teng hvwang*; chin. *tenghuang* 藤黃)

Garrison Army (*zhushoubing* 駐守兵)

Gate of Conciliating Afar (man. *goroki be gosire duka*; chin. *huaiyuanmen* 懷遠門)

Gold (man. *aisin*; chin. *jin* 金)

Gold State (man. *aisin gurun;* chin. *jinguo* 金國)

Gold-Silk-Smoke (*jinsiyan* 金絲菸)

Gold State (man. *aisin gurun;* chin. *jinguo* 金國)

Governor (man. *dutang hergen*; chin. *xunfu* 巡撫)

Grand Commandant (man. *xeobei*; chin. *shoubei* 守備)

Grand Coordinator (man. *dutang*; chin. *dutang* 都堂)

Grand Coordinator of Ningyuan (*ningyuan dutang* 寧遠都堂)

Grand Minister Commander (man. *jifi bihe dutang*; chin. *jinglüe* 經略)

Guan'ning Iron Cavalry (*guan'ning tieqi* 關寧鐵騎)

Han Chinese state or people (man. *nikan gurun;* chin. *hanren* 漢人 or *hanrenguo* 漢人國)

Heaven's-mandate-universal-treasure (*tianming tongbao* 天命通寶)

Hedong region (man. *birai dergi*; chin. *hedong* 河東)

Heje (man. *heje*; chin. *hezhe* 赫哲)

Hong Taiji (man. *hong taiji*; chin. *huangtaiji* 皇太極)

Imperial Son-in-law of Fusi (man. *fusi efu*; chin. *fuxi efu* 撫西額駙)

Investigating Censor (man. *qa yuwan hergen*; chin. *jiancha yushi* 監察御史)

Jianzhou Tatars (*Jianzhou dazi* 建州獚子)

Judges (man. *beidesi*; chin. *shenshiguan* 審事官)

Jurchen (man. *nioiji* or *juxen*; chin. *nüzhi* 女直 or *nüzhen* 女真)

Kaiyuan Circuit Intendant (man. *kai yuwan i dooli;* chin. *kaiyuandao* 開源道)

Liao Rations (*liaoxiang* 遼餉)

Liaoyang Circuit Intendant (man. *liyoodung ni dooli;* chin. *liaoyangdao* 遼陽道)

Liaodong City (man. *liyoodung ni heqen*; chin. *liaodong cheng* 遼東城)

Magistrate of silver treasury (man. *menggun ku i da*; chin. *yinku zhang* 銀庫長)

Manchu (man. *manju*; chin. *manzhou* 滿洲)

Manchu Banners (*manzhou baqi* 滿洲八旗)

Maoqin blue cloth (man. *moqin*; chin. *maoqinbu* 毛青布)

Mandate of Heaven (man. *abkai fulingga*; chin. *tianming* 天命)

Matchlock (man. *qang poo* or *miyooqan*; chin. *niaoqiang* 鳥槍)

Mercury sulfide red (man. *okto qinuhvn*; chin. *yinzhu* 銀朱)

Metropolitan Graduate (*jinshi* 進士)

Ming empire (man. *daiming gurun;* chin. *damingguo* 大明國)

Minister (man. *aliha amban*; chin. *chengzheng* 承政)

Ministry of Mongol Affairs (man. *monggo jugan*; chin. *menggu yamen* 蒙古衙門)

Ministry of Revenue (*hubu* 戶部)

Ministry of War (*bingbu* 兵部)

Mobile Corps Commander (man. *iogi hergen i hafan*; chin. *youji* 遊擊)

Mobile Corps Commander of Gaizhou (*gaizhou youji* 蓋州遊擊)

Mobile Presidential Council (*xingtai shangshusheng* 行台尚書省)

Mongol Banners (*menggu baqi* 蒙古八旗)

National language, riding and shooting (*guoyuqishe* 國語騎射)

New Manchus (man. *iqe manju*; chin. *yiche manzhou* 伊徹滿洲 or *xinmanzhou* 新滿洲)

New Manchu Script (man. *tongki fuka sindaha hergen*; chin. *xin manwen* 新滿文)

Noil cloth (man. *miyanqeo*; chin. *mianchou* 綿綢)

Old Manchus (man. *fe manju*; chin. *fo manzhou* 佛滿洲 or *jiumanzhou* 舊滿洲)

Old Manchu Script (man. *tongki fuka akv hergen*; chin. *lao manwen* 老滿文)

Orpiment (man. *xi hvwang*; chin. *shihuang* 石黃)

Outer-Vassal Mongols (man. *tulergi goloi monggo*; chin. *waifan menggu* 外藩蒙古)

Panning-wash (man. *werembi*; chin. *taoxi* 淘洗)

Peng Silk (man. *pengduwan*; chin. *pengduan* 彭緞)

Pigment green (man. *da lu*; chin. *da lü* 大綠)

Plain Yellow Banner (man. *gulu suwayan gvsa*; chin. *zhenghuangqi* 正黃旗)

Plumbum Rubrum (man. *hvwang dan*; chin. *huangdan* 黃丹)

Provincial Administration Commissions (*buzhenshisi* 布政使司)

Rank Badges (man. *puse*; chin. *buzi* 補子)

Red-Barbarian Cannons (*hongyi dapao* 紅夷大炮)

Red-Hair Large Weapons (*hongmao daqi* 红毛大器)

Regiment (man. *jalan*; chin. *jiala* 甲喇)

Regimental Commander (man. *qiyanzung*; chin. *qianzong* 千總)

Regional Commander (man. *zung bing guwan*; chin. *zongbing guan* 總兵官)

Regional Commander of Guangning (*guangning zongbing* 廣寧總兵)

Regional Military Commission (*duzhihuishisi* 都指揮使司)

Regional Vice Commander (man. *fujiyang*; chin. *fujiang* 副將)

Right Censor-in-chief (*youduyushi* 右都御使)

Rice-Sack Flower (*mi'nanghua* 米囊花)

Saw blade (man. *fufungge huwesi*; chin. *judao* 鋸刀)

Scholar (man. *baksi;* chin. *bakeshi* 巴克什)

Secretary in Ministry of Rites (*libu zhushi* 禮部主事)

Secondary Mongol chieftain (man. *taiji*; chin. *taiji* 臺吉)

Shahukou frontier (man. *xurgei duka*; chin. *shahukou* 殺虎口)

Shanhai Pass (man. *xanaha*; chin. *Shanhai guan* 山海關)

Shamanistic sites (man. *tangse*; chin. *tangzi* 堂子)

Sibe (man. *sibe*; chin. *xibo* 錫伯)

Silver (man. *menggun*; chin. *yin* 銀)

Six Ministries (man. *ninggun jurgan*; chin. *liubu* 六部)

Solon (man. *solon*; chin. *suolun* 索倫)

Subprefectual Magistrate (man. *ting pan xi hafan*; chin. *ting pan shi guan* 廳判事官)

Superintendent Commander (man. *hontoho;* chin. *guanling* 管領)

Supreme Commander of Jiliao (*jiliao zongdu* 薊遼總督)

Ten cash (*dangshi* 當十)

Three Eastern Provinces beyond Shanhai Pass (*guandong sansheng* 關東三省)

Three Highest Administrative Institutions (*Sanfu* 三府)

Three Palace Academies (*neisanyuan* 內三院)

Tribe (man. *gurun*; chin. *bu* 部)

Twelve Heads (man. *juwan juwe uju*; chin. *shi'er zitou* 十二字頭)

Twice-a-year tax policy (*liangshuifa* 兩稅法)

Vice Minister in Ministry of War (*bingbu shilang* 兵部侍郎)

Vice Commanders-in-chief (man. *meiren i ejen*; chin. *fudutong* 副都統)

Vice Director in the Ministry of War (man. *qoohai jurgan i aisilakv hafan*; chin. *bingbu yuanwailang* 兵部員外郎)

Vice Regional Commander (man. *fujiyang*; chin. *fujiang* 副將)

Voile (man. *xa*; chin. *sha* 紗)